ENGLISH FOR BUSI

English for Business Studies

A practical course for use in
secondary schools and colleges

Third Edition

L. GARTSIDE
MBE, B Com, FSCT
*Chief Examiner in Commercial Subjects,
College of Preceptors*

MACDONALD AND EVANS

Macdonald & Evans Ltd
Estover, Plymouth PL6 7PZ

First published 1969
Reprinted (with amendments) 1971
Reprinted 1972
Reprinted 1973
Second edition 1975
Reprinted (with amendments) 1975
Reprinted 1976
Reprinted 1977
Reprinted 1979
Third edition 1981
Reprinted 1982

0 7121 0582 4

Printed in Great Britain by
Hollen Street Press Ltd
Slough

Preface to the Third Edition

Since the second edition of *English for Business Studies* was published in 1975, changes in the requirements of examining bodies and the introduction by the Business Education Council (BEC) of its assignment-based courses have made significant changes in ˙the demands upon students preparing for examinations in English Language. In this new edition the opportunity has been taken to up-date material in areas affected by these changes. Chapter One, which deals with Language and Communication, is largely new, and the chapters on Speech and Reading have been rewritten and extended. The book as a whole has been restructured and is now set in two Parts. Part I concentrates on the use of English in different types of communication, including the essay, the business letter and other forms of business writing. It caters for a wide range of the learning activities involved — reading, writing, listening and speaking. Part II deals with the associated grammatical disciplines and with matters of punctuation, spelling, usage and other aspects of English that affect standards in the communication process. This presentation of subject-matter in two parts is felt to be convenient especially for readers who have acquired a standard of formal accuracy in the use of language and wish to use Part II mainly as a reference source. A recommended Reading List and a reference to the assignment-based courses of BEC are included in Appendixes.

In its rearranged form this new edition preserves the general aim of earlier editions — to provide an essentially practical approach to the use of English in business in keeping with the modern trend towards forms of expression that are natural and unaffected, with the emphasis throughout on clear and concise expression. It offers a fully comprehensive course in English suited to the needs of students preparing for most examinations in English Language at both school-leaving and professional-examination level. Exercises include a generous selection of questions from these examinations and offer a wide range of practice material at different levels of attainment. Chapters Eleven, Twelve and Fourteen include questions similar in substance, if not in form, to assignment-based problems of the type favoured by BEC. For readers who care to use them for audio-typing and shorthand-dictation practice some of the exercises in Chapters Fifteen to Seventeen on Comprehension and Précis Writing have been counted.

The foundation and development of effective communication is heavily dependent upon an acceptable standard of grammatical competence and a clear awareness of syntax and usage. It is a principal aim of this new edition to help those who use it to develop the skills involved.

The inclusion in the exercises forming part of each chapter of questions from past examination papers affords useful guidance to students preparing for examinations, and my thanks are due to the examining bodies whose names appear below for permission to make a selection of questions from papers set by them.

My thanks are due also to the following publishers for permission to use in the text the various extracts mentioned:

To the publishers of the *Concise Oxford Dictionary* and Chambers *Twentieth Century Dictionary* and for the facsimiles reproduced on p. 46; to H.M. Stationery Office for the extracts from *Plain Words* by Sir Ernest Gowers (pp. 27–8); to the Royal Bank of Canada for the paragraphs on *Discipline* from *Monthly Letter* (p. 269), the quotation at the head of Chapter 11 (p. 157) and the paragraphs on *Communication* (pp. 207–8); to Methuen & Co. Ltd. for the extracts from *In Search of England* by H.V. Morton (p. 68); to Penguin Books for the extract from *John Citizen and the Law,* by R. Rubenstein (p. 71); to Ernest Benn Ltd. for the extract from *William Shakespeare* by John Masefield (p. 71); to J.M. Dent & Sons Ltd. for the extract from *Epping Forest* by Sir William Addison (p. 71); and to the Blackpool and Fylde College of Further and Higher Education for the example Assignment in Appendix II.

Examining Bodies

E.M.E.U.	East Midland Educational Union
I. of B.	Institute of Bankers
I.C.S.A.	Institute of Chartered Secretaries and Administrators
L.C.C.I.	London Chamber of Commerce and Industry

L.C.C.I. (Priv. Sec. Dip.)	London Chamber of Commerce and Industry (Private Secretary's Diploma)
N.C.T.E.C.	Northern Counties Technical Examinations Council
N.W.R.A.C.	North Western Region Advisory Council for Further Education
R.S.A.	Royal Society of Arts (various examinations)
U.E.I.	Union of Educational Institutions

June 1981   L.G.

Contents

PART II
GRAMMAR AND SYNTAX

PART I

COMMUNICATION

CHAPTER ONE

Language and Communication

"I don't want to talk grammar.
I want to talk like a lady."
George Bernard Shaw: Eliza Doolittle *(Pygmalion)*

THE IMPORTANCE OF LANGUAGE

Language is inseparable from almost every human activity. It is the central instrument of all education because in its various forms it is basic to the acquirement of all knowledge and skills. Whether spoken or written it is directly involved in the learning process, whatever the subject. It has been described as "a vehicle of thought"; but it is very much more. It is a creative power, a means by which in a sort of inner speech we do much of our thinking. It also has important social implications: it helps to make us what we are and to determine the level on which we establish relations with other people.

Language is only one of a number of means of communication. In recent years emphasis has been given to forms of expression and to means of learning other than words. The visual arts afford a means of expression and of learning which some people find more suitable than the language of words. And there are other means: pleasure can be communicated by a smile, approval by a nod, and the deaf have evolved a complete sign-language of their own. But even so, in its spoken and written forms the language of words remains by far the commonest medium whereby we communicate with one another.

It is useful to distinguish between two main aspects of language. There is on the one hand a body of rules and precedents handed down from generation to generation to which we must conform if we are to communicate effectively within a language community.

1

These rules are the tools of communication, bequeathed to us in the form of grammar, with which we form relationships in business and social life. On the other hand, there are the individual personal variations and modifications of these rules and precedents in our everyday and more intimate personal relationships. Thus, language operates at two levels. There is the formal grammatical element bequeathed from the past and the informal element of a lighter and more imaginative kind which, though based on the grammatical code, is more flexible, more colourful and more neighbourly. The distinction is important, though the latter is not without influence on the former and as time goes on grammatical rules tend to be modified, if only slowly, by the influences of everyday educated usage.

Communication in business traditionally operates at the formal level. This is to be expected since the communicating parties are often unknown to each other. There was a time when formality was strained to the extent that it actually interfered with efficient communication in business. But the cold formal style of business writing that was once fashionable is fast giving way to a more flexible and sensitive style. We do not communicate effectively merely by observing rules of grammar; we are dealing with fellow human beings and to communicate with them effectively we must do so on a more personal level, remembering that, like us, they have feelings and sensibilities that must be respected. One of the things we all look for in our business relationships is a spirit of friendliness in those with whom we work and with whom we seek to do business.

Society has become more complex and so has the language of communication. The growth of large-scale undertakings has extended lines of management and supervision within the undertaking. Advances in science and technology have created a need for new terminology. Because of these developments it is now more difficult to establish successful business relations and our dependence on effective communication has increased. To share fully and adequately in the benefits of these changes in the pattern of economic life we have to familiarize ourselves with new forms of expression while still preserving the ability to communicate our ideas and feelings in language that is simple, clear and readily understandable.

THE MEANING OF COMMUNICATION

Communication has sometimes been described as the art of transferring information and ideas from one mind to another; but it is very much more. In its vital sense communication means a sharing of ideas and feelings in a mood of mutual understanding, a two-way process in which the speaker must have a listener and the writer a reader to share his experience. This understanding can be achieved only if the parties "speak the same language", only that is if the words communicated have the same meanings to both and are used in the same sense. For his part the person communicating must first be clear about his aim — what he wants to say and wants the receiver to know, and how he wants him to react to what he tells him. He must then express it in language free from ambiguity and also appropriate to the receiver's level of understanding. These conditions are essential as a prelude to successful business relationships through communication; it is equally true of relationships within the organization and the outside world.

"The written word is not merely a symbol on a piece of paper, nor is the spoken word a mere vibration in the air"; it is a tool of communication and to perform its function what is written or spoken must mean the same thing to both sender and receiver. If you enter a shop for a metre of cloth or a kilo of sugar it doesn't matter very much how long a metre is or how heavy a kilo. What is important is that when you specify *metre* or *kilo* it means the same thing to the shopkeeper as it does to you. This identity of meaning is the basis of all effective communication; it is the key to the use of all language in business and society.

THE COMMUNICATION PROCESS

Effective communication is always a two-way process starting with a message by a sender, who transmits it to a receiver, who in turn decodes it and interprets it and finally confirms to the sender that his message has been received and understood.

When the sender transmits the message he wants to know three things:

(a) whether his message has reached the receiver;

(b) how the receiver feels about the message;

(c) what further action, if any, is he as sender likely to have to take.

The answers lie in the response he looks forward to from the receiver. If there is no response or feed-back of any kind communication is incomplete. The sender does not even know whether his message has been received or, if received, understood. Nor can he be certain that the words he used and the way he used them accurately represented his idea or, if they did, whether the receiver's interpretation was the one the sender intended.

The cycle of communication between sender and receiver passes through a number of stages:

Conception
The process begins with the sender's decision to communicate an idea, and is effective only if it reflects in the receiver's mind a true

image of the idea communicated; only, that is, if the message received is understood and interpreted in the sense intended by its sender. If it takes the form of a business letter it will be a good letter only if it prompts the response hoped for or expected.

Selection

The sender must choose the method of communication to be used — written, verbal, or visual by photograph, drawing, chart, etc. Written communication provides a record for future reference. It invests communication with precision where details are important, as where a quotation is given or a contract concluded. Problems of interpretation may well arise if not enough care is taken with the details. Does the quoted price, for example, cover the cost of delivering the goods and, if so, to what destination; does it state the period within which and the conditions under which it must be accepted, and does the customer realize that although a quotation is an offer to perform a specified kind of service, the sender is not legally bound by it? Until the quotation has been accepted the sender remains free to amend it or even withdraw it altogether.

Verbal communication is more appropriate for matters that are urgent or involve detailed discussion and exchange of views and opinions. It also provides the sender with an immediate response or feed-back, if not in so many words, then in the listener's attitude — his facial expressions and his gestures and, if communication is by telephone, his tone of voice and general attitude.

Where communication is visually supported, illustrations and samples submitted stimulate recollection, simplify understanding and reinforce what has been said or written.

Transmission

The choice of medium for transmitting the message depends on a number of sometimes complicated factors — geographical distance, degree of urgency, nature and complexity of message, personal relationship between parties, and so on. The post, telex and the telephone are available to meet the claims of distance, however far or near, whereas a private visit, attendance at a meeting or use of a messenger may be more satisfactory if the parties reside in the same locality and personal contact is possible.

Comprehension

Before he can act upon the message the receiver must absorb and understand it. This may not be easy if the sender has failed to make himself clear, or has used technical language unfamiliar to the receiver, or expressed himself in terms above the receiver's level of comprehension. To get the response he seeks the sender must take into account the receiver's background and personality and express himself in language he is likely to understand. If he is communicating with a foreigner he must keep his language simple enough for his receiver to grasp its meaning first time. If he does not already know the receiver he must try to imagine what he is like; a letter from him, or his speech and manner on the telephone may provide a clue. But however much or little knowledge the sender has of the receiver, he must look at things from the receiver's angle and, by imagining himself to be the receiver and not the sender, try to sense the feelings his message is likely to arouse and the reaction it is likely to set up. He must ask himself, "How would I feel if I were to receive the message?". Only then can the sender decide on the best way to put his message over and avoid using language the receiver may not understand. This ability to adapt oneself to the outlook and point of view of the other party is the outstanding quality of a good communicator.

Interpretation

Besides understanding the message the receiver must be able to interpret it correctly. We owe it to those with whom we communicate to express ourselves clearly and to make their task as easy as possible. Clarity is achieved through natural forms of expression, the use of familiar words and the logical arrangement of subject-matter. In business letter-writing and report-writing the language used should be as natural as the language of good everyday speech, but without its colloquialisms and slang expressions. We should write as plainly as we would speak, at the same time remembering that we do not always speak as clearly as we might.

It is surprisingly easy to express ourselves in sentences capable of more than one meaning. If a writer fails to make himself clear he is liable to be misunderstood, and this is something no businessman can afford. To express himself clearly he must think clearly and have a clear awareness of the purpose of his message and what he wants it to achieve. Clear thinking and clear expression go hand in hand. He must choose words that say exactly what he wants them to say and use them in sentences framed to leave no room for misunderstanding. What, for example, are we to make of the following?

No cleaner shall be employed on any day when the office is closed *for a longer period than four hours.*

Does it mean that no cleaner must be employed when the office is temporarily closed or, what seems more likely, that no cleaner must be employed for more than four hours? If so, then *for more than four hours* should immediately follow *employed.*

Many ambiguities can be removed by restructuring sentences so as to bring together those words most nearly related to one another.

No unnecessary force was used to put an end to the uproar *by the organizers of the meeting.*

Does this really mean that the organizers created the uproar, or that the organizers did not use unnecessary force to end the uproar? If the latter, then *by the organizers of the meeting* should be placed immediately after *used,* to which it is related in thought; and similarly with:

I have known Mr. Jones for the past ten years and can recommend him for the post he has applied for *with the utmost confidence.*

If it is the recommendation and not the application that is made *with the utmost confidence,* the phrase should immediately follow *recommend.*

And again, this time from an insurance policy:

The policy holder shall within 30 days of any loss or damage to the property insured *at his own expense* submit a claim.

The phrase *at his own expense* presumably relates to submission of the claim and not to the damage to the property, and should be placed at the end of the sentence, after *claim.*

Even when the sender's words and expressions are exactly the right ones there is no certainty that the receiver will read exactly the same meaning into them. Much will depend on his level of understanding, but at least the sender will have discharged his primary duty of making himself clear.

Conclusion

When communication is verbal the response the sender looks for has the advantage of being immediate. The speed with which it takes place is one of the advantages of verbal over written communication. The ancillary manifestations of the listener's facial expression, his gestures and tone of voice all form part of the response the speaker looks for. They are its unconscious and involuntary components and carry their own message. They add a subtle colouring to the words used. In addition, the listener can ask questions or state his views and in this way invest his response with precision. But unless subsequently confirmed, verbal communication provides no record to support what was said and disputes may arise over what was agreed. The written message cannot draw on these ancillaries of verbal communication and must rely solely on the language used. Written communication also suffers from being the slower medium — telex, letters and reports all take time. But by whatever means and in whatever circumstances the receiving party makes his response, this response or feed-back is an essential factor in all communication. It resolves uncertainties, smooths out differences, and by helping to remove misunderstandings harmonizes relationships and provides firm ground for subsequent action.

COMMUNICATION AND GRAMMAR

Grammar is the name given to the system of rules underlying the use of language. It is concerned with accidence (i.e. changes in the form of single words) and syntax (i.e. the linking of words together to form sense groups). To use a word in its wrong form, or to link words in a way contrary to accepted practice, is to be guilty of bad grammar. Even so, we must not allow ourselves to be slaves to the niceties of grammar. Grammar and syntax have important rules in all written communication, but they must not be slavishly adhered to at the expense of that naturalness of expression which is important in all communication by language. Language is not after all a static thing, and what is fashionable among the writers of one generation may come to be condemned by those of another, while what was once frowned upon may later carry favour. Nowhere is this more evident than in the field of letter-writing. The hackneyed and meaningless forms of expression characteristic of the old-fashioned business letter, with its *beg to inform* and *have to acknowledge,* are rapidly giving place to a style of writing more akin to that of good conversation. The modern trend is towards forms of expression that are natural and unaffected, even if it sometimes means infringing the strict rules of the grammatical purist.

LIMITATIONS OF GRAMMAR

Grammatical rules are not the most important things in language. They follow rather than dictate the fashions of language. We often learn to speak and write perfectly grammatical English, yet with little knowledge of grammatical precept. A person may claim that he knows nothing about grammar and yet be able to speak and write perfectly good English. What he really means is that he is ignorant of the technical terms used in discussing language structure, and that he writes and speaks without being aware of the rules he is unconsciously observing. Through environment and by reading and

writing he has acquired an adequate ability to express himself correctly. There is truth in the claim that impressions developed in
favourable circumstances of home and school and social connections
are the best guide to the correct use of language; it may also be true
that grammar by itself cannot teach the art of effective communication. But not everyone is fortunate enough to be exposed to favourable external influences, and there are many who would benefit
from the technical help afforded by grammar. If you are one of
them you need not be unduly worried. Effective communication
does not call for an intimate knowledge of grammar; a simple knowledge of the main rules, combined with a little common sense, is
often all that is needed to rid us of many of the mistakes we sometimes make, as the following examples show:

Having seen that we are well equipped with modern machinery we invite you (say: *you are invited*) to place your order with us.	*Having seen* is wrongly attached to the second pronoun *we*.
As a user (say: *As you are a user*) of our dictation machines I am wondering whether you know about our latest model.	The person writing is not the user. The opening phrase is wrongly attached to the pronoun *I*.
I had a good look at the town, travelling by train (say: *Travelling by train, I had,* etc.).	The sentence departs from the natural order of expression.
The hall was erected to the memory of our Chairman, who was killed in action as a mark of affection by the Company (say: *The hall was erected as a mark of affection by the Company* to the memory of, etc.).	Here again there is a departure from the natural order of expression.
We laid (say: *lay*) on the grass for over an hour.	Confusion between the verbs *lay* and *lie*.

GRAMMATICAL FLEXIBILITY

Effective communication does not depend merely on obedience to
the rules of grammar. It is in fact better to break a rule and be natural
than to observe it and seem to be affected and artificial. But before
we break the rules we should know what they are and it is one of
the purposes of Part II of this book to provide an outline of them.

Some examples of conventional expressions that offend strict grammatical rules are given below with their strict grammatical forms:

Conventional form	Grammatical form	Rule broken
It is a Society *whose* work is well supported.	It is a Society the work *of which* is well supported.	Inanimate use of *whose* (p. 287).
None of our customers *are* able to pay *their* way.	None of our customers *is* able to pay *his* (or *her*) way.	*None* as a singular noun (p. 276).
Ask him *to kindly reply* to my letter.	Ask him *kindly to reply* (or *to reply kindly*) to my letter. (Besides being clumsy these forms express meanings different from that of the conventional form.)	Split infinitive (p. 282).
He made *quite a lot* of mistakes.	He made *a great many* (or *a large number*) of mistakes.	Use of adverb *quite* as an adjective (p. 292).
Less than a dozen members attended.	*Fewer* than a dozen members attended.	*Less* refers to quantity, *fewer* to number (p. 292).
We *only* received your letter yesterday.	We received your letter *only* yesterday.	Misplacement of *only* (pp. 293–4).
I couldn't find anyone to go *with*.	I couldn't find anyone *with whom* to go.	Prepositional ending (p. 297–8).

These examples are enough to show that we must not be afraid to give our speech and writing a natural touch. Rules like those about splitting infinitives and ending sentences with prepositions may be all very well in their place, but we must not allow them to force us into an unnatural style of communication. We must treat grammar as our servant and not as our master. Even so, it is important to remember that the letters we write are expected to be in good English, and that good English will generally be the kind of English that conforms to the accepted rules of grammar. These rules are, after all, the result of long experience and are based on common sense. Representing as they do the accumulated experience of generations we cannot ignore them lightly. They have, moreover, a social significance since their observance is one of the accepted marks of an educated person. We may not, for example, use *like* as a conjunction (p. 297), or *which* without an antecedent (pp. 285–6); nor may we substitute *me* for *I* in a sentence such as *It is I who am to blame,* though usage sanctions it in the expression *It is me.* Except therefore where usage clearly sanctions departures from the rules, the disciplines of grammar should be accepted and the rules observed. With the increasingly rapid development of facilities for communication English is quickly becoming a universal language, and if we are to share our linguistic heritage with the rest of mankind we must conform to the accepted disciplines and do nothing that will depress the standards of what is recognized as good English.

GRAMMATICAL DISCIPLINE

The essential purpose of grammar is to make communication clear. Its rules are no more than a summary of what experienced writers and speakers have found to be the best insurance against obscure and ambiguous expression. Some rules are more important than others. Disregard of the more important often creates doubt about meaning and therefore seriously interferes with the effectiveness of communication. Disregard of other and less important rules may not create problems of communication, but it lowers the standing of those who fail to conform to the accepted levels of correctness. Wherever possible therefore it is important to communicate not only clearly but also correctly in accordance with educated usage.

In the conflict between what is grammatically correct and what is conventionally permissible we must remember that the essential qualities of good communication in business are sincerity, simplicity and especially clarity. The more we can give expression to these qualities in terms that are friendly without being familiar and natural without being commonplace, the more will our manner of communicating approach the style appropriate to business. If to achieve this we must occasionally disregard the strict functions of grammar no one will blame us, so long as we express ourselves sincerely, simply and clearly, with reason and good sense as our guide.

EXERCISES

1. Test your comprehension of Chapter 1 by answering the following questions:

   (*a*) Language operates at two different levels. What are they?
   (*b*) What is meant by effective communication?
   (*c*) What is meant by "feed-back", and why is it important?

(*d*) Mention in their logical sequence the various stages in the communication process.

(*e*) What are the advantages of oral over non-verbal communication?

(*f*) What are its disadvantages?

(*g*) What is the outstanding quality of a good communicator?

(*h*) What can he do to ensure that his message is free from ambiguity?

2. Assess the importance of grammar as a factor in communication.

3. Read the following passage carefully and then answer the questions that follow it, *using your own words where possible.* Your answers should be written *concisely* in *complete sentences,* unless you are otherwise instructed:—

CHANGES IN SHOPPING HABITS

Social habits change slowly, but a revolution in our shopping habits is gradually getting under way. Within a fairly short period we are likely to look for a good many of our shops not in town centres, but on their outskirts, for shopkeepers and their customers alike will regard it as a matter of course that shopping should be done by car.

In the United States it is already commonplace for a family to own two cars, one for the husband to go to work in, and one for his wife to take the children to school, to go shopping and to go visiting in the afternoon. We may expect, therefore, that some form of private motor transport, in addition to her husband's, will be considered as indispensable as the vacuum cleaner by the average West European housewife in the near future.

For most of human history "near" or "far" from one's home has been measured in terms of distances that have to be covered on foot. "Near shops" in an Estate Agent's advertisement will normally mean that shops are five or ten minutes' walk away. In the oldest parts of our towns every two or three streets of houses have their attendant group of small shops, and as long as household shopping has to be done on foot it is natural as well as convenient to shop as near to home, in terms of distance, as possible.

Yet, even without a private car, the realities of shopping distances have long been changing. On a good bus route it may be more convenient and even quicker to go to shops a mile or two away than to shops within half a mile that have to be reached on foot. Moreover, since shopping also involves transport of one's purchases, there are other advantages in shops that can be reached easily by bus.

With private motor transport, shops within ten miles of where one lives can be considered close at hand. If the shops are also planned for motorised shopping, with all normal needs catered for in one block, a morning's shopping may in fact be got through more quickly, as well as far more comfortably, than by walking from shop to shop in the traditional shopping street within walking distance of a residential area.

(*a*) What change is likely to take place in the situation of many of our shops in the near future?

(*b*) Why will shopkeepers and their customers find this change acceptable?

(*c*) Mention *three* ways in which a second car is used by housewives in the United States.

(*d*) To what does the phrase "near shops" refer in an Estate Agent's advertisement?

(*e*) In what circumstances is it natural for people to do their shopping in their own district, according to the passage?

(*f*) Mention *three* possible advantages of using a bus to go shopping.

(*g*) Give *three* reasons why, according to the last paragraph, the housewife of the future is likely to use private motor transport for shopping rather than walking.

(*h*) Explain *very briefly* what is meant by any *four* of the following words or phrases as they are used in the passage:—

> (*i*) a matter of course (line 4)
> (*ii*) indispensable (line 10)
> (*iii*) Estate Agent (line 14)
> (*iv*) traditional (line 28)
> (*v*) residential (line 29)

(L.C.C.I. Elem.)

4. Read the following passage and answer the questions that follow it.

Gold is the metal-worker's ideal medium: he may draw it into wire as fine as a hair, or beat it into leaf so thin that light will pass through it. It may be cast to the contours of a thumb print or smelted into short fibres one-fourteenth of a millimetre in diameter. Pure gold is remarkably stable and impervious to the ordinary processes of corrosion and decay.

Gold is almost always found in its native metallic state, often in white quartzite rock, or as dust and nuggets in the beds of rivers. Raw gold is seldom pure but mixed with silver, copper or even iron. If the silver content is more than one-fifth it is regarded as another metal, electrum.

Once placer, or alluvial gold, was concentrated by panning. Gold-bearing river gravel was agitated in a shallow pan, the heavier gold being separated by gravity. Sometimes the skin of a newly-killed sheep was anchored to the river bed with stones. Gold dust moving in the current would lodge in the greasy wool. After a time it would be taken out and burned, and the gold washed from the ashes. This could well have given rise to the legend of the Golden Fleece.

(*a*) Why is gold the metal worker's medium?

(*b*) What may have given rise to the legend of the Golden Fleece?

(*c*) What other metals might raw gold be found mixed with?

(*d*) Give the meaning of each of the following:

> (*i*) electrum;
> (*ii*) placer;
> (*iii*) panning.

(*e*) In about 100 words say what you consider to be the main attractions of gold.

(N.W.R.A.C.)

5. What is meant by the term "the grapevine"? Explain the reasons for its existence in large organizations, the drawbacks of this form of communication and the best ways of forestalling them.

(I.C.S.A.)

6. "The best system of communication is that achieved with the least paper-work." Say how far you agree with this statement and explain the advantages of *(a)* oral, *(b)* written communication in business.

(I.C.S.A.)

7. Write notes on each of the following:

charts;
diagrams;
graphs;
tables;

as an aid to effective communication.

(I.C.S.A.)

8. What do you understand by the term "readability"? How would you assess the readability of a lengthy printed document intended for unskilled workers?

(I.C.S.A.)

9. "A picture is worth a thousand words." Explain with examples the meaning of this statement.

(I.C.S.A.)

CHAPTER TWO

The Use of Words

Words are like leaves; and where they most abound
Much fruit of sense beneath is rarely found.

A. Pope: *Essays on Criticism*

CURRENT PRACTICE

No living language is or can be static; the fact of living implies growth. What was incorrect in the past becomes correct in the present, and words and phrases take on a new significance. In our own language many new words are reaching us from America, and while at first some may be regarded by the English mind as offending good taste, their constant use frequently wins them a place in the accepted English vocabulary: we now *contact* a person, call on a *prospect,* and *finalize* a transaction.

In business letter-writing we must adopt what is considered to be the best practice for the time being, neither clinging to what is no longer currently accepted—the commercialese of the Victorian business letter, for example—nor adopting words and phrases that are still novel. In our own day the best practice in business letter-writing has come to mean two things: a plain straightforward style, and obedience to the accepted rules of grammar—a style that uses *write* rather than *communicate, about* rather than *in connection with;* that does not confuse *lay* and *lie, between* and *among,* or *less* and *fewer.* This is the style called for. Neither adornment nor bad grammar has any place in the modern business letter.

IMPORTANCE OF VOCABULARY

"For those who have learned to play it the English language is a wonderful instrument." The great *Oxford Dictionary* contains nearly half a million references. A number of our single-volume dictionaries will contain as many as 150,000, but not many people use more than three or four thousand of them.

English is a rich language. It is so mainly because of its growth from a multitude of sources. The Norman Conquest added a large number of new words, and in the fifteenth and sixteenth centuries the Renaissance created a new intellectual atmosphere, and added large numbers of new Greek and Latin words. Travel abroad has brought many new words from French, Italian, and Spanish sources, and still stranger words from the countries of the East.

A person with a wide vocabulary is able to choose the most effective words and phrases for each occasion. The power to use words effectively is a precious possession, and in business a most desirable accomplishment. Reading and the patient use of the dictionary is the best means we have of increasing our knowledge of words. You should look up every new word in your dictionary and learn its meaning. It is an excellent and indeed an essential plan to keep a list of such words, and to take the opportunity to use them in speech and writing whenever the occasion presents itself, for only by actual use will new words become part of your vocabulary.

CHOOSE THE RIGHT WORD

Even when you know the meaning of a word the exercise of care in its use is still necessary if you are to say precisely what you want to say, because words that appear to have the same meaning often carry fine but nevertheless important distinctions. Such words are called *synonyms.* On the face of it *big* and *great,* and *strong* and *powerful,* may appear to mean the same thing, but a man, for example, can be *big* without being *great,* and *strong* without being *powerful.* He can be a *politician,* yet not a *statesman,* and *uphold* a cause without *supporting* it, while measures he adopts may be *effective* but far from *effectual.*

Study for a moment the different shades of meaning expressed by the synonyms of the simple word *said* in the following sentence.

He said (stated, asserted, claimed, maintained, declared) that the goods had not been delivered.

To *say* means to express in words; *state,* to express in a formal manner; *assert,* to express strongly; *claim,* to express as being true; *maintain,* to uphold; *declare,* to make known.

Such discriminations may appear to be trifling, but the writer who wishes to think clearly and to convey his thoughts with exactness—and which writer does not?—will respect them.

Words are the vehicle of thought, and to convey your thoughts clearly you must choose the right words. A short, carefully prepared paragraph, written in words chosen because they are just the right words, serves its intended purpose better than a whole page of matter expressed in words that are no more than nearly right.

You must first be clear about what you want to say, and then careful about the way you say it. You must at least choose the right words; words that are only nearly right are not good enough. You must make no attempt to express an idea until it has been clearly formed in your mind. Clarity is of the essence of good writing, and you cannot express clearly an idea that has not itself been clearly and fully formed. Once you know what you want to say, the words with which to say it will come all the more readily. Perhaps Lewis Carroll had this in mind when he parodied the well-known proverb, and cautioned us to "Take care of the sense, and the sounds will take care of themselves".

When a word is grossly misused for another which it resembles it is called a *malapropism,* from the French *mal à propos,* meaning ill-suited to the purpose. The term derives from Mrs. Malaprop, the character in Sheridan's play *The Rivals,* noted for her use of words in the wrong sense. She did not wish her daughter, she said, to be a *progeny* (for prodigy) of learning, but she would send her to school to gain a *supercilious* (superficial) knowledge in accounts, and be instructed in *geometry* (geography) so that she might learn something of the *contagious* (contiguous) countries. But above all, her daughter must be a mistress of *orthodoxy* (orthography), so that she might not misspell and mispronounce words so shamefully as girls usually do.

Chosen wisely and used imaginatively, words will convey not only the sense of a message but the spirit of it as well.

CHOOSE THE SIMPLE WORD

One of the main faults in present-day letter-writing is the tendency to prefer what is complicated and roundabout to what is simple and direct. We write:

We shall be in a position to effect delivery.

when we mean:

We shall be able to deliver.

and:

Have you come to a decision regarding the installation of the machine?

for:

Have you decided to install the machine?

It is better to write simply than to write elaborately, though writing simply is often more difficult than writing elaborately. It is said of Bernard Shaw that, having on one occasion written a long letter, he apologized for not having time to write a short one. People who are perfectly able to express themselves in plain spoken language somehow get the idea that the short, simple words they used in conversation are not respectable enough for a place on paper. Where they would say, *We have closed the deal*, they would write, *We have finalized the transaction.*

Preference for the roundabout phrase is linked with a preference for the long word rather than the short. But of the two the short word is the better: it is easier, it is clearer, and more in keeping with good English style. Never use a longer word, therefore, if there is a shorter word that gives the same meaning. Instead of *acquainting* your customer with the details, *tell* him about them; don't *solicit* his custom, *invite* it; and don't *dispatch* the goods, but *send* them to him.

The shorter words in the following list are preferred to their longer equivalents:

Instead of	Say	Instead of	Say
approximately	about	majority	most
assist	help	materialize	occur, take
commence	begin (less		place
	formal)	peruse	read
communicate	write	prevent	stop
communication	letter	purchase	buy
description	kind, sort	request	ask
experience	feel	requirements	needs
implement	carry out	sufficient	enough
inform	tell	terminate	end
initiate	begin, start	transmit	send
locality	place	utilize	use

Nor should *feel* be used as if it were the same thing as *think; feeling* is the result of intuition, and business decisions, which should result from reasoning, should not be expressed as if they were the results of intuition.

By writing simply and avoiding what is elaborate and complex we not only convey our meaning more clearly but also create a feeling of sincerity and integrity. For who can be suspicious of a person who writes and speaks plainly?

EXERCISES

1. Study the following synonyms, and frame sentences to illustrate the different shades of meaning in each set:

        (*a*) abbreviate, abridge   (*c*) association, society

        (*b*) centre, middle   (*d*) balance, surplus

(e) produce, product   *(h)* advise, inform
(f) find, discover   *(i)* receive, acquire
(g) fault, mistake   *(j)* renew, repair

2. Express in a single word the meaning of the words printed in italics in each of the following sentences:

(a) No letter should be sent in handwriting *that cannot be read.*
(b) The scheme was *one that could not be put into practice.*
(c) The proposal was adopted *with full agreement of everyone present.*
(d) The explanation given was *capable of bearing more than one meaning.*
(e) One of the essential qualities of money is that it must be *capable of being carried from place to place.*
(f) The report on the company's activities covered a *period of ten years.*
(g) Our chairman is *a man who always looks on the bright side of things.*
(h) As a civil servant he was entitled to *a pension payable on retirement.*
(i) The two chairs are by the same maker, and are *the same in every respect.*
(j) The problem that presented itself seemed to be *one that could never be solved.*

3. In each of the following sentences substitute a single word that could exactly replace the phrase in italics:

(a) The type of vehicle popular ten years ago is now *going out of use.*
(b) The office manager and the cashier were appointed *at one and the same time.*
(c) The two firms decided to *work in association with each other* in the production of office furniture.
(d) The local tradesman was *unable to pay his debts.*
(e) The secretary was asked to submit a *word for word* report of the meeting.
(f) The capital sum invested provided *a fixed annual sum of money.*
(g) Saving is one of the means we employ to provide for *possible future events.*
(h) The chairman announced that the candidate was *not, under the rules, qualified for election.*
(i) The *programme of business for the meeting* had been circulated to members of the committee.
(j) We prefer to send the goods by road because they are *easily broken.*

4. Words printed in italics in the following letter are used in the wrong sense. Recast the letter substituting the correct words probably intended.

Dear Sir

We have received an *anomalous* letter from a customer who has a grievance that, I assure you, is quite *imaginative.* The *inflammable* tone of the letter suggests that the writer is very angry. His complaint refers to an *incidence* that occurred during the period when work in our factory was *temporally* suspended owing to an *unofficious* strike. The letter is written in French and I am enclosing a *literary* translation of it.

It is not our *practise* to treat *anomalous* letters seriously, but in this *instant* we feel the nature of the complaint to be such that an *inquisition* should be made into the alleged circumstances. We would therefore be glad if you would *precede* to make *judicial* enquiries to find out who the writer is. We *fervidly* hope your *inquisition* will enable him to be identified, because we are most anxious to preserve *harmonical* relations with all our customers and to do business with them on terms that are both fair and *equable.*

Yours faithfully

5. Rewrite the following paragraph without once using the word "got". Do not alter the original meaning in any way:

A little boy once got a bicycle which he soon got used to. As he got bigger, however, it got too small for him, so he got rid of it and got a larger one. At first he got a lot of trouble with his new machine. Once when riding in the country he got a puncture. He got off to repair it, and by the time he had got it done it had got dark. Luckily he got home safely.

(R.S.A. Elem.)

6. Improve the following sentences by using simpler words and phrases for those in italics:

(a) We *discovered* the lorry *in close proximity* to our premises.
(b) The accident is likely to *impair his capacity* for work.
(c) The changes made will appeal to *the great majority* of our customers.
(d) Clerical employment does not *involve the necessity of obtaining* a medical certificate.
(e) *The position with reference to the shortage of labour* is now very serious.
(f) We shall be glad to *render you any assistance in our power.*
(g) When asked if she had typed the report she *answered in the affirmative.*
(h) Because of the recent floods the delivery of the goods by rail is not *a practical proposition.*
(i) We regret the enclosure was *inadvertently omitted.*
(j) The damage caused by the fire was *of a very far-reaching character.*

7. Express the following sentences in simpler form without changing the meaning:

(a) We dispatched the goods to you yesterday per passenger train.
(b) If you will advise us of your requirements we will do our utmost to assist you.
(c) When we received your communication we experienced a sense of deep disappointment.
(d) We anticipate being able to place an order with you for approximately 500 tables.
(e) We venture to express the hope that you will deal with the matter as expeditiously as possible.
(f) The difficulties we had expected to encounter in acquiring the site did not materialize.

(g) The enclosed brochure contains full details of the operations we have in mind, and we trust you will peruse it at your convenience.

(h) We wish to terminate the service agreement to which you make reference in your letter.

(i) There is insufficient work to enable us to utilize the services of a third shorthand typist.

(j) The order for shirts, which you dispatched to us last Friday, has been transmitted to our factory for attention.

8. Each of the following sentences includes a slightly informal expression which is printed in italic type. Replace each of these expressions with ONE word which does not change the meaning of the sentence. (You do not need to write out the whole sentence again.)

e.g. He is always *getting at* me — nagging (He is always *nagging* me).

(a) "What are you *getting at,* Inspector?"
(b) Fortunately, the cat cannot *get at* the goldfish.
(c) If you straddle the white line, other cars cannot *get by.*
(d) We do not have a lot of money, but I am sure we will *get by.*
(e) You have to have charm to *get on* in this world.
(f) "Does she know how to *get on* a horse?"
(g) "I do hope the criminals *get away!*"
(h) "Is there no way of *getting round* that problem?"
(i) "I must *get back* home, immediately."
(j) He can only *get about* with the aid of a stick.
(k) He must be *getting on for* seventy.
(l) The view when we *get to* the top is terrific.
(m) "We must *get together* for a meal sometime."
(n) Mr. Smith can always be relied upon to *get up* a collection.
(o) News *gets around* quickly in these parts.

(E.M.E.U.)

USE ADJECTIVES AND ADVERBS SPARINGLY

Used sparingly and properly adjectives and adverbs can both help; but do not use them unless they contribute something to the meaning of what is said. A thing that is *right* is not more correct when it is claimed to be *definitely right;* nor is *delay* more prolonged merely because it is *undue.*

Care must be taken, too, to use adjectives and adverbs with their proper meanings. *Incidentally* must not be used, as so often it is, to introduce a piece of essential information; nor must we talk of a *fantastic salary* or a *fabulous film-star. Fantastic* means fanciful or *unreal* and *fabulous* pertains to fable or what is *not true.*

Adjectives

Adjectives that denote *kind* are more likely to be correctly used than adjectives that denote *degree.* You can write correctly about a *social problem, good-humoured opposition, unexpected danger,* or a *train disaster,* but need to take care with adjectives in phrases such as a *real problem, considerable opposition, substantial danger,* and *major disaster.* They are not necessarily wrong, but they are often used when it would be better to leave them out.

Adverbs

What applies to adjectives applies equally to adverbs—you should use them sparingly and with care. By all means say "It is *exactly* three o'clock", "I am *completely* puzzled", "I will see you *presently*", "It is *rather* cold", where the adverbs mean something, but keep a watchful eye on the use of adverbs such as *definitely, unduly, relatively, comparatively, somewhat,* and *rather* in expressions such as *definitely harmful, unduly prolonged, relatively few, comparatively soon, somewhat rare, rather think,* where they contribute little or nothing to the sense. Beware, too, of such overworked adverbs as *absolutely, actually,* and *perfectly.*

Vague words, especially adverbs, are always useless; they mean nothing of value. They form a kind of barricade behind which the timid take shelter from the risks to which clear statements and precise promises would expose them. The following example is typical.

> We *hope* (whatever that means) to send a *substantial percentage* (whatever that may be) of the goods ordered at an *early date* (whenever that is.).

Such a statement tells the customer nothing helpful. If only the writer had put *relatively* before *substantial,* and *comparatively* before *early* his security would have been complete.

Use *relatively* and *comparatively* only when you compare one thing with another. Instead of saying *relatively* or *comparatively few, relatively* or *comparatively small,* state how many or what size. Thus, it is quite correct to say:

> In the accident yesterday fifty people were injured, but relatively few seriously.

where the number injured seriously is compared with the number injured. But you must not say:

> In the accident yesterday relatively few people were injured seriously.

since no comparison is made.

AVOID ABSTRACT NOUNS

The purpose of a letter is to convey a message. The message must be clear, and for this the concrete word is better than the abstract. The concrete word denotes something tangible, such as a *man*, a *table*, a *book*. The abstract word denotes something intangible—a quality or condition—such as *freedom, usefulness, heaviness*. Excessive use of the abstract term is a common fault; its meaning is often vague and leads to roundabout statements. There can be no mistake about what is meant by a *book*, but ideas on what is meant by *freedom* may be widely different. Wherever possible avoid the abstract word and use the concrete, reconstructing the sentence if necessary.

> Rules have been made for the *avoidance* and *settlement* of disputes. (Say: Rules have been made for avoiding and settling disputes.)

> *Achievement* of the results looked for will not be possible without the co-operation of the staff. (Say: The expected results will not be achieved without the co-operation of the staff.)

> Your *entitlement* to a pension will be dependent upon length of service. (Say: Whether or not you are entitled to a pension will depend upon length of service.)

The italicized words in these sentences are all abstractions and lead to unsatisfactory ways of saying something that is said more simply and effectively if the sentences are recast as shown.

Large numbers of words ending in *tion* and *sion* are abstract; you should give them careful thought before accepting them. *Position* and *situation* are among the common snares.

> The *position* in regard to the supply of coal may become serious. (Say: There may be a serious coal shortage.)

> The *situation* with reference to the supply of skilled engineers is not likely to improve. (Say: The shortage of skilled engineers is likely to continue.)

> *Conditions* in reference to employment are more favourable than for many years past. (Say: Employment prospects are better than for many years past.)

> *Application* of the new salary scales has caused disappointment. (Say: The new salary scales have caused disappointment.)

> I will arrange for the *preparation* of the programme at once. (Say: I will arrange for the programme to be prepared at once.)

AVOID NEEDLESS PREPOSITIONAL PHRASES

Another common failing in business letter-writing is the use of phrases where a single word would do. Phrases ending with prepositions are often no more than cumbersome substitutes for single words that do the work better. The following are examples of the unnecessary use of such phrases, the word that should be used being shown within brackets.

> We have increased prices *in order to* (to) reduce our losses.
> The equipment is needed *in connection with* (for) the new office block.
> I have received you letter *on the subject of* (concerning) the new machinery.
> We are *in a position* (able) to supply the goods immediately.
> Please insert particulars *in respect of* (for) last week.
> I am writing *on behalf of* (for) Mr. Watson.

The following are phrases of a similar kind.

Instead of	*Say*
approve of	approve
by means of	by, through, with
consequent upon	after
for the purpose of	for
having regard to	concerning
in spite of	although
in the case of	by, for
in the course of	during
in the event of	if
prior to	before
shall take steps to	shall
so as to	
with a view to	to
with the object of	
in relation to	
on the question of	
with reference to	about, concerning
with regard to	

Before using a phrase ending with a preposition make sure that it cannot be replaced by a single word meaning the same thing:

> *During* his speech he talked *about* security.

is shorter, simpler, more direct, and much better than:

> *In the course of* his speech he talked *on the question of* security.

EXERCISES

1. Examine critically the use of the words and phrases in italics in the following sentences, and recast the sentences in good English.

(a) We have in stock a *considerable quantity* of folding tables, which we can offer you *at a reasonable price*.

(*b*) It is expected that work on the new site will be completed *at a comparatively early date.*

(*c*) The *true facts* are as given you in my letter last week.

(*d*) The contractors have been informed *of the likelihood of substantial delay* in the delivery of the steel girders.

(*e*) The gradual rise in prices *represents a real threat to* the standard of living.

(*f*) We *are necessarily anxious* to do everything we can to help.

(*g*) We *rather hope* you will not allow the lower prices offered by our competitors to *unduly influence* your policy.

(*h*) Since the workmen arrived *there has been relatively little opportunity* to deal with correspondence.

(*i*) We *are somewhat at a loss to* understand why we have received no orders from you during the past six months.

(*j*) There is likely to be an *appreciable rise in price* within the next year or so.

2. Rearrange the following sentences in plain, straightforward English, without using the abstract nouns and the phrases in italics (for examples, see p. 22).

(*a*) There is early *expectancy* of a vacancy on the technical staff of the power station.

(*b*) Most of our customers *express a preference for* the older style of furnishings.

(*c*) *The use of* road maps is a *necessity* for the modern motorist.

(*d*) There will have to be a careful *perusal* of the estimates before *a decision on the matter can be arrived at.*

(*e*) It will be for members of the technical staff to decide on the *suitability or otherwise* of the new machine.

(*f*) We *express regret* that we cannot accept *responsibility* for the mistake *that has occurred* in the delivery of the goods.

(*g*) We *have pleasure in announcing* that on 31st July we shall be taking over the business of Blake and Nunn, estate agents.

(*h*) The *appointment* of a new office manager will be made by the Board at their meeting next Thursday.

(*i*) *In all probability* we shall need a *considerable quantity* of new typewriters after the end of this year.

(*j*) We are glad *to have your assurance* that the work on the new plant will be completed by the end of August.

AVOID EXAGGERATION

In conversation we often exaggerate to produce a striking effect. To offer a *thousand apologies,* to feel *terribly hungry,* to *kill oneself with laughing* are expressions that may be harmless enough in speech, but they seldom appear in the written vocabulary, and certainly have no place in the business letter. Avoid saying *stupendous, tremendous, gigantic, immeasurable,* when you mean no more than *large,* or *considerable.*

> The storm caused *immeasurable* (say *heavy,* or *considerable*) damage to the factory.
>
> The labour shortage is creating a *tremendous* (say *great*) problem.

Nor must words such as *awfully, terribly, jolly* be used for *very* in connections like *awfully sorry, terribly inconvenient, jolly glad.*

The use of strong and colourful adjectives such as the foregoing is no doubt inspired by the wish to be interesting and to attract attention in much the same way as swearing. In a business letter attention must be attracted by original ideas and the clarity with which they are expressed, and not by the use of strong and often ill-fitting words. Choose those words which express just what you mean. When a person says he *loves* kippers, *loves* tennis, and *loves* Julie he is using the same term to express quite different feelings, a term that means only one thing—affection. But one can hardly have an affection for kippers, or even for tennis. The meaning may be clear enough to those who are accustomed to such loose expressions, but loose and vague expressions are out of place in a business letter, where what is meant must be said. If we *like* kippers, or *enjoy* tennis, we must say so, and reserve our affection for those we really love.

AVOID FOREIGN PHRASES

When there are English expressions that serve just as well, foreign expressions, particularly Latin tags, are also out of place in the business letter. The English language is usually rich and vivid enough to say all that needs to be said, and you should not as a rule use tags such as the following.

Instead of	Say
a priori	by deduction
ad hoc	for the special purpose
ad lib.	at pleasure
au fait	well acquainted with
bona fide	in good faith
en bloc	as a unit, wholesale
en route	on the way
ex gratia	as an act of grace, or a favour
ex officio	by virtue of the office or post held
fait accompli	already done
faux pas	a false step, a mistake

in toto	entirely
inter alia	among other things
inter se	among themselves
ipso facto	by the fact itself, automatically
modus operandi	mode of operation
non sequitur	it does not follow
quid pro quo	something in return, an equivalent
per annum	yearly
per se	in itself
prima facie	at first sight
pro rata	in proportion
pro tem.	for the time being
seriatim	in the order given
sine die	indefinitely
sine qua non	a necessity
status quo	the present position
sub judice	under consideration
ultra vires	beyond one's authority
vice versa	conversely
viva voce	orally

These and expressions like them have their uses in other fields, but in the business letter they must be used with restraint. English is rich enough not to need the help of alien phrases. Nevertheless, some of these phrases such as *ad hoc, bona fide, en route,* and *ex officio* have established themselves in the technical vocabulary of business, probably because of the economy with which they express the ideas they stand for. It would therefore be against reason to deny them a place in the business letter when it is appropriate to use them. It is different with phrases such as *per annum, pro rata, pro tem,* and *vice versa;* they have no special merit to commend them. They say nothing that cannot be said more simply and clearly in the language they stand for, and while it may be permissible to use them in other departments of business, they are out of place in the business letter.

Foreign phrases are not signs of superior education; they have become much too hackneyed and commonplace for that, and in the interests of that simplicity which is one of the marks of the good business letter it will usually be better to avoid them.

AVOID TAUTOLOGY

Tautology means needless repetition. Avoid using redundant, that is superfluous, words and phrases. Never, for example, associate *quite, very, most* with such words as *unique, perfect, ideal, supreme,* which in themselves express the highest degree possible. Expressions such as *quite unique, quite perfect, very ideal,* and *most supreme* are wrong.

Some other examples of redundancy are given below, the superfluous words being shown in brackets. Be careful to avoid similar mistakes.

He (voluntarily) offered his services.	An offer is in itself voluntary.
He declined (to accept) our offer.	Decline means not to accept.
The goods must be restored (again) to their rightful owner.	Restore means give back again.
He received the news with equanimity (of mind).	Equanimity is evenness of mind.
They exercise an (exclusive) monopoly.	Monopoly is exclusive control.
The reason is (because).	Because means for this reason.
There was world-wide recognition (by all).	World-wide means by everyone.
We returned (back) to this country.	To return is to come back.
He travelled with three (fellow) companions.	A fellow means a companion.
The (true) facts are not known.	A fact is necessarily true.
I am a (new) beginner.	A beginner is necessarily new.
In (close) proximity.	Proximity means nearness.
(A high degree of) perfection.	Perfection is the highest form attainable.
To co-ordinate (together).	Co-ordinate means to bring together.

To provide a fitting conclusion to this chapter on the choice of words it is apt to quote from the advice given by Sir Ernest Gowers in his *Plain Words*—a "book written to help officials in their use of written English". It is a book that everyone concerned with business letter-writing should read.

> What we are concerned with is not a quest for a literary style as an end in itself, but to study how best to convey our meaning without ambiguity and without giving unnecessary trouble to our readers.

He then proceeds to give three rules for writing.*

> Use no more words than are necessary to express your meaning, for if you use more you are likely to obscure it and to tire your reader. In particular do not use superfluous adjectives and adverbs and do not use roundabout phrases where single words would serve.
>
> Use familiar words rather than the far-fetched, for the familiar are more likely to be readily understood.

*Gowers: *The Complete Plain Words,* 2nd ed., H.M.S.O., p. 51.

Use words with a precise meaning rather than those that are vague, for they will obviously serve better to make your meaning clear; and in particular prefer concrete words to abstract, for they are more likely to have a precise meaning.

EXERCISES

1. Improve the following sentences by using more reasonable expressions for the exaggerations printed in italics.

(a) Considering the bad state of trade our turnover last year was *truly magnificent*.

(b) If I've told him once about coming late I've told him *hundreds of times*.

(c) Wait for me downstairs; I'll be with you in *half a second*.

(d) Meetings can waste such a lot of time and I *simply hate them*.

(e) The applause following his speech *literally brought the house down*.

(f) It is *ages* since we last heard from you.

(g) It's *absolute heaven* to work in our new office block.

(h) A good secretary is *worth her weight in gold*.

(i) He is a director of six companies and has *tons of money*.

(j) "One picture is worth *ten thousand words*." (Chinese proverb.)

2. The following sentences all contain unnecessary words. Rearrange each sentence, improving it by using fewer and simpler words, but without changing the sense.

A

(a) He was completely inaudible, and no one could hear him.

(b) We were sitting alone, all by ourselves, when he arrived.

(c) We enjoyed our holiday this year equally as well as last year's.

(d) It is very doubtful as to whether he will gain the promotion he is expecting.

(e) Applicants for employment in our factory abound in great numbers.

(f) There is no question whatever but that the mistake was his own.

(g) Our salesman will call on you if and when you ask him to do so.

(h) When the new clerks arrive each will be told what his respective duties are.

(i) A quite unique feature of the firm's new lorries is their low petrol consumption.

(j) We have received your letter and the same shall have our urgent and immediate attention.

B

(a) She has resigned from her post as invoice clerk.

(b) One way out of the difficulty still remains open.

(c) In the event of your wishing me to do so, I will call on you next week.

(d) I have been unable to reply before owing to the fact that I have only just returned from abroad.

(e) The two assistants were mutually antagonistic to each other.

(f) His appointment dates as and from March 1st.

(*g*) The two vehicles collided with each other at considerable speed.

(*h*) The true facts of the situation are not yet in our possession.

(*i*) As a shorthand-writer she has attained a high standard of perfection.

(*j*) I asked him to call and see me, but he declined to accept my invitation.

3. Improve the following sentences by omitting superfluous words, indicating in each case the reason for your omission.

(*a*) His future prospects were not very promising.

(*b*) As chairman of three different companies he possessed very unique experience.

(*c*) The surrounding circumstances do not justify an advance of more than £2,000.

(*d*) The company has a complete monopoly of the market.

(*e*) We were warmly welcomed as soon as we entered into the room.

(*f*) Descending down the staircase she slipped and hurt herself.

(*g*) The repairs you asked us to carry out are now quite completed.

(*h*) The production of gramophone records has now reached a high degree of perfection.

(*i*) We enclose herewith a copy of the report.

(*j*) We managed to trace the original source of the quotation.

CHAPTER THREE

The Abuse of Words

Words are the dress of thoughts, which should no more be presented in rags, tatters, and dirt than your person should.

Lord Chesterfield: *Letters*, 25th January, 1750

CLICHÉS

Cliché is a French word used in English to denote a phrase that has become stereotyped and threadbare through excessive use. A cliché is another of the faults in style that must be avoided in business correspondence; it indicates poverty of language and an unwillingness to think for oneself. Letters packed with clichés can never be fresh and original, since by its very nature a cliché is something that is second-hand.

A cliché that is unacceptable as standard English becomes slang; if it is frequently used as part of the vocabulary of a particular branch of writing, business correspondence for example, then it becomes what is known as jargon.

The following are some of the commoner clichés, many of which find their way into business letters.

as a matter of fact	for the time being
as a rule	for your information
at all events	goes against the grain
at this moment in time	if the worst comes to the worst
axe to grind	in any shape or form
be that as it may	in point of fact
bear in mind	in the first place
better half	in the meantime
bound to admit	in the near future
by and large	in view of the fact
by the way	in well-informed circles
conspicuous by its absence	inclined to think
cut out the dead wood	it goes without saying
explore every avenue	last but not least
face facts	leave no stone unturned
fact of the matter	look on the bright side

make the most of the opportunity	psychological moment
minor matters	rising generation
need hardly say	second to none
needless to say	shrewd suspicion
no room for complacency	take the rough with the smooth
on the contrary	the man in the street
over and above	to all intents and purposes
plus the fact	unparalleled success

What is a cliché is a matter of opinion. If the phrase is used because it is the fittest way of expressing what one wants to say there can be no objection to it; otherwise it should be avoided.

Figurative expressions like *break the ice, a bull in a china shop, a bee in one's bonnet, on the tip of one's tongue,* are telling and picturesque, and in their proper place are acceptable. Nevertheless, if at any time you find yourself about to slip into a familiar phrase, think twice before using it, and then use it only if it is the best way of saying what you have to say.

SLANG

In all communication we have to learn to adjust our language to the circumstances in which and the person with whom it is used. The kind of language that is suitable between close friends would not be appropriate for a business letter, and when communicating with an individual we have to adjust our style to suit his age, his status, his intelligence, his education and probable range of vocabulary particularly in technical matters. When communicating in speech we may be formal and serious or informal and light-hearted depending on circumstances and the kind of person we converse with. A report to a senior, giving a talk at a club, chatting with close friends, answering the telephone at work all involve a different style of language, and a large part of the art of effective communication lies in our choice of the appropriate style. Must it be conventional and "proper" or may it be intimate and colloquial? There may even be circumstances when slang is permissible.

The *Shorter Oxford Dictionary* defines slang as "language of a highly colloquial type, considered as below the level of standard educated speech". *Slanguage* is a term coined to describe the use of slang in speech and writing. Words and phrases that are unacceptable as standard English are often used in familiar and informal speech, and in moderation and in their proper place there is no harm in so using them. But they are certainly out of place in business letters and in serious writing. In conversation you can say *Do the needful* for *Do what is necessary*, *Get a move on* for *Hurry up*, and *It is up to you* for *It is for you to decide*. These and similar expressions are entirely the language of informal conversation, to which their use must be confined. On no account must you give them a place in the business letter.

The dictionary contains hundreds of words noted as slang. Most of us can recognize them at sight and would not hesitate to condemn them out of hand as offending good taste. We should no more think of using *posh* in our letters than we should *quid* for *pounds*, *grand* for *one thousand pounds* or *blower* for *telephone*. We don't tell our correspondent he has *had it*, *put his foot in it*, or *fallen for it*. We say he has *been unfortunate*, *made a mistake*, or *been deceived*.

At all costs, then, avoid the use of slang in the business letter.

JARGON

True jargon consists of the technical terms and specialized terminology of some profession, trade, or occupation. We all know that groups of specialists must, among themselves, use a special language; they acquire words and ways of saying things that help them in their work. Medical men could not discuss medical matters without the use of medical terms. In this sense jargon forms a valuable and necessary part of the English language and serves a useful purpose. *Sales promotion* in marketing, *elasticity of demand* in economics, *budgetary control* in accounting, *job evaluation* in industry, *inferiority complex* in psychology, and *retro-rocket* in space travel are all useful terms that are well understood within their specialized fields. They are jargon in the true sense; to those who use them they are a form of verbal shorthand.

But jargon in the popular sense has come to mean long-winded and involved expressions used for their own sake. It is a term now applied to a style of writing that is pompous, obscure, and verbose, full of clichés and hackneyed expressions that add little or nothing to the meaning of what is written, and which are sometimes hard to understand.

Jargon in this sense is a style of writing still sometimes found in government departments (called *officialese*), and in second-rate journalism (called *journalese*). It was the characteristic feature of the business letter of fifty years ago, with its stereotyped, roundabout and meaningless terminology—a legacy from the correspondence of our Victorian ancestors. We even held special classes in what was termed *commercial English*, as if the English for commerce was in any way different from the English for other purposes. It is probably fair to assume that such classes actually taught the use of monstrosities like *beg to advise, your esteemed enquiry, thanking you in anticipation,* and *assuring you of our best attention at all times.*

In more recent times business men and commercial schools and colleges have come to recognize how absurd and futile this style of writing is. In their aim to improve the style of their correspondence some of our larger business concerns have even published their own Guides to Letter Writing, and *Plain Words,* by Sir Ernest Gowers (H.M.S.O.), was written for the civil servant at the special invitation of the Treasury. With these and similar influences at work the standard of business and official letter-writing has improved, though phrases we should do better without still linger in the vocabulary of our correspondence. Perhaps in time the efforts now being made to produce better business letters, and the growing awareness of what is good style in letter-writing, will enable us to write *We have received* rather than *We are in receipt of* without feeling that our behaviour is unusual.

EXERCISES

1. In the following sentences substitute fresher expressions for those printed in italics.

A

(a) He *saw fit* to tender his resignation *on the spot.*

(b) Be that as it may, we owe much to his kindness.

(c) If he doesn't mend his ways he will soon be *on the carpet.*

(d) Strange as it may seem I like my present job and have no wish to change it.

(e) I like to be out of doors, though I dislike sport *in any shape or form.*

(f) The electric typewriter we have just put on the market is *second to none.*

(g) We have suffered all the *trials and tribulations* associated with a prolonged strike.

(h) When I learned I should have to work overtime for the next month I felt *it was the last straw.*

(i) Needless to say I hope to be present at tonight's meeting.

(j) Without a shadow of doubt he is the person to blame.

B

(a) We hope the new design will appeal to *the man in the street.*

(b) It stands to reason that when prices rise the value of money falls.

(c) You may not agree with his views, but *when all is said and done* he is the expert.

(d) At the meeting last night the Member for Oxbridge was *conspicuous by his absence.*

(e) The speech he made after dinner was *too funny for words.*

(f) It goes without saying that a good name is better than riches.

(g) The suggestion to build another garage is *without rhyme or reason.*

(h) As a matter of fact I shall be in Manchester on business next week.
(i) Believe it or not his salary is now over £20,000 a year.
(j) Her shorthand wasn't *up to scratch* and as a result she *missed the bus.*

2. Distinguish between a cliché, slang, and jargon, and give two examples of each.

3. Copy the following letter, and underline the phrases that consist of clichés and jargon.

Dear Sirs

Needless to say we are pleased to receive your esteemed favour of 5th August enclosing illustrated catalogue, which arrived at the psychological moment. There is no doubt whatsoever that good orders could be obtained for many of the items in your catalogue, but on the whole we feel you are severely handicapping both yourselves and us by requiring cash settlement. As a matter of fact nearly all business in this area is done on a credit basis, the period of credit varying from as little as one month to as much as three months and more often than not to six months. It goes without saying that custom will be discouraged unless credit can be given.

We further respectfully suggest that the prices you quote are for the most part too high, and by and large you will find it difficult to compete with other manufacturers unless you reduce them.

We trust you will give favourable consideration to our suggestions with respect to both credit and price.

Assuring you of our best attention at all times,
We are
Yours faithfully

4. Express in good English the letter given in Exercise 3.

5. Translate each of the following slangy sentences into good conversational English.

(i) You've got to be joking.   *(vi)* He's got the gift of the gab.
(ii) He was fired on the spot.   *(vii)* I'm fed up to the back teeth.
(iii) Do you get me?   *(viii)* It's a wash-out.
(vi) What's the damage?   *(ix)* He went off the deep end.
(v) He's got the wind up.   *(x)* He's got a screw loose.

COMMERCIALESE

Like most other activities, business has acquired its own technical terms, and these you must use whenever necessary, because they replace what you would otherwise have to say in many words. Many of these terms are now represented by recognized abbreviations such as *C.W.O.* (cash with order), *E. and O.E.* (errors and omissions excepted), *c.i.f.* (cost, insurance, and freight), *D/A* (documents against acceptance). Others such as *carriage forward, paid on account,* and *drawn payable to order* are universally accepted and well understood within the business community. Apart from these and similar specialized terms, the common usage of English provides all that is necessary for business correspondence; ordinary language is good enough. Secretaries deal with ordinary people, and there is no advantage in avoiding the ordinary, friendly words of common speech.

The old-style business letter was shrouded in a jargon that came to be termed *commercialese,* or *commercial English.* Even in the modern business letter much of the influence of the old style remains to keep writers in a strait-jacket of remote and meaningless expressions, hampering their efforts to write the kind of letters they wish to write. The following are some examples.

Instead of	*Say*
Openings	
Adverting to your favour	Referring to your letter
Re (your letter)	*or*
Replying to your letter	Thank you for your letter
The writer wishes to acknowledge	I (We) acknowledge, *or* Thank you for your letter
We are in receipt of	
We beg to acknowledge	We have received
We have to acknowledge	
We beg to inform you	We are writing to inform you
We beg to thank you	We thank you
Your esteemed favour to hand	
Your letter to hand	We have received your letter
Yours to hand	Your letter has been received
Endings	
The favour of your early reply will oblige	I shall be glad to hear from you soon
and oblige	
Assuring you of our best attention at all times	
I am	
Thanking you in anticipation	Omit all these.
We beg to remain	
We remain	
Awaiting the favour of your early reply	

Miscellaneous

as per	according to
at your earliest convenience	as soon as possible
enclosed please find	I (We) enclose (are enclosing)
of even date	of today
only too pleased to	very glad to
per	by
please be good enough to advise us	please tell us
same	your letter, the goods, etc.
take an early opportunity	as soon as possible
under consideration	being dealt with
idem, inst., prox., ult.	name the month
your communication	your letter, phone message, etc.
your good self	you
your favour	your letter
under separate cover	separately; or better still, by registered post, etc.

Hereto, herewith, thereto, therein, thereof, therewith are also expressions to be discouraged. They introduce into letters a legal flavour that is best avoided. A slight rewording of the sentence is usually all that is necessary to avoid them.

Instead of	*Say*
in the First Schedule *hereto*	in the First Schedule
we enclose *herewith*	we enclose
any information relative *thereto*	any information relating to it
the information contained *therein*	the information it contains

Avoid also such unnecessary phrases as *it should be noted that, it will be appreciated that, I am to point out that.* Such expressions are mere padding. They contribute nothing to the meaning of what is said, in no way help the reader, and are a blemish on style. Omit them; go straight to the point and say simply and directly what has to be said:

	Say instead:
It will be appreciated that owing to fluctuations in price, it is impossible for us to give you a quotation.	Owing to frequent price changes we cannot give you a quotation.
It should be noted that all prices include delivery.	
I am to point out that the prices quoted are subject to a trade discount of 25%.	Omit the words in italics.

The use of stereotyped and hackneyed phrases makes it difficult for letters to be, as they should be, friendly, sincere, and natural. Could what you have said in a letter be said to someone on the telephone and still sound natural? If so, it is a good letter. *We are sorry to tell you* sounds more natural than *we regret to inform you; we are sending separately* is better than *we are sending under separate cover,* and *as soon as possible* is certainly preferable to *at your earliest convenience.*

A good business letter will be written to the point and will use no more words than are necessary to convey a clear message. But this does not mean that it need be discourteous. It is no discourtesy to say *Will you please send* instead of *we should esteem it a favour if you would kindly send,* or to say *as soon as possible* instead of *at the earliest possible moment.*

The following letter is a typical piece of commercialese.

> We beg to acknowledge receipt of your favour of the 26th inst. with regard to the estimate and plans required for the erection of a bungalow on the vacant site in close proximity to the Argosy Theatre, and shall have pleasure in arranging for our architect to call on you with a view to a discussion of the matter on Friday next, the 3rd prox. at three o'clock, which we trust will meet your convenience. In the meantime, we enclose herewith plans of a type of bungalow we can recommend, and beg to remain.,
>
> Yours truly

The writer of such a letter would no doubt claim that there was no time in business to adopt the style of good literature; but it is because so many of our letters fail to include the qualities of good literature that they not only fall short of being good English but also lack the essential qualities of a good business letter, by failing to be clear and to the point.

The foregoing letter is set out below with a corrected version in the right-hand column.

Instead of	*Say*
We beg to acknowledge receipt of your favour	We have received your letter
of the 26th inst.	of 26 February
with regard to the estimate and plans required	requesting an estimate and plans
for the erection of a bungalow	for erecting a bungalow
on the vacant site in close proximity to the Argosy Theatre	on the vacant site near the Argosy Theatre
and shall háve pleasure in arranging	We will arrange

for our architect to call on you	for our architect to call
with a view to a discussion of the matter	to discuss the matter
on Friday next, the 3rd prox. at three o'clock	next Friday, 3 March, at three o'clock
which we trust will meet your convenience	if convenient to you
In the meantime	Meanwhile
we enclose herewith	we enclose
plans of a type of bungalow we can recommend	plans for a bungalow we recommend
and beg to remain	(omit this)

Now read through the two versions and see which is the better. The second says all that is said in the first, and in fewer words—57 instead of 94. It has the further merit of being clearer. Although much shorter, it contains no suggestion of discourtesy.

To summarize the suggestions given in this and the preceding chapter—cultivate a good vocabulary; express yourself concisely and to the point; prefer the short word to the long, and the concrete word to the abstract; use adjectives sparingly, reserving them for occasions when precision is called for; and finally, avoid commercialese. Short, simple statements, well arranged, are what your correspondent will best understand.

EXERCISES

1. The following sentences contain commercialese. Rephrase them in good English.

(a) Thanking you for your communication of the 10th inst.

(b) We trust the goods will meet with your approval.

(c) You may rest assured that any representative from your esteemed house will receive a hearty welcome.

(d) Awaiting the favour of your reply by return.

(e) Yours of the 14th inst. to hand this morning.

(f) Enclosed is a cheque which clears off our indebtedness to you.

(g) We are extremely sorry to learn of the decease of our good friend Mr. Finch.

(h) We are in receipt of yours of the 29th ult.

(i) In reply to yours of yesterday's date, we very much regret the delay in executing the balance of your esteemed order.

(j) In accordance with your suggestion we have today consigned to you twenty cases of Oporto wine, and herewith hand you shipping documents.

2. Rearrange the following letters replacing the words in italics by expressions in straightforward English.

A

Dear Sir

We beg to refer to our communication of 27 April, and shall be glad to learn whether you have yet *come to any decision regarding the installation of* chain drives for which we *had the pleasure of quoting.*

We have *executed a number of contracts for the installation of* these transmissions in several factories in the Midlands, and *have pleasure in stating* that in all cases they have proved satisfactory.

We should be very glad to give you fuller information *regarding* these chain drives on *receipt of* further details of your *requirements.*

Trusting that we shall hear further from you, and that you will *favour us with your valued order.*

Yours faithfully

B

Dear Sir

Your esteemed enquiry of 29th ult. is duly to hand. We now beg to quote you for the supply of 20 tons of zinc ashes, as requested.

We shall be in a position to effect delivery at your works by 29 July for the inclusive price of £322 *per* ton. This is a very *advantageous* price for the quality of ashes you need, and one we are not likely to be able to repeat.

If you decide to *favour us with your valued order,* we shall do our utmost to *execute it to your entire satisfaction,* and shall look forward to further dealings with you.

The favour of your early reply will oblige.

Yours faithfully

3. The following sentences have been taken from business letters. Express them in simpler terms, correcting any faults in style:

(a) We trust that the confidence you have reposed in the firm will in no way be diminished by the altered arrangements.

(b) Thanking you for your kind support and trusting to merit its continuance.

(c) We have great pleasure in advising you that, on and after the 1st prox., Mr. Walter Barton, eldest son of our senior partner, will be admitted a member of the firm.

(d) Trusting that you will favour me with the same generous support that you have always accorded in the past to my predecessor.

(e) Owing to the expiration of our lease, and the acquisition of the site by the Greater London Council, we have been compelled to transfer our business to new premises at the above address.

(f) I have pleasure in enclosing herewith this year's lowest summer price list of fuels, and again beg to solicit the favour of your esteemed orders.

(g) In the matter of price we believe that our figures will, as formerly, show to our advantage when compared with those of any other maker.

(h) Your letter of 26th inst. with enquiry for chain drives is duly to hand, and we have pleasure in sending you herewith our quotation.

(i) We are in receipt of your esteemed enquiry and have pleasure in forwarding a copy of our catalogue under separate cover.

(j) We beg to acknowledge receipt of your order of yesterday's date for 20 cases of oranges, which will be sent carriage forward per British Rail in accordance with your instructions. The invoice is enclosed herewith.

4. Reconstruct the following letters in good English, correcting any faults in style.

A

Dear Sirs

We have to acknowledge receipt of your letter of the 1st inst. and thank you for the kind offer contained therein, which we are very glad to accept with full appreciation of your kind consideration in this matter.

We remain

Yours faithfully

B

Madam

We noticed whilst looking through our books that you have not recently favoured us with your esteemed orders.

We beg, therefore, to enclose herewith a Price List and postcard, trusting to receive a continuance of your patronage, and assuring you that at all times our best attention shall be given to your commands.

We remain

Your obedient servants

C

Dear Sirs,

We are in receipt of your esteemed letter of the 17th inst., with order for four rolls of cloth, but regret to say that on the terms mentioned, we find it impossible to execute this. We are prepared, however, with a view to larger business, to concede you a discount of 20% and a three months' draft.

Thanking you for the support you have hitherto accorded us, and trusting still to maintain our friendly business relations.

We remain

Yours faithfully

D

Dear Sir

With reference to your request that we shall in future send your goods per passenger train, half rate, we have to state that before British Rail will accept parcels on such terms they require us to sign a document making ourselves responsible for any loss or damage in transit.

This, of course, we cannot possibly consent to do, the carriers and railway companies being the agents of the consignee and not ours. You might, however, make a special arrangement with the Company at your end, in which case please advise us.

Trusting that this explanation will be satisfactory, and assuring you of our best services at all times.

We remain

Faithfully yours

E

Dear Sirs

With reference to your letter dated 29th ult., in which you ask to be relieved of your contract for the supply of hand-made nails, we beg to say that we regret the mistake you have made, and, under the circumstances, are willing to pay, in addition to the price agreed upon, half the extra cost of the hand-made over the machine-made article.

Please signify your acceptance of this offer at your early convenience.

Yours faithfully

5. The following is an extract from an essay. Rewrite it, making as few changes in its wording as you can, but making it into an acceptable piece of composition.

If I were Secretary of State for Education, I will asked all children from five to eleven years old be giving an opportunity of learn many subject, as such they can choose later their best ones, and which they will studied at secondary school. And more staffs trained, so that there always enough teacher. And I will make it compulsory training of English and Arithmetic, etc. to school children, and better pay to staffs.

6. Rewrite the following in correct but simple and more forceful English.

(1) Such tentative research as we have conducted into the subsequent careers of the male and female products of our Grammar Schools suggests that the pattern of their adult social life is determined not so much by their early educational environment as by the form and nature of their employment. It must, of course, be conceded that, if social groups are decided by professional status, choice of employment is still largely controlled by the type and quality of a child's school.

(2) A heightened colour and an acceleration of delivery revealed the manager's perturbation at the clerk's brusque interruption so that it was apparent to some of his listeners that what had begun as a mild expostulation would soon harden into a general reprimand.

(I. of B.)

CHAPTER FOUR

The Dictionary

And let a scholar all earth's volumes carry,
He will be but a walking dictionary.

George Chapman: *Tears of Peace*

ON USING THE DICTIONARY

The dictionary is primarily a book of reference; but it is a book worth studying. It is there to supply very much more than just the meanings and spellings of words, though business letters would perhaps contain fewer spelling mistakes if we used it oftener. But it would be a poor compliment to those who have devoted long and arduous years to compiling our great dictionaries if they were used only as casual reference books. Any good dictionary has a wealth of information to reveal in return for so little trouble in using it.

In the passage of years new ideas, new discoveries, new developments in the arts and sciences and in industry and commerce, and altered ways of living find expression in the birth of new words. New words find their way into the accepted vocabulary and establish themselves; others acquire new and modified meanings, while still others fall into disuse and die. All these changes are recorded in the dictionary, where the constantly changing pattern of our vocabulary reflects the constantly changing pattern of human life.

Philology is the name given to the science of language. It includes a study of etymology, which deals with the history of words, the sources from which they are derived, their original meanings and the changes they have undergone in the course of time; it has many interesting things to tell us about words. It tells us, for example, that *assassin* originates in the Arabian *hashshashim* or hashish-eater. Hashish, or Indian hemp, contains intoxicating properties and was supplied to the fanatical Moslem members of the religious and military order, ruled by the "Old Man of the Mountains", notorious for their secret murders of Christian leaders in the time of the Crusades. Hence the name *assassin* for one who undertakes to put another to death by treacherous violence.

Again, our word *battery* originates in the French *battre* (to assail with blows). It was first used to signify a number of guns placed together to enable them to be charged and discharged, that is to deliver blows, simultaneously. It thus became easy to use *battery* in electricity to denote a number of Leyden jars so connected that they may be charged and discharged simultaneously, the term being extended today to any device capable of generating an electric current.

We also learn that *shilly-shally,* denoting hesitation, is a reduplication of *shall I, shall I not?* and that *tire* is a shortened form of *attire* meaning to dress or cover, and that the American *tire* is therefore an etymologically more correct spelling for the "attire or covering of a wheel" than *tyre,* which has been revived in Great Britain to denote the inflated or rubber covering of a bicycle or motor-car wheel.

By using your dictionary to find out all you can about words you will be making a companion of it, and will be amply rewarded. Its regular use will help you to extend your vocabulary, that is your knowledge of words, and your ability to use them. A good vocabulary is one of the hall-marks of an educated person, and a priceless possession both in business and in social life. It is acquired partly from conversation, partly from listening, to the radio, for instance, and partly, and especially, from reading and the regular use of the dictionary. It may seem a far cry from business correspondence to the reading of writers such as John Buchan, Joseph Conrad, and Sir Arthur Quiller-Couch, to quote three masters of English prose at random, yet there is much to be gained from reading them. They are masters of words, and words are the vehicle of thought, as much for the business man as for the author.

Only the right kind of reading, read in the right way, will help you. Into your reading must be introduced the personal element of practice, for, in the words of Aristotle over 2,000 years ago, "What we have to learn we learn by doing". Note immediately any word whose meaning is not clear, and refer to your dictionary. Avoid the temptation, always present, to guess the meaning of a word from its context, otherwise you run the danger of using it wrongly in conversation or, worse still, in correspondence. None of us would wish to be guilty of the mistakes made by Mrs. Malaprop (*see* p. 16). Incidentally, you will find great fun in reading Sheridan's amusing play *The Rivals,* and great gain too if, as you read, you list the malapropisms and look them up in your dictionary.

Use your dictionary freely and study the words you look up. To trace a word back to its root will help you to remember it, and it is an excellent plan to note new words in an exercise book, with a short definition, and a stress mark to indicate the accented syllable. To do this will help both spelling and understanding.

Word	Meaning
cos'monaut	space-man who orbits the earth
discog'raphy	collection, description, etc., of gramophone records
iden'tikit	portrait-building from cards
meg'aton	a million tons
pediat'rics	treatment of children's diseases

A simple list of this kind may serve its purpose, but a more satisfying and effective method is to include in the list notes indicating the etymology, the source and history, of a word and the context in which you first come across it. For example:

Word	Source	Context
cos'monaut	Gr. *kosmos:* the world	the first *cosmonauts* to reach the moon
discog'raphy	Gr. *discos:* a quoit (a ring)	his main interest lay in *discography*
iden'tikit	L. *identitas:* the same	the police issued an *identikit* picture
meg'aton	Gr. *mega:* great	the equivalent of a *megaton*
pediat'ric	Gr. *paed* a child	the *pediatric* ward (in a hospital)

Words arranged in the simple form of the first list, without sources and contexts, become more difficult to remember as the list grows in size. The list becomes more helpful if the details from the second list are included. Knowledge of the origin or history of a word gives the word an added interest that deepens impression and aids recollection; the word becomes more firmly set in the mind. To remember the word in its original context ensures that it is used correctly.

A more business-like method is to arrange the list in card-index form with 5 x 3 in. (127 x 77 mm) cards. A separate card is prepared for each separate word and filed alphabetically. Cards for words

> ## CIRCUMLOCUTION
>
> Roundabout language; the use of many words for few.
>
> L. *circum:* around.
> *loqui:* to speak
>
> His language has a tendency towards circumlocution.

that prove difficult to remember are identified quickly and can be temporarily removed from the set for further study and revision.

But it is not enough to know only what a word means; you must be able to use it. You must build it into your active vocabulary by using it in conversation and writing when the chance occurs, or even by including it in sentences merely for practice. Only in these ways will new words become an effective part of your vocabulary.

Reading will not only improve your vocabulary; it will also widen your knowledge of things, give you new ideas, and provide you with new ways of expressing ideas already held.

The great *Oxford Dictionary,* which is the foundation of all English dictionaries, consists with Supplements, of fifteen volumes extending over some 18,500 pages, and contains nearly half a million references. Its outstanding feature is the inclusion of well over a million illustrative quotations, arranged chronologically, showing how words have been used by different writers and at different periods. No other dictionary gives all this information, and most of us have to be content with a dictionary contained in a single volume. Even so, many of these one-volume dictionaries are excellent for everyday purposes.

Having chosen your dictionary, do not plunge headlong into it for the word you want. First make yourself familiar with the plan of the dictionary. You will find this in the Introduction or in explanatory notes, and the time spent in studying these will save time and trouble in the long run, especially with new and unusual words.

THE DICTIONARY PLAN

The basis on which a dictionary is arranged is, of course, alphabetical, though only the key words are arranged alphabetically in some dictionaries, derivatives, that is words that are not root words or primitives, being given under their key words.

The two methods are illustrated by the facsimilies given below.

The Concise Oxford Dictionary
(Arrangement strictly alphabetical)

abou′t *adv.* & *prep.* **1.** All round from outside (*compass it about*; *go a long way about*; *He is about my path*; BEAT[1] *about the bush*); all round from a centre (*look*, LAY[3], *about you*). **2.** Somewhere near (HANG[1] *about*; *people* or *objects about us*; *have* or *keep* one's WIT[2]s *about* one); carried with (*have no money about me*); here and there (*in* a place, or abs.) (*measles is about*; *move*, ORDER[2], *about*; PUT[1] *about*; *dotted about the fields*; *man about* TOWN); **out and ∼**, (of person, esp. after illness) engaging in normal outdoor activity; **up and ∼**, arisen after sleep or illness. **3.** Near in number, scale, degree, etc., (*about half, fifty, right, midnight, my size, the best*); (colloq., in iron. understatement or comparison; *I'm about tired of this*; *about as exciting as cold semolina*). **4.** Facing in opposite direction (RIGHT[1] *about turn* or *face*; *the wrong way about*); **∼ turn** or ***face** (as Mil. command). **5.** In rotation (*take turns about*; *on duty (week and) week about*). **6.** Occupied with (*about my father's business*; *send him about his* BUSINESS; *what are you about?*); **am ∼ to do**, am on the point of doing (so all vbs. forming fut. participles). **7.** In connection with, on the subject of, (*quarrels, a book, about money*; *something wrong about it*; *have read, do not know, about it*; SET[1], SEE[1], GO[1], *about*); in relation to (*symmetry about a line or plane*); **how about**, = WHAT *about*. **8.** In the course of events (*I brought it about*; *it came about*). **9.** (Naut.) On or to the opposite tack (*go about*; *put about*). [OE *onbūtan* (on A[3], *būtan* BUT[1])]

about-fā′ce, about-tūr′n, *n.*, & *v.i.* (Make) reversal of direction, opinion, policy, or behaviour. [f. Mil. commands (ABOUT 4)]

abo′ve (-ŭ′v) *adv., prep., a.,* & *n.* **1.** *adv.* At or to a higher point; overhead, on high; upstream;

upstairs; in heaven. **2.** On the upper side; earlier in a book or article (*as was remarked above*; *the above-cited passages*; *the above-mentioned facts*); in addition (*over and above*). **3.** *prep.* Over, on the top of, higher than (*above average*, PAR[1]; *heard above the din*; *head above water*); **∼ ground,** alive; *above* one's HEAD[1]; **∼ oneself,** carried away by high spirits, conceit, etc.; **∼-boar′d** *adv.* & *pred. a.*, undisguised(ly), fair(ly), open(ly) [metaph. f. card-playing]. **4.** More than (*above a hundred*); upstream from; further north than; (arch.) to an earlier time than (*not traced above the third century*); out of reach of (*above criticism, suspicion, my understanding*); too great or good for (*above meanness, ideas above* one's *station*); more important than (*above all*); of higher rank than. **5.** *a.* Preceding, previous (*the above statements*). **6.** *n.* That which is above. [f. A[3] + OE *bufan* (be BY[1], *ufan* above)]

ab ovo (ăb ō′vō) *adv.* (Relating tediously) from the very beginning. [L, = from the egg)]

Abp. *abbr.* Archbishop.

ăbracadǎ′bra *n.* Spell, magic formula; gibberish. [cabbalistic word supposed when written triangularly, and worn, to cure fevers etc.; L f. Gk]

abrā′de *v.t.* Scrape off, wear away, injure, (skin, rock, fabric, etc.) by rubbing. [f. L AB(*radere* rasscrape)]

A′brahǎm-mǎn (ā′-; -a-h-) *n.* (*pl.* **-men**). (Hist.) Wandering beggar of 16th c., usu. feigning insanity; **sham Abraham,** feign illness or insanity. [perh. after Luke 16]

abrā′sion (-zhon) *n.* Scraping off, wearing away, (of skin, rock, etc.); damaged area resulting from this. [f. L *abrasio* (as ABRADE; see -ION)]

Reproduced by courtesy of the Oxford University Press

Chambers Twentieth Century Dictionary
(Key words arranged alphabetically)

about, *ə-bowt′, prep.* round on the outside of: around: here and there in: near in place, time, size, etc.: on the person of: connected with: concerning: engaged in.—*adv.* around: halfway round, in the opposite direction (e.g. *to face about*): nearly: here and there: on the opposite tack: in motion or activity.—**about′-face,** (orig. used in U.S. as command) act of turning to face in the opposite direction: complete change of opinion, attitude, etc.—Also *v.i.*—Also **about′-turn.**—*prep.* **abouts′** (*Spens.*), about. —*v.t.* and *v.i.* **about′-ship′,** to put (the ship) on the opposite tack.—*n.* **about′-sledge,** a heavy blacksmith's hammer.—**about to** (do, etc.), on the point of (doing, etc.); **be about,** to be astir: to be on the point of (doing something); **bring about,** to cause to take place; **come about,** to happen in the course of time; **go about,** to prepare to do; **put about** (see put); **turn about,** alternately: in rotation. [O.E. *onbūtan*—*on,* in, *būtan,* without—*be,* by, *ūtan,* orig. a locative—*ūt,* out.]

above, *ə-buv′, prep.* over: in or to a position higher than that of: beyond in degree, amount, number, importance, etc.: too magnanimous or proud for:—*adv.* overhead: in a higher position,

order, or power: in an earlier passage: in heaven.—*adj.* mentioned, stated, or given in an earlier passage.—*adjs.* above′-board, open, without deception; above′-ground, alive: not buried; above′-mentioned; above′-named.—above oneself, elated: conceited. [Late O.E. *ābufan*—O.E. *ā-*, on, *bufan,* above—*be,* by, *ufan,* above.]

ab ovo, *ab ō′vō, -wō,* (L.; 'from the egg') from the beginning. See *Quotations from Latin.*

abracadabra, *ab-rə-kə-dab′ra, n.* a magic word, written in amulets: a spell or conjuring word: gibberish. [Found in a 2nd-cent. poem by Q. Serenus Sammonicus.]

abrade, *ə-brād′, v.t.* to wear down or off.—*adj.* and *n.* **abrā′dant,** abrasive. [L. *ab,* from, *rādĕre, rāsum,* to scrape.]

Abraham-man, *ā′brə-həm-man′,* **Abram-man,** *ā′brəm-man′, n.* originally a Bedlam inmate let out to beg: a sturdy beggar, esp. one shamming insanity (*arch.*).—**to sham Abraham,** to feign sickness. [Said to be from an Abraham Ward in old Bedlam, London:]

abraid, abrade, *ə-brād′,* or (*Spens.*) **abray,** *ə-brā′, obs. v.t.* to awake, rouse.—*v.i.* to start: to awake. [O.E. *ābregdan*—intens. pfx. *ā-,* and *bregdan*; see braid (1).]

Reproduced by courtesy of W. & R. Chambers Ltd.

You will notice that in *Chambers,* the word *about-face* is placed under *about* as a derivative, and not in strictly alphabetical position after *about,* while in the *Concise Oxford Dictionary, about-face* follows *about.*

The word arrangement adopted for any particular dictionary, as well as many other items of useful information concerning the plan of the dictionary, will usually be explained in an Introduction, which you should carefully study. It would be very shortsighted and time-wasting not to make yourself thoroughly familiar with the contents of the Introduction, since its sole purpose is to help those who use the dictionary to do so intelligently and with understanding, and so to get the greatest possible benefit from it.

PRONUNCIATION

Any worthwhile dictionary will indicate how words should be pronounced. This is done by the use of signs and symbols. There is no universal scheme; each dictionary has its own and explains it in the Introduction. For example, four well-known dictionaries variously indicate the pronunciation of *dictionary* as follows.

dik'shən-ə-ri	*Chambers Twentieth Century Dictionary*
dik'shûn ar i	*New Elizabethan Reference Dictionary*
di·kʃənāri	*The Shorter Oxford Dictionary*
di'ctionarÿ	*The Concise Oxford Dictionary*

In the first three examples the word is respelt phonetically; in the last the symbols are added to the word itself.

Correspondence is not, of course, concerned with matters of pronunciation, but many business contracts are of the personal kind or by telephone, and if a good impression is to be created with educated business acquaintances correct speech is essential. The pronunciation of most words in everyday use is probably quite familiar to most people, but guidance is often needed with unusual words, and this the dictionary provides. The different symbols used in the examples given above do not indicate different pronunciations of *dictionary,* but merely different ways of indicating the same pronunciation; hence the need to understand the particular scheme of symbols employed and to recognize the symbols at sight.

When a word consists of more than one syllable it is necessary to know which of the syllables takes the stress. Accentuation, as it is called, is specially marked, usually by a dash placed immediately after the stressed syllable, though the *Shorter Oxford Dictionary* uses, not a dash, but a dot. Indicated stress is not at all hard to follow, but it is important to know it.

Transfer of stress from one syllable to another sometimes alters the grammatical function as well as the meaning of a word. Thus, *ab'stract*, with the stress on the first syllable, is a noun and means *a summary*, while *abstract'*, with the stress on the second syllable, is a verb and means *to take away*. Similarly, *in'cense* is a noun and means *a spice*, while *incense'* is a verb and means *to make angry*. Many other words behave in the same way.

There are also other words with identical spellings whose vowel sounds as well as their accentuation differ. Thus, *minute* may mean either sixty seconds or something extremely small, according to the way it is pronounced. Again, having bought *prod'uce* we must *produce'* the means to pay for it.

Yet another class of words is a frequent source of trouble. It consists of those words with similar pronunciations but with different spellings and different meanings—*forgo* (to go without) and *forego* (to go before); *principle* (a rule) and *principal* (the chief one); *cession* (to yield up) and *session* (a period of time); *role* (a part played) and *roll* (something rolled up) are among the many words in this class. The following are other well-known words in this class.

assent (agreement)	ascent (going up)
berth (a room)	birth (being born)
broach (to mention)	brooch (jewellery)
cereal (food)	serial (an instalment)
check (a test)	cheque (money)
complaisant (obliging)	complacent (self-satisfied)
complement (to supplement)	compliment (to praise)
council (an assembly)	counsel (a barrister)
dependant (a person)	dependent (subordinate)
draft (a document)	draught (a breeze)
exercise (to exert)	exorcise (to expel)
flair (aptitude)	flare (a flame)
feint (a pretence)	faint (weak)
freeze (temperature)	frieze (decoration)
hoard (a store)	horde (a gang)
licence (a permit)	license (to allow)
mask (a covering)	masque (a drama)
meter (equipment)	metre (measurement)
passed (verb)	past (adjective)
plain (simple)	plane (smooth)
practice (noun)	practise (verb)
sew (to fasten)	sow (to scatter)
stationary (still)	stationery (writing materials)
storey (building)	story (a legend)
their (pers. pronoun)	there (adverb)

| whose (possess. pronoun) | who's (who is) |
| wrapped (folded) | rapt (engrossed) |

Then there are those words that are not the same but which bear some resemblance, and which in consequence are frequently confused. They include words such as *accept* (to receive) and *except* (to exclude), *confident* (assured) and *confidant* (one entrusted with a secret), *elicit* (to draw forth) and *illicit* (unlawful). Words of this kind form a very considerable class that calls for special care. (*See* list on pp. 383–4).

And finally, the passage of time has not only given birth to new words, but has also given new meanings to old ones, with the result that the same word has progressed through a number of changes and come to mean different things. The dictionary tells us, for example, that the simple word *bar* means:

> a pole; an obstruction; a strip of metal below the clasp of a medal; a bank of sand at the mouth of a river; the place in Court where prisoners are placed; the profession of barrister; a room in a tavern where liquor is served; and in music, a vertical line on the stave, dividing the piece into equal time parts.

SYNONYMS

In Chapter Two we noticed that the same idea can often be represented by different words that appear to have the same or nearly the same meaning, but which carry fine but nevertheless important distinctions. The idea of *teaching,* for instance, can be represented by *lecturing, instructing, training, tutoring, coaching,* etc., each of which places its own particular emphasis on the form of teaching in mind. These different words, with their different shades of meaning, present a choice of language that makes it possible to describe in precise and accurate terms the idea we have in mind, and to communicate it in words that most nearly represent the impression we want to create. *Teaching* is an amalgam of different techniques; it embraces all the other activities mentioned, and more. It differs from *lecturing* by imposing on the learner the obligation to play an active part in the teaching process and himself to do much of the work, whereas lecturing demands from him no more than the role of a passive listener, except perhaps for his occasional question. *Instructing* and *training* are relevant to the learning of skills, such as the manual skills of typewriting, dressmaking and engineering. *Training* has the wider meaning; it involves instruction and, in addition, what is taught must be rehearsed and regularly practised till the skill is mastered. *Tutoring* and *coaching* signify personal supervision of individuals and small groups, with a distinction between studies under a tutor and training in practical pursuits under a coach. Choices of the kind portrayed here make it possible to ensure that the words we use are those which most accurately fit the circumstances; otherwise we risk creating wrong impressions in the minds of those with whom we communicate.

AREAS OF MEANING

Just as we have different words that mean the same (or nearly the same) thing, so we have words that mean different things — words with more than one meaning. Many of the words in everyday use are of this kind. Used in isolation *recorder* means different things to different people. To some it will mean a person engaged in keeping records of one sort or another — a book-keeper, a statistician, a shorthand-writer. To a lawyer it will mean a registrar or a city magistrate; to a musician, the flute-like instrument now actively taught in some of our schools. To others it will mean some kind of recording apparatus like a tape recorder. Each of these different interpretations represents a different "area of meaning". When a word is used in isolation there may be doubt as to the area of meaning intended; it is only when the word is used in a context that its meaning becomes clear. Even with words that have only one meaning, their precise shade of meaning cannot be known until they are used in a sentence.

But most words in common use have more than one meaning and a great number, such as *bar* illustrated in an earlier section, have many. This may seem confusing, but in practice the context in which the word stands will provide the clue to the meaning intended, and with a little commonsense this can usually be found from the dictionary without much trouble.

The exercises that follow are included specially to help you to know more closely words you will find useful in correspondence, and of course to afford practice in the use of the dictionary.

EXERCISES

1. Refer to your dictionary and write brief notes on the plan which it follows.

2. *(a)* The following paragraph has been copied from a dictionary. Explain in detail what it means.

Till, til, *n.* A drawer for money in a shop—*prep.* To the time of—*v.t.* To cultivate

(b) Explain *briefly* and *clearly* the difference between a dictionary and an encyclopaedia.

(R.S.A. Elem.)

3. The following paragraph has been abstracted from a dictionary. Explain it fully.

While, whīl, *n.* A space of time.—conj. During the time that.—v.t. pret. & pp. *whiled,* whild; ppr. *whiling,* whīling. To cause to pass pleasantly; usually with *away.*

(R.S.A. Inter.)

4. Use each of the following words in a sentence to show the different meanings of the words forming each pair.

(a)	appro'priate	com'bine	con'duct	con'flict	con'tract
	appropriate'	combine'	conduct'	conflict'	contract'
(b)	del'egate	discrim'inate	elab'orate	ex'port	incor'porate
	delegate'	discriminate'	elaborate'	export'	incorporate'
(c)	pres'ent	prod'uce	sub'ject	subord'inate	trans'port
	present'	produce'	subject'	subordinate'	transport'

5. Distinguish the meanings of the words forming each of the following pairs.

A	B
alternate, alternative	elicit, illicit
beside, besides	eligible, illegible
continual, continuous	emigrant, immigrant
credible, creditable	exceptional, exceptionable
deduce, deduct	expropriate, appropriate
defer, differ	exterior, external
deficient, defective	forceful, forcible
deprecate, depreciate	human, humane
disburse, disperse	industrial, industrious
effective, effectual	equable, equitable

C	D
imply, infer	necessary, necessitous
impressive, impressionable	negligent, negligible
ingenious, ingenuous	official, officious
insolvent, insoluble	ostensible, ostentatious
inventory, invention	popular, populous
judicial, judicious	practical, practicable
machinery, mechanism	precede, proceed
masterful, masterly	preventative, preventive
memoir, memorandum	punctual, punctilious
momentary, momentous	receipt, recipe

E

requisite, requisition
résumé, resume
social, sociable
spacious, specious
stimulant, stimulus
student, scholar
superficial, superfluous
temperate, temporary
ultimate, ultimatum
unsatisfied, dissatisfied

6. Refer to a good dictionary and write down what you can find out about the origin of the following commercial terms.

(a) catalogue, commerce, creditor, importer, insurance;
(b) Messrs., mortgage, prospectus, quotation, transport.

7. As nouns and verbs each of the following words has several meanings. Referring to your dictionary as may be necessary give *three* of these meanings for each word.

(a) article, balance, charge, commission, labour;
(b) lighter, negative, net, office, report;
(c) return, review, second, shop, station;
(d) subject, tender, tramp, trunk, well.

8. Replace each of the following phrases by a single word.

(a) The programme of business for a meeting;
(b) The occupier of a rented house;
(c) A collection of goods sent for delivery by rail, etc.;
(d) A record of the proceedings of a meeting;
(e) The decision arrived at by a jury;
(f) The identification of a disease by its symptoms;
(g) The fraudulent making or alteration of any writing;
(h) The act of setting a person free from bondage;
(i) A person chosen by parties to decide between them;
(j) The taking over of an industry by the State.

9. (a) Express in one word each of the following.

(i) The tidal mouth of a river;
(ii) a row of houses curved in shape;
(iii) the amount of curve from the centre to the edge of a road;
(iv) money paid as instalment to confirm a contract;
(v) official examination of accounts.

(b) Write what you would expect to find in a dictionary under these words: interest; rent; claim.

(*R.S.A. Inter.*)

10. Replace each of the following phrases by a single word. (The first and last letters and the number of letters in the word required are given in brackets.)

(a) A document issued by a company charging its assets with the repayment of a loan. (d . . . . . . e)

(b) A prepared set of written questions for the purpose of compiling or comparing information. (q . . . . e)

(c) A detailed list or schedule of goods, furniture, etc. (i . . . . y)

(d) The official survey of a country's population. (c . . . . s)

(e) The needless use of words that merely repeat something already said. (t . . . . . . y)

(f) Not bearing upon or related to the matter in hand. (i . . . . t)

(g) A formal written order for the supply of goods or materials. (r . . . . n)

(h) Not biased in favour of either side in a contest or argument. (i . . . . l)

(i) The fall in the value of a thing due to wear and tear. (d . . . . n)

(j) A person to whom money is paid. (p . . . e)

11. Express the meaning of each of the following phrases by a single word beginning with *con* or *com*.

(a) Consolidated stock forming part of the national debt.

(b) To call a meeting.

(c) A legally binding agreement.

(d) Living at the same time.

(e) A comprehensive view or survey.

(f) To bring all one's attention to bear on the matter in hand.

(g) A well-informed judge in the arts, etc.

(h) An event or occurrence that may or may not happen.

(i) A syndicate or association of trading companies.

(j) A settlement of differences by mutual concession.

12. (a) Supply one word for each of the following phrases:

too ready to believe

showing extreme care over details

the practice of copying ideas and extracts from authors without acknowledgment

separated by a non-conductor

not in accordance with recognized authority

one appointed by two parties to settle disputes between them

local variation of language

dependent on chance

(b) *either* Give brief definitions of the following words:

stoic; gamut; subterfuge; siesta; innuendo; valetudinarian; matutinal; bibliography;

or State the difference in meaning between the following pairs of words:

anomalous, anonymous   precedent, precedence

corporal, corporate   comparison, caparison

and Show that you know the meaning of the following phrases by using them in sentences:

salubrious neighbourhood   impecunious relative
histrionic talents   rudimentary principles
                    heterogeneous mass.

(L.C.C.I. Priv. Sec. Dip.)

13. *(a)* Select four of the following phrases and show that you understand their meaning:

contemporary writers   reciprocal courtesies
fallacious argument   prima facie evidence
                    collective security

(b) By using them in sentences distinguish between the meaning of the following pairs of words:

complacent   deprecate   equable   vicarious   presumptive
complaisant   depreciate   equitable   precarious   presumptuous

(L.C.C.I. Priv. Sec. Dip.)

14. *(a)* Distinguish between the meaning of the following pairs of words:

unconscionable, unexceptionable   cursive, cursory
capitation, caption   endemic, epidemic
                    chantry, chanty

(b) Explain the meaning of each of the following:

to beg the question   a laissez-faire policy
a Party shibboleth   to lose caste
                    their name is legion.

(L.C.C.I. Priv. Sec. Dip.)

15. Some words have two or more totally different meanings while keeping exactly the same spelling. Write sentences which show the possible meanings of the following words (15 sentences in all). For example: *calf.* (1) The cow has just given birth to a calf. (2) She had hurt her calf muscle.

(a) refuse (2 meanings)
(b) cheek (2 meanings)
(c) stick (2 meanings)
(d) vault (2 meanings)
(e) show (2 meanings)
(f) cross (2 meanings)
(g) still (3 meanings)

(E.M.E.U.)

16. Choose two words from each of the following groups *(a)* to *(e)*. Write ten sentences, each containing one of the chosen words, to show the different shades of meaning between the chosen words in each pair.

(a) grave sober despondent funereal (adjectives)
(b) hunger appetite fast famine (nouns)
(c) gilded blond sallow sandy (adjectives)
(d) reputation prestige glamour aura (nouns)
(e) bestow reward present compensate (verbs)

(N.W.R.A.C.)

THE NEED FOR EXACTNESS

The written word is not merely a symbol on paper, nor the spoken word a mere ripple of sound waves. Words are tools of communication and it is important that the same word holds precisely the same meaning for the reader as it does for the writer. This is the essential basis of successful communication. Care must therefore be taken not to use words to express meanings they do not bear. The exactly right word must be used, not a word that seems right and which may be no more than nearly right. You must not say *alternate* when you mean *alternative, proposal* when you mean *proposition,* or *disinterested* when you mean *uninterested.*

Ability to choose and use the right words depends upon the range of one's vocabulary, and this will be adequate only if opportunities are taken to talk with educated people, to read critically, and to use and study the dictionary.

Words change their meanings; some tend to encroach on others that are better. The use of such encroaching words should therefore be avoided. The following list includes a number of encroaching words and also others that are commonly misused.

Do not confuse this	*with this*
accept (to receive, agree)	except (to exclude)
achieve (to attain by effort)	get, reach (to obtain, possibly without effort)
acquaint (to make aware)	inform (to tell)
address (formal, and may be written)	speech (less formal, and presumed to be spoken)
advise (to offer counsel)	inform (to tell)
affect (to produce an effect)	effect (to bring about, to accomplish)
aggravate (to make worse)	annoy (to irritate)
allude (to refer to something indirectly)	mention (to call attention to)

Do not confuse this	*with this*
alternately (first one, then the other)	alternatively (offering a choice)
amateur (not professional, but may be highly skilled)	novice (a beginner)
answer (relates to questions)	reply (relates to arguments and statements)
anticipate (to act in advance, to forestall)	expect (to wait, to look for)
appreciate (to set value on anything)	realize (to understand clearly)
appropriate (fitting, suitable)	relevant (applicable)
audience (hearers)	spectators (onlookers)
capacity (power to receive or retain)	ability (power to do)
comprise (to contain, include)	compose (to put together)
conference (a meeting, esp. large)	talk (conversation)
confirm (to verify, make sure)	corroborate (to make doubly sure)
continuous (without a break)	continual (recurring frequently)
credible (believable)	creditable (praiseworthy)
defective (lacking in quality)	deficient (lacking in quantity)
dependant (a person)	dependent (an adjective)
discreet (prudent)	discrete (separate, distinct)
disinterested (unbiased, impartial)	uninterested (not interested)
distinguish (to recognize a difference)	discriminate (to make fine distinctions)
e.g. (for example)	i.e. (that is)
enquiry (a question)	inquiry (an investigation)
exceptional (unusual)	exceptionable (objectionable)
expect (to wait, look for)	believe (to accept as true)
evidence (proof)	testimony (a sworn statement)
kind (sort)	description (as described)
farther (more distant)	further (in addition)
feasible (practicable, capable of performance)	probable (likely)
find (to come across)	discover (to uncover, detect)
imply (to mean indirectly)	infer (to deduce)
individual (has a disparaging flavour)	person (a human being)
integrate (to combine the parts of, form a whole)	co-ordinate (to range together)
likely to (probably)	liable to (suggests something detrimental)
loan (something lent)	lend (the act of lending)
meantime (noun)	meanwhile (adverb: say *meanwhile*, but *in the meantime*)
mutual (reciprocal)	common (applying to many)
neglect (a careless omission)	negligence (habitual neglect)
nice (exact)	attractive (inviting, charming)
party (a legal term)	person (a general term)
practical (useful in practice)	practicable (feasible)
practically (opposite to theoretically)	almost (nearly)

Do not confuse this	*with this*
pretence (make-believe)	pretension (advancement of a claim)
proposal (an offer)	proposition (something proposed for discussion)
quantity (how much)	number (how many)
remember (to recall without conscious effort)	recollect (to recall with conscious effort)
requirements (wants)	requisites (essentials)
site (a specific spot)	situation (general surroundings)
state (to present formally)	say (to speak)
transpire (to become known, come to light)	occur (to come to pass)

Examples of the right and wrong use of some of these words are given below.

Wrong	*Right*

Advise, inform

We will *advise* you as soon as the goods are ready. (Say *inform*.)

We *advise* you not to accept the price offered. (i.e. give you counsel.)

Allude, mention

The matter *alluded* to in your letter will be considered at our next meeting. (Say *mentioned*.)

He was *alluding* to one of us. (i.e. hinting at someone not actually mentioned.)

Anticipate, expect

We do not *anticipate* any difficulty in meeting your request. (Say *expect*.)

We *anticipated* your request for quick delivery and sent the goods this morning. (i.e. acted in advance.)

Appreciate, realize

You will no doubt *appreciate* that we cannot allow a discount. (Say *understand, realize*.)

Your help is very much *appreciated*. (i.e. valued.)

Appropriate, relevant

We shall study the part played by the *appropriate* financial institutions in providing the capital needed. (Say *relevant*.)

The speech made by the chairman was not *appropriate* for the occasion. (i.e. not suitable.)

Capacity, ability

He has an unusual *capacity* for sketching. (Say *ability*.)

His *capacity* for foreign languages is quite remarkable. (i.e. his power to acquire.)

Wrong	*Right*
Comprise, compose	
The twelve members who *comprise* the committee all hope to attend the the meeting. (Say *compose*, or better still, *form.*)	The committee *comprises* twelve elected representatives. (i.e. includes.)
Disinterested, uninterested	
As I have attended all meetings you can hardly accuse me of being *disinterested*. (Say *uninterested*.)	We suggest the matter be referred to someone who is *disinterested*. (i.e. not biased.)
Expect, believe	
We *expect* you were quite right to decline the offer. (Say *believe*.)	We *expect* to hear from you soon. (i.e. like to hear from you.)
Feel, think	
I cannot help *feeling* that the terms are unreasonable. (Say *thinking*.)	Despite the absence of evidence I *feel* he has acted wisely. (i.e. feel instinctively.)
Individual, person	
He is a most reliable *individual*. (Say *person*.)	A distinction must be drawn between the *individual* and the group. (i.e. the single person.)
Integrate, co-ordinate	
The formation of a pool will *integrate* the work of the typists. (Say *co-ordinate*.)	The advertising department will now be *integrated* with the sales department under the sales manager. (i.e. will form one with the sales department.)
Likely, liable	
We are *likely* to fail in our attempts to increase profits. (Say *liable*.)	It is *likely* that she will take offence if you criticize her. (i.e. probable.)
Loan, lend	
We are willing to *loan* you £200 for a month. (Say *lend*.)	The Council will grant a *loan* of £200. (i.e. a sum of money.)
Meantime, meanwhile	
I shall be away until Friday; *meantime*, perhaps you will complete this report. (Say *meanwhile*, or *in the meantime*.)	The manager will return next Monday; *meanwhile* (or *in the meantime*), Mr. X will act as his deputy.

Wrong	*Right*

Mutual, common

We refer you to our *mutual* friends, Messrs. X & Co. (Say *to X & Co., who are well known to both of us.*)

We are glad to think that our *mutually* good relations will not be impaired by the difficulties that have arisen. (i.e. our relations with each other.)

Practical, practicable

To complete the work by the time stated is not *practical.* (Say *practicable.*)

What is *practicable* is not always *practical.* (i.e. what is possible is not always profitable.)

Transpire, occur

The accident *transpired* as he left the meeting. (Say *occurred.*)

It has *transpired* that the directors could not agree. (i.e. become known.)

EXERCISES

1. Complete the following sentences by selecting from the words in brackets the one that expresses the appropriate meaning.

A

(a) After a long and arduous climb they (*reached, achieved, got to*) the summit.

(b) On (*achieving, reaching*) retirement age all employees qualify for pension.

(c) I will (*acquaint, inform*) him (*with, of*) the facts.

(d) I am writing to (*acquaint, inform*) you that our representative will be in your district next week.

(e) The appointment of a new secretary will not (*affect, effect*) my plans for visiting the Continent.

(f) I hope the appointment of a new secretary will (*affect, effect*) an improvement in the administration.

(g) Threats only serve to (*aggravate, annoy*) those to whom they are made.

(h) The medicine supplied only served to (*aggravate, annoy*) his condition.

(i) The journey to the United States can be made by air or (*alternately, alternatively*) by sea.

(j) They spent the evening at home and (*alternately, alternatively*) listened to music and watched television.

B

(a) I am writing to (*say, state*) that the goods you enquired about are now in stock.

(b) The document (*says, states*) quite clearly that the lease will not be renewed on the same terms.

(c) Many of the points made were not (*relevant, appropriate*) to the argument.

(*d*) The music selected for the occasion was not (*relevant, appropriate*).

(*e*) Our (*proposal, proposition*) for the sale of the premises was not accepted.

(*f*) A (*proposal, proposition*) to abolish overtime will be discussed at the meeting.

(*g*) I (*remember, recollect*) the opera very well indeed.

(*h*) I am afraid I cannot (*remember, recollect*) the details of a transaction that took place so long ago.

(*i*) Things are (*creditable, credible*) or otherwise according to the likelihood of their truth.

(*j*) He gave a very (*creditable, credible*) account of himself.

C

(*a*) The (*discovery, invention*) of the steam engine is attributed to James Watt.

(*b*) His secretary was a very remarkable (*person, individual*).

(*c*) Genius has been defined as an infinite (*capacity, ability*) for taking pains.

(*d*) He is (*apt, liable*) to be called upon to make good the deficit.

(*e*) He was so old and infirm that his handwriting was hardly (*readable, legible*).

(*f*) In moving a vote of thanks the chairman congratulated the lecturer on his (*address, speech*).

(*g*) We have found an excellent (*site, situation*) for the new building.

(*h*) He was unwilling to pay the amount except under (*compulsion, obligation*).

(*i*) His perpetual questions (*aggravated, irritated*) me beyond measure.

(*j*) She possessed no great (*ability, capability*), but she had a special (*faculty, aptitude*) for music.

2. Contrast the meanings of the words included in each of the following pairs by using each word in a sentence. (*Refer to your dictionary as may be necessary.*)

(*a*) address, speech	(*f*) requirements, requisites
(*b*) amateur, novice	(*g*) site, situation
(*c*) answer, reply	(*h*) accept, except
(*d*) neglect, negligence	(*i*) confirm, corroborate
(*e*) quantity, number	(*j*) exceptional, exceptionable

3. Study the following sentences, and comment on the correctness or otherwise of the use of the words printed in italics.

(*a*) We are writing to *acquaint* you with the changes recently made in our price-list.

(*b*) The fall in the prices of dairy produce has been *aggravated* by competition from producers in New Zealand.

(*c*) It is generally *felt* that everything possible should be done to reduce the amount of overtime now being worked.

(*d*) Our agents have written to *advise* us that the consignment should reach you during next week.

(*e*) The prices of the new cars have been *nicely* regulated in relation to production costs.

(f) Practically all our employees have now decided to transfer to the new superannuation scheme.

(g) A scheme is being worked out which, we hope, will meet the *individual* needs of most of our customers.

(h) Fabric of the *description* and quality you refer to should be available early next spring.

(i) We *feel* sure that it will be greatly to our *mutual* advantage if you consent to act as our South African agents.

(j) We assure you that the considerate way in which you have dealt with this complaint is very much *appreciated.*

4. Rewrite the following sentences substituting the correct words for those wrongly used. (Not all the sentences contain errors.)

(a) I think it is desirous to prepare a balance sheet every six months, so that the position can be continuously reviewed.

(b) Your letter brought a most aggravating situation to our notice, and we now have no choice but to find alternate accommodation.

(c) Only a negligible typist would fail to clean her machine regularly.

(d) By his remarks he seemed to infer that the fault was mine.

(e) Over the years we have continuously stressed that persons under 21 are illegible for these appointments.

(f) Far from being complimentary his remarks were derogatory.

(g) Only the chairman's impressionable and masterful handling of the meeting precluded chaos.

(h) It is anticipated that a private secretary will have at least a superfluous knowledge of accounts.

(i) Because of the continuity of the railway strike the meeting arranged for next week is liable to be cancelled.

(j) A judicial choice of questions enabled the candidate to give a most credible performance at the examination.

5. *(a)* An alteration of the stress in pronunciation affects the meaning of the following words. Write two sentences for each word to illustrate this fact:

attribute; invalid; ferment; consummate.

(b) Distinguish between:

embezzlement—forgery   an epitaph—an epigram
tradition—convention   tactics—strategy
projection—projectile

(c) Write a paragraph containing not more than two sentences including the following words. Then rewrite the paragraph, again with not more than two sentences, substituting simple variants for the given words:

inveigle; circumspection; symmetry; perambulate; verbosity; temerity.

(L.C.C.I. Priv. Sec. Dip.)

USE OF TECHNICAL TERMS

In the previous chapter we noticed that certain technical terms and specialized terminology are peculiar to particular branches of activity —*mortgage, probate,* and *tort* for example to law; *equities, consols,* and *arbitrage* to the stock exchange; *annuity* and *actuary* to insurance; *stevedore* and *consignment* to transport; *invoice* and *overheads* to accountancy; *soprano* and *jazz* to music, while economics employs unusual terms such as *duopoly* and *oligopoly.*

The use of terms in their technical settings is not likely to cause trouble. Technical vocabularies are not, as a rule, very extensive, or, for those who need to use them, difficult to learn. More dangerous are those words that may be used in both a technical and a general sense, and care must be taken to avoid using a word in one sense when the other is intended. Any good dictionary will help you not to confuse the general sense of *infant* and *consideration* with their technical uses in law; *market* and *value* with their technical uses in economics; *assurance* and *average* with their technical uses in insurance, and so on.

It is often possible to express a particular idea in a number of different ways. It is even possible to express technical language in non-technical form, and unless it is certain that the use of technical language will be understood by one's correspondent, a message in general terms is to be preferred.

Examine the following sentences.

A trader's capital is the excess of his assets over his liabilities.

A trader ascertains his capital by deducting his liabilities from his assets.

A trader is worth the amount by which what he owns exceeds his debts to others.

By deducting what a trader owes from what he possesses we are able to ascertain his capital.

All four sentences express the same idea, but the language is different. The technical language of the accountant used in the first two sentences is replaced in the last two by terms that can easily be understood by anyone, even if they have had no training in bookkeeping.

EXERCISES

1. Refer to your dictionary, and in a short sentence express the meaning of each of the following terms as used in the business sense:

(*a*) action (*law*), advance, allotment, assets, insurance;

(*b*) bear, bull, carriage, commission, conveyance (*law*);

(c) drawback, drawings, goodwill, infant (*law*), interest;
(d) journal, lease, manifest, plant, protection;
(e) return, royalty, security, statement, stock;
(f) tender, title (*law*), tramp, trust, turnover.

2. Referring to your dictionary as may be necessary, give in your own words a short definition of each of the following commercial terms:

(a) agent, amalgamation, annuity, auctioneer, barter;
(b) budget, broker, cartel, company, consignment;
(c) contract, credit, currency, debenture, demurrage;
(d) depreciation, endowment, factor, guarantee, indemnity;
(e) insolvency, invoice, lien, monopoly, notary;
(f) option, overdraft, partnership, rebate, requisition;
(g) revenue, subsidy, tariff, trustee, wharfinger.

3. Explain in non-technical language, as if for a person who knew nothing at all about business, what is meant by each of the following sentences.

(a) The goods will be sent by rail, carriage forward.
(b) There is a debit balance of £50 on Mr. Harding's account.
(c) The gross profit for the year was £2,800.
(d) The consignment was sent on 15th February, f.o.b. Montreal.
(e) Cheques are not legal tender.
(f) Small payments are made from petty cash.
(g) A person who buys an established business must usually pay for goodwill.
(h) I have an overdraft at the bank.
(i) The society is prepared to lend money on mortgage.
(j) The goods are subject to a trade discount of 30%.

4. In the following sentences replace each of the phrases in italics by its appropriate commercial expression.

(a) A *person to whom money is owing* will often allow a discount for prompt payment.
(b) A retailer usually replaces his stock by buying from a man who keeps a *building in which goods are stored.*
(c) The shopkeeper frequently reckons his profits as a percentage on *the total sales of the business over a period.*
(d) In most offices a particular person is made responsible for *the small sums of money paid to cover miscellaneous expenses.*
(e) It is a requirement of the law that the accounts of a company must be periodically *submitted for examination by an accountant.*
(f) It is the practice in most offices to pay *the amounts due to executives for services rendered* monthly.
(g) *The periodical payment made for the use of another's property* represents an important item of expenditure in most businesses.
(h) If goods supplied on credit are paid for within the time specified it is usual to allow a *deduction from the invoiced price* to the buyer.

(*i*) A *statement setting out the financial position of a company* must be presented to the shareholders once every calendar year.

(*j*) In these days *the publication of information regarding things for sale* is generally considered to be necessary for anything beyond local trade.

5. Give a brief, dictionary-type definition of each of the following words, and then in each case write a sentence illustrating the word's correct use:

implicit;   literally;   nominal;   obsolescent;   mutual.

6. Choose FIVE of the following dictionary definitions, and for each write down the word which is being defined, beginning with *per*. For instance, for *prevail upon (a person) to do something* you would write *persuade*. Number your answers.

(*a*) Stubborn in holding to one's opinion or design; resolute; obstinate;
(*b*) The excrement of moisture through the pores of the skin;
(*c*) Clearness of statement or exposition; lucidity;
(*d*) Situated at right angles to the plane of the horizon, or directly up and down;
(*e*) Make a hole or holes right through; pierce with a pointed instrument;
(*f*) Done as a piece of routine or for form's sake only;
(*g*) Filter, ooze, or trickle through a porous substance or medium.

(*I. of B.*)

7. Choose FIVE of the following dictionary definitions, and for each write down the word which is being defined. All the words begin with the prefix *anti*. For instance, for *an antibacterial substance produced by a living organism* you would write *antibiotic*.

(*a*) Opposing putrefaction or decay;
(*b*) Settled aversion or dislike; repugnance, distaste;
(*c*) The parts of the globe diametrically opposite;
(*d*) An emphatic contrast of ideas;
(*e*) A remedy to counteract the effects of poison;
(*f*) A cover to protect the back or arms of a chair, sofa, etc.;
(*g*) Any event which is ridiculously less important than what precedes.

(*I. of B.*)

8. Write ten sentences, each containing, in its correct meaning, a word beginning with one of the following prefixes; use each prefix once only:

amphi-; ante-; extra-; hyper-; inter-; mono-; poly-; pre-; pro-; psuedo-.

CHAPTER FIVE

Hints on Composition

And, as imagination bodies forth
The forms of things unknown, the poet's pen
Turns them to shapes, and gives to airy nothing
A local habitation and a name.

Shakespeare: *A Midsummer Night's Dream*

THE ART OF COMPOSITION

Composition is an art. It consists in arranging words into sentences and sentences into paragraphs to form a complete piece of writing valued for both its form and its style. It may take a variety of forms. The writing out of a speech, or lecture, the candidate's answer to an examination question in subjects such as history and geography, the writing of a poem or of a business letter are all exercises in composition. It is the last-named with which we are concerned in this book.

In the ordinary course of your work in an office you will not usually be required to write at length on a variety of topics, but practice in the writing of compositions will help you to develop a facility of expression that will prove useful when you come to write letters.

In Part II of this book the mechanics of language are examined. Punctuation, spelling, and grammatically correct sentences are all essential elements of good composition, but they are no more than servants helping to fulfil the purpose for which they exist. The use of good English goes far beyond mere ability to handle the technicalities of language. The whole purpose of writing, like the whole purpose of language, is to transfer thoughts, ideas, and feelings from one mind to another. It is therefore important for the writer to express himself not only with unmistakable clearness and without waste of words but also in such a way that his message is understood in the spirit in which it is sent.

QUALITIES OF GOOD COMPOSITION

To be good a composition must satisfy three conditions:

(a) it must reveal the writer's ability to express himself clearly in good English;

(b) it must have a clear purpose; that is, it must have something to say;

(c) it must have unity and proportion, and be well arranged.

Good English

Of all forms of composition, letter-writing is the most common, and to the writing of a good letter good English is indispensable. As defined by Sir Ernest Gowers, good English is English that is readily understood by the reader. In business letters especially you must be able to say all that is necessary in the fewest possible words. You will need a working knowledge of grammar, a good command of vocabulary, and a critical appreciation of what is good in form and style. In a word, you will need to write grammatically, clearly, concisely, and in good taste.

Something to say

Unless you have something to say that is worth saying, your composition, however good in other respects, will remain nothing more than a dull and lifeless collection of words and sentences. However skilful you may be in your command of language, however cultivated your style, your first need as a writer is to have something to say.

Like the weaving of threads into a piece of cloth, the weaving of words and sentences into a piece of finished composition is a process of manufacture, and as with other processes of manufacture, raw material is needed. As a writer, whether of formal composition, of poetry, or of business letters, your raw material consists of your thoughts, the ideas you hold, and the information you are able to gather from outside sources—from books, magazines, and newspapers, and by observation and enquiry.

Arranging the material

Having gathered your information, the next thing is to arrange your ideas on paper. Before you attempt to write your composition it will pay you to spend a few minutes thinking out what you want to say. Jot down your ideas on a piece of paper as they come, never mind in what order, and when you have finished go through them carefully, striking out whatever seems to be irrelevant. Then go through your list again, this time grouping together ideas that are related and arranging the groups in the order in which you wish to present them. Make sure that each group leads naturally on to the next. Thinking in this way about the points you wish to make will help you to avoid unnecessary repetition and to produce a straight-forward, logically developed piece of work. Do not start to write until you have a clear idea of the framework into which your facts and ideas are to fit. Preparation of this kind will have a marked effect upon the quality of your composition.

The final version
The next and final step is the expansion of your prepared plan into the completed piece of composition. The bare framework of ideas which you built up must now be clothed in words. Develop the theme paragraph by paragraph, making sure that each paragraph deals with its own topic and leads naturally to the next.

Observe proportion
Be careful to keep a sense of proportion, avoiding the temptation to write at undue length on any particular point merely because it specially interests you, or because you have special knowledge of it. Follow the plan you have prepared and devote to each point the amount of space it merits. Above all, keep to the subject.

The opening paragraph
(a) *In general composition.* Your first paragraph should be in the form of an introduction. It must be interesting and strike the key-note of the subject. It must be interesting, since you wish to capture the attention of your reader; it must strike the keynote of your subject so that he knows what to expect. Don't make it too long, but get down to your subject as quickly as possible. You are, after all, writing for your reader, and a long-winded introduction may easily irritate him and kill any interest he might at first have felt. A brief explanation of your theme, an apt quotation, or occasionally a definition will often provide the kind of introduction needed. It will perhaps be useful to study a few of the introductions by well-known writers. The first two are taken from Bacon's *Essays:*

Travel, in the younger sort, is a part of education; in the elder, a part of experience. *(Of Travel)*

Revenge is a kind of wild justice, which the more man's nature runs to, the more ought the law to weed it out. *(Of Revenge)*

In his Introduction to *In Search of England,* H.V. Morton opens with the paragraph:

> This is the record of a motor-car journey round England.

This paragraph, consisting of only one sentence, tells the reader briefly what to expect in the following pages.

And again, in Chapter Four, his opening paragraph consists of only two short sentences.

> There is a strangeness about Cornwall. You feel it as soon as you cross Tor Ferry.

Not all introductory paragraphs need be, or should be, as short as these. The following, introducing an article on "Damages at Law", is longer, and prepares the way for a defence of the apparent inconsistencies associated with the award of damages for breach of contract:

> The average layman is prone to feel that "The law is an ass", but that is only because he is often quite ignorant of the general principles that guide the Courts, whose decisions, admittedly, may sometimes seem unreasonable or even inconsistent.

The following, introducing an article on "The Art of Examining", consists of a quotation:

> Examinations are formidable even to the best prepared, for the greatest fool may ask more than the wisest man can answer.

These openings are widely different in kind, but they have a common purpose—to arouse interest. This indeed is what you must try for—to engage and hold the reader's attention from the beginning.

(b) In business letters. It is just as important to create interest in the opening paragraph of a letter as of any other piece of composition. If your letter is in reply to one received you may count upon its being read; but if it isn't there is every chance of its not being read unless you succeed in creating interest at the outset.

It has become the fashion to start reply business-letters with phrases such as *In reply,* or *In answer, to your letter; With reference to your letter; Referring,* or *Replying to your letter;* and so on. Such openings are dull and monotonous—worn threadbare from over-use. You can avoid them by going straight to the point; you wouldn't be writing your letter if you weren't replying to one. But if you feel a reference to the letter you are answering is needed a little ingenuity will enable you to give your own a better send-off. Try beginning your letter in one of the following ways.

Express pleasure or regret:

I was glad to receive your letter of . . . .
I am sorry not to have been able to reply sooner to your letter of . . . .

Show that some action has been taken:

On receiving your letter of 10th March I telephoned our head office.
I have made enquiries about the cost of the repairs you mention in your letter of . . . .

Ask or answer a question:

Before I can deal with your letter of . . . I shall need to know . . . .
You are right in assuming that the price mentioned in your letter of . . . is subject to a discount of . . . .

Here are some more examples:

Fashionable	*Better*
In reply to your request of . . . we have much pleasure in enclosing our catalogue.	It gives us great pleasure to enclose the catalogue for which you asked in your letter of . . . .
In answer to your enquiry of . . . concerning Mr. Harris, I am able (or pleased, or sorry) to inform you (or worse still, I have, or beg, to inform you) that I have known him since	Mr. Harris, about whom you enquire in your letter of . . ., has been known to me since . . . .
With reference to your order of . . ., we have sent the goods to you by passenger train.	The goods which you ordered on . . . have been sent to you by passenger train.
Referring to your advertisement in this morning's *Daily Telegraph*, I wish to apply for the post of shorthand-typist.	I wish to apply for the post of shorthand-typist advertised in this morning's *Daily Telegraph*.

Your letter may not, of course, be a reply to another, but may be taking the initiative in seeking or giving information, making a request, or promoting a sale. In any event, the same rule applies—

you must give it an interesting send-off, otherwise it will not get the attention you want it to have; it may not even be read beyond the first paragraph. Direct your opening to the reader's personal interest, and thus prompt him to read on to find out more. His interest may be that of being important, doing good, making money, saving time, keeping fit, and so on. But whatever it is, address your appeal to it. There is a type of opening for every occasion. Here are just a few.

An opening seeking advice:

> It is sometimes said that the highest compliment one can pay a person is to ask him for advice, and we are writing now to ask for yours on a problem that has worried us for some time. (Appeals to self-importance.)

An opening requesting help:

> Have you ever stopped to think what it is to be blind; what it means not to see your loved ones, to watch television or read a book? There are many like this, and they need your help. (Appeals to sentiment.)

An opening promoting a sale:

> Wise men learn from the experience of others. Would you like to learn from ours and cut your laundry bills by half? Then read what follows. (Appeals to money-saving.)

These openings are again all widely different; but they have one thing in common—they are directed to the personal interest of the reader.

The closing paragraph

(a) *In general composition.* The last paragraph is just as important as the first. It will naturally summarize the preceding matter, and draw conclusions. Like the opening paragraph, it should not be long. When you have said all there is to say bring your composition to an end with a paragraph that leaves your reader with an impression of finality and completeness —that leaves him in no doubt that he has come to the end. A brief summing up, an apt quotation, a quick look into the future, and so on, will often provide a suitable finish.

The following is the closing paragraph of an article on "The Techniques of Teaching". It draws together the two main ideas that formed the theme of the article.

But whatever methods we use, there will never be much wrong with our teaching if we steadily observe the two basic propositions with which we set out, namely: that the student must be taught to learn by doing, and that he must be taught to think for himself.

The following are other examples of suitable closing paragraphs by modern writers:

From Ronald Rubenstein's *John Citizen and the Law* (a Pelican Book):

And that was that! When John Doe and Richard Roe, like good old soldiers, faded away in 1852, after new and simplified legal forms had been introduced, they received no funeral oration. There were "No flowers by request", but there are still a few lawyers who may say, "Thanks for the Memory".

From John Masefield's *William Shakespeare* (Home University Library):

Our knowledge of Shakespeare is imperfect. It can only be increased by minute and patient study, by the rejection of surmise about him, and by the constant public playing of his plays, in the Shakespearean manner, by actors who will neither mutilate nor distort what the great mind strove to make just.

And finally, an example from Sir William Addison's *Epping Forest*. The paragraph concludes a chapter on Bishop Hall of Waltham Abbey:

Perhaps he is remembered best now for his defence of episcopacy, which so roused the anger of Milton. At the end of his life he settled in the modest living at Higham, near Norwich, dying there in 1656, aged eighty-two.

(b) In business letters. Like any other piece of composition, a business letter must have an effective close. This does not mean that every letter must have a closing paragraph, but it does mean that the letter must end on a natural note. The well-planned letter that has followed a logical sequence, for example, brings itself to a natural close, and to add to it may well weaken rather than strengthen its force.

Often, however, a closing paragraph is needed. The type of close will depend upon the type of letter it is. If you are answering a request for something you cannot do you will explain why you cannot do it, and express regret; if you are acknowledging an order you will express thanks for the chance to be of service; if you are applying for a post you will hope for an interview; and if you are trying to sell you will invite an order, send a representative, arrange a demonstration, or do whatever seems to be called for. The ways of closing a letter are as numerous as the different purposes that letters serve.

The paragraph may consist, on the one hand, of nothing more than a simple and graceful exit, as where *Any visit you care to make to our showrooms will be very welcome,* or, on the other hand, of a strong inducement to act, as where *The special discount now offered can be allowed only on orders placed by January 31st. After that date full catalogue prices will be charged.*

There is one kind of ending you must always avoid, and that is the old-fashioned ending beginning with a participle, as *Trusting to hear from you, Thanking you for your trouble, Hoping you will place an order,* and so on. Such endings are relics of a past letter-writing age; they lack definiteness, mean nothing, and serve no useful purpose. Finish your letters with a direct statement that means something—a statement that forms an essential part of the letter and is worthy of the room it takes up. Otherwise, you will become involved in meaningless jargon that merely wastes time. Thus:

> Looking forward to hearing from you soon
> We are

is much better written as

> We look forward to hearing from you soon
> Yours faithfully

and

> Thanking you for your interest
> We remain

could well become

> We thank you for your interest
> Yours faithfully

The following are some examples of suitable closing paragraphs used in correspondence:

Acknowledging an order that cannot be met (and assuming the reason has already been explained):

> We are indeed sorry we cannot on this occasion supply the kind of material you need, but enclose a book of samples showing our full range of polyester fabrics, and hope you will give us the chance to serve you another time.

Acknowledging an order that can be met:

> We thank you for your order and are arranging to send the crockery by British Road Services tomorrow. We hope you will be pleased with it, and look forward to further orders from you.

Getting an order:

> We have no wish to rush you into a decision, but as repeat orders are constantly coming in, and as our stocks are very limited, we strongly urge you to place an order at once. The completion and return of the enclosed card is all that is necessary.

Applying for a post:

> When you have considered my qualifications and heard from my referees I hope you will grant me an interview and give me an opportunity to prove that, if appointed, I would give you complete satisfaction.

Revision

The writing of the final paragraph of a composition or a letter does not complete your task. You must now look through what you have written, and if necessary revise it. You must be on the alert for errors of grammar, spelling, and punctuation, or a faulty construction that might have crept in. It is better for you yourself rather than for your reader to detect mistakes of this sort. Read through each sentence critically, and if you find any faults correct them clearly. If your corrections are to a business letter you have no choice, of course, but to retype it.

EXERCISES

1. The following opening paragraphs are taken from business letters. Avoiding as far as possible the use of the traditional openings, and making any other improvements, rewrite or type them. You may think it necessary to use more than one sentence.

(a) From an application for a junior clerkship:
In reply to your advertisement in today's *Liverpool Courier*, I beg respectfully to offer my services for the post of junior clerk.

(b) From a letter of appointment:
With regard to our recent interviews, we have the pleasure to inform you that we have decided, subject to your references proving satisfactory, to appoint you to the managership of our London office.

(c) From a letter relating to a reference:
We should esteem it a favour if you would kindly let us know by return whether Mr. James Smith, who has applied to us for a situation as ware-

houseman, was in fact formerly employed by you, and if so, whether you found him satisfactory.

(d) From the reference given:
In answer to yours of yesterday's date, we have to say that Mr. James Smith was in our employ about eighteen months and was, much to our regret, discharged last Saturday owing to slackness of trade.

(e) From a letter announcing removal of premises:
Owing to the expiration of our lease and the acquisition of the site by the G.L.C. for street-widening purposes, we have removed to the above address immediately in the rear of our late premises.

(f) From a reminder concerning a quotation:
We beg to refer to our quotation of 27th April for six "Carnegie" chain drives complete, and shall be glad to hear whether you have yet come to a decision regarding the installation of these transmissions.

(g) From a reminder concerning samples:
We have been expecting to hear from you with regard to the samples we sent you on the 7th instant.

(h) From a letter regretting inability to supply goods ordered:
In reply to your postcard re Tarentalla tomatoes, we have to say that at the moment it is impossible to give you another fifteen cases.

(i) From a letter cancelling an order:
If you will refer to our order, No. 94,672, given into your hands on the 26th May last, you will find that delivery of the goods was required on or before 1st August. We are therefore cancelling the order.

(j) From a reply to a complaint:
We are in receipt of your letter complaining of the make of cloth delivered to you in February last, and must at once say that, in our opinion, you are unreasonably exacting in your criticism.

2. Write, or type, final paragraphs to letters suitable in the circumstances outlined below.

(a) Your employer, a nurseryman, has just had a new illustrated rose catalogue printed, and asks you to prepare a circular to send to prospective customers with the catalogue. Remembering that many who will receive the catalogue have not previously dealt with your employer, write a persuasive final paragraph to the circular.

(b) You are the owner of a drapery store that has recently been damaged by fire and are preparing a circular to your customers. Draft a suitable final paragraph explaining that there are many attractive bargains in the salvaged stock, and invite the customers to visit the shop to take advantage of them.

(c) You are writing a letter to a married friend setting out the advantages of life assurance and trying to persuade him to insure his own life. Write, or type, a suitably persuasive final paragraph.

(d) A customer has written to complain of incivility and inattention when he visited your stores. Draft a conciliatory final paragraph regretting the circumstances and hoping for continued custom.

(e) A supplier has delivered goods which arrived late and are now of no use to you. Draft the final paragraph of a letter cancelling the order and asking him to take the goods back. Express yourself courteously.

(f) You find yourself unable to settle an account for goods supplied. Your supplier has already given you one extension of credit, and you now ask for a further extension. Prepare a suitable final paragraph. You expect to be able to settle the account by the end of next month.

(g) A business friend of yours, who was once bankrupt but has since voluntarily paid his creditors in full, has gone into business again and you receive an enquiry about his financial standing. Write a favourable final paragraph.

(h) Harold Watts has bought a haulage contractor's business. He prepares a circular announcing a change in the name of the firm, but does not propose to make any change in the policy of the business. Write, or type, a final paragraph asking former customers to continue to do their business with the new firm.

(i) A firm of cycle manufacturers are having difficulty in finding an agent in Canada for the sale of their machines, and have been advised to approach Messrs. Hardacre & Co., Toronto. The firm write to Hardacres offering them the agency and outlining the advantages of their machines. Draft the concluding paragraph of the letter, but avoid showing that you are over-anxious for them to accept your offer.

(j) A small fire has occurred at your shop premises and you write to the insurance company giving details of the circumstances and the extent of damage. You are very anxious that the premises should be restored in good time before Christmas, but cannot arrange for this until the insurance company settles with you. Draft a suitable final paragraph stressing the urgency.

3. Write short compositions on the following subjects, making use of the outlines given and including any ideas of your own:

(a) Punctuality
Its meaning; its advantages; disadvantages resulting from want of it; the loss to ourselves by being unpunctual, and the loss to others; reflections on punctuality in a concluding paragraph.

(b) Travel
The need to travel; methods of travelling; the pleasures of travelling; travelling abroad; travelling as a means of increasing knowledge and removing prejudices; conclusion.

(c) Music
Music as a means of expression; types of music—instrumental, operatic, religious, dance, etc.; great musicians of the past; modern music; should music be encouraged, and why?

(d) Canals
Definition of; history of; some examples of international fame; decline of

canals in Britain; comparison with Continental canals; uses and advantages of canals; unsuited to modern conditions; a look ahead.

(e) Choosing a career
Importance of right choice; difficulty of choosing at an early age; aptitudes and inclinations as a guide; personal qualities best suited for particular careers—the Ministry, the army, politics, industry, commerce; advantages and disadvantages of different careers; in a concluding paragraph—the dangers of idleness and the value of voluntary services for people of means.

4. Write compositions on the following subjects, making use of the outlines given and including any ideas of your own:

(a) The self-service store

(i) Definition
A modern development
Shop organization

(iv) Disadvantages to owner
Wrapping and price labelling
Pilfering

(ii) Advantages to owner
Economy in staff
Impromptu buying by
    customers

(v) Disadvantages to customer
Temptation to buy
Impersonal service
Absence of credit
No delivery service

(iii) Advantages to customer
Goods on display and priced
Personal choice
Reminder of needs
Quick service
Cleanliness—foodstuffs wrapped

(vi) Future of such stores

(b) The Post Office and the business man

(i) History
Before 1840
Rowland Hill's reforms

(iii) Services rendered
Postal
Remittance facilities
Savings bank
Giro
Miscellaneous services

(ii) A public corporation
A monopoly
Profit-making

(iv) Conclusion
A valuable national service
Indispensable to business man

5. Using the information given on the next page, describe the different duties performed by the Queen.

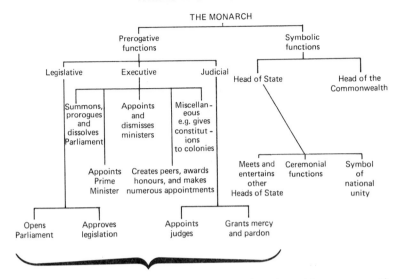

On the advice of the P.M. or other responsible minister (but the Monarch can advise, encourage, warn)

SOME CAUTIONS CONCERNING COMPOSITION

Here are some of the more common pitfalls you must try to avoid when writing a composition.

Avoid the pronoun "I"

A composition should usually be written impersonally in the third, not the first, person. Therefore, unless you are relating personal experiences, avoid using the pronoun "I". A reader is interested in the ideas presented rather than in the writer who presents them. Hence, keep yourself in the background and let your ideas speak for themselves.

Avoid mixing tenses

Do not mix tenses. Use throughout the tense with which your composition begins.

Consider the following well-known passage from *Oliver Twist*.

A council *was held*; lots *were cast* who should walk up to the master after supper that evening, and ask for more; and it *fell* to Oliver Twist.

The evening *arrived*; the boys *took* their places. The master, in his cook's uniform, *stationed* himself at the copper; his pauper assistants *ranged* themselves behind him; the gruel *was served* out; and a long grace *was said* over the short commons. The gruel *disappeared*; the boys *whispered* each other, and *winked* at Oliver; while his next neighbours *nudged* him. Child as he was, he *was desperate* with hunger, and reckless with misery.

Sometimes, however, the subject will call for a change of tense, as in the writing of narrative into which conversation is introduced.

> He rose from the table; and advancing to the master, basin and spoon in hand, *said,* somewhat alarmed at his own temerity—
> "Please, sir, I *want* some more."
> The master was a fat, healthy man; but he *turned* very pale. He *gazed* in stupefied astonishment on the small rebel for some seconds, and then *clung* for support to the copper. The assistants were *paralysed* with wonder; the boys with fear.
> "What!" *said* the master at length, in a faint voice.
> "Please, sir," replied Oliver, "I *want* some more.
> The master *aimed* a blow at Oliver's head with the ladle, *pinioned* him in his arms, and *shrieked* aloud for the beadle.

Avoid monotony

Variety is as necessary to a piece of composition as it is to an attractive garden. The monotony born of sameness has a chilling effect and may well kill any interest the reader might otherwise have had. You can avoid it by using some of the devices dealt with at length in Chapter Sixteen—by varying the length and form of your sentences, mixing long sentences with short and loose with periodic, and sometimes by changing the normal word order of subject and predicate.

Avoid exaggeration

Be discreet in your choice of words and avoid any that exaggerate. Hyperbole, as gross exaggeration is called, is a figure of speech that may be all very well in popular language when it is recognized as such, but it has no place in the business letter. Exaggeration tends to weaken rather than strengthen the effect of a statement intended to be taken seriously, since it calls in question the writer's general regard for sincerity and accurate statement. Avoid especially the use of such expressions as *tremendous* or *gigantic* for *big, unbearable* or *intolerable* for *annoying.* And don't write *scores of times* for *several times, exhaustive enquiries* for *careful enquiries,* or express *astonishment* when you are merely *surprised.* Avoid also the popular though improper use of words such as *terrible, dreadful, awful, disastrous,* and *frightful.* Strong words lose their power when used unnecessarily. Besides, if you refer to a lost cricket match as a *disaster* or to a sleepless night as *terrible,* what have you left that is vivid enough to describe a train crash or an atom bomb?

Avoid bombast
Guard against the inflated kind of language known as bombast. Write simply and naturally rather than elaborately and artificially. Accept the following as your guiding lights.

(a) Reject the pompous phrase that so often litters our writing, especially in business letters.

(b) Choose the simple word rather than the elaborate that means the same thing, preferring *sent* to *forwarded, use* to *utilize,* and *ask* to *request* (pp. 16—17).

(c) Use adverbs sparingly, keeping them for those occasions when they add something to the sense (pp. 20—1).

(d) Reserve adjectives for making your meaning more exact, and eye with suspicion those which merely serve for emphasis. Refer by all means to a *real diamond,* but be chary about referring to a *real danger* or a *real difficulty* (p. 21).

(e) Avoid abstractions and needless prepositional phrases (pp. 22—3).

(f) Avoid tautology (pp. 26—7).

All these are snares for the careless writer.

Avoid hackneyed expressions
Avoid above all the use of slang expressions and be on your guard against clichés, jargon, and quotations that have become threadbare from over-use (pp. 30—3). Be fresh and original.

No two people think or write alike. Each has, or should have, his own style. This will vary not only with himself but also with the subject. A person writing a letter to a friend adopts a style that is homely; a lawyer to a client, a style that is legalistic and precise; a business man to a customer, a style that is direct and clear. For each different occasion there is a separate style.

Avoid circumlocution
And finally, don't waste words; write to the point. Express your ideas in direct, preferably short, simple statements, and arrange them in well-organized order. When tempted to litter your sentences with conjunctions like *and, but, consequently,* and *however,* try a full-stop instead. This will help to keep your sentences short, and

make it easier for your reader to grasp their meaning. He may quite naturally feel annoyed if he has to read a sentence twice before he can understand it.

EXERCISES

1. Explain in detail:

(a) how to keep fit;
(b) the duties of a private secretary;
(c) the importance of electricity in modern life;
(d) how to prepare for an examination;
(e) how to write good English;
(f) how you would furnish your own room, and why;
(g) the value of learning a foreign language;
(h) the importance of first-aid in the home;
(i) the value of any youth organization to which you belong;
(j) which month of the year you prefer, and why.

2. Construct outlines for compositions on the following subjects:

(a) roads *v.* railways;
(b) the influence of the Press;
(c) the use and abuse of strikes;
(d) public libraries;
(e) discipline;
(f) examinations;
(g) the value of school games;
(h) hire purchase;
(i) the value of insurance;
(j) the value of a commercial course.

3. Making use of the outlines you have prepared, write short compositions on the subjects included in Question 2.

4. Write a paragraph of 100-150 words, describing the scene at the beginning of a Christmas party, following and filling out the plan given below. State the number of words you have used.

Arrival of some of the guests—decorated hall—talk and laughter—into room arranged for party—fire burning brightly—holly and mistletoe—paper hats—Christmas tree in corner—table laid attractively for tea—many good things to eat.   *(R.S.A. Elem.)*

5. Expand the following outline into a carefully written paragraph of about 150 words. Pay close attention to building of sentences, choice of words, and punctuation, and, at the end, state the number of words used.

Summer evening—country cottage—garden with flowers—old man in chair (describe him)—setting sun— sleeping cat—mouse nibbling crumbs—a sudden noise—what happened next.   *(R.S.A. Elem.)*

6. Expand the following outline into a carefully written paragraph of about 140 words.

A sunny day—a high cliff by the sea—four climbers—their appearance—the view from a ledge on the cliff—a fall of rock—a miraculous escape.

(R.S.A. Elem.)

7. Write a short article, about 150 words, on each of the following subjects:

(a) gramophone records;
(b) road signs;
(c) summer holidays;
(d) weather forecasts;
(e) town planning;
(f) television;
(g) one-way traffic;
(h) mass production;
(i) correspondence courses;
(j) the cost-of-living.

8. In a short composition of about 200 words examine the case for and against one of the following.

(a) Should smoking be abolished?
(b) Should co-education be encouraged?
(c) Is ambition a good thing?
(d) Should corporal punishment be abolished?
(e) Can capital punishment be defended?
(f) "Man for the field, woman for the hearth;
   Man for the plough, but for the needle she."

9. Write a paragraph supporting or opposing ONE of the following propositions. Your paragraph should be convincing in expression, should contain two or three arguments, and should consist of about 150 words:

(a) that tidiness is a much over-rated virtue;
(b) that girls employ their leisure more profitably than boys;
(c) that "hitch-hiking" is degrading and should not be allowed;
(d) that too much attention is paid to punctuation in the writing of English.
(R.S.A. Inter.)

10. Write a suitable paragraph expanding ONE of the following ideas.

(a) The cinema, as a form of entertainment, is losing popularity;
(b) The standard of cookery in canteens is not high enough;
(c) Men's dress is too dull and drab.   *(R.S.A. Inter.)*

11. Develop ONE of the following ideas in a well-planned paragraph of about 170 words.

    (*a*) A world-language is necessary for world progress.
    (*b*) Manners maketh man.
    (*c*) Money must be the servant of a man and not his master.
    (*d*) Honesty is the best policy.
    (*e*) Atomic power.   (*R.S.A. Inter.*)

12. Write a paragraph of about ten lines on ONE of the following debatable subjects (you may agree or disagree with the proposition).

    (*a*) Television is a time-waster.
    (*b*) Record-breaking flights should be discouraged.
    (*c*) The output of private motor-cars should be severely limited in future.
    (*d*) Parents provide too much pocket-money for their children.

13. Write a composition of about 300 words on ONE of the following subjects:

    (*a*) Doing the week's shopping.
    (*b*) End-of-season sales.
    (*c*) Saturday morning at the shops.
    (*d*) The work and duties of a private secretary.
    (*e*) Big stores compared with small shops:
        (*i*) from the customer's point of view;
        (*ii*) from the shop assistant's point of view.

                                                           (*R.S.A. adapted*)

14. Write about 200 words on ONE of the following topics.

    (*a*) Tea *or* rice.
    (*b*) My views on violence in television programmes.
    (*c*) Some duties of a good citizen.
    (*d*) Unemployment among young people.
    (*e*) Some qualities a secretary looks for in an employer.
    (*f*) Working in the city *or* in a new office building in the countryside.
                                                        (*L.C.C.I., Elem.*)

15. Write for about 45 minutes on ONE of the following.

    (*a*) Community service.
    (*b*) "If wildlife is not protected, there is not much chance for us."
    (*c*) Old age as an economic and social problem.
    (*d*) "We live in an age of personalities."
    (*e*) The problem of litter.
    (*f*) Journalism: its use and abuse.
    (*g*) "The customer is always right."

                                                           (*R.S.A., Adv.*)

CHAPTER SIX

The Essay

Abstruse and mystic thoughts you must express
With painful care, but seeming easiness;
For truth shines brightest through the plainest dress.

Wentworth Dillon: *Essay on Translated Verse*

PERSONAL WRITING

The highest form of literary prose is that which the writer endows with a personal quality—the form of writing in which he expresses his own feelings on some particular topic or circumstance and which bears the imprint of his personality by revealing his own opinions and imaginative qualities. It is this form of subjective or personal writing that distinguishes the essay from the form of writing concerned with the objective recording of actualities and generally referred to as "Composition". The essay is a form of reflective writing devoted to an expression of the writer's views rather than to an account of some external reality; it is concerned with sentiments rather than with facts, involves feeling as well as thinking, and permits considerable freedom of style and method. It is essentially individual and no two people would write on the same topic in quite the same way.

Personal writing becomes possible only when the writer reaches maturity and is able to respond more intensely to his experiences and to exercise a more healthy discrimination in his choice of language. It is of course natural for the student taking a vocational course to question the relevance of personal writing to his vocational needs and to feel that the time devoted to it could be more profitably spent in other ways. But he has no cause for concern. His activities in note-making, letter-writing and précis writing provide ample scope for the impersonal style of writing predominantly needed in business. It is generally accepted that the most striking improvements in the use of language are achieved when the study of English is not confined to its more utilitarian aspects. Personal writing and impersonal writing both have their uses, the former as a cultural force and the latter as a vocational accomplishment. The two are in fact complementary; each needs the other. On the one hand, practice in personal writing has an important bearing on the power and quality of the form of writing used in business, while on the other hand imaginative writing is partly dependent on the form of training employed in the cultivation of English as a practical skill. All that has been said in earlier chapters is therefore as relevant to essay writing as it is to any other form of written composition.

GATHERING MATERIAL

As already stated, treatment of an essay is essentially individual, and different people writing on the same topic may be expected to handle it in different ways. This, however, is not to say that method is unimportant; it is indeed more important than in most other forms of writing. The pre-requisite is to have something to say, and here much may be done by systematic reading, by keeping in touch with current events through the Press, radio and television, which provide excellent material, and by interested observation and enquiry. These and other sources provide a serviceable store of ideas for use when the time comes.

CHOOSING A SUBJECT

When asked to write an essay you will usually be offered a choice of subject. In an examination you will naturally choose to write on the subject about which you know most, since you will have no opportunity to look things up. It is good examination technique to avoid a subject likely to be chosen by a great majority of the candidates if there is another on which you feel you can write equally well. Examiners welcome a break from the tedium of marking an unbroken succession of essays on the same subject. In making your choice it is useful to remember that essays calling for subjective treatment, as where they involve explanation, discussion or expression of opinion, usually commend themselves more favourably to examiners than those whose character is purely narrative or descriptive.

Examiners realize that candidates are motivated by different interests and that if a candidate is to write he must have something to write about. Accordingly, a very diversified choice of subject, often conforming to a pattern sequence, will usually be offered. Some inkling of this pattern may be gleaned from a glance back at the papers set in earlier examinations. Thus, in four out of six consecutive papers recently set by the Institute of Chartered Secretaries and Administrators one of the subjects was "Education" under the following titles.

(*a*) The most important features of a good education.

(*b*) The educational policy and requirements of the country in which you live.

(*c*) The significance for your country of its present educational programme.

(*d*) Many adolescents are bored by their experiences in school, which seem to have nothing to do with life.

Each of these six papers also included at least one question on current affairs and one on politics, while five included a question on economics. In most professional examinations an important feature is the emphasis given to current affairs, while all papers regularly include questions, and usually more than one, of a general nature, of which the following are typical.

The beauties of the countryside The charm of gardens A most unusual holiday Market day in a country town Simple pleasures	Institute of Bankers
Spectators at games What makes a holiday successful Changes I should like to see in my town or village Umbrellas	London Chamber of Commerce and Industry (Intermediate)

The emphasis on current affairs confirms the need to maintain touch with current news and views, through the news columns and leading articles of a good daily newspaper and the other sources mentioned earlier.

PREPARING A PLAN

Having settled upon your subject your next step is to draw together and jot down your scattered ideas and then marshal them and prune them, following the procedure suggested on pp. 66–7. This helps to give form to your essay and, in an examination, provides a yardstick by which you can check your timing and adjust your material to the time that remains for it. You must take care to observe the essential qualities of unity, coherence and emphasis referred to in the chapters on *Sentence Building* and *The Paragraph. Unity,* as applied to the essay as a whole, prescribes that ideas not immediately relevant to the subject must be discarded; *coherence,* that a logical sequence of thought must be preserved throughout, so that the topic dealt with in each paragraph leads smoothly and naturally into that of the next; and *emphasis,* that all parts are given the amount of space proportionate to their relative importance. Opening and closing paragraphs should also have special attention. All these are matters that are treated more fully in other chapters, and in particular in Chapters Five and Sixteen, and before attempting any of the exercises at the end of the present chapter you are recommended to study relevant portions of these chapters, and especially the *Hints on Composition* in Chapter Five.

WRITING THE ESSAY

The plan having been prepared, thought must be given to the writing of the essay itself, with special attention to the three other essential qualities of style, relevance and proportion.

Style

The style must be appropriate to the subject-matter and may vary from the serious to the humorous, from the dignified to the colloquial, depending on the nature of the topic. For the type of essay usually set in examinations a plain style is the most suitable, a style, that is, which is free from elaborate and high-sounding expressions, a style that is natural and free from effect. But if you have a wide vocabulary, by all means make use of it, but with discretion and not to show off; long and uncommon words used for ostentation do not help. Language that is homely has the most telling effect, but slang, colloquialisms and abbreviated forms such as *can't, won't* and *didn't* should be avoided. Study to be simple and natural and in this respect emulate the style of many of our best writers. Match the words you use to the sense you wish to convey, avoiding the sententious style of the preacher on the one hand and the rhetorical style of counsel on the other hand, while at the same time remembering that the language of the essay should be more literary, more copious in its vocabulary, more dignified in the matter of style and less elliptical than the forms used in ordinary speech.

Essay subjects are often of the controversial kind, requiring examination of different points of view. Essays of this kind are often presented in the form of quotations which, as a rule, put forward one side of some personal or general problem, which the candidate is invited to discuss, but with which he may not agree. In essays of this type ideas should be presented impersonally in such forms of words as, "There are some who feel that ...", "It is generally assumed that . . .", but when drawing on your own experience, or when you hold decided views, you may quite legitimately express yourself in the first person and say, "I remember the occasion when . . .", "I spent several years in . . .", "It is my own opinion that . . .", and so on. The occasional introduction of a personal note in this way adds a touch of life and reality to the essay, but apart from this special use the first person should be avoided.

Relevance

What you have to say must, of course, be relevant to the subject on which you are invited to write. Once you have made your choice from the topics included in the question your first task is to decide what is involved in its treatment. Thus, in the title "The uses of atomic power" the scope of your essay is clearly defined, though you are still free to treat the topic in your own way. But if the title is the more general one of "Atomic power", it leaves you free not only to determine the manner of treatment but also to decide which aspects of the topic you will deal with, and the inclusion of the history and development of atomic power, its uses and the problems it creates would all be relevant, but not if the subject of the essay were merely "The uses of atomic power". If the subject is "Examinations", you receive no help in deciding what line to take. At the lower level a candidate might deal with the topic in a purely personal way and write about his dread of examinations, his efforts to prepare for them, his feelings on entering the examination room, and the anxiety with which he awaits the result. If on the other hand the subject should be "The uses and abuses of examinations", "The purpose of examinations" or "The value of examinations" the scope of the subject is clearly defined and restricted and the approach to the topic is necessarily different in each case. In dealing with the last-named, for example, one would expect to deal with the advantages and drawbacks of examinations from both the teacher's and the student's point of view, but a discussion of such matters would not be relevant to an essay on "Uses and abuses" or on "Purpose", though they would be so to an essay on "Examinations". Clearly, having made your choice of subject, you must take care to observe its precise scope and avoid introducing matter not strictly relevant to the title.

Proportion

If you are asked to write on a topic that calls for a treatment of two opposing aspects—old and new fashions, former and present-day transport, the case for and against examinations, for example—you must maintain a proper balance between the two and resist the temptation to write expansively on one at the expense of the other merely because you are more interested in it, or know more about it, or hold personal views in favour of or against it. This does not mean that you must not express your personal views. On the contrary, if the topic is controversial you must not hesitate to express your point of view, provided you are careful to support it by evidence and argument in the effort to win the reader over to your way of thinking.

REFLECTIVE COMPOSITION

Many of the subjects set in examinations are chiefly narrative or descriptive. You will find examples in the lists included in the earlier section on p. 85. For their adequate treatment subjects of this kind require no more than clearness of expression and an orderly arrangement of facts. Treatment of such subjects becomes reflective only when one might wish to generalize, make comparisons or draw conclusions.

But in dealing with subjects that involve discussion of abstract principles, such as justice, perseverance, courtesy, modesty and ambition, the method of treatment must be mainly reflective, and as differences of opinion on abstract subjects vary widely, so will the method of treatment. The practised writer will naturally pursue a course of his own, but for the learner the following will usually provide a suitable line of approach:

(a) Introduction, including definition of subject.
(b) Judgment or personal opinion.
(c) Arguments in support of views held.
(d) An example.
(e) Conclusion.

The paragraph with which you open your essay is important and you should refer again to what has been said about this on pp. 67–8. The paragraph should bear directly on the subject. In the treatment of abstract subjects that involve discussion the subject must be clearly defined. The definition must not include the term defined or any of its derivatives; nor must it consist of a single word synonymous with the given term. To say that "Perseverance consists in perseveringly following a set objective", or that "Perseverance is determination" takes the reader no further and does not constitute a definition. But if we say that "Perseverance is the mental quality that enables us to continue steadfastly in a course of action in face of difficulties, and to overcome them", we bring out the two essential characteristics of an exact definition, namely, *(i)* the general nature of the term defined and *(ii)* its particular nature. The general nature "the mental activity" is that which perseverance has in common with other mental qualities, such as courage and ambition, while the rest of the definition particularizes perseverance, that is, distinguishes it from other mental qualities.

A definition of terms in this way, to which is added an indication to the reader of how you propose to treat the subject, will usually serve as a satisfactory introductory paragraph. For example:

> Perseverance is the mental quality that enables us to continue steadfastly in a course of action in face of difficulties and to overcome them. It is a desirable quality in everyone. The will to persevere not only brings success but also creates self-respect and cultivates a sense of pride in achievement. But it must not be confused with obstinacy and an unwillingness to be deflected from one's course or to change one's opinion when it would be reasonable to do so.

Since the whole treatment of the theme will rest upon the judgment or opinion you express, take care not to express yourself too strongly, but take a calm and unbiased view of the subject. Thus, in writing on "Pride", don't make the wild statement that "Pride is a weakness to be avoided", because there are forms of pride that are excusable or even commendable, such as pride in one's children and pride in one's country.

Any judgment you make or opinion you express must naturally be supported by examples, illustrations and arguments. You can draw supporting material of this kind from books and the Press, from history, geography, the radio and your own experience. If you have stated that a particular quality is desirable or otherwise, of universal or of limited benefit, you must explain the grounds on which you base your opinion and draw comparisons and provide examples in the form of anecdotes and quotations, where any of these would be appropriate. You should remember that while the general conclusions you draw are in the last resort the most important parts of your essay, it is the arguments and the material upon which you draw to support them that provide the greatest interest for your reader, who may well be your examiner.

The way in which an essay is brought to a close calls for special care. There are several reasons for this. Some of them have already been mentioned in the section headed *"The Closing Paragraph"* on pp. 70–1. Moreover, it is from the closing sentences of the essay that the reader gathers his last thoughts and impression of your effort, and these are therefore likely to be a strong influence in affecting his judgment on the merits of your essay as a whole.

THE EXTENDED ESSAY

Choosing the subject
There may be occasions when you are required to prepare what is termed an extended essay, of the type required for the former Ordinary National Certificate and Diploma examinations. Essays were prepared in the candidates' own time and consisted of some 3,000 to 5,000 words on topics chosen by the candidates themselves, and approved provided they were recognizably related to some aspect of business studies, using the term in a broad sense. Among the topics included in one approved scheme were the following, given here mainly as examples to show the wide range of choice available.

Advertising	Middlemen
Competition and monopoly	Subsidies
Cost of living	Trade unions
Equal pay	Vocational guidance
Full employment	Wages structure

Should you be required to choose a topic for an essay of this type avoid the mistake of making your topic too wide, out of fear that you may not have enough material for an essay of the length required. If your topic is too wide, you become involved in a mass of information incapable of adequate treatment, and the essay tends to become little more than a catalogue of flat and uninspiring generalities. *Advertising,* for example, is much too wide a subject to be treated, within the length permitted, with the degree of depth required for an interesting essay. Less wide-ranging titles, such as *Modern Advertising Media* and *The Case For and Against Advertising,* offer ample scope and provide better opportunities for a lively and satisfactory treatment.

By the same token *Competition and Monopoly* could be restricted to *The State Control of Monopoly; Subsidies,* to *Agricultural Subsidies in Britain; Trade Unions,* to *Trade Union Development in the last Fifty Years,* and so on.

Sources of information
Having decided on the field in which to write, your next step is to make use of your school or college library, and your local public library if necessary, and examine books on the subject. This will help you to decide on some particular aspect of it as the essay title. Then discuss your choice with your teacher and seek his advice on information sources. These may include not only books and articles

in encyclopedias, magazines, trade periodicals and Government publications, but also first-hand contacts with business concerns. Tactfully approached, most firms will be willing to provide literature and illustrations and to answer questions that do not involve detailed investigation. Government departments and most large firms have publicity and public relations departments and, if approached in the right manner, can always be relied upon to co-operate.

A London schoolboy of sixteen, asked to write an essay on the fruit and vegetable market, voluntarily rose at five one morning and went to the market to gather his material at first hand. He accepted the disciplines involved in all investigation, sifted through his own mind what information he was able to gather and, when he came to write his article, impressed it with the stamp of his personality. All these are important advantages of knowledge gained by personal investigation, and to them may be added the valuable psychological reactions that spring from satisfying the creative instinct.

The great drawback of books as sources of information in a constantly and rapidly changing world is that they may not be up to date. This applies even to the books most recently published, because of the frequently long interval between the publisher's acceptance of a manuscript and the date of publication; hence the need for the other sources mentioned.

Preparing the plan

As you gather your information you will of course make notes. These should indicate sources in case you want to go back to them later. Especially if your subject covers material that is subject to change, you are advised to use either a notebook in loose-leaf form or a set of record cards of card-index type. This is a useful arrangement even where, as in an historical treatment, the subject-matter is static. Each page, or card, should be suitably titled and later insertions made at the appropriate points. The arrangement also assists the planning process—sheets or cards can be sorted, and if necessary resorted, until you are satisfied that you have them in the best order for a logical development of your theme.

Planning follows the procedure mentioned earlier but, because of the length of the essay, calls for more care than in planning the shorter type of essay. Provide for an opening paragraph that gives the essay a good send-off and for a closing paragraph that provides a good round-off. In Chapter Five you will find examples of both.

The success with which you plan will have a marked bearing on the quality of the subsequent essay. Having drafted your plan, try putting it aside for a while, say for a day or two, and give yourself time to think about it. Then go back to it and with the freshness of a second look try to view it from the reader's angle and add the finishing touches.

Writing the essay

Now, in your own words, prepare your essay in draft form, making sure that what you state as fact is not in doubt and that the opinions you express are soundly based. If you introduce quotations to give point to an idea, you must use quotation marks as explained on pp. 355—6 and state sources, either in the text or in the form of footnotes. (On p. 355 you will find examples of both methods.) Your examiner can then distinguish between your own writing and the material you have taken from the writing of others.

Read carefully through your draft, preferably aloud, marking points where the flow of reading does not run smoothly and give them a second look. Then read the draft again, this time with an eye to spelling and grammar. You can now submit the draft to your teacher knowing that you have done all you can to produce a satisfactory piece of work. He will no doubt wish to discuss your draft with you and have suggestions. You can now prepare your essay in final form.

Attractive presentation is important because it creates a good first impression. You will find the following suggestions helpful.

(*a*) Arrange if you can for your essay to be typed; it makes for easier reading, especially if double line-spacing is used.

(*b*) Prepare a title-page on the lines of the following:

Business Education Council
National Certificate
Essay on

RECENT TRENDS IN COMMERCIAL AVIATION
by
Charles Loeber

Southdown Technical College
1981—82

(*c*) If your essay includes diagrams, cuttings and similar material, position them appropriately in relation to the text, adding captions to show their relevance.

(*d*) If your essay is arranged in sectional form, include a *Table of Contents,* giving titles of sections and page numbers.

(e) Secure the pages in a suitable cover bearing your name and that of your school or college, as in the example above.

Illustrative material of the kind mentioned in paragraph (c) must not be overdone. Your effort is, after all, an essay and not a project, and your examiner is an examiner in English. It is therefore to be expected that he is primarily concerned with your powers of expression, your skill in organizing your material and your ability to present it as a logically developed theme expressed in good English prose.

EXERCISES

1. Write approximately 200 words on *one* of the following topics.

(a) Fashions.
(b) My ideal house.
(c) Likes and dislikes.
(d) The preparations for a party.
(e) A short description of a book which I have enjoyed reading, with reasons for my choice. *(U.E.I., Prelim.)*

2. Write approximately 200 words on *one* of the following.

(a) Gardens.
(b) Furnishing a house.
(c) Of poems, plays, novels, which do you prefer? Give reasons for your choice and refer to works which you have seen or read.
(d) You have missed your connection at a busy railway station and have several hours to spend. Describe how you would pass the time.
(e) "Advertising should be strictly controlled." Discuss. *(U.E.I., Prelim.)*

3. Write an essay on *one* of the following.

(a) Dancing.
(b) A camping holiday.
(c) The day when everything went wrong.
(d) Television advertisements. *(U.E.I., 1st yr.)*

4. Write an essay on *one* of the following.

(a) An afternoon in a large department store.
(b) The Highway Code.
(c) The advantages and disadvantages of television.
(d) The Common Market.
(e) Faces. *(U.E.I., 1st yr.)*

5. Write an essay of about 250 words on *one* of the following subjects.

(a) A walk along the sea-shore.
(b) A wedding.

(c) My most treasured possessions.
(d) Motor-cycles.
(e) Good companions.   (L.C.C.I., Elem.)

6. Write an essay of about 250 words on *one* of the following subjects.

(a) A procession.
(b) Preparing for a holiday.
(c) An outbreak of fire in a forest *or* in a factory.
(d) A country fair.
(e) "When father papered the parlour."   (L.C.C.I., Elem.)

7. Write an essay of about 300 words on *one* of the following subjects.

(a) Synthetic fabrics in modern life.
(b) Good and bad advertising.
(c) Motorways.
(d) Some buildings I like *or* dislike.
(e) Spectators at games.   (L.C.C.I., Inter.)

8. Write an essay of about 300 words on *one* of the following subjects.

(a) Favourite haunts of mine.
(b) Paper-backs.
(c) People who would never be missed.
(d) A portrait of myself as I expect to be in ten years' time.
(e) How I would make my office *or* schoolroom more attractive.
                                                            (L.C.C.I., Inter.)

9. Write 400-500 words on *one* of the following subjects.

(a) Identify and comment on the occupations that can be termed "commercial".
(b) Argue the advantages and disadvantages of road versus rail transport in your country.
(c) Through what official departments does the government influence the trade and commerce of your country? What is the nature of this influence?
(d) Describe and contrast the work of chain stores and cooperative retail societies in a national system of retail distribution.
(e) Prepare a report recommending the supply of electricity rather than gas to the new offices of your firm.
(f) Does the influence of Western science and technology pose dangers for the developing countries of the world?   (L.C.C.I., Higher)

10. Write 400-500 words on *one* of the following topics.

(a) What difference would it make to the commercial life of a country if insurance did not exist?
(b) Discuss differing patterns of organisation which can be found in the retail trade. What advantages accrue to the consumer from such kinds of organisation?

(c) Why is foreign trade of great importance to your country? Indicate the different ways in which exporters can obtain orders from abroad.

(d) Describe the various ways in which manufacturers can advertise their goods. How is the consumer protected against misleading advertising?

(e) Prepare a report for your company recommending participation in a Trade Fair.

(f) Evaluate the importance of oil in world affairs today.

(g) How may measures taken by a government to deal with a balance of payments deficit affect commercial and industrial firms?   (L.C.C.I., Higher)

11. Write for about 45 minutes on *one* of the following subjects. Great importance will be attached to the quality and logical arrangement of your ideas.

(a) Describe the scene in a busy central post office.

(b) Holiday camps.

(c) The annoyance of office life.

(d) Discuss the rival advantages of the cinema and of television as forms of entertainment.

(e) You are going on a week's holiday with your family. Your cousin and her husband, who have visited your home on only one or two occasions, are coming to stay in your house while you are gone. Write a letter explaining all they need to know, and what preparations you have made for them.

(R.S.A., Inter.)

12. Write for about 45 minutes on *one* of the following subjects. Great importance will be attached to the quality and logical arrangement of your ideas.

(a) Rivers.

(b) Choosing a new car *or* a new bicycle.

(c) "The telephone like many another modern device is both a blessing and a curse." Discuss this opinion.

(d) Our local grocer *or* parson *or* milkman.

(e) Your local newspaper has offered a prize for the best account (to be published abroad) of the area within a ten-mile radius of your home. The account is to include information about the occupations of the people, industry and agriculture, communications, and famous historical places or beauty spots.

(R.S.A., Inter.)

13. Write a carefully planned essay of about 600 words on *one* of the following.

(a) Waste

(b) "Despite what its founders thought, there is no limit to the money the National Health Service can consume." Given that medical services are continually expanding, what future do you see for the NHS?

(c) Photograph albums

(d) A defence of advertising

(e) Small pleasures

(*f*) The delights and difficulties of "Doing-it-Yourself".

or:

(*g*) A carefully planned short story entitled "Neighbours".

(*R.S.A., Adv.*)

14. Write an essay on *one* of the following topics.

(*a*) "The study of the past has little value for the present." Discuss this statement.

(*b*) It has been said that there is a close connection between status symbols and commercial advertising. Do you agree?

(*c*) Discuss the influence which supermarkets may have on the formation of new social habits.

(*d*) Discuss recent developments in Britain's relationship with the rest of Western Europe and the outlook for the future. (*U.L.C.I., Senior*)

15. *Either* write an essay on *one* of the following titles:

(*a*) The value of endurance tests.

(*b*) The circus as a form of entertainment is out of date.

(*c*) How I should like to appear to other people.

(*d*) "Necessity is the mother of invention."

(*e*) The charm of gardens.

(*f*) Advertising methods of today.

(*g*) "The old order changeth, yielding place to new,
   And God fulfils Himself in many ways,
   Lest one good custom should corrupt the world."
                              (Tennyson: *Morte d'Arthur.*)

(*h*) A defence of examinations.

or

Write a short story with the title "Where ignorance is bliss."

(*I. of B.*)

16. *Either* write an essay on *one* of the following:

(*a*) The kind of music you like best.

(*b*) Mechanical aids in banking.

(*c*) What qualities make a nation great?

(*d*) "Educate men without religion, and you make them but clever devils."

(Wellington)

(*e*) Customers.

(*f*) The future of the trade unions.

(*g*) An outstanding personality of today.

(*h*) "But it is pretty to see what money will do." (Samuel Pepys)

or

Write a short story ending with the words ". . . and that was the last I saw of him." (*I. of B.*)

17. *Either* write an essay on *one* of the following titles:

(*a*) Prestige symbols.
(*b*) The pollution of our coasts and rivers.
(*c*) Violence in nature.
(*d*) Can "indirect taxation" be defended on moral grounds?
(*e*) "There's a fascination frantic
      In a ruin that's romantic." (W.S. Gilbert: *The Mikado*)
(*f*) Market day in a country town.
(*g*) Why should we seek to limit the size of towns and cities?

or

Write a short story beginning: "My uncle Tom could never abide cheese."
                                                        (*I. of B.*)

18. *Either* write an essay with *one* of the following titles:

(*a*) Britain's motorways.
(*b*) The qualities that make a good bank manager.
(*c*) "A haunt of ancient Peace." (Tennyson)
(*d*) The fascination of maps.
(*e*) The "brain drain".
(*f*) Tradition.
(*g*) Jobs about the house.
(*h*) "A woman's place is in the home."

or

Write a short story in which the principal characters are identical twins.
                                                        (*I. of B.*)

19. Write an essay on *one* of the following subjects.

(*a*) The significance for your country of its present educational programme.
(*b*) Recent developments, and their importance for the future, in one area of Africa or Asia.
(*c*) The present relationship between trade unions and management.
(*d*) The effects of an expanding television service.
(*e*) Lord Acton's statement: "Power tends to corrupt and absolute power corrupts absolutely".   (*I.C.S.A.*)

20. Write an essay on *one* of the following subjects.

(*a*) The present state of East—West relations.
(*b*) The most important features of a good education.
(*c*) The work of a composer or musician you admire.
(*d*) President Johnson's statement: "Moderation in the affairs of the nation is the highest virtue".   (*I.C.S.A.*)

21. Write an essay on *one* of the following subjects.

(*a*) Automation: its significance for management and labour.

(*b*) Is an independent judiciary essential to democracy?

(*c*) Earlier this year rival teenage gang leaders in a town near Birmingham were invited to meet senior police officers to try to halt the growth of hooliganism. Indicate the ideas that you, as one of the leaders, would have put forward.

(*d*) Can the nationalization of industry be justified?

(*e*) Field-Marshall Lord Montgomery's statement: "I hold the view that anybody who thinks Britain should not be a nuclear Power must be mad—indeed, absolutely mad."   (*I.C.S.A.*)

22. Write an essay of approximately 400 to 500 words on *one* of the following topics.

(*a*) On being interviewed for a post.

(*b*) "The man who is supremely happy in his work has no need of leisure."

(*c*) Describe the impact which has been made on you by any great work of man (e.g. a painting, a piece of music or literature, or a building).

(*d*) Christmas is a lot of humbug.

(*e*) The argument that taking part in an international sporting event is more important than winning is merely an excuse for failure. Discuss.

23. Write an essay of approximately 400 to 500 words on *one* of the following subjects.

(*a*) The tyranny of routine.

(*b*) "One had as good be out of the world, as out of the fashion."

(Colley Cibber)

(*c*) Lovable faults and unpleasant virtues.

(*d*) The state of a nation's development can be judged by the status of its women.

(*e*) "If only youth knew; if only age could." (*Henri Etienne*)

(*f*) The finest city I have ever seen.

CHAPTER SEVEN

Comprehension and Interpretation

So from the world of spirits there descends
A bridge of light, connecting it with this,
O'er whose unsteady floor, that sways and bends,
Wander our thoughts above the dark abyss.

Longfellow: *Haunted Houses*

IMPORTANCE OF COMPREHENSION

For business purposes of every kind and at every level of performance, whether routine or administrative, efficiency is liable to turn, not only upon the clarity of the information conveyed, but also upon the facility and accuracy of its interpretation. Efficient communication is essentially a two-sided activity and the need for higher standards of both expression and interpretation grows constantly with the increasing complexity of modern business. This ability to distinguish clearly what is important and what is not is not a matter of scholarship or learning; rather is it a matter of perception and common-sense—qualities for which comprehension tests provide both regular and systematic training. To be able to grasp quickly the gist of a report or of a group of letters or other documents is an accomplishment of the greatest value to anyone engaged in business or professional life. A sub-editor must condense a long report into a few brief paragraphs; a solicitor must prepare a "brief" of his client's often involved law case; a judge must grasp and summarize the essential details from a mass of evidence. A business executive does not always have time to read all that has been written on a subject, or all the details of a transaction, and frequently calls upon his staff to prepare a summarized version from which, in a few moments, he can master the essential facts. The preparation of such summaries calls for a firm grasp of the main ideas expressed in the material to be summarized. This is not always an easy matter, because basic ideas must often be sifted from masses of illustrative and explanatory material, or writers may have allowed themselves to become engaged in digressions only remotely connected with the main theme. Nevertheless, a firm grasp of the subject-matter to be summarized is essential. The matter *as a whole* must be clearly comprehended because comprehension and summarizing go hand in hand. It is impossible to present ideas in summarized form, or indeed in any other form unless they are thoroughly understood.

Précis writing is a process that proceeds by three clearly defined stages, consisting of interpretation, assimilation and compression. We cannot assimilate the ideas in a passage we have read until we have interpreted them, that is to say until we can express clearly and correctly, and in our own words, the underlying meaning of what we have read. As a first step, then, we must read and re-read the subject-matter until its main theme has been grasped with certainty and assurance. Full comprehension of what is to be summarized is the essential condition precedent to all satisfactory précis writing.

```
                                      1 Margate Road
                                      St. Annes-on-Sea
                                      Lancs.
                                      FY8 3EG

                                      15th May 19..
    The Superintendent
    The Union Assurance Company
    25 Queen Street
    PRESTON
    PR1 8RA

    Dear Sir

    When I moved from London to St. Annes last year I
    was compelled, by the terms of the lease of the land
    on which my house had been built, to transfer to the
    Reliance Insurance Company that portion of the premium
    which, over a long number of years, I had paid to your
    company to cover the insurance of my house property.
    It would have been more convenient for me to transfer
    also that portion of the premium which covered the
    contents of the property, but on account of the special
    rebate to which I was entitled at the time it was to
    my advantage to keep it with your company.

    When I retired from teaching my membership of the
    A.T.T.I., which had entitled me to the rebate, ceased,
    and the question now is whether, as a retired teacher
    and a former member of the A.T.T.I., I can continue
    to be entitled to the rebate. I should be glad if you
    would kindly say "Yes" or "No", so that if the answer
    is "No" I may reconsider my insurance under the various
    policies I have taken out with you.

    Yours faithfully
    W. Harrison
    W. Harrison
```

Read the letter through twice and then, to test your comprehension of its contents, answer the following questions without reference to the letter. Then test the result by referring to the letter itself.

(a) What change was made in the writer's insurance arrangements when he removed to St. Annes?

(b) What compelled him to make the change?

(c) Why didn't he transfer the whole of the insurance (property and contents) to the Reliance Company?

(d) What occurred when he retired from teaching?

(e) What is the question he now raises with the Union Assurance Company?

(f) For what reason does he ask the question?

Answers to these questions may not have proved difficult, but in examinations, questions on comprehension are sometimes asked that call for the exercise of a keen sense of deduction. Examine for example, the following passage taken from *Oliver Twist,* and then try to answer the questions that follow.

A WORKED EXAMPLE

It was not until he was left alone in the silence and stillness of the gloomy workshop of the undertaker, that Oliver gave way to the feelings which the day's treatment may be supposed likely to have awakened in a mere child. He had listened to their taunts with a look of contempt; he had borne the lash without a cry, for he felt that pride swelling in his heart which would have kept down a shriek to the last, though they had roasted him alive. But now, when there were none to see or hear him, he fell upon his knees on the floor; and hiding his face in his hands, wept such tears as—God send for the credit of our nature—few so young may ever have cause to pour out before Him.

For a long time, Oliver remained motionless in this attitude. The candle was burning low in the socket when he rose to his feet. Having gazed curiously round him and listened intently, he gently undid the fastenings of the door, and looked abroad.

It was a cold, dark night. The stars seemed, to the boy's eyes, farther from the earth than he had ever seen them before; there was no wind; and the sombre shadows thrown by the trees upon the ground looked sepulchral and death-like, from being so still. He softly reclosed the door. Having availed himself of the expiring light of the candle to tie up in a handkerchief the few articles of wearing apparel he had, set himself down upon a bench to wait for morning.

(a) What impression do you form of Oliver?

(b) Refer to the sentences from which you form your impression.

(c) How do you account for Oliver's emotion when he found himself alone?

(d) What prompted him to look abroad into the night?

(e) Why would the stars seem to be more remote than ever?

Concerning *(a)* one gains the impression that Oliver must have been very young, and that he was proud, sensitive, thoughtful and courageous. As to *(b)* the following are some of the references that give a clue to his age and character: the references to a "mere child" and "few so young" indicate that he must have been very young. That he was obviously proud is evident from his determination to hide his feelings from those who had ill-treated him. From his display of emotion once he was alone it is clear that the insults and cruelty heaped upon him had affected him deeply. From what immediately follows the sentence "For a-long time Oliver remained motionless" on his knees, it is also clear that he had been deep in thought and had at last come to a decision. This decision to escape, despite the forbidding and unknown conditions of the world outside, showed his total disregard of the possible dangers that faced him, but he was prepared to take his chance. The emotion referred to in question *(c)* was a perfectly natural reaction to a situation in which he had suppressed his feelings in the presence of those who maltreated him. As to *(d)*, it was equally natural that he should look out into the night on the world into which he would step next morning. No doubt the action gave him a sense of reassurance and helped him to collect his thoughts about the morrow. As to the last question, friendless and isolated, Oliver must have felt a sense of loneliness so deep that he even imagined that the companionship of the stars had deserted him.

COMPREHENSION IN EXAMINATIONS

Types of test

Examinations in English language tend to give increasing emphasis to tests in comprehension. Tests usually follow the pattern of the preceding examples and form part of a printed question paper, but they sometimes consist of pages read aloud, candidates then being required to reproduce the subject-matter within set time limits. Both types of test are essentially tests of understanding; both are also alike in calling for written answers that reveal degrees of competence in expression, logical arrangement, vocabulary, spelling and punctuation. Another variant of the test is the printed page placed in the hands of candidates for only a limited time, when it is withdrawn and candidates are served with questions to answer. Like the aural comprehension test, this variant of the printed test is a test of memory as well as of understanding.

Treatment of words and phrases

Comprehension tests disclose two main faults, namely:

(a) inability to discriminate between what is relevant and what is not;

(b) failure to give full answers to the questions asked.

To correct the first, re-read the passage until you thoroughly grasp its main theme. To correct the second, read the questions closely, make sure you know just what is wanted and then give your answers in complete sentence form, except where you are asked to explain individual words and phrases, when short-phrase or even single-word answers are all that is needed. Be careful to retain the part of speech of the term you are explaining—nouns or noun phrases to explain nouns, adjectives and adjectival phrases to explain adjectives, and so on. You will then find that the new words can be substituted for the originals in the passage.

> They will refer the case to *an arbitrator* if they can't agree (*a person appointed to settle a dispute*).
> The explanation given was *ambiguous* (*capable of bearing more than one meaning*).
> If the proposal is adopted *unanimously* we shall be surprised (*with the full agreement of all present*).

Depending on its context the same word often carries different meanings—the word *service* for example.

> We provide good after-sales *service* (benefits to customers).
> Before marriage she spent several years in *service* (domestic employment).
> Morning *service* was well attended (worship).
> I shall be happy to render you a similar *service* (favour).
> He saw active *service* in France (warfare).
> My stereo has given me good *service* (performance).

When explaining multi-purpose words such as this, give only one meaning—the one appropriate to the text.

Deal with phrases and sentences as you would with single words—explain fully, but in the fewest words possible. Avoid, if you can, words contained in the original, as in the following:

> *A temporary redundancy* (a surplus of labour for the time being);
> *Fallacious argument* (deceptive or misleading claims);
> *Man stands poised on the era of universal exploration* (man is now at the stage when he is ready to explore the universe).

A work-plan

To summarize: You will find it helpful to work to the following plan.

(*a*) Read the passage carefully, more than once if necessary, until you thoroughly grasp the writer's theme.

(*b*) Then read through the questions and underline in the passage those parts which you consider to be relevant.

(*c*) Answer the questions fully but briefly in your own words, and answer them precisely. To comment on the writer himself, for example, is not an answer to a question asking you to comment on the writer's views.

(*d*) Except when explaining the meanings of individual words and phrases, answer the questions in sentence form.

(*e*) Take care to retain the grammatical form (i.e. the same part of speech) of the word (or words) you explain.

(*f*) When a word has more than one meaning, make sure to give it the meaning it has in its context.

(*g*) When asked to *explain* a lengthy phrase or sentence, take care to provide what is asked for, namely an explanation and not a paraphrase. Consider the following quotation:

> "*I warmed both hands before the fire of life;*
> *It sinks, and I am ready to depart.*"

The difference between explanation and paraphrase may be illustrated as follows.

(*i*) A figure of speech relating to life and death (*explanation*).

(*ii*) While it was possible, I lived my life to the full. Now that I can no longer do so, I am ready to die (*paraphrase*).

(*h*) Finally, look at the question again to make sure that you have supplied all the information asked for, and check your answers for grammar and spelling.

INTERPRETATION OF STATISTICS

The nature and uses of statistics

Statistics and the conclusions and inferences drawn from them play an increasingly important role in the social and economic life of the community. We conduct opinion polls for forecasting political trends, the B.B.C. conducts audience research as a guide to programme policy, the Government relies on statistical techniques to estimate potential demand for pensions, the health service and unemployment pay. The national budget, which influences every aspect of our economic life, is itself based on estimates of the probable consumption of taxed commodities, prospective income levels and income from land development, capital transfers and other sources. Most of this work is the province of the professional statistician, but no businessman today can afford to ignore the value of regular and accurate information on such matters as output, production costs and turnover, and there are many occasions when he must himself collect and assemble the data relating to his activities and take action on what his findings reveal. When planning for the future he cannot afford to build on vague impressions.

The essence of statistics lies in comparison, because the significance of one set of figures cannot be appreciated until it is compared with others of the same kind. The managing director of a company may be interested to learn that sales during last month touched £45,000, but the information has no statistical significance until it is related, for instance, to sales in the corresponding month of the preceding year. Comparisons are valid only when made between quantities expressed in identical terms. We cannot compare weekly earnings as a measure of living standards between two periods if, in the first, the working week is one of forty hours and in the second, one of thirty-eight. Nor can we validly compare the monthly values of imports and exports unless we take account of the number of working days in each of the months compared. For official purposes the "month" is taken to be twenty-six working days, and official import and export figures are adjusted accordingly.

Presentation of statistics

Statistics are commonly presented as a series of figures in table form. This method has the merit of showing information in detail, but it suffers from the drawback that its salient features are not readily recognizable. Masses of figures hold little interest for the layman and where the aim is to get the main points across and detail is not essential, diagrams are often the preferred method of presentation. Statistical diagrams take a variety of forms—graphs, bar charts, pie diagrams and pictograms—some being more suitable for particular purposes than others. The pie diagram, as its name suggests, consists of a circle divided into sectors of varying sizes. The pictogram is a pictorial diagram that compares statistical data by repeating symbols representing the type of data presented. As most diagrams reduce the data to an absolute minimum it is important to remember that while they may be factually correct they may be presented in ways that mislead; hence the need to read them critically and with care. The two diagrams below are both factually correct, but an alteration of the scale and the omission of its lower half creates the impression that the number of council houses built by Authority A is double the number built by Authority B, whereas it is only a quarter more (Fig. 1).

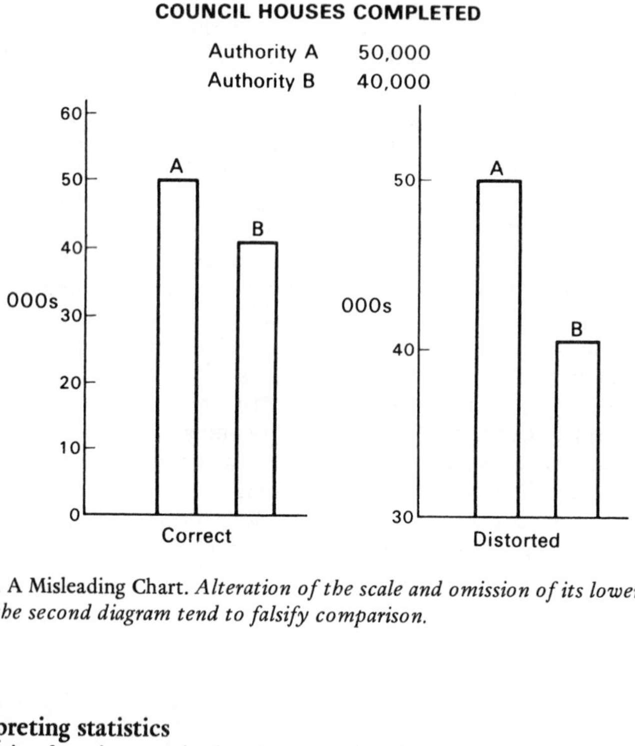

COUNCIL HOUSES COMPLETED

| Authority A | 50,000 |
| Authority B | 40,000 |

Fig. 1. A Misleading Chart. *Alteration of the scale and omission of its lower half from the second diagram tend to falsify comparison.*

Interpreting statistics
Statistics forming a series involve a study of two types of movement:

    (a) short-period fluctuations;
    (b) general movements or trends.

Tables and graphs compared
Interpretation depends upon an understanding both of fluctuations and of trends. The simplest device for this is the *line graph*. It represents quantities in a way that immediately catches the eye and establishes clear relationships. To spot these relationships is much more difficult when figures are presented in table form as in the following example.

Consumption of Electricity

Quarter	Year 1	Year 2	Year 3	Year 4	Year 5
	£	£	£	£	£
March	15.00	15.90	16.10	15.70	16.75
June	12.30	12.60	13.20	13.12	14.20
September	11.14	12.15	12.30	12.60	12.75
December	14.20	14.14	15.00	14.10	15.30
	52.64	54.79	56.60	55.52	59.00

Expressed in graphical form quarterly consumption would appear
as in Fig. 2.

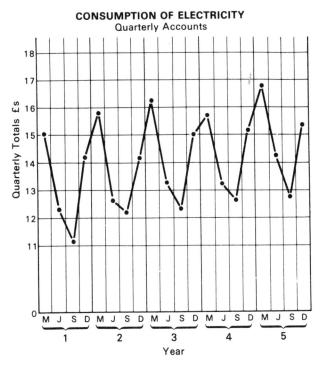

CONSUMPTION OF ELECTRICITY
Quarterly Accounts

Fig. 2. Line Graph Showing Seasonal Variations. *A line graph representing
seasonal variations tends to obsucre the main trend.*

The above graph provides a clear picture of the quarterly expenditure, but it tends to obscure the general trend. This trend is clearly
revealed if, instead of plotting the actual quarterly expenditure, we

plot the quarterly moving average of the expenditure. To calculate the quarterly moving average we first obtain the moving annual totals. The first of these totals is the aggregate expenditure for the whole of Year 1 (£52.64). The second is the aggregate for the last three quarters of Year 1 plus the first quarter of Year 2 (£53.54). The third is the aggregate for the last two quarters of Year 1 plus the amount for the first two quarters of Year 2 (£53.84), and so on for the whole of the five years. Each of the moving annual totals calculated in this way is then divided by four to represent the separate quarters. The quarterly results are then plotted as in Fig. 3.

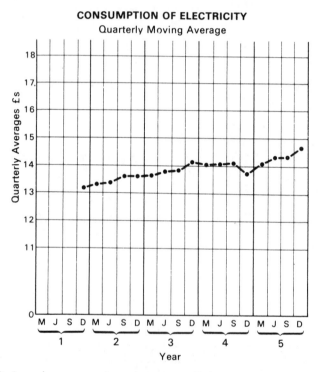

Fig. 3. A moving average. *A moving average eliminates seasonal variations and clearly reveals the direction of the main trend.*

In whatever form statistics are presented, interpretation must begin with an appreciation of their main features.

(*a*) The title must be studied carefully so that the nature and purpose of the data are clearly understood.

(b) The degree of accuracy to which the figures are quoted must be noted.

(c) It is important to remember that graphs, pictures and summarized tables are used to emphasize only certain main features and that they do not tell the whole story.

The examples below illustrate the method of simple statistical interpretation.

Interpreting a table
From the table below we can draw a number of interesting conclusions.

(a) Nearly two million dwelling-places were built in the seven-year period.

(b) The total number completed each year remained fairly constant throughout the period.

(c) Local authorities' share which, in the first year, was more than half the total completed, fluctuated from one year to another on a downward trend, until in the final year it fell to just over one-third.

(d) The private sector's share, considerably less than half the total in the first year, rose to more than half in the final year.

(e) This increase is marked by a trend that remained steady throughout the period.

(f) The picture presented by the table poses the interesting question why building for local authorities should have fallen so drastically over such a short period. The implications may or may not be political.

NUMBER OF HOUSES AND FLATS COMPLETED
in
ENGLAND AND WALES

Year	For Local Authorities	For Private Owners	For Others	Total
1	137,584	122,942	8,127	268,653
2	113,146	124,087	4,292	241,525
3	99,456	146,476	3,449	249,381
4	103,235	162,100	3,891	269,226
5	92,880	170,366	5,586	268,832
6	105,302	167,016	6,349	278,667
7	97,015	168,242	5,398	270,655

Interpreting a graph

In reading a graph it is not enough merely to take in the overall picture. The type of graph, its intended purpose, choice of unit (money, articles, persons, etc.), choice of scale and the true meaning of the slope of the curve all need careful scrutiny (Fig. 4).

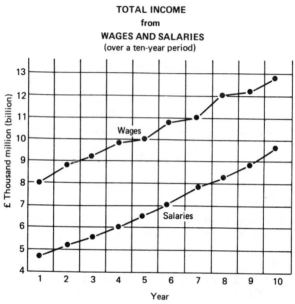

Fig. 4. Wages and salaries compared. (Annual Abstract of Statistics - Abridged)

Questions

(*a*) What is the usual distinction drawn between wages and salaries?

(*b*) Study the two curves in Fig. 4 carefully and state what conclusions can be drawn from them concerning fluctuations and trends.

(*c*) Write a short paragraph giving reasons that might explain why the increased amount paid to salaried workers over the period is substantially higher than the increased amount paid to wage earners.

Answers

(*a*) Salaries are fixed payments made periodically, usually monthly or quarterly (or at other longer intervals than a week) for regular services of a non-manual or non-mechanical kind. They are often calculated on an annual basis. Wages are payments of remuneration, usually made weekly, to manual workers of all kinds. They vary with the number of hours worked or the amount of work done. It is a requirement of the Truck Acts 1831-1940, that wages, but not salaries, must normally be paid in legal tender, but under the Payment of Wages Act 1960 wages may be paid direct into a bank account, or by cheque or postal order where an employee makes a written request for payment in one of these ways.

(b) Annual amounts paid in both wages and salaries show a steady increase throughout the period. Increases in total wages for Years 8 and 10 were greater than for any other years, the increase in the intervening Year 9 being relatively very small. Salaries, on the other hand, increased at a steadily progressive rate throughout the period. Total annual wages and total annual salaries both follow a similar steady and substantial upward trend, but the *rate of increase* for salaries (111%—from £4.6 billion to £9.7 billion) is nearly double that for wages (61%—from £8.0 billion to £12.9 billion).

(c) The greater rise in the amount paid to salaried persons may be due either to substantial pay increases (a very likely cause) or to increases in the number of salaried staff employed as more sophisticated methods of administration and control are adopted. What is very probable is that it is a combination of both.

Some dangers of misinterpretation

Statistics are very often neither exact nor accurate in the arithmetical or accounting sense. Strict accuracy is not usually possible, but since statistics are concerned mainly with aggregates, averages and general trends, strict exactness to the nearest ton or £ is not necessary for practical purposes. What is more important than strictly accurate figures is the reliability of the sources supplying the data, the method of presenting the data, and the relevance of the adopted method to the questions to which answers are sought.

Statistics can be of great help to those who make business decisions, but they are full of pitfalls for the unwary. Some of the ways in which diagrams may be misleading have already been referred to and one must constantly beware of all charts designed to emphasize some particular feature or prove some particular point.

It is always necessary to examine carefully the scale markings on a line graph. Injudicious choice of a vertical scale can create a completely false impression of the range of fluctuations recorded. If the vertical scaling is too wide, fluctuations are exaggerated; if too narrow, they become inconspicuous. Similar results follow if the horizontal scale is not aptly chosen. A graph that does not show any scale is quite worthless, and perhaps deliberately deceptive.

Many statistical figures, too, are based on averages. These are easily misunderstood. The difference between an arithmetical average and a weighted average should be noted carefully, otherwise one may get a completely false impression. If a car is driven 100 miles, the first 25 at 30 m.p.h., the second at 40 m.p.h., the next at 50 m.p.h. and the last at 60 m.p.h., the arithmetical average of its four speeds is 180/4, or 45 m.p.h., but its average speed over the 100 miles is only a little over 42 m.p.h. since speed is a matter of the time taken to cover the distance.

Want of attention to the definitions used in presenting statistics is another cause of error. When considering "Total value of merchandise imported", it is important to know what is included in "merchandise" and what is meant by "imported". It is important, too, to know something of the sources from which the statistics have been drawn and the manner in which they have been compiled. In many cases, explanations are given in footnotes to official reports, but in other cases, where information is not forthcoming, caution is necessary. Sometimes the figures are stated to be "seasonally adjusted". This means that the actual figures are replaced by an average taken for a corresponding period to eliminate the effect of unusual factors, as where exports for a particular month are unduly affected by a dock strike.

There are pitfalls, too, when we come to compare values. To know whether imports or exports have increased (or decreased) allowance must be made for changes in the value of money. If prices have risen, an increase in the *value* of exports may spell a decrease in *quantity.* Even when correctly adjusted, figures showing an increase in exports provide only a very limited picture, since the increase may well be accompanied by a decrease in the share of world trade if the export trades of other countries are expanding.

Finally, a good deal of information is based on samples and unless these are free from bias and are representative of the whole, the figures can easily provide a false picture. Sampling is a method widely used. The B.B.C. use it in audience research, the businessman in market research, and in opinion polls it is used to discover what the public think and what they want. Experience shows that there are dangers in relying too much upon these methods.

EXERCISES

1. Read the following passage carefully, and answer the questions based on it.

Switzerland is a much misunderstood country. People think it consists chiefly of the Alps, and that the Alps are white. The Alps are thickly green most of the way up; the valleys are level-floored; there are fertile plains and gently undulating hills. There are palm trees as well as pines, for Switzerland runs down into the hot south on Lake Maggiore.

Peace-lovers are always meeting in Switzerland, and this too causes misunderstandings. The Swiss are not pacifists, but a nation of soldiers, fortified, provisioned for a siege, armed to the teeth. Practical intelligence, not pacifism, has caused the Swiss to keep clear of international power politics. Their geographical position made it possible, their neighbours found it an advantage, but their cool sense of real values brought it to pass.

Practical intelligence is also the basis of Switzerland's economy. She has no ores to speak of, no natural resources except water power and her people's ability to do things. But this ability is so developed that barren Switzerland has probably the highest average living standard in the world.   *(178 words)*

(a) Explain briefly in your own words the two misunderstandings referred to here.

(b) What is meant by Switzerland's economy?

(c) Explain the reference to "water power". What other natural resources might be found in other countries?

(d) What indications would you expect to find when visiting Switzerland of the "high average living standard"?   *(R.S.A. Elem.)*

2. Read carefully the following passage and then answer the questions set below. You are advised to spend not less than 30 minutes on this exercise.

I learned grammar when I was a private soldier on the pay of sixpence a day. The edge of my berth, or that of the guard-bed, was my seat to study in; my knapsack was my book-case; a bit of board, lying on my lap, was my writing table; and the task did not demand anything like a year of my life. I had no money to purchase candle or oil; in winter-time it was rarely that I could get any evening-light but that of the fire, and only my turn even of that. And if I, under such circumstances, and without parent or friend to advise or encourage me, accomplished this undertaking, what excuse can there be for any youth, however poor, however pressed with business, or however circumstanced as to room or other conveniences? To buy a pen or a sheet of paper I was compelled to forgo some portion of food, though in a state of half-starvation; I had no moment of time that I could call my own; and I had to read and to write amidst the talking, laughing, singing, whistling and brawling of at least half a score of the most thoughtless of men, and that too in the hours of their freedom from control. Think not lightly of the farthing that I had to give, now and then, for ink, pen, or paper! That farthing was, alas! a great sum to me!   *(244 words)*

In answering the following questions [except questions (a) *and* (e)*] use complete sentences and, where possible, your own words.*

(a) Suggest a suitable title for the passage.

(b) Describe *two* of the difficulties that the writer of this passage had to overcome in order to study.

(c) What was his most frequent source of light in the winter?

(d) State what the writer used as: *(i)* a seat to study in; *(ii)* a bookcase; *(iii)* writing table.

(e) Give other words or phrases that could be used to replace the following, without changing the sense of the passage: *(i)* circumstances; *(ii)* accomplished; *(iii)* pressed with business; *(iv)* brawling; *(v)* a great sum.

(f) How do we know that the writer had to teach himself?

(g) What sacrifice did he make in order to purchase a pen or a sheet of paper?

(h) Indicate, using *only two* sentences, what this passage suggests to you about the character of the writer.   (*R.S.A., Elem.*)

3. Read the following passage carefully and then answer the questions that follow it, *using your own words where possible.* Your answers should be written *concisely* in *complete sentences,* unless you are otherwise instructed.

The Future of Mankind

Most people are fascinated by the attempt to forecast something of the conditions of life and social activity as they will be in the centuries ahead. We live in an age in which scientists, engineers and inventors have increased both our knowledge and the number of our mechanical contrivances beyond the dreams of our predecessors. Hence we naturally tend to assume that such progress will be as continuous in the future as it has been in the past, and that the mechanical, industrial and inventive activity of our own age will be as far exceeded in the coming centuries as the achievements of the past have been exceeded in our age.

Whether such an assumption is justifiable or not, only time can tell. It is even conceivable that history may repeat itself, and that periods of intense activity and material progress, such as occurred in the past, notably in the civilizations of ancient Egypt, Babylonia, Greece and Rome, may again be succeeded by periods of inactivity and the consequent loss of much of the previous gain.

Yet there is a fundamental difference between our civilization and the ancient civilizations. Our civilization is world-wide and all-embracing, whereas the ancient civilizations which preceded it were confined within the narrow limits of particular countries. Thus it is extremely unlikely that a relapse similar to those which have occurred in the past can again be possible.

We may ask whether the happiness and well-being of mankind would not be better conserved by a general slackening of the intense activity and competition of the present age. However, as there is little sign of any such tendency at present, we must face the fact that a considerable increase in material progress and industrial activity in the years to come is not only possible but extremely probable. If this happens, we are bound to recognize that it must involve immense changes in many of the conditions of life which we are apt to regard as settled features of the present or of any future age.

(a) State *two* ways in which scientists, engineers or inventors have, in your opinion, benefited our conditions of life.

(b) Why do we assume that man's material progress will be as continuous in the future as it has been in the past?

(c) What do you understand by the statement, "History may repeat itself"?

(d) What difference between our civilization and ancient civilizations makes it unlikely that man's material progress will be checked in the future?

(e) Justifying your answer from the passage, say whether you think the writer entirely approves of modern civilization.

(*f*) In what ways does the writer think it probable mankind will advance in the future?

(*g*) Explain *very briefly* what is meant by any *four* of the following words as they are used in the passage:—

    (*i*) contrivances (line 4)
    (*ii*) predecessors (line 5)
    (*iii*) fundamental (line 16)
    (*iv*) relapse (line 19)
    (*v*) conserved (line 22)   *(L.C.C.I., Elem.)*

4. Read the following passage carefully and then answer the questions that follow it, *using your own words where possible.* Your answers should be written *concisely* in *complete sentences,* unless you are otherwise instructed.

Why the Value of Money Changes

If all the people in a country suddenly obtained twice as much money as before, they could only buy the same quantity of goods, because the total stock in shops and warehouses would not have altered. The natural result would be that prices would rise, as buyers competed with each other, and the same amount of goods would be purchased at the higher prices. Although such an event is unlikely to happen, it illustrates an important principle of economics: the value of money at any given time is determined by the quantity of money available in relation to the number of goods and services for sale. The more money there is available for making purchases, the less its value. The smaller the amount of money in relation to the things for sale, the more value each unit of money will have.

The fact that we do not always spend the money we receive at the same rate has an important bearing on the changing value of money. Sometimes we spend our money very slowly; at other times we spend it as soon as we get it. If there is a depression in trade, we postpone buying whatever we can do without, until we see what is going to happen. The effect is just the same as if there were less money, and prices begin to fall. On the other hand, if we feel confident that we shall continue to earn good wages, we may spend our money almost as soon as we earn it. The effect then is the same as if there were a larger quantity of money, and prices go up.

Once prices have begun to rise or fall noticeably, the tendency is for the change to be exaggerated. If general prices are rising, people hurry to buy articles they had intended to buy later, before they become more expensive, and by so doing cause prices to rise still further. On the other hand, when prices begin to fall, they delay their purchases, in the hope that the goods will cost less and, as there is less money circulating, the level of prices goes down still further.

(*a*) If each of us was suddenly given twice as much money as before why could we not buy more goods?

(*b*) *Using your own words,* state what determines the value of money at any given time.

(*c*) (*i*) When does money become more valuable?
    (*ii*) When does money become less valuable?

(*d*) What relation is there between our rate of spending money and

    (*i*) falling prices?
    (*ii*) rising prices?

(*e*) *Using your own words,* state briefly what happens when prices have begun to rise or fall noticeably.

(*f*) (*i*) What happens to rising prices if people immediately start buying things they want?

    (*ii*) What happens to falling prices if people delay their intended purchases?

(*g*) Explain *very briefly* what is meant by any *five* of the following words or phrases as they are used in the passage:—

    (*i*) principle (line 6)
    (*ii*) determined (line 7)
    (*iii*) unit (line 11)
    (*iv*) a depression in trade (line 15)
    (*v*) postpone (line 15)
    (*vi*) circulating (line 26)   (*L.C.C.I., Elem.*)

5. Read the following passage and answer the questions below.

After a lifetime of some 250,000 years on earth only the last 6,000 of which are a *matter of approximate historic record,* man has conquered earth gravity and *stands poised on the era of universal exploration.* It is, however, imperative that the significance of the earth satellite be measured in terms of man's new capacity to *extend his citizenship to the universe.* The principal need today is to *tap our intelligence* and moral imagination to the fullest in creating a working design for a better tomorrow in which all the world's people can share. We have to accept a *complete commitment* to a *pooling of authority* and a *sharing of human knowledge for the human good.*   (*119 words*)

(*a*) Explain the meaning of the phrases in italics.

(*b*) Give words of similar meaning to conquered, significance, capacity, principal.

(*c*) Write a paragraph of three sentences in which you state qualities you would like in a "better tomorrow".

(*d*) Discuss the appropriateness of the word "working" (design). What do you understand by the expression?

(*e*) Add three sentences that make a logical continuation of the above passage.
(*L.C.C.I., Priv. Sec. Dip.*)

6. Read the following passage and then answer the questions below.

"Man's imagination is limited by the horizon of his experience. When he attempts by guess-work to outgo the bounds assigned, his frailty and ignorance stand apparent; he is like a child explaining the world by its doll's-house. The irremovable boundaries of knowledge are the same for every age; human sense is feeble, human reason whimsical and vain, human life short and troubled. But every now and then, in the long history of the race, there is a rift in the cloud, or a new prospect gained by climbing. These are the great ages of the world. Creation widens on the view, and the air is alive with a sense of promise and expectancy. Thus it was in the age of Elizabeth. The recovery of the Classics opened a long and fair vista backwards; the exploration of the New World seemed to lift the curtain on a glorious future. And the English, the little parochial people, who for centuries had tilled their fields and tended their cattle in their island home, cut off from the great movements of European policy, suddenly found themselves, by virtue of their shipping, competitors for the dominion of the earth. It is no wonder that their hearts distended with pride, and, hardening in their strength, gloried. A new sense of exaltation possessed the country, the exaltation of knowledge and power." (Professor Walter Raleigh.)   *(225 words)*

(a) Express in your own words the thought contained in the first sentence.

(b) What are the "irremovable boundaries of knowledge"?

(c) Comment on the force of any *two* metaphors in this passage.

(d) According to Professor Raleigh, what two factors made the Elizabethan Age one of the "great ages of the world"?

(e) What aspect of their economy contributed to the greatness of the English in the time of Elizabeth?

(f) Explain the force of the adjective "parochial" in "the little parochial people".   *(I. of B.)*

7. Read the following passage and then answer the questions below.

"The enjoyment of physical possession of things would seem to be one of the prerogatives of wealth which has been little impaired. Presumably nothing has happened to keep the man who can afford them from enjoying his Rembrandts and his home-grown orchids. But enjoyment of things has always been associated with another prerogative of wealth which is the distinction that it confers. In a world where nearly everyone was poor, this distinction was very great. It was the natural consequence of rarity. In England, it is widely agreed, the ducal families are not uniformly superior. There is a roughly normal incidence of intelligence and stupidity, good taste and bad, morality and immorality. But very few people are dukes or even duchesses, although the latter have become rather more frequent with the modern easing of the divorce laws. As a result, even though they may be intrinsically unexceptional, they are regarded with some awe. So it has long been with the rich. Were dukes numerous, their position would deteriorate. As the rich have become more numerous, they have inevitably become a debased currency."   (J.K. Galbraith: *The Affluent Society*,)   *(183 words)*

(a) Give, in your own words, the meaning of the opening sentence.

(b) Why does the writer associate "his Rembrandts" and "home-grown orchids" with wealth and what is the force of "his" and "home-grown"?

(c) How does the writer amplify his contention that, in England, "the ducal families are not uniformly superior"?

(d) Why have ducal families and rich people been regarded with awe by other people?

(e) What is the significance of the reference to the more numerous rich as "a debased currency"?

(f) Quote any one sentence which reveals the author's sense of humour and explain the humour.   *(I. of B.)*

8. Write a short account (about 150 words) stating what deductions can be made from the following table.

Index Numbers of Wage Rates and Normal Weekly Hours
(All industries and services; Year 1 = 100)

Year	Weekly wage rates				Normal weekly hours	
	All Workers	Men	Women	Juveniles	All Workers	Men
2	110.0	110.0	109.7	111.3	99.9	99.9
3	114.0	113.8	114.0	115.8	99.7	99.7
4	117.0	116.8	117.0	119.0	99.6	99.6
5	120.0	119.7	120.8	123.2	98.0	97.9
6	125.0	124.6	125.3	130.3	95.9	96.0
7	129.6	129.1	130.3	135.6	95.1	95.1

9. Write a short composition (about 200 words) on "The uses and abuses of statistics".

10. What is the purpose of using graphs? Suggest an occasion when a graph might be of value in:

(a) your college or school;
(b) an office.   *(R.S.A. Inter.)*

CHAPTER EIGHT

Listening and Note-Making

Take a note of that; his Lordship says he will turn it over in what he calls his
mind.

Nash: *Life of Lord Westbury*

THE ART OF LISTENING

It is through the activity of listening that we get most of our knowledge of the world and the people we meet and know. For effective
communication by speech the hearer must listen. Hearing and listening are not the same thing. Hearing is a passive activity that calls for
no effort from the hearer; listening is essentially an active and pur-
poseful process in which the listener participates and makes a positive
contribution by bringing his powers of concentration to bear on
what he hears. As defined in the *Oxford Dictionary* listening is a
skill involving conscious effort in following what is spoken, in recognizing the main points and making sure that they are understood.

Concentration is the essence of effective listening. In this context
concentration means giving exclusive attention to the matter in
hand and this is not easy for any length of time unless we chance to
be deeply interested in what is being said. Even then attention is
apt to be distracted by what goes on around us — the chirp of a
sparrow, the sight of a bee, any small thing in fact of which we
become consciously aware. Like reading, listening is a receptive
activity and it is easy to lose concentration and the ability to listen.
Concentration is easiest where interest is deepest and if concentration is to be sustained interest must be maintained. Where interest
is present it will not usually be difficult to concentrate, but there
are times when we need to apply our minds to things in which we
have little interest. The spontaneous concentration that springs
from interest is then lacking and attention becomes a deliberate
effort of will. Distractions are less likely to trouble us if we watch the
speaker. His gestures and facial expressions add meaning to his
words, and the fact that he is aware of being watched helps him to
feel that he has the interest and attention of his listeners. This may
improve the quality of his communication and in turn help his
listeners to understand him more easily.

Making notes is part of the skill of listening. In the words of Dante's *Divine Comedy*, "He listens well who takes notes". Besides providing a record for future reference making notes improves the quality of listening because it compels concentration and effort in comprehension.

Making notes while listening is the most difficult of all forms of note-taking because it involves not only the skill of listening but also the essential art of selection. This requires the listener to distinguish what is important from what is less so and calls for close concentration. In taking notes of an address there is time to note only the lecturer's main points, but before we can do this we have to be able to detect them. This calls for close attention and critical listening. In speech things are said once only; if we miss them there is no repeat and no opportunity to hear them again. Familiarity with the subject-matter helps us to recognize main points more easily than if the subject-matter is strange, and a teacher dealing with subject-matter that is new will sometimes helpfully suggest the points of which notes should be made.

SOME USES OF NOTES

Taking and making notes are essential activities in all subjects in which the aim is to acquire knowledge rather than to develop skill, especially where lectures form part of the teaching.

We cannot do without notes. We need them to remind us of things that have happened and of things to be done. Notes from the past serve as guidelines for the future. Speaking, writing and reading all rely upon the ability to take and make notes. Verbal reports, telephone conversations, compositions, essays, business letters and book learning all make use of notes at some time or other. During every hour in a business office the worker is either listening to instructions or giving them, interviewing or being interviewed, or speaking on the phone. Notes of these things assist recollection and provide reliable information upon which to act. The businessman attends many meetings and conferences. He makes notes of matters he wants discussed and of suggestions he proposes to make. At the meeting itself he takes notes of what is said and of decisions reached. He also makes notes before drafting a report or dictating an important business letter. For the student, much that is useful is to be found in books, magazines and the Press and one of the marks of the serious student is the practice of making notes. He must grasp the essentials of what he reads. He may be a quick thinker and he may have a good memory, but thinking needs facts with which to work and on which to build ideas. Facts must be recallable when they are wanted and note-making is the only certain way of ensuring that they are.

As explained in Chapter Twenty-one note-making consists of jottings which, oftener than not, are not in sentence form. This is so with note-taking too, but note-making differs from note-taking in that it combines the art of selection with the art of arrangement. In the course of a lesson or lecture it is not always possible to restrict the notes taken to essential matters, or to arrange them in the order most suitable for future reference. This suggests the need for two notebooks—a rough temporary notebook for use in class and a permanent notebook for notes written up after they have been sifted, and classified and combined with notes from subsequent reading or other sources.

Where the notes are on a subject that is undergoing constant change, as in commerce and law, a notebook in loose-leaf form permits later insertions to be made at points where they belong. It is a good plan, too, to confine the original notes to the right-hand page, leaving the left-hand page free for notes to be added from later reading, or for inclusion of cuttings from magazines and the Press where these up-date existing information or give new information likely to be of use.

DICTATED NOTES

Note-taking is not a universal gift and students often welcome advice on it. If you are one of them let it be said at the outset that the form in which you keep your notes is an entirely personal matter, but for clarity and quick reference a suitable tabular method has much to commend it. Some suggestions are made later in this chapter. The more conscientious you are, the stronger will be the temptation to make elaborate notes and to turn your notebook into a mini-textbook. As a process of learning this is not good. The main purpose of notes is after all to provide an epitome of leading facts and principles, and only where a particular point is not treated adequately in your textbook should it be necessary to make a detailed note.

Nor is it good learning to rely on notes provided in hand-outs or dictated, much as you welcome them. There are at least three important objections to dictated notes:

(a) they relieve you of the effort you should be making for yourself;

(b) they provide you with information that has not passed through your mind and which you may not understand;

(c) they take up time in class that could be spent more profitably in other ways.

It is important that your notes should be your own and not those of somebody else, otherwise you are being robbed of the chance to do your own thinking. Nothing is more calculated to blunt a person's mind than for his thinking to be done for him. It is therefore to your benefit that dictated notes should be given sparingly and confined to occasions where some formula or statement needs to be learned in precise language. The occasions for this should be rare. But although dictated notes are normally taboo, there is no objection to the practice of indicating points on which notes should be made.

THE USE OF SHORTHAND

The main reason for learning shorthand is utilitarian and if you are a shorthand-writer there are good reasons for using your skill in both taking and making notes, provided that when taking notes you confine yourself to essentials and avoid the temptation to turn lectures into dictation-practice sessions. You cannot take a verbatim note and at the same time concentrate on the import of what is being said.

If you decide to keep your permanent notes in shorthand, you are recommended to set them out under longhand headings and sub-headings. The different items then stand out clearly from what would otherwise be an unbroken mass of shorthand notes, and this enormously simplifies subesquent reference. The notes retained in shorthand should be brief, otherwise they lose much of their value by being overloaded with detail—essential points are obscured by unnecessary verbiage. Try to grasp the essential points and record them as far as possible by short phrases, or even by single words where these are significant.

POINTS ON NOTE-TAKING

(a) Unlike a précis, notes need not be in sentence form. Short phrases and even single words are sometimes enough.

(b) Pick out the essential points and note them briefly. You can later fill in the details from other sources.

(c) Make sure that your note is not so brief that you can't make sense of it later on.

(d) Use abbreviations if they will help, e.g. shd. (should), wd. (would), info. (information), C.20 (twentieth century), and any others you care to devise.

(e) Use headings and sub-headings, numbering them and lettering them as suggested in the following section on tabulated notes.

(f) Underline notes that are particularly important, or which you may specially wish to remember.

(g) When making notes from a book, employ the method suggested for précis, but less elaborately.

(b) Note the source from which you get your information, e.g. *J.B.L., Apl. 19.., p. 25* (Journal of Business Law, April, 19.., Page 25).

TABULATED NOTES

A schematic arrangement in which notes are classified and grouped under headings and sub-headings is the one most convenient for revision. A well-displayed set of notes arranged in this way makes for quick reference: particular sections or items can be spotted at a glance. What is known can then be passed over quicky and attention concentrated on what still needs to be learned. The following is an example of simple tabulation.

MAIL ORDER SELLING

1. *Causes of rapid growth*
      Credit purchase (probably main cause)
      Unwanted goods returnable
      Large numbers of housewife agents
      Convenience of "armchair shopping"

2. *Types of Mail Order Business*
   Manufacturers
      Direct selling eliminates middleman
   Department stores
      Separate M.O. departments to supplement normal selling
   M.O. warehouses
      Specialize in M.O. selling only (e.g. Gt. Universal Stores, Grattan Warehouses, Empire Stores)

3. *Methods of Payment*
   Goods on appro.
      Usually seven days
      C.O.D. ⎫
      C.W.O. ⎬ Refund guaranteed if not satisfied

4. *Advantages to Supplier*
      Bulk buying (e.g. from manufacturers)
      Inexpensive sites (e.g. factory premises in North)
      Low-cost labour (mainly female)

5. *Drawbacks to Supplier*
      Costly advertising
      Costly catalogues
      High operational costs (e.g. agents' commissions, packing and postage)
      Large stocks (involve risks from obsolescence and falling prices)
      No personal contact with customers

6. _Future Prospects_
    Good, for following reasons:
      Urban transport problems ⎫
      Working housewives ⎬ create more postal shopping
      Spreading to higher income groups (as better class of goods are offered)
      Extensive potential market (only 3% of total sales at present)

The following is a more elaborately-planned example of tabulated note-making. It is similar in form to that on p. 205 used in making reports and, like it, consists only of headings on a five-point scheme, with centralized main headings, side headings and three types of sub-heading.

I MODERN TRENDS IN RETAILING

A. _Self-service_
  1. _Rapid Development_

  2. _Store Organization_
    (a) Layout
      _(i)_ Open shelving
      _(ii)_ Frozen foods

    (b) Psychological strategy
      _(i)_ Shelf arrangement
      _(ii)_ Promotion lines
      (iii) Special offers

  3. _Advantages_
    (a) To trader
      _(i)_ Increased sales
      _(ii)_ Impulse buying
      (iii) Economical staffing

    (b) To customer
      _(i)_ Self selection
      _(ii)_ Quick service
      (iii) Reminder of needs
      _(iv)_ Lower prices

  4. _Drawbacks_
    (a) To trader
      _(i)_ Pilfering
      _(ii)_ Lack of customer contact

    (b) To customer
      _(i)_ Impersonal service
      _(ii)_ Involuntary shoplifting
      (iii) Impulse buying

B. *Supermarkets*
C. *Mail-order Marketing*
D. *Discount Stores*   (With appropriate sub-heads as in Section A)
E. *Mobile Shops*
F. *Auto-vending*

II TYPES OF RETAIL BUSINESS

This Section would deal with the following:

A. The Small Retailer
B. The Specialist Shop
C. The Department Store
D. Multiple Shops and Chain Stores
E. Mail-order Selling
F. Co-operative Societies

arranged with sub-headings as in Section I.

Sometimes notes can usefully take the eye-catching form of the genealogical table.

THE FUNCTIONS OF GOVERNMENT

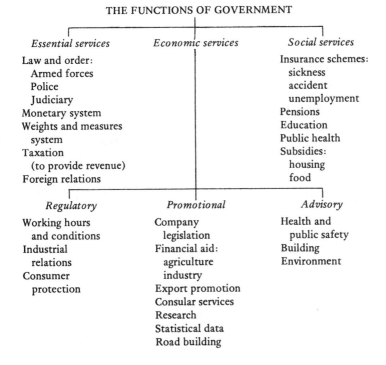

Essential services	*Economic services*	*Social services*

Law and order:
  Armed forces
  Police
  Judiciary
Monetary system
Weights and measures
  system
Taxation
  (to provide revenue)
Foreign relations
		Insurance schemes:
		  sickness
		  accident
		  unemployment
		Pensions
		Education
		Public health
		Subsidies:
		  housing
		  food

Regulatory	*Promotional*	*Advisory*

Working hours
  and conditions
Industrial
  relations
Consumer
  protection
	Company
	  legislation
	Financial aid:
	  agriculture
	  industry
	Export promotion
	Consular services
	Research
	Statistical data
	Road building
		Health and
		  public safety
		Building
		Environment

WRITING FROM NOTES

Related to note-taking is the inverse process of expanding notes into full literary form. Like note-taking, the process of expansion is constantly being employed in everyday life. The author, the lecturer, the businessman and many others all make use of it. Their notes record only the minimum of information, but they are enough for their users to be able to recall the underlying thoughts, feelings and arguments for which the notes stand. Sometimes, a short phrase or even a word will supply all the information the user needs for producing an extended piece of writing or preparing a lengthy speech. It is surprising how memory can be kindled or trains of thought set in motion by the suggestive power of a single word from a carefully garnered set of notes. Many public men record much of their experience in the form of notes filed in a card-index or some other sort of filing arrangement to which they turn when needing an illustration, a quotation or a point of view. The literary man, the preacher, the lecturer and the businessman will each use his notes for his own particular purpose in his own special way, but whatever the purpose for which the notes are kept they are there to help to produce an end-product in the form of a worthy piece of expanded prose.

NOTES OF MEETINGS

Guiding principles

Unquestionably the easiest way to take notes at a meeting is to use either shorthand or a tape recorder. A complete note of the proceedings can then be available, but in practice this is rarely needed. Instead, the notes made will usually be selective. Members attending the meeting must usually make their own, and the notes of those who do not write shorthand will need to be highly selective and concentrated on the substance of what is discussed and decided. The amount of detail needed to serve as a sufficient reminder varies considerably with the individual. Those who take fairly full notes may find that doing so prevents them from contributing fully to the proceedings; those who are satisfied with an occasional note may find that their notes are of little help as reminders when they come to use them. Between these two extremes the individual must find by experience what is right for himself, but as a guiding principle it should be accepted that the notes made should be the minimum needed to serve their purpose. When the notes come to be written up in permanent record form, it is probable that some can be discarded. Those retained should be systematically classified and arranged in logical order under headings and sub-headings in the manner already outlined. The work of selecting, compressing and arranging the notes follows the principles for précis writing and employs precisely the same skills. Practice in either of the two activities will help to improve performance in the other.

Minutes of meetings

The agenda
An agenda is simply a list of the matters to be discussed during a meeting. Copies are circulated several days before the meeting to all who are entitled to be present. The purpose of an agenda is two-fold:

(a) to guide the chairman through the meeting;
(b) to give those invited to attend prior notice of what is to be discussed.

For most informal meetings agenda are not prepared, though the convenor is well advised to make a note for his own benefit of the matters he wishes to be discussed. Matters discussed at the meeting will normally follow the sequence laid down in the agenda and a written record of the proceedings, known as *minutes*, will later be prepared by the secretary from the notes he or someone for him takes at the meeting.

The minutes
Minutes are a summarized record, written in the third person and in the past tense, of what has taken place. They state the date and place of the meeting, the names of those present, the matters discussed and the decisions reached. They are prepared by the secretary and presented by him at the next meeting and after they have been read and agreed are signed by the chairman as a correct record.

Besides setting out the wording of all propositions, the names of the proposers and seconders, and the votes cast in favour and against, the minutes may also record the main points raised in discussion and the names of the persons making them.

The three essential qualities of a set of minutes are accuracy, clarity and brevity, in that order. They must be accurate as presenting a true record of what took place; they must be clear so that persons not present at the meeting can be fully informed of what took place; they must be brief so as to provide a summary of the principal matters discussed and the decisions taken. An adequate left-hand margin should be left for sub-headings if necessary. Matters recorded should appear in the following order:

(*a*) a description of the meeting and a note of the time, date and place;

(*b*) the names in alphabetical order of those present, with the name of the chairman first and the names of officials last;

(*c*) apologies for absence;

(*d*) minutes of last meeting to be read and approved;

(*e*) matters arising from the minutes;

(*f*) correspondence;

(*g*) the business discussed—first the business stated in the agenda, followed by any other business;

(*h*) date of the next meeting.

SPECIMEN MINUTES

College of Further Education, Oxbridge

Minutes of a meeting of Heads of Department held at
14.30 hours on 10 February, 19.. in the Board Room.

Present

Dr. H. Lowery (Chairman)	Mr. H. Cooper
Mr. W. Aldred	Mr. R. Jukes
Mr. G. Andrew	Mr. W. Godfrey (Secretary)
Mrs. L. A. Brazier	

Apology

The secretary read a note from Mr. L. Groves regretting his absence from the meeting through illness.

Minutes

The minutes of the last meeting were read and approved, and signed by the chairman.

Matters arising

Mr. Jukes reported that arrangements with local firms to provide employment experience for second-year students in the secretarial department had now been concluded, and that the scheme would operate as from the beginning of next session, on 21 September.

Correspondence

The chairman reported that he had received a request from the Camford High School for use of the college swimming-bath on an additional half day a week as from the beginning of next term. To grant the request would involve some rearrangment of departmental time-tables. After some discussion, Mr. Andrew proposed and Mrs. Brazier seconded, and it was

AGREED that existing swimming facilities granted to the Camford High School be extended to include Tuesday mornings as from the beginning of next term.

Course in Motor Engineering

Mr. Cooper reported that he had been in touch with the local Trades Council and the local branch of the Employers' Federation and that both welcomed the proposal to offer a course in motor engineering and would give it full support. There was discussion on workshop accommodation for the course, during which Mr. Aldred offered to give up one of his drawing offices in the workshop block in exchange for a classroom in the college main building. Mr. Cooper said he could provide the classroom and proposed, and Mr. Aldred seconded, and it was

AGREED that the new course should be offered when the college reopens after the summer vacation.

Any Other Business

The secretary reported that arrangements were well in hand for the forthcoming staff dinner arranged for 24 April.

Next meeting

The next meeting was agreed, and fixed for 10 March at 14.30 hours.

Chairman

In a business organization the minutes of directors' and shareholders' meetings, committee meetings and conferences are important and confidential. They will normally be kept under lock and key to ensure restriction of access to authorized persons only. Pages in the minute book are numbered serially so that pages cannot be removed undetected.

EXERCISES

1. What do you understand by the words "effective listening"? What are the main features that are needed in a good listener?   (I.C.S.A.)

2. Reproduce the following passage in the form of notes to bring out the main points.

The institution of marriage in Britain is not in decline as is so vehemently argued by its critics, but is simply undergoing a process of change whereby it is adjusting to the twentieth century with its highly industrialized, complex western society.

The emancipation of women, together with shorter working hours, earlier retirement, the Welfare State, family planning, and new attitudes to children and the elderly, have all had their effect on marriage, but they have modified it, not destroyed it.

Divorce is often quoted as being evidence that the institution of marriage is under a strain and indeed, about to break up. However, the high divorce rate may be said to be due to the fact that people have higher expectations of marriage than they used to. Personal relationships and compatability are more important in a marriage than ever before. The fact that more marriages end up in divorce nowadays points to the courage of people to publicly terminate their marriages rather than privately suffer, as formerly. It does not mean that there are more unhappy marriages.

In Ronald Fletcher's words ". . . the picture of marriage in modern Britain is, surely a picture of considerable health, considerable stability and an enlarged degree of opportunity and happiness".

The Family and Marriage in Modern Britain: R. Fletcher   *(N.W.R.A.C.)*

3. Make notes on the following passage in not more than 110—120 words. Five or six headings should be used. Any work which is **not** in note form will lose at least ten marks.

In concluding, let me make a few observations about the activity of financial institutions serving international trade. Two of the essential qualities of the banking profession are flexibility and inventiveness, and those who prove to be lacking in those qualities will sooner or later be by-passed by competitors who offer quicker, cheaper or more comprehensive services to their clients. The strong competitiveness of banking, particularly in a period of high international liquidity, tends to reduce profitability, however, and this may sometimes lead to the acceptance of greater risks.

In trade financing this latter tendency has been showing itself in the acceptance of longer terms and weaker borrowers than would have been considered only a few years ago. On the other hand, one must admit that the dynamic growth of world trade and the enormous investments required for the development of natural resources and infrastructure do require far greater efforts from financial institutions, both as regards the amounts involved and the geographical area to be covered. This situation has stimulated the establishment of specialized organizations, often backed up by a group of large banks, engaged in medium-term lending and international capital market operations of considerable magnitude. During the last five years some of these finance companies have grown in size far beyond anything that was expected at the time of their founding. Their strength lies not only in their powerful shareholders and in the expertise they have acquired, but also in the fact that, as joint ventures, they can sometimes accept risks which each individual shareholder-bank might hesitate to take.

On the other hand, groups of banks from different countries have joined forces by establishing common operations in third countries and by granting combined credit facilities to multinational customers. In doing all these things they have followed the requirements of the market and at the same time stimulated the international operations of their industrial and commercial clients.

Jointly and individually, many banks have, furthermore, increased the range of their services by introducing not only new types of credit such as euro-currency roll-overs, multi-currency global credit lines and international leasing facilities, but also entirely new services such as cash-management. It seems justified to conclude that, in spite of present disturbances, the financial community is playing a constructive role in furthering international trade, and that it is in the interest of both the developed and the developing parts of the world that it should continue to do so in the greatest possible freedom.

(From "International Trade Finance", by K.H. Beyen—delivered at the 26th International Banking Summer School)   *(I. of B.)*

CHAPTER NINE

Reading

The mind, relaxing into needful sport,
Should turn to writers of an abler sort,
Whose wit well manag'd, and whose classic style,
Give truth a lustre, and make wisdom smile.

W.Cowper: *Retirement*

THE SIGNIFICANCE OF READING

Reading is a more important source of most people's command of language than is sometimes realized, and it is probably true of the young that standards of expression and spelling, about which employers continue to complain, have suffered from the modern shift away from reading as a leisure-time activity to attractions of another kind. Reading may not be an activity whose practical value equals that of writing and speaking, but like listening it plays a vital role in comprehension. It is also an important source of information and culture. As one writer put it:

> "Where the power to get enjoyment and information from books is lacking, the development of a satisfactory personal life is unlikely to be realized."*

And think for a moment of the effect of good reading upon our powers of self-expression. It provides the material to raise conversation above the level of gossip and to express our ideas and feelings in clearer and more interesting ways. Whoever we are and whatever our calling we all have much to gain from a well-planned pattern of reading. It was not the job of writers like Walter Scott or Winston Churchill, to quote two masters of English prose at random, to write business letters for a living, but as we ourselves prepare for business there is much we can learn from reading writers such as these. They made it their business to express their feelings and convey their ideas clearly and simply enough to ensure for themselves a considerable and intelligent class of readers. They were masters in the handling of words, and words are the vehicle of thought whether the thoughts are those of the professional writer or of the businessman.

*A.F. Watts: *The Language and Mental Development of Children (Harrap)*.

READING FOR INFORMATION

Reading for information is highly significant in both business and social life. The businessman must keep himself informed of developments in his own specialized field, and for all of us reading as a source of information opens up new avenues of interest leading to wider and more satisfying social relationships. The businessman who never gets around to reading books not directly associated with his trade or profession is depriving himself of the skills, the understanding and the increased freedom of thought which reading outside his specialized field would give him. The reading to be found in technical books and in trade and professional journals forms a necessary part of his way of making a living, but this kind of reading should not be the end. It is only one aspect, admittedly an important one, of the use of books. The accumulated knowledge of past generations is far too great to be acquired through experience in a single lifetime, but we can acquire it vicariously from books.

READING FOR STUDY

Of our reading for information much of it will be concerned with study, the study of a textbook for example. For this type of reading the most rewarding approach is first to get the gist of, say, a chapter or other section of convenient length, by reading it quickly for a general grasp of the whole, and then follow with one or more readings until the section as a whole has been clearly understood, marking with a pencil those passages felt to be important. The marked passages can then provide the basis for notes. On note-making you will find some suggestions in Chapter Eight. Some students preparing for examinations take their note-making a stage further and condense their notes into still briefer notes, brief enough perhaps to be contained on a postcard for rapid revision shortly before the examination.

READING AND VOCABULARY

Reading is not only a most valuable source of information; it is also one of our most powerful means of widening vocabulary. But like mere listening it is no more than a passive sort of activity, lacking in that vital element of personal practice which enables us to "learn by doing". Hence the need to put into use the new words we come across. We throw away one of our best opportunities for self-improvement if we fail to look up words whose meanings we are not sure of. The temptation to by-pass new words and to "go by the context" and accept a rough-and-ready interpretation is strong, but it is a temptation we must resist if we are to get the best from our reading. New words should be studied and then used as soon as possible. As a first step look them up in your dictionary, note their meanings and how they are pronounced, and make sure you can spell them. Then add them to your notebook or card-index and, with the more difficult and unusual words, record the context in which you found them. Finally, establish them as part of your permanent vocabulary by using them in writing and conversation, practising them if necessary in sentences of your own making. If on average you add only one new word a day to your list you will in the course of a year add more than three hundred to your vocabulary. Listed in one of the ways explained in Chapter Four and practised as suggested they will become a permanent part of your linguistic armoury and add to your ability to communicate fluently in terms that are unmistakably clear and readily understood.

READING AND LITERATURE

From the standpoint of culture and its bearing upon personality, character and behaviour, reading in its literary form has an even deeper significance. In some measure it enables us to experience life vicariously and become acquainted in a purely impersonal context with some of the problems we ourselves may one day have to face. If we define literature as language used with the greatest skill in writings esteemed for their beauty of form and style, then reading without literature would be a poor relation indeed.

Recent years have seen the publication of many good books of travel, biography, natural history and popular science, all of which provide excellent reading for those seeking to widen their literary horizon beyond popular fiction. Not that there is anything wrong with fiction as an instrument of culture, provided it shares the one characteristic of all good reading — that it is the work of authors who convey their thoughts and feelings in language that is simple, lucid and eloquent, with some degree of emphasis on style and a certain elegance of expression. Fiction is a main field of imaginative literature. It is the kind of literature that appeals strongly to most of us and is a most effective means of establishing the habit of reading and of influencing taste. It influences conceptions of life and standards of behviour that may have a determinant effect on the kind of persons we are or wish to be. Our enormous variety of fiction and non-fiction offers a choice to suit all ages and tastes. There is no justification for the feeling held by some that good literature is dull reading. Much of our best literature is among the most interesting and exciting. The books listed in Appendix I as recommended reading have been included as much for their interest as for their intrinsic beauty and literary qualities. You will enjoy reading most of them.

Besides serving as a source of information and a means of raising the cultural level, reading is an instrument of thought and has an important bearing on our ability to think. It is one of the means whereby we understand not only what others are thinking and feeling, but also what we within ourselves are thinking and feeling. Of this bond between thought and reading the Government's pamphlet *Language* quotes as follows from a publication by the Association of Assistant Masters in Secondary Schools:

> . . . our powers of thinking consciously and feeling consciously are, to a great extent, limited by our ability to clarify and put into words our own thoughts and feelings.*

EFFICIENT READING

Reading and comprehension are inseparably linked as parts of the same process — that of understanding the meaning and significance of the printed word. Ability to read efficiently is a valuable personal skill and one in which we must raise standards if we are to make the most of our rapidly-growing literary heritage. On the whole most of us tend to read too slowly, many of us much too slowly. We assume an inverse relationship between reading speed and comprehension, and that a rise in speed brings about a fall in comprehension. This is not so. The truth is that, within limits that vary for each one of us, reading speed and comprehension tend to rise together. The result of slow reading is more often poorer comprehension, not better; we grasp the meaning better when we read faster. Slow reading is a handicap we can overcome with practice to the benefit of our reading standards in both speed and comprehension. It may seem strange but tests have shown it to be true that, to a point, comprehension improves as reading speeds increase. The quality of comprehension will of course suffer if we attempt to read at speeds that have not been cultivated and become habitual with practice.

Reading rate varies a good deal with a number of factors, particularly with the type of subject-matter, the purpose for which we read and the level of the writer's language. It is higher when we read solely for pleasure — fiction for instance. Our interest in the plot, the characters or the topic, provides its own driving force. It is lower when we read for information, for then we must read with understanding and some regard for what must be remembered. The rate is lower still when we settle to read poetry because of its often unfamiliar form of language and the imaginative effort needed to interpret the poet's thoughts and emotions. If the passage for

The Teaching of English (Cam. Univ. Press, 1952).

reading is one of any length, a chapter or other section in a book for example, it is a good strategy to first read through the section at speed to get a general grasp of the whole, and then to re-read it paragraph by paragraph, making notes as necessary until the whole is completed.

Reading speeds also vary a good deal between individuals. Most of us talk on average at a rate somewhere between 120—200 words a minute, but the range in our average reading speeds is probably greater. There are people who read as slowly as 100 or 120 words a minute, with the average reader and an average book at somewhere around 200—300 words a minute. For the efficient reader the range may well be very much higher. If your own reading speeds are habitually low, remember that you are likely to read with better understanding if you raise them. You can do this by systematic practice timed at so many words a minute until you achieve the speed level at which you feel you perform at your best. Aim always at a speed as close as possible to your upper limit of each piece you read.

There are people who habitually read at 400 words a minute or more, and if your own habitual speed is lower than half of this, then there is a good case for trying to raise it. What in fact is your average reading speed? You can find out by testing yourself with the following passage.

It seems hard to credit now, but Christmas Day was/once abolished by Act of Parliament. That was in 1644,/at the climax of the Puritan ascendancy, and it did/not last. Charles the Second restored the festival, in England
50 /at any rate; the Scots did not follow him. (Hence/the importance of Hogmanay in Scotland.) The point to remember/is that the Puritans had some grounds for what they/did. For centuries, Christmas had gradually been getting out of/hand. The feasting and drinking, the games and
100 masques, directed/by a Lord of Misrule, had come to last longer//and longer; Christ's birthday had almost disappeared in a riot./This is no doubt an overstatement, but it is how/many saw it. It was time for a call to/ order, and the gaiety shrivelled as if in a frosty/wind.
150   It sounds a terribly sour thing to say today,/of all days, but are we in danger of abusing/Christmas again? The threat does not now come from the/Lord of Misrule and all he stood for, but rather/from Mammon, leading Christmas on to become too elaborate, too/expensive, too artificial,
200 too far removed from the stirrings of//heart and soul.
    The present danger is that of the/merriment becoming too dependent on material things; synthetic, no longer/able to rise spontaneously, as it did and should, straight/from warm human contacts among families and friends—dependent instead/for its impetus on ever-increasing quantities of
250 drink, food, organized/entertainment, ever more expensive and elaborate presents: a salesman's Christmas,/with reverberations running from October

to the January sales. We/have not yet reached the point at which a revul-
sion/against Christmas as potent as that of the Puritans might/make itself
300 felt strongly enough to throw a cold shadow//on the festival. But we should
beware of going further/that way. How pitiful it would be if Christmas
did/become tarnished by our misuse of it; no other festival/has so deep an
impact on us, and if elders/sometimes weary of traditional customs, there
350 is always a generation/to whom they are new, and to whom their repeti-
tion/through the years of childhood fixes the day's image in/their minds
ineradicably.   *(373 words)*

Now answer the following questions to test the quality of your
comprehension.

(a) Why did the Puritans abolish Christmas?

(b) Who restored the festival?

(c) How do you explain the Scots preference for celebrations at
the New Year?

(d) For what reasons does the writer suggest that Christmas could
be abolished yet again?

(e) What does he suggest is the proper attitude towards Christmas?

(f) What special reason does he give for preserving the Christmas
tradition?

READING TECHNIQUE

Not every piece of writing is of equal importance, and while we
may quite properly talk about "average" reading speeds, a flexible
approach to reading is necessary for the best results. Different kinds
of subject-matter and the varied aims of readers call for different
treatment. There are many kinds of subject-matter not important
enough to justify close atttention and to plod conscientiously
through these and maybe pages of irrelevant matter is just a waste
of time. Reading must be concentrated on what is important, and
that depends on its intended purpose. In the words of Francis Bacon:

> Some books are to be tasted, others to be swallowed, and some others to
> be chewed and digested: that is, some books are to be read only in parts,
> others to be read, but not curiously; and some others to be read wholly,
> and with diligence and attention.   *(Essays: Of Studies)*

Henrik Ibsen, the Norwegian poet and dramatist, put the same point
more briefly when he said:

> "One should not read to swallow all, but rather see what one has use for."
> *Peer Gynt: Act IV*

Effective reading calls first and foremost for clarity of purpose and a flexible approach. For different kinds of material and different aims there must be a range of reading speeds "geared" to suit the reader's own needs and requirements — rapid reading for an overall picture, slower reading for reflection and study, and skimming for what is of little importance to the purpose in view. Skimming is not reading in any sense; it may even consist of little more than flicking pages over as we would the pages of a directory. It nevertheless serves a number of useful purposes:

(a) It provides a general overall picture of the subject-matter and is useful as a preliminary to closer reading.

(b) It helps to pinpoint material likely to be needed.

(c) It serves as a substitute for reading when time is short.

As a rule, a preliminary skim enables subsequent reading to be done at a significantly higher speed than would be possible without it.

Effective reading combines a flexible approach with successful gearing. It is a most valuable skill and the foundation on which high standards in all other subjects are built.

REFERENCE BOOKS

It is true that the next best thing to knowledge is to know where to find it. To establish the habit of searching for information and to know where to look for it forms an important part of a sound training in the English language. Every public library has a reference section where one may expect to find copies of most standard reference books. *Whitaker's Almanack,* itself a mine of information on almost every subject of contemporary interest, lists more than two hundred annual reference books covering an extensive range of the arts, the sciences, trades and professions. Any book that contains required information may of course be used for reference, but properly speaking, reference books are books compiled and arranged specially to make it easy to look up particular items of information.

As a student of the English language you should certainly have a working knowledge of such reference books as encyclopaedias and dictionaries. Both vary considerably in size. Encyclopaedias range from the thirty-volume *Encyclopaedia Britannica* to single-volume editions such as *Pear's Cyclopaedia* and the *Daily Mail Year Book,* with *Chambers Encyclopaedia* (fifteen volumes) and *Everyman's Encyclopaedia* (twelve volumes) in the middle range. An encyclopaedia may not contain information relating to contemporary affairs; it then becomes necessary to consult *Whitaker* or one or other of the specialist year books.

What now remains of this present chapter relates to reference books of special interest to you as a student of English language, foremost of which is the English Dictionary. What it can do for you and how you should use it are matters already discussed in Chapter Four. The great *Oxford Dictionary*, with Supplements, comprising fifteen volumes, is the foundation of all English dictionaries, but for general and business use you will find the *Concise Oxford Dictionary* and *Chambers Twentieth Century Dictionary*, and similar one-volume dictionaries excellent for your purpose.

The main purpose of the dictionary is to explain the meanings of words, the idea they are intended to convey. The word whose meaning is required is given first and its meaning (or meanings if there is more than one), i.e. the idea, follows. For example:

> **freedom:** the state of being free, exemption
> from restraint, liberty, independence.

Roget's Thesaurus of English Words and Phrases works the other way round. It first states the idea and then lists the word or words, the synonyms, by which the idea may be fitly and aptly expressed. Thus:

> **shorten:** abbreviate, abridge, compress, condense,
> contract, curtail, epitomize, reduce, summarize.

The words for which synonyms are given are indexed alphabetically in a separate part of the book; the words themselves are numbered and grouped in the general body of the book according to a plan of classification set out at the beginning of the book.

The *Thesaurus* has come to be as widely acceptable and as indispensable to writers as a dictionary. It is a book that should certainly find a welcome to your bookshelf. Each synonym has its own special meaning or application and can be correctly used where other words synonymous with it would fail to convey the intended meaning precisely.

Fowler's Modern English Usage, recognized as an authority of grammar and the correct use of words, is another valuable book. Items dealt with, sometimes at length, are arranged alphabetically as in a dictionary. But it is much more than a dictionary. It is a commentary on the use of language as it should be, though it also deals, as its title suggests, with language as currently used. For example, an article dealing with the alternative uses of "i" and "y" in such words as *tire* (of a wheel) and *tyre; stile* (a hedge) and *style* (in manner) explains that from the fifteenth to the seventeenth century *tire* and *tyre* were spelt indifferently, but that *tyre* became generally obsolete before 1700 and *tire* remained as the regular form, as it still does in America, but that in Great Britain *tyre* has now become the accepted usage, though there is no apparent justification for the change. One more example will be enough to bring out the different purposes served by *Fowler* and the dictionary. The dictionary tells us that *appreciate* means *to rise in value,* but in dealing with this word, *Fowler* has this to say: "The word is overworked as a synonym of *understand* or *recognize* in official and business letters", especially in such phrases as *You will appreciate* (for *understand) my concern; I appreciate* (for *recognize) that you have a problem.* The dictionary gives only the meaning of the word; *Fowler* explains when it should not be used.

The *Complete Plain Words* by Sir Ernest Gowers (H.M.S.O.), written primarily to raise standards of letter writing and report writing in the civil service, is a guide to the use of plain straightforward English. You will find a reference to this very useful book in the closing paragraphs of Chapter Two.

The *Oxford Companion to English Literature* is another useful book. It contains information about different aspects of literature and literary characters.

Dictionaries of quotations are useful if you want to trace the author of a particular quotation, or to check the precise wording of of a quotation. Most dictionaries of quotations have an index in which the key words in each quotation are arranged alphabetically, with numerical references to pages in which the quotations are given. The quotations themselves are usually arranged in alphabetical order of author. In the reference section of your local library you are almost certain to find the *Oxford Dictionary of Quotations,* and similar books by Stevenson and by Bartlett. There are also smaller dictionaries of this kind, such as the *Concise Oxford,* the *Penguin* and the *Everyman* for use at home or in the office. Treat yourself to one of these smaller books — you will find that it makes fascinating reading.

EXERCISES

1. Read the following passage twice at what you feel to be your best speed and, without referring back, answer the questions that follow:

Happiness arises largely from the mental qualities of contentment, confidence/serenity and active good-will. It includes the pain of losing/as well as the pleasure of finding. It thrives best/in a crowded life. The men and women who are/ recorded in history and biography as the most happy
50 were people/with always somewhat more to do than they could possibly/ do. Every waking hour of their lives was occupied with/ambitious projects,

literature, love, politics, science, friendship, commerce, professions, trades, / their religious faith, and a thousand other matters. The secret / of happi-
100 ness may be found by making each of these // interests count to its utmost as part of the fabric / of life.

We need to avoid the extremes of sluggish / placidity and feverish activity. We are not going to be / satisfied with felicity which resembles that of a stone, unfeeling / and unmoving, but will look back from future years with
150 / sorrow and regret if we run to and fro, giving / in to what Socrates called "the itch".

Happiness obviously includes / two sorts of behaviour: active and passive. We may say / that the active part consists in searching and sharing, while /
200 the passive part is made up of security and possession. // Neither part is complete in itself, and neither yields full / satisfaction if it is over-emphasized. Philosophers from the ancient / Greeks to the present day have been extolling a balanced / life as the most happy life, and many unhappy people
250 / can, when they face the issue, trace their discontent to / imbalance.

The recipe for happiness cannot be given in any / single word, because its many virtues have to be combined / in their proper quantities, at the proper times for proper / purposes.

It is legitimate to seek happiness. We cannot help / observing that while
300 followers of some schools of thought are // telling us to avoid seeking happi-ness, they intimate that if / we do so we shall be happy.

The search requires / a plan. We need to know what sort of happiness / we seek, what the ingredients are, what are our strongest / wants, and what
350 we have to start with. We should / train ourselves to keep the programme simple, and free from / complications and side trips, to pay attention to little things, / to deflate quickly after being praised and to bounce back / quickly from disappointment, to seize to create opportunities to put / our
400 special abilities to work, to seek excellence in everything // we do, to remain modest, and to review and revise / periodically.

Most of us do not really have to seek / far and wide. Happiness grows at our own fireside, if / we cultivate it.

Royal Bank of Canada: Monthly Letter   (433 words)

(a) What, in broad terms, is the writer's recipe for happiness?
(b) Happiness includes two sorts of behaviour. What are they?
(c) What does the writer mean when he talks about a balanced life?
(d) Mention some of the things we should do when planning for happiness.
(e) Where does happiness grow?

2. Name the title and author of a book that has impressed you most, and describe the contents of the book.   *(E.M.E.U.)*

3. Shakespeare wrote comedies, tragedies, histories and poems. Which do you prefer, and why?   *(E.M.E.U.)*

4. From a novel you have read recently relate an incident which illustrates human courage or endurance, and briefly discuss the chief character taking part in the incident.   *(U.E.I.)*

5. Which books have you read this year? Which has been your favourite? Why?   (N.C.T.E.C.)

6. In about 100 words say how much you use your library (local, college or school) and what section of it you find particularly helpful.   (N.C.T.E.C.)

7. Write an account in 100/150 words of a book you have read recently, using the following guide:
Name of the book — its author — the main characters — the story briefly — if you liked it or not — and why.   (R.S.A., Elem.)

8. Name a book which you have enjoyed, dealing with nature, or country life, or the sea and show what you have learnt from it.   (R.S.A., Elem.)

9. What is the attraction in reading highly imaginative stories, with characters and incidents very unlike those of real life? Illustrate your answer by reference to one or more such books.   (R.S.A., Elem.)

10. What makes a best seller, do you think? Refer to one you have read, giving your opinion of it.   (R.S.A., Elem.)

CHAPTER TEN

Speaking

Speak clearly if you speak at all;
Carve every word before you let it fall.

O.W. Holmes: *A Rhymed Lesson*

THE IMPORTANCE OF GOOD SPEECH

Clear speech and good handwriting have been called "the good manners of language". Both are important, but for many people to be able to speak well is more important than to be able to write well. In its spoken form language remains by far the commonest means of communication. It increases in importance more and more as radio, television and the telephone tend to replace the printed word as a means of communication and culture. The social value of good speech cannot be too much emphasized, and its practical significance in the life of everyone becomes clear when we reflect that for every sentence we write we speak hundreds.

Reference was made in Chapter One to the importance of communication in business at all levels of activity, routine as well as administrative, and to the need to raise standards of both written and oral expression in keeping with the growing complexity of business. Advances in mechanization have increased the importance of the spoken word as a medium of communication both within the firm and between the firm and the outside world. The telephone has lessened our dependence on writing, but it has increased our dependence on speech. The use of audio systems in the office, too, has given added importance to good speech standards and to the need for high standards of dictation.

Speech, too, has obvious sociological implications. It has an important bearing on education in the widest sense and is a highly desirable social accomplishment. As an element in personality it influences a person's whole being. Indeed, speech and personality tend to develop together. Each reacts upon the other and a young person whose speech standards are at a poor level is not only at a social disadvantage, but also at a disadvantage in business where, in his competition with others, inadequate speech standards may rob

142

him of the promotion for which his abilities would otherwise qualify him. Those have the best command of language who have been brought up in an environment where agreeable habits of speech, a wide vocabulary and the habit of reading are characteristic, and as far as possible an important aim in formal education must be to reproduce these conditions in the classroom. The raising of oral standards adds to cultural bearing and gives the student confidence, not only when he takes his place among persons of education in business, but also in the wider field of his social relationships.

THE ELEMENTS OF GOOD SPEECH

What we mean by good speech is speech that is clear, so that what is said is heard and received without effort. In this, diction and tone and pitch of voice all play a part. To these qualities we must add accent in the sense of stress upon particular word syllables—a very different thing from accent characteristics of particular parts of the country.

Accent

Accent in the latter sense, i.e. accent as a manner of speech is less important than accent in the sense of syllable stress. Most of us show in our speech some trace of the accent of the district where we were bred, but this is nothing to be worried about. Provided one's manner of speech is easily understood and is in no way unpleasant, no-one is going to bother very much whether the accent is standard B.B.C. or that of one's home town. If we speak plainly people will understand us; if we speak pleasantly they will enjoy listening to us.

The idea that there is only one correct accent has lost much of its one-time force, and the short plain vowels of the Northerner in such words as *ask, class* and *past* (pronounced with the short vowel *"a"* as in *cat*) no longer offend the ears of the Southerner who pronounces these and similar words with the longer vowel sound *"ah"* as it occurs in *alms*. It is interesting to note that in his phonetic shorthand system Isaac Pitman, himself a southerner, employed the shorter North-country vowel sounds. He also adopted the Northerner's pure vowel sound *"ay"* in such words as *paid, take* and *cake* rather than the diphthongized vowels of the Londoner, sounded in these words as *pay-eed, tay-eek* and *cay-eek*. There are many shades of sound between the pure vowel *"ay"* in *mail* and the dipthong *"i"* in *mile*. Those who use the pure vowel can be readily understood, but those who tend towards the *"i"* sound, as some Cockneys still do, run the risk of being misunderstood as their listeners hear the word *paint* as *pint*, *pail* as *pile* and *mail* as *mile*.

What may be termed the received or accepted accent of our time is that which we hear in the B.B.C.'s news and programme announcements. Because of its use by the B.B.C. and the wide audience it reaches, it has come to be regarded as the standard English accent. But we should not set out deliberately to cultivate or imitate it, for then we cease to use it naturally. It becomes artificial, and certainly the last thing we want to encourage is the "refaned" accent of those who "put it on".

Radio and television have done much in recent years to reduce our dialectal differences. Even as recently as half-a-century ago it was not always easy for a person from the South to understand the speech of some Northerners. Today, radio and television broadcasts are readily understood in all parts of the country, and in time we may expect that repeated listening to broadcast news and television announcements will have a modifying effect on regional accents. Some regard this as a desirable trend, though differences of accent and intonation ought not to matter. Provided intelligibility does not suffer, variety of accent is not something to be discouraged; some regional accents are in fact quite pleasant to listen to. To quote from a pamphlet produced by the former Ministry of Education (now the Department of Education and Science):

> If the language is audibly uttered, if the consonants are given full force, if uncouth provincialisms of vocabulary are eliminated and if the intonation is pleasantly modulated, there are few regions of England (though there are some) that have not their own agreeable and acceptable varieties of English.*

Accentuation

Accent in the sense discussed in the preceding section must be distinguished from what is termed *accentuation,* or syllable stress, whose effect is to give prominence to particular syllables in words. Whereas regional accent is not of material importance so long as it is easily intelligible and not unpleasant, the correct use of accentuation is important. Not only does it bear the mark of an educated person, but also it sometimes affects the meanings of words. Transfer of stress from one syllable to another frequently changes both function and meaning. Such words are termed *homographs.* Obvious examples are the nouns *com'bine, des'ert, en'trance, ob'ject, pres'ent, pro'ject,* all of which have a different function as verbs when the stress is transferred from the first to the second syllable.

Language, Ministry of Education Pamphlet No. 26. H.M.S.O., 1954.

The question of stress is interesting, too, when we study the compounds that abound in the English language. In some, particularly the older, compounds the stress falls on the first syllable, as in *post'man, bed'room* and *rain'bow*. In others each of the two elements in the compound carries equal stress, as in *first-aid, one-sided, red-hot*.

Wrong pronunciation can be embarrassing to the speaker. Many common errors of pronunciation are due to faulty accentuation. The following are notable examples.

Wrong	Right
advertise'ment	adver'tisement
chastise'ment	chas'tisement
compar'able	com'parable
contrar'y	con'trary
controv'ersy	con'troversy
gondo'la	gon'dola
hor'izon	hori'zon
invent'ory	in'ventory
irrepar'able	irrep'arable
manda'tory	man'datory
mischiev'ous	mis'chievous
prefer'able	pref'erable
primar'ily	pri'marily
rem'onstrate	remon'strate
respite'	res'pite
seden'tary	sed'entary
tel'epathy	telep'athy
thea'tre	the'atre

Diction

Present-day speech standards as far as many people are concerned are on the whole far from good. We have the authority of the former Ministry of Education for the following statement:

> Most teachers are familiar with the local employer who complains that the products of his town's schools cannot spell, punctuate, compose, or hold themselves up straight and speak audibly at an interview.*

That was in 1954. What was true then is still true today. One has to listen most carefully to know what some people are saying. These people suffer from what may be termed *speech inertia*. They put insufficient effort into the mechanics of speaking and instead of

Language, op. cit.

clear-sounded consonants and well-formed vowels we get either slurred speech or incoherent mumblings. There is nothing more trying than having to listen to people who cannot or will not speak plainly. We cannot expect to sound our consonants clearly if we do not give adequate movement to our lips and tongue; nor can we produce good vowel sounds if we hardly move our mouth. Consonants impose a limit on the length of vowel sounds and in many words supply the final element in what is being said. If we take the sound in the word *lay,* we can add to it consonants that in turn will produce *late, laid, lake, lace, lame, lane* and *lair.* Not until the final consonant is supplied can we know what word is intended. Clearly then, well-sounded consonants especially at the ends of words are an important element in good diction.

There is a similar problem when two or more words different in origin and meaning are pronounced alike. Such words are said to be homophonous, or *homophones* of each other. When they are used out of context their meanings cannot be known; we must await completion of the phrase or sentence in which they appear before comprehension becomes possible. There is no such problem when homophones occur in reading. Anyone reading *draft* or *draught; heart* or *hart; vein, vane* or *vain; they're* or *their; sun and air* or *son and heir* is immediately informed, but when homophones are used in speech we must await future words to resolve our doubts by context.

Tone

In Chapter Eleven we refer to the importance of tone in a business letter. Tone in speech is every bit as important. Tone of voice often provides a better clue to a person's feelings than the words he uses and may either help or hinder communication. A tone that is cold, aloof, impatient, or condescending may easily antagonize the listener and make it much less likely to get from him the response we seek. A warm, friendly tone does much to foster that sense of considerateness and tolerance which makes for happy personal relations. When a person talks to another he must consider the way in which he wants to influence his listener and express himself accordingly. The tone he adopts must suit both the occasion and the purpose, being persuasive, apologetic, conciliatory, friendly, firm, and so on as circumstances require. However good it may be in other respects an oral communication delivered in the wrong tone may affect the listener in a way very different from that intended.

Pitch

Allied to tone is what we term "pitch", or the way the voice rises or falls on the musical scale. Failure to vary the pitch makes speech uninteresting. As one writer has put it, "a dull, flat voice has about as much charm as a fishmonger's slab". It is monotonous and dreary and soon tires and bores the listener. He may even stop listening. Certainly, an important part of the art of speaking is to sound pleasant, alert, even lively, and interested in what is being communicated, even if it requires a conscious effort to do so.

Timbre

Timbre of the voice is something quite different from tone and pitch. Nor has it anything to do with softness or loudness. It is the individual quality of voice we associate with a certain person. We all know people whose voices are pleasant to listen to, not because of accent, but because of the quality of their voices. Such people are fortunate in possessing a valuable asset. Not all of us have this desirable quality, but there are many of us who could improve our speech and the manner in which we use our voices by making a conscious effort to do so. Some ways in which we can do this are considered in the sections that follow.

CULTIVATING GOOD SPEECH

Speech should be natural, easy and expressive, and there are several ways of encouraging these qualities.

Importance of example

The first and simplest is example. The ear is usually a perceptive learner, and for those who are still at school the mere fact of listening regularly to teachers who speak well will achieve something for most students, and for some a great deal. For those who have left school, radio and television broadcasts provide good opportunities for careful and critical listening to news, plays, talks, debates and readings of both prose and poetry, all of which usually provide examples of good speech by experienced and accomplished speakers. When the news is read, for instance, notice in particular how clearly consonants are sounded and the way in which the aspirate, also a consonant, is used.

Use of drama and literature

Secondly, there are those arts in which the voice is used to interpret the language of others—in drama and poetry for example. Speech is likely to be improved as an understandable consequence of engaging in dramatic art, though that may not be the main reason, or even any reason at all, for joining a drama group. The reading of poetry and prose aloud compels a close study of the meaning of what is read and the appropriate use of the voice. The same may be said of speaking aloud passages that have been learned by heart.

Practice in conversation

Thirdly, there is conversation in the form of discussion and debate, and also the quiz, all of which provide opportunities for improving speech. A face to face conference is the most satisfactory form of communication in many areas of business and private life. As a method of communication it is both speedy and effective. Oral debate in groups enables suggestions to be exchanged, ideas to be examined and policies to be settled, and thus provides not only speech practice but also opportunities to influence the thinking of others.

Use of voice recordings

Those who are conscious of having speech habits which they believe to be to their disadvantage are often guilty of no more than a slight suggestion of local, but not faulty, speech. With a little care this can be eliminated. Much more difficult to lose is slovenly speech, with its dropped aitches, glottal stops and warped vowels, because those who use it are often not aware of it. To banish faults such as these we need first to create an awareness of them and then win the offender's co-operation by stressing the importance of good speech. A girl may look attractive, but if her speech is bad she loses her charm as soon as she opens her mouth. To win her co-operation we must persuade her that it is more important to speak well than to dress well. In the tape recorder we have a valuable ally. Speech recorded on tape and immediately played back provides the opportunity to hear ourselves as others hear us. Listening to these recordings with concentration and deep interest will usually do far more to correct bad speech habits than any amount of explanation and exhortation. In this way we may hope to get rid of such faults as the intervocalic R in expressions like *lor (law) and order, I sor (saw) 'im do it,* the opposite fault of omitting the R in such phrases as *there is, hour and a half,* and the replacement of the intervocalic T by the glottal stop in such expressions as *wa(t)er, la(t)itude, i(t) isn't, Car(t)er Pa(t)erson, we shan't le(t) i(t) 'appen, I've 'ad qui(t)e a day.*

Rightly or wrongly, dropping the aspirate is associated with poor education and upbringing. With a little care we can quickly cure this bad fault and, too, avoid the not infrequent ungrammatical use of *of* for *have* in such expressions as *We must of* (for *have*) *been mistaken,* and *They can't of* (for *have*) *thought about it seriously.*

Note here that the "h" should be sounded in such words as *what, why, where, when, which* and *whether.* On the other hand there is a tradition that suppresses the aspirate and uses the indefinite article *an* rather than *a* in such expressions as *an hotel, an historic fact, an habitual late-comer, an harmonious meeting,* where the aspirate forms part of an unstressed syllable. But where the aspirate introduces a stressed syllable it is sounded and takes the indefinite article *a,* as in *a history book, a habit, a holiday, a hospital.* Such niceties of language may have been forgotten and dropped by many, but they have not become archaic and are still accepted as forming a part of correct speech. The aspirate in *heir, honest, honour, honorary, hour* and a few other words is not sounded. These words therefore take *an* as their indefinite article.

Even without the aid of a teacher the use of high fidelity recording apparatus can certainly help to cultivate acceptable speech standards. It is one of the most effective means of building a tradition of good oral habits and of checking any inclination to slovenly speech. A useful exercise is to prepare beforehand and then record and play back a short reading of a piece of selected prose. Some faults will be noticed by the person recording; others would perhaps need to be pointed out by teachers or friends. Later on, similar exercises can be carried out with unprepared material.

Reading aloud

Reading aloud is yet another effective method of raising speech standards. Prepared passages read to small groups offer a useful beginning to be followed by readings not previously prepared. Passages not clearly heard at the farthest point should be re-read until the reader succeeds in projecting his voice so that all can hear. Voice projection has little to do with loudness, but it has a great deal to do with clearly pronounced consonants and well-shaped vowels, and with variations of pitch and adequate pauses to mark punctuation. Training and practice in the spoken word are essential if we are to make the most of our natural gifts. What we need if we would speak well is not so much lessons in elocution as care in expressing ourselves audibly, grammatically, fluently, pleasantly and with good diction, so that "through the magic of words we can make the most of our personality and give eloquent expression to our thoughts and feelings".

SPEECH AND WRITING COMPARED

It is sometimes suggested that we should "write as we talk", but although the boundary between the written and spoken forms of language has become somewhat blurred in recent times, we have not yet reached a stage when these two forms of communication are completely interchangeable. There are a number of reasons why this is so:

(*a*) At any period of time in the development of language certain words and forms of expression, known as colloquialisms, are always acceptable in speech but not in writing. They constitute an important difference between language in its spoken and written forms. *Jack got the sack because he wouldn't toe the line,* may be acceptable in speech but certainly not in writing. The abbreviated speech forms *we'll, they'll, didn't, couldn't* etc. are among the commonest of the colloquialisms we use today.

(*b*) As between speech and writing there are also differences of syntax. Speech is more tolerant and informal and does not always use complete sentences. *Back in a few minutes* and *see you soon* are common enough kinds of expression, but they have neither subject nor finite verb. They nevertheless form part of normal everyday speech.

(*c*) The spoken language also sanctions a number of minor grammatical blemishes so firmly established by widespread usage that to avoid them would sound pedantic, or even wrong. For example:

(*i*) use of the objective instead of the nominative form of pronoun after the verb "to be" — *it is me* (for *it is I*), *that's him* (for *that's he*), *that is them* (for *that is they*);
(*ii*) use of the subject form *who* (for the indirect object or dative form *whom*) — *who did you speak to?* (for *whom did you speak to?*, or *to whom did you speak?*);
(*iii*) use of the accusative instead of the possessive before the gerund or verbal noun — *do you object to me* (for *my*) *going?*

In expressions such as these our speech would sound pretentious and affected if we strictly followed the rules that apply to writing.

(*d*) The various devices used in writing to vary emphasis or produce shades of meaning are considered in Chapter Sixteen. In speech, these effects are produced by stressing some particular word in a sentence: *You should have stayed here with me.* By stressing in turn any one of the three words underscored we convey three quite different impressions to our listener:

(*i*) <u>you</u> (that is, <u>you</u> in particular);
(*ii*) <u>here</u> (that is, <u>here</u> and in no other place);
(*iii*) <u>me</u> (that is, <u>me</u> and no-one else).

Underscoring is a practice sometimes used in informal writing, but apart from this there is no satisfactory substitute for the stress employed in speech.

(*e*) Nor, as with stress, is there any substitute in writing for tone of voice, gestures and facial expression as expedients for varying shades of meaning. They endow the language of speech with qualities not present in the language of writing. In writing, words mean what they say; in speech, they say what they mean, or are intended to mean, by the way they are used to convey variations of emphasis and nuances of pleasure, approval, disappointment, sympathy, irritation, sarcasm and a whole range of other feelings.

ORAL COMMUNICATION IN BUSINESS

Advantages and drawbacks

The scale and scope of modern industry and trade have increased the importance of plain and exact communication, much of which takes the form of verbal intercourse between individuals and groups, oral reporting, dictating letters and telephoning. Oral communication has the advantage of immediate feed-back. It enables us to know at once whether we have been understood. It also provides better opportunities than writing for establishing friendly personal relations. But it suffers from the disadvantage that the hearer may not be listening. Hence the need to adopt a lively tone and to say what has to be said forcefully and with conviction. The listener must be "kept awake". Accent may also be important. A class accent may help or hinder depending on the class of person or group addressed, but this is something one can do little about. Tone on the other hand is something that can be controlled. If it is warm and friendly it assists communication; if it is cold, or overbearing or patronizing it hinders it.

Provided they have been properly prepared, oral reports should present no problem to a person whose speech standards are good. The more formal type of report, such as the reports presented at meetings, calls for fairly full speaking notes; it may even be better if reports of this kind are drafted in advance and then read.

Using the telephone

The operator

The telephone has now become so much a part of normal everyday life that most students entering business for the first time will already be accustomed to using it. It has become an almost indispensable part of modern life and more particularly so in offices, where many transactions of the kind that depend on the telephone could not be carried on without it. The switchboard operator is a significant link between her firm and the outside world and through the effect on callers of her manner of speech and the speed, accuracy and courtesy with which she handles their calls she does far more to enhance or impair the good name of her firm than is often realized. Some preliminary training is therefore desirable. It should be directed to establishing proper habits and desirable qualities in telephone usage—clear diction unaffected and free from any trace of unpleasant accent, and a business-like and pleasant manner. Discourtesy on the telephone is more often than not the result of thoughtlessness. Any form of unnecessary delay is a form of discourtesy. The operator can help to avoid this by keeping a pad and pencil near at hand. She can then take notes without wasting her caller's time. The habit of speaking "with a smile in the voice" is one she must learn to cultivate. To smile when we speak goes far to make the voice pleasant.

Telephone etiquette

The rules of telephone etiquette apply to all who use the telephone in business. They may be summarized as follows.

(a) *Answer the phone promptly,* speak clearly and announce your telephone number or the name of your firm, or both; or, where it is more appropriate, give your name and department, adding *Miss* or *Mrs.* if you are a woman, but not *Mr.* if you are a man. The addition of "Good morning" or "Good afternoon", or "Can I help you?" creates a good first impression. Good speech habits are more than ever necessary on the telephone since interference from other lines sometimes makes even the clearest speech difficult to understand.

(b) *Avoid the greeting "Hello" or "Yes?".* Such greetings are discourteous as well as time-wasting since they put the caller to the trouble of finding out who you are.

(c) *Be polite, courteous and pleasant,* but never familiar, and speak in a warm and friendly tone "with a smile in your voice".

(d) *Avoid slang expressions,* such as "Hang on" (say *Hold the line please*), "O.K." (say *Certainly,* or *Very good*), "Half a mo" (say *Just a moment please*). Avoid, too, the irritating "Yep" for "Yes".

(e) *Offer to ring your caller back* if he wants information that will take you some time to find, but if he decides to wait keep him aware of what is happening.

(f) *If you cannot deal with the caller* and must transfer the call to a colleague, explain to your colleague the nature of the call. It wastes the caller's time and tries his patience if he has to repeat a question he has already asked or information he has already given.

(g) *When speaking on an imperfect line* do not shout, but speak more slowly and with greater deliberation. Shouting causes distortion and makes matters worse.

(h) *Treat with strict confidence* matters you overhear on the phone. Your duty in this is as confidential as the private secretary's in dealing with her employer's correspondence.

The telephone suffers from the drawbacks of cost and the fact that gestures and facial expressions are not there to be relied upon to help to convey feeling. Pleasure, impatience, irritation, anger, boredom—all these feelings come through clearly in the tone of voice. Even such expressions as "It's a pleasure" and "You're welcome" can convey a wealth of ill-feeling if uttered in a cold, hard tone.

Time passes more quickly than one realizes and the system imposes on the telephone user a demand for brevity. Business calls must therefore be restricted to essential talk—there is no time for social chatter. A warm and friendly tone helps to compensate for the inevitable curtness.

Recorded dictation
When dictating a letter, a report, or indeed any other material, you are confronted by a special problem. Your reader will receive your communication in writing and will judge it by writing standards. As the dictator, you are as it were "writing by speaking" and, as we have seen, the spoken and the written languages are not interchangeable. This may create problems and open the way to misunderstandings. There is therefore a need to study your correspondent, to "stand in his shoes" and try to anticipate his reactions. If you use dictation equipment the following suggestions will help you:

Advantages and drawbacks
It is estimated that recorded dictation saves nearly 50 per cent of the time the shorthand-typist spends on correspondence. It has two further advantages:

(a) dictation can take place at any time, even away from the office and during travel;

(b) it eliminates mistranscriptions of shorthand and there can be no doubt about what was said.

With recorded dictation, however, the typist is no longer immediately available for discussion with her executive, or as a source of information, and difficulties arise when details that need elaboration are involved.

Rules for those giving dictation

The success of an audio-typing system depends very largely on the care and skill of those who dictate. Verbal corrections during dictation confuse the typist unless she first plays the dictation through. Those who dictate must express themselves correctly the first time. By observing a few simple rules the user can contribute considerably to the success of the system. These rules may be summarized as follows.

(a) Make brief notes before you begin and have ready at hand any documents you may need to refer to. This ensures straightforward dictation, free from repetitions and corrections and greatly simplifies the typist's task.

(b) Speak clearly and deliberately and at no faster than a reasonable speed, say 100–120 words a minute.

(c) Begin by giving the following information in the order shown:
    (i) your name and reference;
    (ii) size of notepaper to be used (unless you are using an individual dictation machine that carries a scale);
    (iii) number of carbon copies to be taken;
    (iv) correspondent's reference, if known;
    (v) correspondent's name and address, spelling out confusing or unusual names, (e.g. *Mason, Mayson, Leominster* (pronouunced lemster), *Kirkcudbright* (pronounced kircoobri), *Macleod* (pronounced macloud);
    (vi) indicate salutation to be used—*Dear Sir,* or *Dear Mr. . . . .;*
    (vii) state heading, if any, to be given to the body of the letter.

(d) Dictate such instructions as "paragraph" and "bracket". It is also helpful to dictate "period" or "full-stop" as well as less familiar punctuation, such as semi-colons, and dashes to mark parentheses. An experienced typist may not need such help; voice inflexion will usually be sufficient to indicate commas and other more usual punctuation.

(e) Spell out technical terms and, where not obvious, indicate use of capitals.

(f) Dictate nature of subscription—Yours faithfully, Yours sincerely, etc., and also designation of the person who is to sign the letter—*Managing Director, Sales Manager,* etc.

(g) Use short sentences and paragraphs; they are more suited to the business letter than long ones.

(h) Make sure that the letter is what you want it to be by having a play-back of all but simple letters, and keep in mind that your vocabulary and style must be that of writing and not of speech.

(i) State size of envelope needed if the letter is to be accompanied by enclosures.

Where the file containing previous correspondence is passed to the typist it will not be necessary to give all the information mentioned above.

EXERCISES

1. Use each of the following homographs in two sentences to show how change of stress alters the function and meaning of the word:

abstract	incense
compact	record
concert	refill
conduct	refuse
extract	transfer

2. Indicate pronunciation of the following words by placing an accentuation mark immediately after the stressed syllable in each:

advantageous	practicable
antithesis	relative
appreciative	subsidence
euphemism	temporary
interested	transferable

3. Read a short passage on any subject that really interests you and record it on a tape recorder. Then listen carefully to the play-back to notice *(a)* how clearly you speak and *(b)* how interested in the subject you sound.

4. Prepare a short talk on any subject in which you are not very interested (fishing, motor racing, stamp collecting, poetry, a general election, your journey to and from school or college). Record your talk, play it back and listen critically for *(a)* aspirates not clearly sounded and *(b)* consonant sounds at the ends of words.

5. First read the following passage. Then record it and listen to the play-back with a critical ear for tone and pitch of voice:

Courtesy: A Saving Grace

Good manners are everywhere a passport to friendship and respect. In any social situation it is graceful in men and women to think and act with courtesy and with regard for the convenience and feelings of others.

Good manners are the necessary guardians of peace in any society, and yet we hear and read less about cultivating them than we do about diet and daily dozens and all sorts of other things to preserve and enhance physical beauty.

Courtesy, defined as gentleness and politeness, is the settled medium of social exchange, just as money is the medium of economic exchange. It is like an air-cushion: there may be nothing in it, but it eases our jolts wonderfully. A "please" and a "thank-you" may seem trivial things, but they sweeten services and are agreeable to everyone.

Royal Bank of Canada: *Monthly Letter* (adapted)

6. As Office Manager write a circular to members of your staff to suggest ways in which the telephone should and should not be used.   *(I.C.S.A.)*

CHAPTER ELEVEN

Business Letter-Writing I
(Principles of Communication)

We beg to advise and wish to state
That yours has arrived of recent date.
We have it before us, its contents noted,
And herewith enclose the prices we quoted.
Attached please find as per your request
The samples you wanted, and we would suggest,
Regarding the matter and due to the fact
That up until now your order we've lacked.
We hope you will not delay it unduly,
And beg to remain yours very truly.

Royal Bank of Canada: *Monthly Letter*

BUSINESS LETTER-WRITING

The business letter is the chief instrument of external communication in business—the principal means whereby a firm maintains contact with the outside world. Often enough it is the firm's only contact with its customers, who form their impressions of the firm as much from the tone and quality of its correspondence as from the care and promptitude with which their orders are met. Standards of business letter-writing are better than they have been, but there still lingers a tendency to cling to the outworn clichés of the nineteenth-century business letter and, from either indifference or sheer laziness, to write in the sort of absurd and meaningless jargon that forms the quotation at the head of this chapter. Remember that such expressions as *your favour, esteemed order, 5th instant,* and *to hand* are old-fashioned. As one writer has put it, "They went out with the ark".

Over long distances the business letter is a more economical form of communication than either the telephone or the personal visit it replaces. It serves three main purposes:

(a) it conveys a message, maybe to seek or give information, to place or acknowledge an order, to make an appointment, to forward documents, and so on;

157

(b) it provides a permanent record for future reference and also valuable evidence in the event of legal disputes;

(c) it provides opportunities to increase good will by creating in the mind of the recipient a favourable impression of the writer's firm, and of the writer himself.

THE PERSONAL APPROACH

To accomplish its third purpose your letters must be written on a personal level in warm and friendly terms. The use of impersonal constructions tends to produce a tone that is cold and aloof. Consider the following letter.

> Your order of 15th March has been received and is having attention, but it is regretted that the goods cannot be supplied until the end of this month. It is hoped the delay will not inconvenience you in any way.

Now compare it with the same letter written on the personal level.

> We have received your order of 15th March and are giving it our attention (or better: are dealing with it); but we are sorry we cannot supply the goods until the end of this month and hope the delay will not inconvenience you in any way.

In the second of these letters the writer identifies himself with his firm and, by using the first person *We,* introduces a warmth of tone and strikes a note of genuine regret, both of which are lacking in the impersonal style of the first letter.

Unlike that of the private letter, the aim of the business letter is purely utilitarian, and as a letter it will be satisfactory only if it achieves its purpose. This means that before beginning to write you must be clear about what you want your letter to do and in what way you want it to influence your reader. You must therefore know something about him. You must ask yourself, "What is he like?", "What does he know already?", "What does he want to know?", "What do I want him to know and what is likely to be his reaction to what I tell him?" In all letters concerned with business matters the dominant need is for exactness expressed in terms that are absolutely clear. What you have to say you must say naturally, sincerely and without waste of words; it must be to the point. What you write will be judged, not by its merits as a piece of polished literature, but by whether it does the job intended in an efficient and workmanlike manner.

THE FORM OF THE BUSINESS LETTER

The business letter must be considered from two points of view, first as an exercise in arrangement and secondly as an exercise in composition. If you are following a secretarial course, with type-writing, you may already have learned something of business-letter form and layout, in which case you can pass quickly over this section.

The modern business letter is nearly always typed and it will be useful to look at the style and layout now commonly adopted. The style illustrated on p. 160, known as the "semi-indented" because the paragraph first lines are indented while the inside name and address is in block, is a style that has enjoyed popularity in the past, but it is now being rapidly overtaken by what is termed the "fully-blocked" style shown on p. 162, on the grounds that it is a time-saver. Those who like this style claim that it has a business-like look; those who dislike its appearance claim that it is side-heavy and unbalanced.

Apart from the letter-head, which usually includes such items as telephone number, telegraphic address, directors' names and spaces for references, the business letter consists of the following six princi-pal parts.

The date

The customary form is *25th October, 19...,* but there is a modern tendency to omit the *th* and other equivalent letters and also the comma following the month. There is no full-stop after *th* (since it is not an abbreviation) or after the year (since the date as a whole is not a sentence). The name of the month should be neither abbre-viated nor stated in figures. To give the date in figures might easily be confusing in correspondence with the United States, where it is the practice to write dates in the order of month, day and year.

The inside name and address.

Except when transparent-window envelopes are used it is not neces-sary to include the correspondent's full address, though it continues to be standard practice to do so in typewritten letters. *Esq.* (for *Esquire*) is legally restricted to certain classes of persons (e.g. judges, magistrates and barristers and eldest sons of knights). But according to the *Shorter Oxford Dictionary* the title is "allowed by courtesy to all who are regarded as gentlemen", and it is customary to use it when addressing men with letters after their names (e.g. *H. Parker Esq., M.P.*). *Esq.* should not be used when writing to a person in a foreign country; instead, use the appropriate foreign equivalent of *Mr.*, but where there is doubt address the person as *Mr.* Except in the special cases mentioned, *Mr.* is the more appropriate mode of

Directors: G. B. Davis, R. B. North,
M. W. Beevers, W. D. J. Argent

Macdonald & Evans Ltd

Estover Road, Plymouth PL6 7PZ
Telephone: Plymouth (0752) 705251
Telegraphic Address: MACEVANS Plymouth
Telex: 45635

Your ref: Our ref: Date: 24th September, 19..

Mrs. Frank Fairclough,
31 Dunster Road,
GUILDFORD, Surrey.
GU2 9LU

Dear Mrs. Fairclough,

Semi-indented Letter-Style

       This style is a modified version of the fully-indented style. The main differences lie in the inside name and address, which is typed in block form, and in the complimentary close, which is typed evenly to fall across the centre of the typing line, with the designation similarly centred. Some typists using this style prefer to place the complementary closure and signature to the right of the typing line instead of in the centre.

       The closed pattern of punctuation has been adopted. This makes free use of commas, for example in the date after the name of the month, at the end of each line of the inside address except the last, and after both the salutation and the complimentary closure.

       Another point to note about the pattern of punctuation is the absence of full stops after the date, and also at the end of inside name and address unless the name of the county is abbreviated, when the normal abbreviation full-stop is used.

       The pattern of end-punctuation used does not of course affect the punctuation used in the body of the letter, to which the normal rules apply.

Yours sincerely,
for MACDONALD & EVANS LTD.

R.B. North
Managing Director

REGISTERED OFFICE ESTOVER PLYMOUTH REGISTERED NO 488168 ENGLAND

Example 1

Some people still regard this as the most attractive of all letter styles. The blocked inside name and address is liked because of its compactness and the added tidiness it gives to the left-hand margin. The placement of the complimentary close and signature data over the centre of the typing line provides a fitting counterpart to the inside name and address.

This style continues to appeal to the more conservative reader, who likes the indented paragraphing which reading of printed matter (contd. on p. 161)

address for use in business correspondence and should be adopted. *Messrs.* (the plural of *Mr.*) is reserved for firms (i.e. partnerships) whose title includes a personal name. It is not used for limited companies and other incorporated bodies, which should always be addressed through the secretary or other official. Nor is it used in addressing partnerships when the firm's name is impersonal, or contains a courtesy title, or begins with *The*. The following illustrate current practice in this matter:

Messrs J. Hughes & Co.
    but
Universal Radio Stores   } partnerships
Sir John Hughes & Co.
The Hughes Advertising Agency.

The Personnel Manager,
J. Hughes & Co. Ltd.   } an incorporated body

In all typed letters the blocked style of name and address is now customary. Conventional or "closed" punctuation is as shown below, with commas at line-endings, but not before *Ltd.*, which is part of the company's name as registered. Except when the county name is abbreviated (e.g. *Lancs.* for *Lancashire*) a full-stop at the end is unnecessary:

Mr. G.B. Davis,
Macdonald & Evans Ltd.,
Estover,
Plymouth
PL6 7PZ

What is termed "open" punctuation has now become fashionable (see pp. 342—3).

The salutation
The customary salutation is *Dear Sir* (*Dear Sirs* for a partnership, though *Dear Mr. . . . .* is often used to set a friendly tone to the letter, especially between persons known to each other).

Subject headings
Subject headings summarize the theme of the letter and are useful time-savers, especially where correspondence on a subject is likely

---

has made so familiar. He claims that it makes for easy reading. Others dislike the indentations; they claim that they are time-wasting for the typist, and that the style has now been used for so long that it has become old-fashioned. In this example closed punctuation has been used.

Directors: G.B.Davis, R.B.North,
M.W.Beevers, W.D.J.Argent

Macdonald & Evans Ltd

Estover Road, Plymouth PL6 7PZ
Telephone: Plymouth (0752) 705251
Telegraphic Address: MACEVANS Plymouth
Telex: 45635

Your ref: Our ref: **RBN/PRF**   Date: **13th Feb. 19..**

Miss Elizabeth Groves
11 Osborne Road
WATFORD Herts
WD6 4PA

Dear Miss Groves

Fully-blocked Letter Style

This letter-style is very modern and is now being increasingly
used in this country. Its outstanding feature is the
commencement of all typing lines, including those
for the date, the inside name and address, the subject
heading and the complimentary close, at the left-hand
margin.

Some people who use this style prefer to place the date
in its usual position on the right, because it helps to
give to the letter a more balanced appearence. It also,
as in this example, enables the date to be more readily
identified in filing.

For this letter the open pattern of punctuation has been
adopted; that is to say, none except essential punctuation
marks are used outside the body of the letter. You will
notice, for example, a complete absence of punctuation
marks from the date, the salutation, the complimentary
close and from the ends of lines forming the inside
name and address.

Yours sincerely
for MACDONALD & EVANS LTD.

R.B. North
Managing Director

Example 2

This letter-style has become increasingly popular in recent years and is now
firmly established as the modern style. Those who like it claim that it has a
business-like appearance and that the absence of indentations reduces typing-
time. There may be some loss of clarity due to the absence of indentations,
but this can be made good by increasing the number of line-spacings between
paragraphs from two to three. The open pattern of punctuation used in this
example is in keeping with the modern letter-style, but is not essential to it.
If closed punctuation is preferred, it could be used.

to lead to a series of letters. If your correspondent has already used a heading, follow his lead and use the same heading. If you are replying to a query about an order it will clearly be helpful to head your letter:

<u>Your Order No. . . .</u>

Headings are typed two line-spacings below the salutation and underscored. Unless it makes a complete sentence, and this is unusual, the heading does not take a full-stop.

Confidential and Personal

These words indicating the status of special letters should be prominently displayed at the head of the letter, above the the inside name and address. If the letter is intended for your correspondent in his purely private capacity make it *Personal* rather than *Confidential.* A personal letter will remain unopened, but one marked as confidential will be dealt with by his deputy. Envelopes should also be correspondingly marked to indicate the special status.

The message

The foregoing are no more than the formalities of business letter-writing. Conventionally, they may be important but are only ancillary to the main purpose of the letter, which is to communicate a message. A good deal has been said in earlier chapters about the need to write good English, English, that is, which is easily understood. To do this you must write simply and avoid needless elaboration. Do not say *express a preference for* when all you mean is *prefer,* or *give consideration to* in place of *consider.* Be quite clear in your own mind what you want to say and then say it simply and in straightforward language, preferring short words and phrases to long ones. For *in the course of my enquiries* say *during my enquiries,* and do not say *I am writing on behalf of,* since *I am writing for* is much more natural and does just as well. Use short sentences and keep your paragraphs short—each one with a clear-cut message. Avoid the temptation to show off; write for your reader's benefit—not your own.

Avoid, as far as possible, such words as *herewith, aforesaid, inasmuch, whereas* and *undermentioned* and reserve them for the legal documents to which they properly belong. Avoid, too, using *ultimo, instant, proximo* and their corresponding abbreviations. They represent commercial jargon at its worst, and there is no conceivable reason for preferring them to the names of the months. There is indeed every reason not to use them since their meaning is not always clear. What, for example, are we to make of the following letter from a City insurance broker to a client?

> In my letter of the 3rd instant I mentioned that your underwriters required doctor's confirmation of date by the 8th proximo. This should have read the 8th instant. The letter was dictated on the 30th ultimo and typed on the 3rd instant. Hence the error.

Remember that a letter is "a piece of conversation by post" and write naturally. Say quite simply just what you mean. Would you say on the phone, *"I have received you communication of the 10th instant, for which I thank you"*? Of course you wouldn't. You would say quite simply, *"Thank you for your letter of the 10th"*, and that is what you should say in your letter.

The complimentary close
The subscription *Yours faithfully* in formal business letters is correct for all occasions and there is little point in bothering too much about other forms of closure that may be right in particular circumstances. *Yours sincerely* is strictly correct only between friends, or between persons well known to each other, though its use has now become common in association with the salutation *Dear Mr. . . .*, with the highly commendable motive of introducing a warmer and more personal note into business letters.

The signature
Never sign a letter with a rubber stamp. If a letter is worth sending, it is worth the trouble of reading by the sender and to add a signature takes no more than a few seconds. As most signatures today are illegible it is good practice to type the name of the signer at the foot of the signature space. If you sign a letter for someone else, sign it *for* . . . . It is now common practice to type the name of the company, preceded by *for,* below the complimentary close, as in the specimen letters on pp. 160–2, but when headed paper is used there seems to be no good reason for continuing the practice, except when the letter is written in the plural *we.*

The correct signature of a partner signing for his firm is that of the name of the firm, without the addition of his own name or initials.

Enclosures
It is the responsibility of the person who makes up the post to ensure that material intended to accompany the letter is enclosed. He must have some means of knowing at a glance which letters

need enclosures. The method most commonly used is to type the word *Enclosure* or an abbreviation of it in the bottom left-hand portion of the letter, with a figure indicating the number of enclosures if there is more than one (e.g. *2 Encl.*).

Alternatively, a horizontal line, or a solidus (/), or a line of dots, may be placed in the left-hand margin of the letter immediately opposite the line that mentions the enclosure. This is the most effective method, especially with long letters, because it indicates at a glance what enclosures should be sent.

STYLE AND TONE

The essential qualities of a good business letter are sincerity, simplicity and clarity and these are not to be found in such flowery and senseless verbiage as the following.

> We are in receipt of *or* We beg to acknowledge (for We have received)
> Your esteemed favour to hand (for We have received your letter)
> The favour of your early reply will oblige (for I shall be glad to hear from you soon)
> At your earliest convenience (for as soon as possible)
> Your good selves (for you).

Just as there is style in literary writing, so there is style in business letter-writing. What is wanted is not the florid prolixity of the style enshrined in such phrases as the foregoing, but a plain style—a style that is simple, clear and easily understood. The important thing about a business letter, or indeed any letter, after the information it conveys, is the impression it leaves with the receiver. Its tone and style must be of the sort to create a good impression of the writer's firm, and also of the writer himself as an efficient person anxious to be of service. This means that you must put yourself in the receiver's shoes and try to sense his feelings and anticipate his reactions to what you write. You must constantly ask yourself, "If I were to receive this letter, how would I feel about it?" Only in this way can you decide how best to set down what you have to say.

The importance of style in letter-writing lies in its impact upon the receiver. The writer must first of all be clear about the purpose of his letter and what he wants it to achieve, and then adopt a style and tone suited to the occasion and the purpose. The primary concern is to make sure that the message is clear and to the point, so that it is understood and acted upon in the way the writer intends. The tone of the letter as a whole must be right—friendly, firm, persuasive, apologetic, conciliatory as may be necessary. However good in other respects a letter in the wrong tone may produce an effect very different from the one intended. Letters of complaint, for example, call for restraint—a tone that is firm but not aggressive or in any way offensive. Nothing is to be gained by sarcasm or rudeness; one is much more likely to get what one wants by being courteous. Replies to complaints must be conciliatory and reassuring.

Consider the following letter sent by the manufacturer to a customer who has had trouble with an alarm clock recently purchased.

Dear Sir

We were very surprised to learn from your letter of 15 July that the "Senator" alarm clock you bought recently does not work.

These clocks are all individually inspected and thoroughly tested before leaving the factory, and yours is the first and only complaint we have received about their performance. We suspect that the bell does not ring because you have failed to release the "Stop" button at the back of the clock. If you will check on this we think you will find that the clock works satisfactorily. If it does not, please write to us again.

Yours faithfully

The tone of this letter is hostile and condescending and likely to create resentment because it implies that the customer is foolish and incompetent. In the following alternative reply the manufacturer shows a genuine interest in the complaint. He writes in a friendly tone, addresses the customer by name and does everything possible to ensure customer satisfaction. Moreover, the considerate manner in which he treats the complaint helps to build for himself a reputation for reliability and fair dealing.

Dear Mr. Johnson

Thank you for your letter of 15 July enclosing the "Senator" alarm clock, received this morning.

We find your comments on the performance of your clock very interesting and have passed it to our engineers for inspection and a report. Meanwhile, we are arranging to replace your clock with a new one, but before sending the replacement are submitting it to a series of tests to ensure that it is free from the fault to which you refer and in full working order. We will send it to you as soon as the tests have been completed.

We apologize for the trouble and inconvenience this matter has caused you, but are confident that the replacement clock we are sending will prove satisfactory and give you the service you are entitled to expect from our products.

Yours sincerely

The primary purpose of language is communication; but there is much more to language than the mere conveying of messages. The way in which it is used is important in its effects on personal relationships in both business and social life. It is not enough for a letter to be grammatically correct. So long as its message is clear, its tone and effect on the feelings of the recipient are more important than its grammar. The two letters that follow convey the same message, but in very different terms:

Dear Sir

I have to thank you for your application for the post of personal assistant to our managing director, and to inform you that the post has now been filled.

Yours faithfully

There is nothing grammatically wrong with the above letter, but it is cold and distant and does nothing to allay the disappointment the applicant is bound to feel. Now compare it with the following.

Dear Mr. Barrington

Thank you for your application for the post of personal assistant to our managing director. We received a large number of applications, including some from persons with experience in the special field of electronics in which we operate. The appointment has now been made, but as our work continues to expand there are likely to be other vacancies in which you may be interested. I hope you will feel able to apply to us again when they are advertised.

Yours sincerely

This letter conveys the same basic message as the first, but its tone is warmer, more understanding, less discouraging and kinder to the applicant's feelings. It addresses him by name and treats him as a human being, and aims to lessen his disappointment at not getting the job. Unlike the earlier letter its tone is likely to encourage him to try again.

The tone of a letter reflects the spirit in which the writer projects his image to his reader. If the message is to be effective and evoke the response the writer is seeking it must establish rapport with the reader and be accepted favourably by him. Good tone in correspondence creates its own psychological impact and does much to foster that sense of considerateness which makes for happy personal relations. In business such relations are important and the power to say what has to be said in an effective, finished and even graceful way is a cardinal part of the art of good business letter-writing.

THE OPENING AND CLOSING PARAGRAPHS

If your letter is well planned it will start and finish on the right note. The opening paragraph is the place where you will refer to previous correspondence or, if there is no previous correspondence, to the subject-matter you are writing about. For example:

> During last May you serviced my Super 60 electric shaver at a cost of £8.75, but the result has not proved satisfactory.

Where there has been previous correspondence it has become fashionable to start reply letters with such phrases as *In reply to your letter, With reference to* (or *Referring to) your letter* and *Thank you for your letter.* Such openings cannot be criticized as being either commercialese or ungrammatical, but they are flat and unenterprising—worn threadbare from overuse. By using a little ingenuity you can give your reply a much more interesting send-off, as by expressing pleasure or regret, by showing that some action has been taken, or by asking or answering a question. You might, for example, use such introductions as the following.

> I was glad to receive your letter of . . .
> On receiving your letter of . . . I at once consulted our works manager.
> Before I can deal with the matter raised in your letter of . . . I shall need to know . . . .
> On 24th January you were good enough to send me two brochures . . . .

These and similar introductory forms give your letters a much more interesting start than the formal phrases they replace.

If you do begin a letter with *In reply to* (or *With reference to) your letter* be careful to follow with the first-person pronoun *I* or *We* and then say what you are doing about it. It would be perfectly correct for you to write *In reply to your letter of yesterday, I am sorry to report* . . . but if you say *In reply to your letter of yesterday, our managing director died this morning* your correspondent would be astounded that his innocent enquiry had produced such a tragic result. Similarly, you cannot say *With reference to your letter of 10 March, you are right in thinking that our offices close on Saturdays,* since your correspondent is not replying to his own letter. Nor can you say *With reference to your letter, it is correct that our offices close on Saturdays*—the opening phrase must be expressly linked with the person who is replying.

The ways of closing a letter are as numerous as the different purposes letters serve. What is important is that the letter should end on a natural note. A closing paragraph is not always necessary; the ending may consist of no more than a graceful exit in the form of a very brief observation—*We shall deal promptly with any order you give us; We are sorry there should have been any misunderstanding; We are glad to have been of service,* and so on.

Avoid closing your letters with phrases introduced by participles, of which *Thanking you in anticipation* and *Assuring you of our best attention at all times* are arch-offenders.

Instead of	*Say*
Awaiting your futher instructions.	We await your further instructions.
Thanking you for the interest you have shown in our enquiry.	We thank you for your interest in our enquiry.

Quite apart from being ponderous, wordy and too formal, the participial phrase is grammatically incomplete unless followed by the implied pronoun to which the participle relates and which it is usual to provide in such expressions as *I am, We remain* and *I remain.* There is nothing grammatically wrong with the participial closure, but do not use it; it is a starchy form of commercialese that belongs to a past age.

On pp. 68—73 you will find more examples of opening and closing paragraphs used in business letters.

EXERCISES

1. State the main features of a good business letter. Enumerate some undesirable features the writer of a business letter should avoid.

2. Imagine that a friend of yours has died. Write a letter to the parents, whom you know slightly but not very well, expressing your sympathy with them and mentioning some of your friend's good qualities. The body of the letter should contain no more than 100 words.   *(R.S.A. Elem.)*

3. The following letter is badly worded. Rewrite it in improved form, *using not more than 50 words.*

Dear Madam

In answer to yours of the 12th inst. we acknowledge receipt of your letter re "Dragon" bicycles. We are very pleased to tell you that the supply situation is at last improving, although the small models are still in short supply. It was only yesterday that we instituted the necessary enquiries re these small models and it will be our endeavour to despatch at least six prior to the holiday rush. We will advise you immediately we can furnish particulars about despatch.

We await your reply in anticipation.

Assuring you of our best attention at all times.

Yours faithfully   *(R.S.A. Inter.)*

4. The following letter is badly constructed; the sentences are short and the style is jerky and lacking in "flow". Moreover, some of the words are badly chosen. Retype it in improved form, making any corrections necessary and paying careful attention to choice of words, punctuation and paragraphing.

Dear Sir

We are surprised to hear from your letter of 12th May that the case of tinned pears has got lost. It was sent with the other groceries on 3rd. We cannot tell how the accident happened. We have carefully checked over your order. All the articles were despatched at the same time. Our despatch clerk says that your address was marked plainly on each case. Enclosed is the railways receipt. Kindly return it after you have looked at it. We have written the railway company. They have been asked to make an enquiry. You should receive it in the next few days. If you do not receive the case in a week, write again.

Yours faithfully   (R.S.A. Inter.)

5. Write a letter to a Continental hotel, booking accommodation for yourself and a friend *or* a party, and stating your requirements and probable time of arrival.   (U.E.I. Elem.,)

6. As Secretary of your Youth Club you are planning next year's programme. Write a letter to a well-known person inviting him (or her) to visit your Club and to give a talk to the members. Give briefly a few details of the activities of the Club which would help in planning the talk.   (N.C.T.E.C., Elem.)

7. You are secretary to a large firm of electrical manufacturers. You have put on the market a new appliance for which there have been huge orders. Unfortunately, there has been a hold-up in production and you are far behind in deliveries. Write a circular to your retailers explaining the delay, and promising satisfaction as early as possible.

Pay special attention to the tone and layout of your letter. (U.L.C.I., Inter.)

8. Write a letter to a distributing firm, in connection with an advertisement of a domestic appliance, such as a vacuum cleaner or a washing machine, inserted by them in your daily paper, requesting them to send a representative to your home in order to give you a free demonstration of the working of the appliance. Be careful to offer them a choice of days and time.   (L.C.C.I., Elem.)

9. You wish to buy a house in a district to which you are moving later in the year. Write a letter to an estate agent, describing the type of house and amenities you would like, and requesting him to send you details of some suitable properties. Be careful to give full particulars of your requirements, which should include some indication of the amount you are prepared to offer for the house.   (L.C.C.I., Inter.)

10. On behalf of the general manager of your firm, write a letter to a private motor coach company, which has served you well in the past, in order to arrange transport for your annual staff outing to a popular seaside resort.(*L.C.C.I., Inter.*)

11. Write *one* of the following.

(*a*) A letter to a customer who, on retirement, proposes to leave the neighbourhood and has asked if his account may be transferred to the branch of your bank nearest his new home.

(*b*) A letter to your local transport manager pointing out that the provision of buses on your route, from the suburbs to the centre of the city, is inadequate at certain times of the day.   (*I. of B.*)

12. The branch office in which you are employed is finding that the turnover of clerical staff is increasing and that it is becoming difficult to obtain reliable assistants. Write a letter to your senior member of staff at head office giving possible reasons for the problem and suggesting any remedies you think appropriate.   (*I.C.S.A.*)

13. A large section of the manufacturing plant owned by the company you work for has been damaged by fire. Draft a letter, to be sent to the company's customers, explaining the position and outlining any plans the company is making to meet its orders. Your letter should contain 150–200 words.
                                                                (*I.C.S.A.*)

14. Write one of the following letters.

(*a*) From a commercial director to customers indicating that price increases on all goods are inevitable. He states at least four good reasons, expresses regret, but points out that several developments in company policy in other matters will mean better service to customers.

(*b*) From a solicitor to an industrial client who has a case on which counsel's opinion has been obtained. He advises that there is little point in proceeding with the case, states reasons and indicates another method by which some satisfaction might be obtained.   (*L.C.C.I., Priv. Sec. Dip.*)

15. (*a*) Your employer is a local councillor whose term of office has expired and who is submitting himself for re-election. He asks you to draft a circular to be sent to his constituents. He wishes to remind them of his service (he is a member of the Housing, Public Relations and Finance Committees) and to ask for their support at the coming election.

or

(*b*) The company for which you work has a branch overseas, and the general manager of the branch wishes to send his 18-year-old son, a Brazilian, with a sound knowledge of English, to spend six months in England to improve his knowledge of English and English institutions. He asks for the help and advice of the managing director of the British company, on whose behalf you draft a letter. You make suggestions on points such as education and training; places of interest; social activities; accommodation; direct association with the company; period of work in the British company; possible costs; and any specific programmes you think of interest.   *(L.C.C.I., Priv. Sec. Dip.)*

CHAPTER TWELVE

Business Letter Writing II
(Examples)

Since truth and constancy are vain,
Since neither love nor sense of pain,
Nor force of reason can persuade,
Then let example be obeyed.

George Granville: *To Myra*

The following examples are offered not as models for imitation, but as guides to letter-writing in a variety of circumstances. To copy someone else's letters is a mistake; learn to be original and write your own. What you write will then reflect your own personality and not merely that of another.

A TESTIMONIAL

```
                                           2 June 19..

The Chairman
H. Baxter & Co. Ltd.
LONGHOPE Glos.
GL17 OPD

Dear Sir

It is with great pleasure and confidence that I support
the application of Mr. Gordon Ellis for the post of
personnel manager with your company.

Before joining us as our personnel manager six years
ago, Mr. Ellis had wide and varied business experience
in a number of responsible positions, both at home | and
abroad. His services to the company and his help to me
personally have been invaluable. In his dealings with
employees of all classes he is tactful, understanding and
sympathetic. As an organizer he is efficient  and far-
sighted and, as an administrator, level-headed.

If his application is successful it will mean a great loss to
my company and to me personally, but I feel bound to pay
tribute to his outstanding qualities and to wish him the
success which, in my opinion, he thoroughly deserves.

Yours faithfully

R. Curtis
Managing Director
```

A testimonial solicited by a prospective employer should be addressed by name to the person making the request. The writer should not make a biased recommendation, but should confine his statement to facts that provide a true picture of the applicant and make it clear when he is merely stating an opinion, as in the closing paragraph of the example.

APPLICATION FOR A POST

```
                                        18 Bedford Avenue
                                        Chingford
                                        E4 5BN

The Secretary                           23 May 19..
E.K. Arnold and Sons
25 Tudor Street
EC4 OAD

Dear Sir

I feel I have the right qualifications and experience for
the post of foreign correspondence clerk currently adver-
tised in The Guardian.

I am twenty-three years of age and was born of English
parents in Paris and came to England with my family when
I was eleven. I was a pupil at Walthamstow Grammar School
and left at eighteen with G.C.E. passes at "A" level in
English, French and German and a pass at "O" level in
eight subjects, including Spanish. Since leaving school
I have regularly visited the Continent and speak French
and German fluently, Spanish fairly well.

For the past five years I have been employed by W. Harding
& Co., a firm of City export merchants with extensive
connections abroad. Regular dealings with overseas customers
have given me valuable practical experience in using my
languages and I should welcome the opportunity that a post
as foreign correspondense clerk would give me to make
even greater use of them. A post of the kind you are offer-
ing is what I have been hoping for a long time to find.

I enclose çopies of testimonials from Mr. N. Wharfe and
Mr. J. Hughes, and refer you to Mr. R. Barlow, M.A., my
former headmaster, and to my present employers for further
information.

I hope you will grant me an interview, when I can give you
information about my qualifications and experience in
greater detail.

Yours faithfully

A.H. Brooks
```

This application is business-like and to the point. It includes all the essential information—personal details, qualifications and experience, the reason for the application and particulars of testimonials and references.

Useful hints on how to apply for a post are given in the author's *Modern Business Correspondence.* His *Model Business Letters* contains over six hundred specimen letters covering a wide range of transactions of the kind handled in business every day.*

ENQUIRY AND REPLY

The enquiry explains very simply what is wanted, and why, and, as it seeks a favour, is accompanied by a stamped, addressed envelope for the reply. The Secretary's reply is most helpful and its tone is warm and friendly; the form of salutation and complimentary closure help to make it so.

Enquiry

```
                                              18 Rufford Road
                                              Clacton-on-Sea
                                              CO1 9UZ

                                              18 March 19..

        The Secretary
        International Metal Exchange
        Oxbridge Raod
        LONDON
        WE4 8TW

        Dear Sir

        I am writing a book on Modern Business Training for publication
        by a London firm of publishers and in the proposed chapter
        on Commodity Markets and Exchanges and would like to include
        a short account of the organization and work of your Exchange.

        I am most anxious that the account should be up to date,
        accurate in detail and thoroughly reliable and should be
        grateful if you would send me any literature or other infor-
        mation you may have that would help me in preparing the
        text.

        I enclose a stamped, addressed envelope and am of course
        willing to defray any cost that may be involved.


        Yours faithfully

        J. Hudson

        J. Hudson
```

*Both books are published by Macdonald & Evans.

Reply

```
                                        20 March 19..
J. Hudson
18 Rufford Road
CLACTON-ON-SEA
CO1 9UZ

Dear Mr. Hudson

I was interested to learn from your letter of 18th March
that you propose to include an account of this Exchange
in your book on Modern Business Training.

You will find enclosed one or two pamphlets and I hope
they will be of some help yo you, but if you find the
information is not enough for your purposes and will let
me know, I shall be pleased to enlarge upon it.

Perhaps the best course would be for you to call on me on
a day and at a time mutually convenient. I could then arrange
for you to visit the "floor" of the Exchange and see for
yourself how dealings are conducted.

Yours sincerely

W.A.Bell

W.A. Bell
Secretary
```

A BUSINESS TRANSACTION
(Enquiry, Quotation, Order and Acknowledgment)

Enquiry

```
Messrs. Harrison, Mayson & Co.        12 October 19..
Tulketh Mills
BOLTON
BL8 7YZ

Dear Sirs


We have recently received a number of enquiries
from customers for cotton fitted bed-sheets and should
be glad is you would send us full particulars of your ranges,
including sizes, colours and prices inclusive of packing
and delivery charges. If illustrated brochures or pamphlets
are available it would be helpful if you would send us copies.

When replying, please state delivery period, discounts
and terms of payment.

Yours faithfully
for L.A. BIRD & SONS LTD.

R.G.Bennett

R.G. Bennett
Secretary
```

This letter contains the essential qualities of a satisfactory enquiry. It states clearly and concisely, and yet fully, exactly what is wanted and leaves no margin for error or misunderstanding.

The name of the company is included after the complimentary close because the enquiry is written in the first-person plural.

Quotation

```
                                           14 October 19..
The Secretary
L.A. Bird & Sons Ltd.
Vulcan Walk
TORQUAY
TQ6 4TJ

Dear Sir

Quotation No. 965

We were pleased to receive your enquiry of 12 October and
enclose a copy of our illustrated brochure showing our various
ranges of fitted bed-sheets. The sheets are made in four
standard sizes, from 75 cm to 150 cm and supplied in pink, blue
and primrose. They are made both in cotton and in polyester-
cotton material of exceptional wearing quality. Wonderlon
is very reasonably priced and we can strongly recommend it.

The prices quoted in the brochure cover packing and delivery
and are subject to 35% trade discount. Terms of payment are
2½% one month from date of invoice. We can promise delivery
within ten days of receiving an order.

We look forward to receiving an order from you, but if either
you or your customers would like more information, we should
be very happy to arrange for one of our representatives to
call on you.

Yours faithfully


HARRISON, MAYSON & CO.
```

The essential quality of a quotation is that it should be explicit and state clearly and fully the nature and quality of the goods quoted for.

The above is a satisfactory and helpful reply to the enquiry. It covers all the points raised and shows the firm's willingness to go out of its way to be of service. It is the kind of letter that helps to build good will.

The correct signature of a partner signing for his firm is that of the name of the firm, as in the above example, without the addition of his own name or initials.

Order

```
                                          19 October 19..
Messrs. Harrison, Mayson & Co.
Tulketh Mills
BOLTON
BL8 7YZ

Dear Sirs

Order No. 322

Thank you for the brochure and other information received
with your letter of 14 October. We find the terms of your
quotation No. 965 acceptable and shall be glad if you will
supply the following;

12   Nylon fitted bed-sheets        blue   105 cm
12        do.              primrose  120 cm
12   Wonderlon fitted bed-sheets    blue   105 cm


Please acknowledge this order and be good enough to inform us
when you depatch the goods.

Yours faithfully
for L.A. BIRD & SONS LTD.

R. G. Bennett

R.G. Bennett
Secretary
```

Acknowledgment of order

```
The Secretary                            21 October 19..
L.A. Bird & Sons Ltd.
Vulcan Walk
TORQUAY
TQ6 4TJ

Dear Sir

Your Order No. 322

We thank you for your order of 19 October for three dozen fitted
bed-sheets. These will be sent to you tomorrow by National Carriers
and should reach you within a day or two. Our invoice is enclosed.

We hope you will like the sheets and look forward to the pleasure of
serving you again on future occasions.


Yours faithfully


HARRISON, MAYSON & CO.
```

An order placed on the basis of a quotation must be linked with the quotation by reference number and date, as in the example. The letter is concise, yet says all that is necessary and says it politely and in a business-like manner.

The acknowledgment satisfies the three essentials of such letters:

(a) an appreciatory acknowledgment of the order;

(b) a reference by name to the goods ordered;

(c) an assurance that the order is being attended to.

Although not essential, the inclusion of an offer to be of further service helps to stimulate future business and to create good will.

LETTERS OF COMPLAINT

Letters concerning complaints are among the most difficult of all to write and call for the greatest restraint on both sides. Delay in delivery, or delivery of the wrong type of goods, may give rise to anger and resentment, but this must not be revealed in the subsequent letter of complaint, if only because it may turn out that the other party is not in fault. In any case, it is well to remember that even the most efficient concerns may sometimes fall short of the best standards and that oneself is by no means infallible.

Making complaints

When making a complaint, stick to the following rules.

(a) Assume that the other party will receive your complaint with understanding and deal with it sympathetically. As a matter of business it pays him to do so.

(b) Avoid assuming that the other party is to blame; he may have a perfectly good defence, as in the correspondence given below.

(c) Confine your complaint to a statement of facts and a polite enquiry as to what the other party proposes to do about it.

(d) Do not suggest how the mistake may have occurred or how it should be remedied; these are matters for the other party.

(e) Above all, avoid rudeness; at best it will only create resentment and may give rise to an unwillingness to co-operate and be helpful.

The following is a very tactful letter of complaint. It is confined to the facts, with a request for urgent attention. The writer is careful

COMPLAINT

```
The Secretary                          12 September 19..
J. Watkins & Sons Ltd.
28 Victoria Street
SW1H OET

Dear Sir

On 15 August last I sent you an order for fifty copies of
Modern Commercial Correspondence for Schools by D. Collins,
stressing the importance of delivery at the latest by 10
September, the date on which the new session was due to
begin.

No acknowledgement of the order has been received, nor have
the books been delivered. Failure to receive them on time is
causing grave inconvenience and I shall be glad if you will
look into the matter as one of urgency and let me know when
the books can be expected.

Yours faithfully

J. Durate

J. Durate
Principal
```

to say *No acknowledgment has been received* and not *There has been no acknowledgment* since it is possible that an acknowledgment was sent and has either gone astray or been mislaid.

Dealing with complaints

"The customer is always right"—so it is said. It is at any rate a sound plan to assume that a complaint received has been made by a reasonable person in good faith and that "The customer *may* be right". No firm can afford to put its goodwill at risk by ignoring complaints or by treating them lightly. Any complaint is a matter for concern and must be dealt with promptly, otherwise delay will increase resentment. If the complaint requires investigation likely to take some time, it should be acknowledged, with an explanation that it is being looked into and the promise of a full reply later. If the complaint turns out to be unfounded, this should be pointed out politely and without reproach. If on the other hand, the firm is at fault, the only proper course is a frank admission, an expression of genuine regret and an undertaking to put matters right.

The promptitude with which the suppliers took steps to investigate the complaint reveals their genuine concern that anything should have gone wrong with the order.

Acknowledging consideration shown

When a complaint has been dealt with promptly and with fairness, the one making it should acknowledge this. To do so is no more than elementary courtesy. At the same time it helps to create a

REPLY TO COMPLAINT

```
The Principal                          13 September 19..
Camford Technical College
High Street
CAMFORD
CF1 3RS

Dear Mr. Durate

We were surprised to learn from your letter of yesterday that the
fifty copies  of Modern Commercial Correspondence for Schools,
ordered by you on 15 August, have not reached you. Your order was
received by us on the 17th and, as our stock records showed the
books to be available, we passed it to our warehouse staff the
same day.

We phoned the warehouse manager this morning and he confirms that
the books were collected by British Rail on 22 August, for delivery
to you carriage paid.

We very much regret the delayed delivery and the inconvenience
it is causing you. We have, however, already taken the matter up
with the railway authorities at this end and as soon as we have
any information about the consignment we will phone you. Meanwhile,
may we suggest that you make similar enquiries at your end.


Yours sincerely
for J. WATKINS & SONS LTD.

L. Elphick

L. Elphick
Secretary
```

good relationship and may mean that any future complaints will be
received and treated with understanding.

COLLECTION LETTERS

Another kind of letter calling for considerable tact and patience is
what is termed the collection letter, that is the letter seeking payment of an overdue account. No one likes being asked for money,
least of all those whose payments have fallen behind, and, unless
the letter is framed with care, offence may be caused where none is
intended and where it can be ill-afforded.

The purpose of the collection letter is to persuade the debtor to
pay up while at the same time retaining his custom and good will. A
bad payer is naturally a source of irritation, but it is unwise to allow
any suspicion of irritation to creep into the request for payment. It
is even more unwise to threaten legal proceedings until all other
means have been tried and have failed. There may be a number of
reasons for the failure to pay, some of them deserving more of
sympathy than of anger. There is of course always the plausible
debtor, expert in making excuses, who needs watching. Nevertheless, collection letters must be framed politely and even the ultimate
letter threatening legal proceedings must be written "with regret".

Reminders for payment frequently take the form of a statement of account to which are added some such words as "Account Overdue", "Second Application" and "Please remit immediately" and it is not usual to send a collection letter until a series of these monthly statements has failed to produce results. A cautious approach is always necessary since the firm requesting payment may itself be in fault, as where a ledger-posting error continues to show as a debtor a customer who has already settled his account.

The following are examples of the kind of approach recommended:

LETTERS COLLECTING PAYMENT

First application

```
Mr. W. Ryan                                    10 April 19..
25 Elms Road
SOUTHPORT
PR8 3PS

Dear Sir

Account No. 5387

According to our records our account for the paint and wallpaper
supplied on 3 January last has not yet been settled.

We enclose a detailed statement, which shows the amount owing
to be £49.37, and hope you will be able to make an early
settlement.

Yours faithfully
for H. HOPKINSON & CO. LTD.

        J.G. Gartside

J.G. Gartside
Secretary
```

Second application

```
                                               12 May 19..
Dear Sir

Account No. 5387

Not having received any reply to our letter of 10 April,
we are writing again to remind you of the amount still owing on
your account, namely £49.37, and should be glad if you would now
send us your cheque in settlement.

Yours faithfully
```

Third application

---

23 June 19..

Dear Sir

Account No. 5387

We do not appear to have received any reply to our two previous
requests for payment for the sum of £49.37, still owing on
your account.

With the utmost regret we have now reached the stage when we must
press for immediate payment and hope that by the end of the month we
may receive your cheque for the full amount due. Failing settlement
by that date I am afraid you leave us no alternative but to place the
matter in other hands, but we trust this will prove unnecessary.

Yours faithfully

EXERCISES

1. Write a letter to your local paper, about the appearance of your town as it probably strikes visitors from abroad, and urge that something should be done to increase its attractiveness.   *(U.E.I., Elem.)*

2. Write a letter to a firm enquiring the price of a certain product in which your own firm is interested, and the conditions of sale and delivery. (About 80 words.)   *(U.E.I., Elem.)*

3. Write a letter in reply to the following advertisement.

Accountants require junior clerk; prospects good, especially for those with shorthand; experience not essential; state age and qualifications in writing to: Paulson's, 147 City Road, New Cardington-on-Sea, Co. Durham.
        (N.C.T.E.C., Pre-Senior)

4. Write a letter to your local bus company complaining about irregularity in the service and the refusal of drivers to stop and pick up passengers. Draw a frame 114 X 162 mm and address an envelope.   *(N.C.T.E.C., Senior)*

5. Write:

(a) A letter of complaint to the head office of a large retail concern with many branches, about a particular branch near your home, making the following points: *(i)* poor quality of product; *(ii)* indifferent service; *(iii)* insufficient variety and choice of goods.
(b) A suitable reply from the managing director.   *(N.C.T.E.C., Senior)*

6. Write a letter as from the sales manager of a firm manufacturing paraffin heaters, in reply to a customer's complaint of delay in executing their order for 50 single-burner and 20 double-burner convection heaters. You need *not* include full headings: begin with "Dear Sirs" and end with "Yours faithfully".

(E.M.E.U.)

7. Imagine that you wish to stay at a seaside hotel for a fortnight. Write to the manager, setting out your letter in business style, enquiring if he has a single room vacant for the period of your holiday, and asking him, if so, to send you particulars, and the cost with full board. State that you enclose a stamped, addressed envelope for his reply. Show also how you would address the envelope to him.   *(R.S.A., Elem.)*

8. Imagine that a new neighbour of yours uses her wireless almost all day long and likes it to be very loud. As you work at night and sleep during the day, this has become very troublesome to you. Write a friendly letter to her, explaining the position, and trying to persuade her to see your point of view.

(R.S.A., Elem.)

9. You have bought from Messrs. Jones and Smith, Holington, London, a chair advertised in a catalogue which the manager sent you. Delivery was promised in a fortnight. A month has passed and the chair has not arrived. Write a concise, firm, but polite letter to the firm, enquiring about the delay and urging early delivery. Send out the letter in correct form and, in a suitable framework, show the envelope, properly addressed.   *(R.S.A., Elem.)*

10. Imagine that you have left school and are applying for a job, and have decided to ask your former head teacher to act as a referee for you (that is, to provide a confidential report about the kind of person you were when you were at school for the employer to whom you are applying for the job). *Using between 150 and 200 words* in the body of the letter write a letter to your former head teacher asking him or her to act as referee. State when you were at school, give details of the job for which you are applying, and any other information which you think may help the head when writing the reference.

(R.S.A., Elem.)

11. Write *one* of the following.

(a) A letter to the manager of an insurance company protesting that an increase of premium to cover damage to your house in respect of storm, tempest and flood is excessive.

(b) A letter to a business acquaintance declining politely the request that you should be named as an executor in his will.   *(I. of B.)*

12. Write *one* of the following.

(a) A circular letter to the members of a social club of which you are secretary, giving details of an outing you have arranged, and seeking to enlist their support.

(b) A letter to a responsible person who has known you well, asking him to act as a referee in support of your application for a better post. Include a brief outline of your progress during the two years since you saw him last.   *(I. of B.)*

13. Write *one* of the following.

(a) A letter to the secretary of a club to which you belong, declining the offer of a place on the club's committee.

(b) A letter to a manufacturer, complaining that one of his accredited dealers, from whom you have bought an expensive article, has given poor after-sales service.   *(I. of B.)*

14. *(a)* Write a letter to your employer asking for an immediate increase in salary, giving reasons for your request.

(b) Write the employer's reply explaining why it is not possible to grant the request.   *(I.C.S.A.)*

15. Write a letter in reply to the following advertisement.

Assistant, qualified or qualifying, required by a large commercial group of companies in the department of the company secretary. Starting salary dependent on qualifications and experience. Applications giving concise particulars of education, present and past employment and stating age, present salary and when available, should be sent to Box A, *The Chartered Secretary*, London, W.1.   *(I.C.S.A.)*

16. An efficient clerk who used to work under you was asked to resign because suspicion that he was responsible for some petty pilfering was causing ill-feeling against him and hampering the work of the office, although you had never seen any evidence that he was in fact responsible. He has now applied for another post, giving your name as a referee, and his prospective employer has written to you to ask about him. Write your reply.

17. While working as a despatch clerk at Nottingham Hosiery Ltd., Houndsgate, Nottingham NG1 4PL you receive the following letter:

9, Green Street
Newark
Notts.

18 January 1978

Dear Sir

Please send three pairs of wool, winter-weight stockings to the above address.

I enclose a £3 postal order in payment, which should also cover postage and packing. The last time I bought a pair they were 65p a pair but that was a while ago so I am adding the extra money.

Yours faithfully,

F. White (Mrs.)

In fact, Nottingham Hosiery Ltd. no longer make wool stockings. The only winter stockings they make are in acrylic fibre. These cost £1.75 a pair. Reply to Mrs. White as clearly and helpfully as possible.   *(E.M.E.U.)*

18. Mrs. J. Regan, who lives at 24 Meadow Road, very near the school bus-stop is very annoyed by the noisy and even violent behaviour of certain pupils. In the past she has had a high opinion of the school's pupils in general. Write Mrs. Regan's letter of complaint to the Headmaster, the Newton School, Field Lane, Nottingham NG6 2DY.   *(E.M.E.U.)*

19. Write a letter for your company—Electrical Enterprises, Princess Street, London SS8 4NB—to the Advertising Manager of *The Weekly Echo,* Union Street, London JK3 7XZ, informing him of the success of the full-page advertisement your company had in last week's issue of the newspaper. Many readers wrote in for details of the advertised goods and a number of sales has already resulted. Ask the Advertising Manager to send you rates for a similar advertisement each week for the next six months. Lay out your letter correctly.
                          (L.C.C.I., Inter.)

20. Write a letter, of between 150 and 200 words, for your company, Shaw & Co. Ltd., Shaw House, Gill Road, Deantown, Deanshire AB15 7MO, to Mr. J.A. Hutton, 26 Bebbington Lane, Bebbington-by-the-Sea, L18 9YZ, who is the former Office Manager of Shaw & Co. Ltd., and who retired a month ago. Tell Mr. Hutton that all the arrangements for having his retirement pension from the company paid by his local bank have been made and that he can start drawing it immediately. Thank him once again for his thirty years of service to the firm and wish him a happy retirement with his wife in their new home. Lay out your letter correctly.   *(L.C.C.I., Inter.)*

21. You work in the Customer Relations Department of a large firm of holiday tour operators whose head office is in London. You receive a letter from an overseas client who has recently spent a fortnight in the Canary Islands on a holiday arranged through your firm. He claims that he contracted food poisoning at the hotel selected by you and that he will be prevented from working for a further two weeks. He feels that your firm has been negligent and that some financial compensation is due to him.

Reply on behalf of your firm "Southern Sunshine" regretting his misfortune but disclaiming responsibility.   Offer him a 20% reduction on your special Christmas long-weekend in Paris.
                          (L.C.C.I., Higher)

22. Your employers are internationally known manufacturers of heat-resistant kitchenware. Recently a series of complaints has been received from Malaysia alleging that saucepan handles, made under the brand-name "Flame-resist", are not heat-proof and that, in some cases, the material has cracked. An investigation at your Huddersfield works reveals that this defect is confined to

one batch exported to the Far East last April. At the time of production supply difficulties enforced the use of a material slightly different from the usual.

Write a suitable letter of regret and explanation to the aggrieved customers. Assure them that immediate free replacement will be made by your local agent, explain the cause of the problem and thank them for notifying you as you are zealous to guard your reputation for quality and safety.   *(L.C.C.I., Higher)*

CHAPTER THIRTEEN

Summarizing Correspondence

I have made this letter rather long because
I have not had time to make it shorter. (Translation)
Pascal: *Lettres Provinciales*

TWO TYPES OF SUMMARY

It is often necessary in business to have a shortened version of some previous correspondence or of a lengthy document or report. As applied to business correspondence, précis writing is the art of summarizing a series of letters so that the part played by each in the total transaction can be quickly gathered without trouble. The rules that apply to précis writing generally (see pp. 326–8) apply equally to correspondence:

(a) supply a suitable heading;

(b) gather the gist of the correspondence as a whole;

(c) make notes of the main points;

(d) provide an introductory clause in the past tense and retain this tense throughout;

(e) prepare a rough draft, and check it carefully;

(f) write the précis in good prose, using indirect speech in the third person;

(g) state the number of words used, if the summary is made as a whole.

The précis of a lengthy correspondence may take either of two forms.

(a) *Summarization by stages.* It may take the form of a separate summary of the contents of each letter, thus enabling the separate steps in a transaction to be followed in detail.

(b) *Summarization as a whole.* The précis may take the alternative form of a single summary of the correspondence as a whole, thus providing an overall picture of the transaction.

For a busy executive the latter is the more appropriate form, since he is usually more concerned with the broad aspects of a transaction than with its details. In preparing a summary of this kind the essential thing is first to gain a clear grasp as a whole of the main theme or topic with which the separate letters are concerned and then to summarize the substance of the correspondence in narrative form.

The overall summary is the method usually required in examinations and, unless the examiner indicates a contrary intention, is the method that should be adopted.

A WORKED EXAMPLE

Let us suppose that for the information of the manager of Excelsior Electric you are required to summarize the following five letters, using first method *(a)*, i.e. by stages, and then method *(b)*, i.e. as a whole:

Letter No. 1

```
                                        14 Ramsden Road
                                        St. Annes-on-Sea
                                        FY8 3EG

                                        25 March 19..

The Manager
Excelsior Electric Shaver Co. Ltd.
LIVERPOOL
L7 8RP

Dear Sir

I am enclosing my Model 65 electric shaver, together with case
and electric lead, and shall be glad to receive from you a
quotation of the cost of repairing the shaver.

The shaver does not function at all and when plugged into
the mains supply becomes very hot. Even when the shaver did
function, there was often difficulty in starting.

When replying, please state price of a new shaver of a similar
type and whether you could give a trade-in allowance on the one
enclosed.

Yours faithfully

L. G. Carter

L.G. Carter
```

Letter No. 2

```
                                                28 March 19..
Mr. L.G. Carter
14 Ramsden Road
ST. ANNES-ON-SEA
FY8 3EG

Dear Sir

We have examined the shaver enclosed with your letter of
25th March and quote as follows for its repair;

New motor            £5.52
New base and cover   £1.75

We also advise replacement of the present heads, both of
which are badly worn. Replacement would involve a further
charge of £4.50 giving a total charge of £11.77.

The list price of a new shaver of a similar type is £28.97,
against which we could give you a trade-in allowance of
£6.00 (Six pounds).

We await your further instructions.

Yours faithfully

J. Hughes
Service Manager
```

Letter No. 3

```
                                           14 Ramsden Road
                                           St. Annes-on-Sea
                                           FY8 3EG

                                           1 April 19..
The Service Manager
Excelsior Electric Shaver Co. Ltd.
19 Bedford Street
LIVERPOOL
L7 8RP

Dear Sir

Thank you for your quotation of 28 March.

Because of the high cost of repair I am disposed to buy a
new shaver at your trade-in price of £22.97. I notice, however,
that this figure does not include the usual leather-cloth
covered de-luxe case. Would you please state the trade-in price
for this shaver complete with de-luxe case?

Yours faithfully

L.G. Carter
```

Letter No. 4

```
Mr. L.G. Carter                              5 April 19..
14 Ramsden Road
ST ANNES-ON-SEA
FY8 3EG

Dear Sir

I am sorry to say that the de-luxe case about which you enquire
in your further letter of 1 April is no longer supplied. The shaver
is now supplied in a special pack, and this is included in the
price we quoted in our letter of 28 March.

Yours faithfully


J. Hughes
Service Manager
```

Letter No. 5

```
                                          14 Ramsden Road
                                          St. Annes-on-Sea
                                          FY8 3EG

                                          8 April 19..

The Service Manager
Excelsior Electric Shaver Co. Ltd.
19 Bedford Street
LIVERPOOL
L7 8RP

Dear Sir

With reference to your letter of 5 April and our
earlier correspondence, I am appreciative of your offer
to supply a new replacement shaver at the special trade-
in price of £22.97, but I have decided not to take advantage
of it. Instead, I shall be glad if you will arrange for
the repair of my own shaver on the terms quoted in your
letter of 28 March, and enclose a cheque for £11.77 to
cover the cost, including the provision of new heads.


Yours faithfully


L.G. Carter
```

Summary of foregoing correspondence

Method 1 (Summary of the separate steps in the transaction).
By this method the contents of each letter are summarized in date
order under a heading that includes the date of the letter and the
names of both writer and recipient.

<u>Repair of Model 65 Shaver
Correspondence with L.G. Carter, 14 Ramsden Road,
St. Annes-on-Sea, FY8 3EG</u>

25 March, 19 . . .   From L.G. Carter to Ourselves
Mr. Carter enclosed Model 65 shaver and asked us to quote for repair. He
also asked for trade-in price of a new shaver.

28 March, 19 . . .   From Ourselves to L.G. Carter
We replied quoting £7.27 for repair, plus an optional £4.50 for new heads.
We also quoted a trade-in price of £22.97 for a new shaver.

1 April, 19 . . .   From L.G. Carter to Ourselves
Mr. Carter asked for trade-in price of new shaver complete with de-luxe
case before deciding on trade-in offer.

5 April, 19 . . .   From Ourselves to L.G. Carter
We notified Mr. Carter that the de-luxe case is no longer available, and that
a special pack, covered by our quotation, is now supplied instead.

8 April, 19 . . .   From L.G. Carter to Ourselves
Mr. Carter wrote rejecting our trade-in offer and, enclosing a cheque for
£11.77, requested repair of his own shaver, including new heads.

Method 2 (Summary of the transaction as a whole)

On 25 March, 19 . . ., L.G. Carter of 14 Ramsden Road, St. Annes-on-Sea,
FY8 3EG, asked us to quote for repair of his Model 65 shaver, which he
enclosed, and for trade-in price of a new shaver. We quoted for both on
28 March. He enquired on 1 April for trade-in price of shaver with de-luxe
case, to which we replied on 5 April stating that this case had been replaced
by a special pack, covered by our quotation. He decided on 8 April not to
buy the new shaver and requested repair of his own, enclosing a cheque for
£11.77 to cover cost, including supply of new heads.

EXERCISES

1. Prepare a précis of the following letter in about one-third of its present
length.

                                                2 The Avenue
                                                SOUTHPORT Lancs.
The Editor   PR8 5DF
Commercial Education   8 January 19 . .
Caxton House
GLOUCESTER
GL7 28Z

Dear Sir

I hope you will excuse me for not having replied immediately to your letter
of 14 December, inviting me to write another article for *Commercial Educa-*

tion. I will certainly do so; it is just a question of the subject. On the day I received your letter I had to reply to an enquiry from a firm of chartered accountants, the two partners both being women, and this of course raised the question of how they should be addressed. The circumstance reminded me of an article I wrote recently on the use of "Messrs." as a courtesy title. The article has not been published, and if you are interested in it I will send it on to you.

The article was prompted by a number of letters in the *Evening Gazette.* At least one correspondent suggested that it was the duty of the commerical schools and colleges to give a lead on this vexed question of the use of "Messrs.", and I wholly agree. As head of a commercial school I feel we have a duty to ensure that our students know what they are about in a matter that arises nearly every time they type a letter. At the moment they are at sixes and sevens and it is not difficult to argue a case for standard practice. I wrote the article referred to after inspecting about a hundred letters which the editor of the *Evening Gazette* allowed me to see, and I should like to feel that the commercial teaching world has the courage to give the lead that is rightly expected from it.

The article consists of about 3,000 words, and should you feel that this is too long, I could rewrite it to any length you suggest. If on the other hand, you feel that the use or non-use of "Messrs." is too contentious a question for a suitable article in *Commercial Education,* I will prepare something on another subject.

Yours faithfully
G. BANNISTER

(309 words)

2. Your employer and his wife are visiting your agent in Cape Town, South Africa, and have received a long letter from him. Summarize this for your employer.

Dear James

This is a last-minute letter. I hope it will reach you before you leave. Since our final confirmation of all the business arrangements, Joan has made a number of plans for you and Irene. As previously planned, we will meet you at the boat, and drive you straight to your hotel, and hope you will dine with us that night as our guests.

By the way, there is a slight change in the programme for Wednesday. We are due at the steel factory at 10 a.m., instead of 12 noon as planned. Therefore, you will not be able to see Arthur Brown that morning as you hoped, but he has invited you and Irene (with us) to drinks in the evening. If you are not too tired, we hope you will dine with us afterwards at the club. I have been able to arrange for you to see Mr. John Clarke on Friday morning, which I could not confirm when I last wrote to you. Joan has made a hair appointment for Irene on Thursday afternoon, and I am sure they will be able to fill up time shopping and meeting some of our friends. Once again, let me say how much we are looking forward to seeing you.

Sincerely
CHARLES

(217 words)   (R.S.A. Inter.)

3. Prepare a summary in not more than 100 words of the following correspondence. Names and addresses will not be included in the count of words.

6 St. Mary's Avenue
FAREHAM Hants.
PO15 7JR
27 May 19 . .

The Secretary
Teale & Sons Ltd.
76 Tabley Lane
CHELMSFORD
CM2 3RS

Dear Sir

We are holding a large reception at the Archway Hall on Saturday 22 June, and wish to know whether you will be able to undertake the catering arrangements for us at a moderate price. We are expecting about three hundred guests, for whom we wish to provide a dinner, and also light refreshments during the time for dancing, which will continue until midnight.

We shall require an orchestra and public address system and we understand that you may be able to supply these.

We shall be glad to hear from you as soon as convenient, as we are afraid we have already left the enquiries until rather late.

Yours faithfully
MARY A. CASLAKE (Miss)

(118 words)

TEALE & SONS LIMITED

76 Tabley Lane
CHELMSFORD Essex
CM2 3RS
30 May 19 . .

Miss M.A. Caslake
6 St. Mary's Avenue
FAREHAM Hants.
PO15 7JR

Dear Madam

Thank you for your letter of 27 May. We have given careful thought to your enquiry concerning the catering and general supplies for the reception you wish to hold on 22 June. Although we have not had time to go into every detail, we think we can manage to supply all your needs at a sum which we hope you will consider reasonable. We estimate that the cost for three hundred guests would be £4.25 per head, but if the number falls below three hundred the cost per head will increase proportionately.

We cannot make arrangements for an orchestra , although we can supply a public address system. This is provided free of charge for a party of two hundred or more. We suggest you get in touch with Messrs. Christopher & Bayliss, 106 High Road, Chelmsford, who we think can make arrangements for a small orchestra.

We shall do our best to make your reception a very happy event.

Yours faithfully
M. SMITH
pp. Teale & Sons Ltd.

(171 words)

6 St. Mary's Avenue
FAREHAM Hants.
PO15 7JR
1 June 19 . . .

The Secretary
Teale & Sons Ltd.
76 Tabley Lane
CHELMSFORD
CM2 3RS

Dear Sir

We are pleased to learn that you are able to make the catering arrangements for our reception, but we think it would be best, before going further into the matter, for my colleague or myself to call on you to discuss the arrangements more fully.

We suggest next Thursday or Friday 6 or 7 June.

We assume that you are able to provide the necessary tables and chairs.

Yours faithfully
MARY A. CASLAKE

(72 words)   *(R.S.A. Inter.)*

4. Give a clear summary in about 75 words of the following letters. Supply also a heading, in which names and addresses may be given.

CHARLES FOWLER & SONS

38 Castle Street
BEXHILL Sussex
TN39 3DT
15 March 19 . .

Messrs. Stanley & Earl
NEWCASTLE UPON TYNE
NE1 5XR

Dear Sirs

We recently ordered from you one Stokewell Ashfree Stove, which was subsequently delivered to our premises in Jarvis Mill either late evening or early morning when the shop was closed. The stove was left in our yard without a delivery note or signature.

When we discovered the stove, we sent it at once to our client, Mr. Jack Pipe, a plumber, in the packing in which we received it. When Mr. Pipe unpacked it he found that the top and two mica panels in the fire-door were broken.

We realize that a few days have elapsed since delivery, but we hope you will be able to replace the broken parts.

Yours faithfully
CHARLES FOWLER & SONS

(117 words)

STANLEY & EARL

Newcastle upon Tyne NE1 5XR

18 March 19 . .

Messrs Charles Fowler & Sons
38 Castle Street
BEXHILL, Sussex
TN39 3DT

Dear Sirs

We have received your letter of 15 March and note your remarks regarding the Stokewell Ashfree Stove which was delivered when your premises were closed.

We find it hard to believe that our lorry driver would do this as he is a most reliable man, but we will, of course, accept your statement and arrange to despatch the replacements free of charge towards the end of this week.

Yours faithfully
STANLEY & EARL

(72 words)

CHARLES FOWLER & SONS

38 Castle Street
BEXHILL Sussex
TN39 3DT
22 March 19 . .

Messrs. Stanley & Earl
NEWCASTLE UPON TYNE
NE1 5XR

Dear Sirs

We have today received one top for a Stokewell Ashfree Stove together with two fire-door mica panels in good condition.

We wish to point out, however, that we returned to you the fire-door as well as the top and mica panels.

Will you please let us have the door as soon as possible?

Yours faithfully
CHARLES FOWLER & SONS

(60 words)

STANLEY & EARL

Newcastle upon Tyne NE1 5XR

25 March 19 . .

Messrs. Charles Fowler & Sons
38 Castle Street
BEXHILL Sussex
TN39 3DT

Dear Sirs

Thank you for your letter of 22 March. We cannot understand the remarks in your second paragraph as we can find no mention in your last letter of the fire-door being returned. Moreover we have not received the door.

Would you kindly let us know whether the complete fire-door was returned or the right or left door only.

It is of course, unnecessary to remove the fire-door in order to replace the mica, and as the fire-doors are fitted with great precision in our works, due care must be taken to replace them correctly, or the working will be seriously affected.

Yours faithfully
STANLEY & EARL

(109 words)   *(R.S.A., Inter.)*

5. Summarize the following letters *as briefly as possible* but omitting nothing of importance.

The Glade
Ravens Lane
REDBRIDGE Essex
IG4 4BN
9 May 19 . .

The Manager
The Queen's Nurseries
BASILDON Essex
SS6 3DF

Dear Sir

I have bought plants and seeds from you for several years, but, although I have been pleased with the bright colours and large blooms of many of the flowers, none of them in recent months seems to have had any fragrance.

At the back of my present house I have a balcony overlooking the garden about twelve feet above ground level, with approximately forty feet of oak trellis below it. Up this trellis I grow a number of roses, chosen from your last year's catalogue especially for their scent, but there was no fragrance at all.

I wonder whether, in the search for large and colourful blooms the scent of many of our garden flowers has been lost.

Perhaps you would let me know if there is anything that I can order which you can guarantee will have a rich perfume. I did not receive a catalogue from you this year.

Yours faithfully
B.A. BROOKE   *(155 words)*

                                                    The Queen's Nurseries
                                                    BASILDON Essex

Mr. B.A. Brooke   SS6 3DF
The Glade   12 May 19 . . .
Ravens Lane
REDBRIDGE Essex
IG4 4BN

Dear Sir

I am sorry to hear you have had cause to complain about some of the plants bought from our nurseries.

Though it is true that certain flowers have lost the fragrance they once had, many recent introductions have just as much scent as their predecessors and I am quite certain that if you are really searching for subtle or rich perfumes there is no lack of choice.

There are some plants of course, which are grown for their scent alone and not for their beauty. Notable among these is the half-hardy nicotiana. In my opinion it is an untidy plant and its flowers are not graceful or beautiful, but the scent on a summer's evening especially after rain is really delightful.

Even the dwarf varieties have a delicious scent though it may not be quite so strong. A few of these planted near the house in some remote corner would give you a most fragrant scent.

Perhaps you would like to try to grow next year under glass a few sweet peas which have more scent than the outdoor ones, and the Clucana lily is one of the most beautiful and fragrant.

I am enclosing my new "Seed Guide" and illustrated "Plant Catalogue", which you should have received last January. It may be that you did not receive them owing to your change of address but I shall be pleased to send you any late planting flowers if you will let me know immediately.

Yours faithfully
B.S. GOLD
The Queen's Nurseries   *(247 words)*   *(R.S.A. Adv.)*

CHAPTER FOURTEEN

Making a Report

Lord of my love, to whom in vassalage
Thy merit hath my duty strongly knit,
To thee I send this written ambassage,
To witness duty, not to show my wit.

Shakespeare: *Sonnets*

At some time or other most of us find ourselves faced with the task of making a report, even if it is only a report of a telephone conversation, or an interview, or a meeting we have attended. Reports of this kind will usually be short and straightforward accounts calling for no more than an orderly arrangement of relevant facts clearly presented. These reports, like those at meetings of clubs and societies, and in business generally on matters of routine, are often made verbally.

But in business, reports frequently call for very much more. They may involve lengthy investigation and research and run into many pages or even assume the proportions of a small book. But whatever the nature of the report, the object is always the same—to present in adequate form relevant factual information, and sometimes conclusions and recommendations, as a guide to action to be taken. The form taken by the report will vary with its length and subject-matter; but there are certain general principles common to all report writing and it is with these that this chapter is concerned.

THE KINDS OF REPORT

Routine reports

What is said in the pages that follow refers to written reports, but much of it is equally relevant to verbal reports of the kind mentioned. Written reports fall into two classes. They may be either routine reports or special reports. Many of the reports made in business are routine and deal with matters that periodically recur. The reports of sales representatives to their sales manager, the periodical reports of departmental managers on the work of their departments, the reports made at committee meetings and the chairman's annual report at shareholders' meetings are all reports of a largely routine kind and conform to a pattern established by precedent. Presentation of reports of this kind creates no special problem; many routine reports are in fact made on predesigned forms that greatly simplify the work of preparing and presenting them.

Special reports

Special reports are different. They are not submitted as a matter of general practice, but are once-only *ad hoc* reports called for to provide information on matters of particular interest and concern. They cover every conceivable situation in which those asking for the reports may be interested and on which information is sought. They range from reports that are no more than replies to requests for information needed to bring an executive up to date with developments and projects to those which involve prolonged investigation undertaken for the purpose of helping to shape business policy. They may be in summary form and consist of only a single sheet, or they may be detailed and extend over many pages. They may be made by individuals or by groups, by lay members of staff or by specialists. They may be made by committees specially appointed to investigate issues of wide-ranging significance. Most government reports are of the last-named type and sometimes extend to hundreds of pages, but even so, they are still compiled on the same general principles as other special reports.

For reports made by committees and other composite bodies the style of presentation will usually call for the replacement of the first person *I* or *We* by the impersonal third person—*the Committee, the Council,* and so on. They should be signed by all the members, the chairman signing first, the secretary last and the remaining members in alphabetical order of surnames.

ESSENTIAL QUALITIES

Skill in writing, in whatever field it is exercised, means ability to present the subject-matter accurately, clearly and in an interesting way. In report-writing accuracy is paramount. A written report is in every sense a piece of composition and, having gathered your material, you must next deal with it as such and discard what is irrelevant and analyse, group and arrange what remains on the lines suggested in Chapter Five.

A well-written report will have the following qualities.

Completeness

It must be complete and accurate. You must investigate everything that falls within the terms of reference. You must gather your facts carefully, interpret them honestly, distinguishing clearly between what you present as facts and what you state as opinion, and, whether the findings are favourable or otherwise, make sure that the evidence on which you rest your conclusions is both adequate and reliable.

Clarity

It must be clear. Clear writing is the product of clear thinking; if you do not think straight you cannot write straight. Your report will be clear only if you present it as an orderly procession of facts and ideas; otherwise, your reader will find it hard to follow what to you may be clear-cut and easily comprehensible.

The report must of course be written in good English, that is to say in English that is not only grammatically flawless but also easily understood. If it is written for someone who understands the specialized language of his calling, there can be no objection to using the kind of jargon current in his specialized field. Make use by all means of such expressions as *price ex ship* (price on delivery from ship), *prompt day* (the day fixed for settling accounts), *spot price* (the price for goods where they lie) and *put option* (an option to sell) in their proper environment. These and similar expressions have become part of the currency of communication in the specialized fields in which they are used, and within those fields are universally accepted and readily understood. But on the other hand avoid the kind of popular jargon enshrined in roundabout and cliché-ridden expressions that cloud the minds alike of those who use and those who read them.

Conciseness

It must be concise. Conciseness does not consist in using few words, but in using as few words as possible to express what has to be said. The essential point is not the length of the report, which may be long enough to cover several pages, or short enough to be written on a postcard, but economy in the use of words. Your report may still be lengthy and yet concisely written. Follow the advice given on p. 79; write to the point, work to a plan and never make your report longer than it need be.

Readability

It must be readable. Unless the report has been asked for, you cannot afford to assume that it will be read. Nothing you write will get the attention you want it to have if you present it in terms that are pedestrian. The use of bright and colourful language adds interest to a report and makes it more readable. To say, *There were many who disagreed with the proposal, but others greeted it with approval* is pedestrian and dull. *There was a lively and controversial discussion on the proposal* is both brighter and shorter. It is not enough for presentation to be clear; it must be attractive—in a form and in terms

that capture attention. No report is of any use unless it is attractive
enough to at least gain a reading.

FORMS OF PRESENTATION

Reports in letter form

Short reports will usually be cast in the form of a letter addressed
to the person or persons at whose request, or on whose instructions,
the report is made. The mechanical structure will not differ from
that of the ordinary business letter and the report should be signed
and dated as such. It is always helpful, too, if a subject heading is
included above the body of the letter.

Subject-matter will usually be arranged in the following order.

(a) *Terms of reference.* In the opening paragraph a brief mention
of the request for the report and its scope, followed by a formal
statement that the report is now being submitted.

(b) *Procedure.* A statement of the methods of investigation used:
the sources consulted, the enquiries made, the tests if any carried
out, and any other methods used to ascertain the facts.

(c) *Findings.* An orderly arrangement of the facts ascertained.

(d) *Conclusions.* A statement of the conclusions drawn from the
facts.

(e) *Recommendations.* A statement of the recommendations
made, if these have been asked for, will conclude the report.

This five-part format is traditional, but there is nothing compulsory
about it. It is useful for lengthy reports; for short reports simpler
structures could be used so long as essential requirements are covered.
Items (a) and (b) for example could be combined to form an *Introduction,* and *Conclusions* and *Recommendations* could be merged
into a single paragraph.

The following hypothetical letter is given as an example of this
type of report.

The Secretary   3 July 19 . .
The Institute of Business Studies
7 Russell Square
LONDON WC1B 5EH

Dear Sir

Revision of the Syllabus in Commerical Law
for Marketing Students

On 5 June you asked me to investigate and make recommendations
on the changes necessary to bring the present syllabus in Commercial Law into
line with present-day needs of students preparing for careers in marketing. I

have borne in mind that the aim of the course is to provide students with a businessman's rather than a lawyer's knowledge of those aspects of law which are most likely to affect their business relationships. Their needs will therefore be sufficiently met by a selection for treatment of that part of the law which may be regarded as indispensable to the practice of marketing. The instructional core of this selection would include contract, agency and sale of goods, and these are the aspects of law which the course should emphasize.

Investigations
My enquiries have included (i) an examination of several books recently published on various aspects of commercial law, (ii) discussions with the directors of the College of Marketing and of the Institute of Export Managers, (iii) consultations with teachers and examiners, and (iv) a scrutiny of syllabuses and past examination papers of a number of professional bodies conducting examinations in the subject.

Findings and Conclusions
As a result of these enquiries I find that as it stands your syllabus is not entirely suited to the needs of the marketing student, for the following reasons:

1. It is too widely drawn and cannot be satisfactorily covered in the one-session part-time course it has been designed to serve.
2. It could be restricted without in any way imparing its value. Such specialized branches of the law as partnership, incorporated bodies, bankruptcy, liquidation and arbitration at present included are more appropriate to the needs of the company secretary than to those of the marketing specialist.
3. Within the limits of a one-session part-time course any teaching of the specialized branches of law mentioned in the preceding section must inevitably be at the expense of other topics of more importance to the marketer.

Recommendations
Accordingly, I make the following recommendations:

1. That the sections of the present syllabus dealing with bankruptcy, liquidation and arbitration be entirely omitted.
2. That the treatment of partnerships and incorporated bodies be restricted to the following:

(a) the nature of corporate personality—a comparison between partnerships and incorporated associations;
(b) company formation with reference to legal aspects of the memorandum, articles and prospectus, but not to formation procedure;
(c) a comparison of the legal position of shareholders and partners.

3. That a new section dealing with insurance be included to cover:

(a) formation of the contract of insurance, and the effects of fraud, misrepresentation and mistake;
(b) the principles of indemnity and insurable interest.

Yours faithfully,
B. BROOKS

Reports in tabular form

The letter-form of presentation is suitable for short but not for lengthy reports. A lengthy report in letter form makes it difficult for the reader:

(a) to grasp the essential information on a first reading;
(b) to perceive relationships between various parts;
(c) to select those parts in which he may have a special interest.

But a schematic arrangement in which the material is classified and grouped under headings and sub-headings greatly simplifies the reader's task. He can see at a glance what the different sections are about, pass quickly over those that do not concern him and concentrate on those that do. A table of contents makes his task easier still. It gives him a bird's-eye view of the subject-matter covered as well as a close-up of sections that specially interest him. The table will reproduce the main headings and sub-headings of the report and include a list of any appendixes and diagrams. With very lengthy reports it is also helpful to prepare, in addition, a summary of the findings, conclusions and recommendations consisting of no more than a single page.

The following is an outline of the plan usually followed in preparing reports on these lines.

Title page
Table of contents
Summary
The report (sectionalized under headings and sub-headings)
Appendixes

The report itself is headed in the manner shown below and opens with a paragraph setting out the terms of reference. The report should be signed and dated by the person who submits it.

<u>REPORT ON PROPOSED CENTRALIZED TYPING SERVICE</u>
<u>AT</u>
<u>UNIVERSAL INSURANCE CO., LTD., SHEFFIELD</u>

1. Terms of Reference

    On the instructions of the Managing Director dated 17 July 19 . . , to report on the proposal to set up a centralized typing service, and make recommendations.

2. Investigation Procedure
3. Findings
4. Conclusions
5. Recommendations

Date . . . .

Signature . . . .

Designation . . . .

The example below, consisting only of headings arranged on a five-point scheme, with main headings, side headings and three types of sub-heading, illustrates the form taken by an architect's report presented in tabular form. Capitals, numerals, lettering, underscoring and indenting are all employed as devices for presenting the different items with varying degrees of emphasis. Numerals and letters are alternated, with upper-case roman numerals for the most important and lower-case for the least important headings. An important point to notice is that the main heading is centred and that sub-headings are progressively indented as their importance diminishes.

S P A C E D   C A P I T A L S
(Centred for title of Report)

I, II, III etc. Upper-case roman numerals
(Centred for main section headings)

A, B, C etc. (Capital letters for side section headings);
  1, 2, 3 (Arabic numerals for indented sub-headings);
    (a), (b), (c) etc. (Lower-case letters for indented minor sub-headings);
     (i), (ii), (iii) (Lower-case roman numerals for indented paragraphs);

The progressive indentation used in this method enables the reader to run his eye over a page and to grasp the substance of the report more easily. Items on the same level of importance can always be identified by position as well as by numbering.

REPORT BY F. STONE A.R.I.B.A.
ON
PROPOSED ALTERATIONS TO PROPERTY
AT
15 VICTORIA ROAD, EASTBOURNE

I DWELLING HOUSE

A. <u>Kitchen</u>
  1. <u>Door to Conservatory</u>
  2. <u>Boiler</u>
    (a) Type
    (b) Position

B. Lounge
  1. <u>Structural Alterations</u>
    (a) Windows
    (b) Fireplace
  2. <u>Electrical Work</u>
    (a) Power points
    (b) Lighting
      (i) Switch positions
      (ii) Light positions
    (c) Radiators
      (i) Number and type
      (ii) Positions
  3. <u>Decorations</u>
    (a) Ceiling
    (b) Walls
      (i) Painting
      (ii) Papering

II OUTBUILDINGS

A. <u>Garage</u>
B. <u>Greenhouses</u>

The numbering and lettering scheme adopted in the above example is convenient when headings are arranged in five degrees of importance. With headings of three degrees of importance upper and lower-case roman numerals may both be omitted from the schemes, and also the upper-case letters, as in the example in Chapter Eight, pp. 123—4.

An alternative method that makes use of numbered sections only is sometimes used, especially in Government reports:

1, 2, 3, 4 etc. for main sections;
1.1, 1.2, 1.3, 1.4 etc. for subsections;
1.2.1, 1.2.2, 1.2.3, 1.2.4 etc. for subordinate sections, or for paragraphs within the sub-sections.

This method is occasionally also used in the civil service and in local government. Other schemes are equally acceptable provided the one adopted is consistently maintained throughout the report.

Reports in paragraph form

Not all reports are long enough or detailed enough to call for five-point headings; four, or even three (the scheme adopted in this present chapter) are probably more common. What is important is not the choice of scheme but consistent use of the scheme chosen so that headings of equal importance conform to a uniform pattern of display. For very long reports it is sometimes better to follow the simpler arrangement of numbered paragraphs grouped under centred section headings, as in the following passage adapted from a series of articles on *"The Communication of Ideas"*. * This arrangement has the merit of making cross-references easy to follow. It is the arrangement frequently adopted for Government reports.

The Importance of Communication in Business

1. Communication of ideas is an important human activity. Words underlie our whole life, are the signs of our humanity, the tools of our business, the expression of our affections and the records of our progress. The key word in all use of language is "communication". Thoughts locked up in your own breast give no profit or pleasure to others, but just as you must use the currency of the country in which you are travelling, so you must use the right currency in words if your thoughts are to gain a hearing.

2. In business there is no inefficiency so serious as that which arises from poverty of language. The man who does not express himself meaningfully and clearly is a bungler; he wastes his time and that of his associates. Few men are in business for financial reward alone. Business is a means of living and of expressing self-satisfaction. The average businessman is a perfectly normal human being—sympathetic, warm and friendly. He finds it natural and easy to show his real personality in face-to-face contacts, but alas! when he sits down to write a letter he changes completely. He becomes cold, formal and his writing jargon-ridden with *esteemed enquiries, best attentions* and *enclosures herewith.*

A businessman may be firmly attached to such meaningless phrases, but he may be persuaded to part with them when it is pointed out that they add quite considerably to the cost of his letters. He needs to write more imaginatively.

Imagination as an Aid to Communication

3. What is written imaginatively in the daily work of office and industry will get desired results. If the writer looks further, what he writes with imagination will live on when the atomic age is ancient history. Why? Because imagination is the one common link between human minds in all ages.

*Royal Bank of Canada: *Monthly Letter.*

4. Imagination in writing finds expression in the use of accurate and illuminating equivalents for thoughts. One may show imagination by dealing with something unfamiliar; by calling attention to commonplace facts that are generally overlooked; by bringing into view familiar things in new relationships; or by drawing together relevant thoughts in a nosegay tied with one's own ribbon.

5. In letter-writing, imagination creates desirable personal contact. When you call in your secretary to write a letter, you are entering into a personal relationship with the reader. He is no longer a statistic in a mass market; he and you are human beings talking things over.

WRITING THE REPORT

Your first step in writing a report of any kind is to make sure that you know exactly what is wanted; in other words you must be clear about your terms of reference, i.e. what you are required to do. This is no more than common sense. You must keep clearly in mind the defined purpose your report is intended to serve, otherwise you will waste time and effort in dealing with irrelevancies. The purpose will generally be a combination of some or all of the following:

(*a*) to provide information;
(*b*) to submit opinions and ideas;
(*c*) to report findings and the conclusions drawn;
(*d*) to make recommendations.

Unless the terms of reference are lengthy, they can usually be incorporated in the title given to the report:

Report on the
PROPOSAL TO INTRODUCE A CENTRALIZED TYPING
SERVICE
to replace the existing system

Headings to reports should be short, but they should describe and not merely identify their subject-matter. *Revision of the Syllabus in Commercial Law for Marketing Students*, though longer than *Syllabus in Commercial Law*, is better since it describes precisely what the report is about. For the same reason *Centralization of Typing Services* would be a better heading than *Reorganization of Typing Services*.

Writing a report need not be the difficult task it is sometimes thought to be. Like so many other tasks it becomes easier when broken down into its component elements. A breakdown on the following lines is helpful:

(*a*) study your terms of reference carefully;

(*b*) find out what sources of information are available; and

(*c*) identify those upon which you propose to draw;

(*d*) from these sources make notes of the information you need; and then

(*e*) group the information under appropriate headings;

(*f*) prune your information, discarding any that is irrelevant; and

(*g*) use what is left to prepare a draft report;

(*h*) correct your draft and rewrite, or type, it in final form;

(*i*) if the report is lengthy, append a summary of your findings.

In preparing for the report there are four stages:

(*a*) collecting and assembling data;

(*b*) organizing the data;

(*c*) preparing a draft report;

(*d*) revision and checking.

Sources of information

Collecting and assembling relevant information is the foundation of all good report-writing. It is often a more extensive task than the actual writing of the report. Every report has its own special requirements, but certain sources of information are common to all. Information upon which you can draw when writing a report is of three kinds.

(*a*) *That which is recorded.* This includes books, articles in journals, the earlier reports of others, documents and files of correspondence.

(*b*) *That which is investigated.* This includes questionnaires, interviews and conversations with persons who have expert knowledge or first-hand experience.

(*c*) *That which is direct.* This consists of your own observations and the tests and experiments conducted either by you yourself or under your supervision.

Just as in law the evidence of an eye-witness is more valuable than that of a person who testifies by hearsay, so in report writing information acquired direct at first hand is more reliable than that gained from what is recorded by others or obtained from questionnaires and interviews. The written records of others may not always be accurate and information taken from them should always be checked, if possible. There is a danger, too, that answers obtained by questionnaire or to questions at interviews may state as facts what may be no more than opinions held, or even that the answers given may not represent the truth.

Some reports may be so short that the processes of collecting and organizing the data and writing the report can be performed as a single operation, but at the other extreme there is the lengthy report extending to many pages that may involve the writer in long hours spent in collecting facts and in grouping and interpreting them before he can even begin to think about sitting down to write. It all depends upon the length of the report and the amount of detail to be included.

Organizing the material
Proceed as follows:

(a) find a title that makes plain the purpose of the report; this will help you to keep to the point and to shun irrelevancies;

(b) jot down in an exercise book, or on cards or loose sheets, any facts or ideas likely to be useful;

(c) note their sources in case you want to refer back;

(d) after each note leave space for additions;

(e) make liberal use of sketches and diagrams whenever possible.

The order in which you collect the material you need is not important. What is important is that you collect what you consider to be sufficient for your purpose. Having done this you are ready to proceed with the task of collation, as follows.

(a) *Bring together related facts and ideas* and group them into sections under main headings. The use of separate sheets, each headed with its appropriate title, simplifies the next step.

(b) *Arrange the sections in the order in which you propose to write them up.* In an eye-witness account—of an accident for instance —the record of events should be chronological; any other arrangement is liable to confuse the reader. For other kinds of report an arrangement that deals first with the most significant items is preferred. Reports are then better balanced, more interesting to read, and are also probably shorter since a chronological arrangement encourages inclusion of minor points noted when the events occurred, and more important points may be lost in a mass of unimportant detail.

(c) *Within each section arrange your material in a logical sequence;* your narrative or argument will then have an even flow. This arrangement may reveal that some of the information included is unnecessary and that other information is inadequate and needs to be reinforced.

(d) *Transfer to appendixes statistical data and other factual details* used to support statements in the main text. This makes it easier to follow the gist of the report and to grasp its main theme.

(e) *If the report is one requiring you to state your conclusions,* decide whether to give them at the end of each separate section, or to group them in a section of their own at the end. The second of these methods is the more usual, though the first is very suitable for lengthy reports.

(f) *Should your terms of reference ask for recommendations*, give them in a separate section at the end. Your recommendations will suggest the course of action to be taken and indicate the probable results. Any recommendations must be based on facts and free from bias or emotion of any kind. Personal feelings must not be allowed to enter into what is essentially a factual, unbiased and unemotional account of an investigation.

Only by careful organization of your material as described above is it possible to clarify a complex subject and to present a logically developed and readable report.

Drafting the report

Report-writing is a specialized form of written communication and its cardinal merits, like those in business letter-writing, are clarity, brevity, and of course strict accuracy.

The introduction

Having planned the main sections of your report and the conclusion, you must now draft the introduction. It should:

(a) state the terms of reference and how far you have been able to carry them out;

(b) explain the procedure followed in your investigation;

(c) include a table of contents;   but only if the report is

(d) include a brief summary of your   detailed and lengthy.
conclusions and recommendations.

The list of contents and the summary will help readers who are interested only in the subject-matter of particular sections.

The main sections

Because the tone for a report is rather more formal than that for the business letter, it is customary for reports to be written in the third person. Readers of a report are interested, not in the writer but in what he has to say. Use of the first person will often be necessary in an eye-witness account, e.g. *I was standing near the bus shelter when the lorry crashed into it.* But whenever possible the impersonal third person should be used. Instead of:

> For some time we have been publishing reports
> on such subjects as transport, banking marketing,
> and taxation. I recommend that we should now bind

these reports together in handbook form and provide
district managers with individual copies.

write in the third person, as follows:

> It is recommended that the reports published in the
> past on such subjects as transport, banking, marketing,
> and taxation should be bound in handbook form and
> distributed to district managers.

Except for this use of the third person in reports, the rules of
business letter-writing apply equally to report-writing, with emphasis
on relevance, accuracy, clairty and conciseness.

Concentrate on writing one section at a time, and arrange as follows:

(a) use charts and diagrams where they will usefully supplement
the text — each should be placed as close as possible to its textual
reference and bear an identifying caption or title;

(b) use footnotes for quoting source references and so preserve
the unimpeded flow of your writing;

(c) for the same reason, as mentioned earlier, transfer statistics
and other detailed information to appendixes;

(d) finally, review your title and section headings — precise wording
is needed so that subject-matter is described and not merely
identified.

The conclusion

If your introduction contains no more than a summary of your conclusions
and recommendations you will need to give them in full in
your conclusion, which should have a section heading of its own.

It is becoming increasingly common to summarize findings and
recommendations and to present them in the form of a synopsis
immediately after the statement of the terms of reference. This
may not be the most logical practice, but it has the following advantages
for the reader:

(a) it gives him a grasp of the substance of the report and makes
it easier for him to follow the detailed report itself;

(b) being familiar with the main points and recommendations
he can read the report with a critical frame of mind and assess the
relevance and importance of each section as bearing on the recommendations
made;

(c) It saves time for the busy reader who is interested to know
only the gist of the report and its main conclusions.

A synopsis is not intended as a substitute for the report, but it does provide an over-all picture, not only for those who must read the report in detail, but also for those who may be concerned with only certain aspects of the report.

Revising and checking the report

Having completed your rough draft check the facts (especially figures) carefully. Make sure that the factual information is unassailable, appropriately grouped and logically arranged. Be on the look-out for spelling mistakes, grammatical slips and points where punctuation could be improved. In the process try to put yourself in the reader's shoes and visualize the sort of impact your report is likely to have. Strive hard to make your reader's task as easy as the subject permits. "Hard writing makes easy reading."

Having done this you will find it a good plan to put your draft aside for a while, for a day or two if possible, before reading it again. Ask yourself, "Have I left anything out that should be included?" If not, "Is the report too long, and can it be shortened without losing any of its value?" If you check too soon after the report is written, your recollection of what you intended to write may still be strong enough to cause you to pass over the shortcomings of what you actually wrote. It is also a good plan to read the report aloud; then, if it reads easily, you may count upon its being easy to understand. But if in the reading you hesitate at any point, it is the signal for a second look.

REPORTS IN EXAMINATIONS

In the English papers set at their examinations by a number of professional bodies, candidates are frequently called upon to prepare reports and memoranda on a variety of business matters. Sometimes only the barest outline of the circumstances to be reported on is provided, as in the following question, set by the London Chamber of Commerce and Industry.

> Write a report for your general manager on an important trades exhibition which you have attended on behalf of your firm.

Questions of this kind compel candidates to draw on their experience and to exercise their imagination in creating the situations on which they report. They must invent fictitous material so that their reports include enough detail to provide interesting reading as nearly related to real life as possible. Examiners expect that such reports will be long enough, say about 200 words, to display the writer's ability to organize and arrange his material in an effective and convincing way.

Other questions, of which the following is an example taken from a paper set by the Chamber at an examination for the Private Secretary's Diploma, give an outline of the points candidates are required to cover.

> Your employers are proposing that a company library be formed with the aim of making available current technical literature, and of stimulating interest in subjects relevant to the company's activities. No fiction is to be included, but the content of the library is to be as liberal as possible. You are asked to compile a report outlining a scheme for establishing and operating the library. Sections of your report should cover siting of the library; book and journal selection; library service; hours and personnel; conditions of issue; replacement and general buying policy; circulation of journals; cataloguing and inventory, etc.

Even in reports of this kind, where the background material is provided, it is still expected that candidates will use their experience and imagination to help to bring the report alive, and candidates should not hesitate to introduce fictitious material where it is relevant.

Still another type of question will supply details, consisting of facts and ideas from which candidates are required to select those relevant to the specific purpose of the report.

Even candidates with business experience will not always find their first-hand knowledge sufficient for dealing adequately with many of the reports concerned with problems of office organization, typing arrangements, training schemes, selling and advertising schemes, plant extensions, personnel matters and the like. They must supplement their experience from such sources as the daily press, reports of debates in Parliament, reports at shareholders' meetings and articles in association journals and so on. Candidates without business experience must rely entirely on these and similar sources for their information. Unofficial strikes, trade exhibitions, shorter working hours, reports of conferences and on conditions in "new towns" are all among the topics to be found in the exercises that follow this chapter. These and similar topics are frequently the subject of comment and criticism in the sources mentioned. From reading, by attendance at meetings, through conversations with friends and by personal enquiry you should make use of all the opportunities you can to extend your experience and familiarize yourself with topics of current interest, and especially those affecting industry and commerce.

Because of the time factor, reports asked for in most examinations must necessarily be short and, as a rule, presentation in letter form similar to the example on pp. 202—3, will be the most suitable. But if the report forms a main part of the paper, as where it replaces the essay or the précis as in the second of the example questions given above, the examiner will expect a report of some length, when a schematic presentation, subdivided and arranged under headings, may prove to be more suitable.

THE MEMORANDUM

Reports, like letters, are used externally as well as internally within an establishment, but the memorandum is used only within the same establishment. Memoranda also differ from reports in that they are unsolicited and written on the initiative of the persons who present them. An executive will sometimes present what he may term a report to draw attention either to some matter to which he has devoted time, or to circumstances which he feels he should make known. But it is better to refer to voluntary submissions of this kind as *memoranda* and to reserve the term *report* for submissions made in response to requests, or on the instructions of others. A memorandum will usually be headed as follows:

MEMORANDUM	
From	Date . . . .
To	Ref. . . . .
	Subject
Copies to	Signature . . . .
Encl.	

The memorandum is an official form of communication, but it is less formal than an official report and may be written in the first person, and also in note form provided notes can convey the message clearly.

Salutation and complimentary close are both omitted, but the body of the memorandum should be headed to define the subject and, since there are no terms of reference, a short statement at the beginning should explain the circumstances prompting the submission. Space should be provided to indicate to whom copies of the memorandum have been sent and for a statement of any accompanying enclosures. For the rest, the rules that apply to report writing also apply to the memorandum.

EXERCISES

1. Write an account of a football or hockey match, or other sports event, you have witnessed recently.

2. Assume that the principal of your college has asked for an account of the sports facilities provided by your college sports club and for your suggestions as to how they could be improved. Write the report you would submit to him.

3. Prepare a report on any function which you have attended recently, estimating its success and making recommendations for improving similar future functions.

4. Write a report, giving particulars of the course you are taking at school or college, estimate its usefulness to you and, giving reasons, include suggestions as to ways in which you think the course might be improved.

5. Prepare a memorandum for the secretary of the students' union of your college recommending an extension of student activities.

6. You have just returned from a business visit to a foreign capital. Write a confidential report to your general manager, summarizing the results of your errand, and making suitable recommendations.   *(L.C.C.I., Inter.)*

7. Write a report suitable for presentation to the council of one of the "new towns" on the social activities of the young people of the town, making such recommendations as seem desirable to you.   *(L.C.C.I., Inter.)*

8. Write a report for the general manager of a large motor works on the causes, in so far as you have been able to ascertain them, of an unofficial strike, involving about a thousand of the firm's employees, which has seriously interrupted the production of new cars. Make such observations and recommendations as seem desirable to you.   *(L.C.C.I.. Inter.)*

9. Your employer is considering a system of audio-typing at the company's headquarters. The company employs 183 executives, 120 secretaries and shorthand-typists and 30 copy-typists, and the introduction of such a system would have considerable repercussions from both the human and work point of view. You are asked to compile a report, detailing the nature and extent of possible repercussions and offering suggestions on control and corrective methods.   *(L.C.C.I., Priv. Sec. Dip.)*

10. Your employer is head of the publicity department of a holiday resort. He asks you to prepare a report, listing the amenities of the place, detailing the

facilities for holiday-makers, giving all information that they might require and stressing the attractions. The report will form the outline of an article to be used in a journal devoted to holiday haunts. Write the report.

(L.C.C.I., Priv. Sec. Dip.)

11. You are secretary to the chairman of a company employing five hundred office staff. The chairman has asked for your views on two proposals which have been made to him:

(a) that a staff restaurant should be opened, instead of the present system of issuing luncheon vouchers;

(b) that three hundred junior staff at present paid weekly in cash should be paid monthly by bank transfer.

Write a report summarizing your views on *either (a) or (b)*.

(L.C.C.I., Priv. Sec. Dip.)

12. The chairman of the company for which you work is investigating ways in which office procedure could be made more efficient. He is considering, in particular, the introduction of new equipment and the reorganization of staff duties. He wishes to know the views of employees on these matters. Write a memorandum to the chairman, of about two hundred words, indicating your ideas and giving reasons for any changes you may suggest.   *(I.C.S.A. Inter.)*

13. The company for which you work is considering the removal of its office from a building in a crowded city street to premises which are quieter and more spacious but further from the centre. The company wishes to discover the views of its staff about such a change. Write a memorandum to the chairman, of about 150–200 words, expressing your ideas on the subject.

(I.C.S.A.. Inter.)

14. Draft a memorandum to the manager of your organisation to suggest ways of economising in the use of office supplies.   *(I.C.S.A., Inter.)*

15. The company you work for is considering: *(i)* changing its present working hours so that rush-hour travel may be avoided; and *(ii)* introducing a shorter working week if employees are willing to accept a little less time for their lunch break. Write a memorandum to the senior member of staff in charge of these matters, giving your views on the two points and making any relevant suggestions.   *(I.C.S.A., Inter.)*

16. Whilst taking a large sum of money to the bank in the firm's car, you were involved in a collision with a lorry. You were not seriously hurt but were treated in hospital for shock and the car was wrecked. The bag containing the money burst open and twenty pounds were lost. In about 250 words, write a full report of the incident so that your head office can put in an insurance claim.   *(N.W.R.A.C.)*

17. A new refectory block is planned for your college. As secretary of the Students' Union, write a report to the college Catering Committee stating

which aspects of existing catering facilities your members would like to see
continued in the new canteens and what changes they suggest. Your report
may give consideration to such matters as seating, staffing, vending machines,
"no-smoking" areas, menus or anything else you consider important.

$$(N.W.R.A.C.)$$

18. You are the personal assistant of Mr. K. Davison, the manager of Willetts
(Mail Order) Ltd., a firm situated near the centre of Leicester. The firm has 29
employees. The office hours are 8.30 a.m. to 4.30 p.m. but Mr. Davison has
noticed that employees frequently arrive late in the morning. He has asked you
to investigate the causes and prepare a report for him. Here are the facts you
have discovered:

Twelve employees, mostly senior members of the staff, always arrive on
time. They travel by car and are allowed to park in the firm's own car park
behind the office.

The firm's car park can accommodate 17 cars.

Eight employees live on the Gilling Estate, two miles away, and travel to
work by bus. The bus service operates every fifteen minutes. These eight
employees travel on the bus which leaves the Gilling Estate at 8.15 a.m., and
is scheduled to reach to stop just outside the office at 8.26 a.m., but it is
usually several minutes late.

Six employees who come to work on foot are mothers with young children
at school. These employees are often late and the reason they give is that it
takes a long time to get the children off to school.

Three junior members of the staff who travel by car do not have permits
to use the firm's car park. They blame their frequent unpunctuality on
traffic congestion and the difficulty of finding a parking space in the town.

Write the report. You should include any recommendations you consider
appropriate. $$(E.M.E.U.)$$

19. You have had an idea for improving conditions in your college or at
work. The idea you have had may be concerned, for example, with *one* of the
following:— travel and car parking; catering arrangements; safety; changing to
an open-plan office; the purchase of some new equipment; staggering working
hours; or holding an "Open Day". You took the idea to your departmental
head in the hope that he would do something about it. He asked you first to let
him have a written report in which you make clear both your recommendation
and the reasoning behind it. Write the report. $$(E.M.E.U.)$$

PART II

GRAMMAR and SYNTAX

CHAPTER FIFTEEN

Essential Grammar

> Let schoolmasters puzzle their brain,
>   With grammar and nonesense, and learning,
> Good liquor, I stoutly maintain,
>   Gives genius a better discerning.
>
> Goldsmith: *She Stoops to Conquer*

It is not the purpose of this book to provide a comprehensive treatment of grammar and composition; but a study of the sections of grammar that follow may help you to avoid many of the errors that sometimes appear in the routine of business.

THE PARTS OF SPEECH

The special work done by a word in a sentence is called its function. Some words are used to denote the things we speak about; others to say what these things do or have done to them, and so on. There are eight of these functions; they are quite distinctive and easily distinguished. Corresponding to these functions, words are divided into classes called parts of speech, known respectively as nouns, pronouns, adjectives, verbs, adverbs, prepositions, conjunctions, and interjections. To be able to identify the various parts of speech will give you confidence in recognizing the different components of which language is made up.

The rest of this chapter is devoted to a short account of each of these parts of speech. You will find the treatment sufficient to enable you to understand the work of sentence building dealt with in the next chapter.

The noun
The noun is a word used for naming an object of thought. It is the name given to a person *(Mary)*, a place *(St. Albans)*, a quality *(hap-*

piness), an action *(motoring),* or, in fact, to any object of thought about which we want to say something.

Nouns are sometimes classified as follows:

(a) common nouns: everyday objects or ideas:

house, light, flower;

(b) proper nouns: names of persons, places, ships, books, etc. (nouns in this class are spelt with capital letters):

James, Manchester, *s.s.* Eastern Prince, the Pilgrim's Progress;

(c) collective nouns: names of groups or collections: of similar individuals:

flock, committee, tribunal.

The noun phrase

The function performed by a noun may also be performed by groups of words. A group of words that do not by themselves make complete sense is called a phrase, and a phrase that performs the noun function is called a noun phrase.

The financial standing of Mr. Maybank is not in question.

The words in italics form the subject of the sentence and name the object of thought about which the rest of the sentence has something to say. The words form a noun phrase.

The noun clause

A group of words that make complete sense is a sentence. When two or more sentences are combined into a longer sentence they cease to be called sentences and, in relation to the new and longer sentence of which they form part, are called clauses. A clause that performs the noun function is called a noun clause.

We regret *you cannot deliver before the end of the month.*

The words in italics make a sentence. The sentence names the object of the regret, and in the longer sentence becomes a noun clause.

The pronoun

The pronoun is a word used *pro* or *instead of* a noun (e.g. *I, me, mine, he, him, his, she, her, hers),* or for several nouns (e.g. *we, us, ours, they, them, theirs).*

Mr. Wilson told his secretary to type the letters for the director.
    He   her   them   him

Pronouns may also refer to things and actions.

> *It* does not belong to you.
> I don't approve of *that*.
> *What* are you doing?

A pronoun indicates the object of thought without naming it and makes it unnecessary to repeat the same noun over and over again. Consider the following sentence:

> I saw the gardener, and asked the gardener if the gardener would mow the lawn.

By using pronouns we can simplify this sentence considerably and improve its quality, and incidentally its clarity:

> I saw the gardener, and asked *him* if *he* would mow the lawn.

Pronouns are of several different classes.

Personal pronouns
Personal pronouns are so called because they stand for any one of the three persons used with a verb.

(a) First person—the person or persons speaking.

> *I* have just bought a new car.
> My father decided not to come with *us*.

(b) Second person— the person or persons addressed.

> *You* should try to be more punctual.
> This gift is intended for *you*.

(c) Third person—denotes the person or thing spoken about.

> *They* were not successful in the examination.
> You will find *it* in the dining-room.

From these examples you will see that the personal pronoun may be used in the sentence as either subject or object.

Possessive pronouns
Possessive pronouns denote possession, and include: *mine, his, hers, its* (not *it's*, which means *it is*), *ours, yours, theirs, whose.*

> This car is *yours* (i.e. your car).
> The one in the garage is *mine* (i.e. my car).

Relative (or conjunctive, i.e. *connective) pronouns*
The relative pronoun *relates* to some preceding noun or pronoun, called the antecedent. At the same time it performs the function of a conjunction by joining two sentences to form one. The relatives include: *that, which, who* (with forms *whose, whom), what.*

> This is the house *that* Jack built. (i.e. This is the house. Jack built it.)
> She *whom* you met at dinner is my secretary. (i.e. She is my secretary. You met her at dinner.)

To avoid uncertainty a relative pronoun and its antecedent should be kept together in the sentence.

> I waited for a No.38 bus, *which* was 15 minutes late. (The noun *bus* is the antecedent of *which* and comes next to it.)

If other words including a noun come between the pronoun and its antecedent the meaning of the sentence becomes uncertain.

> I have just received the list referred to in the will, *which* had been mislaid. (If *mislaid* is intended to refer to the *list* as antecedent, the sentence will need to be reconstructed.)
> I have just received the will. Included with it is the list, *which* had been mislaid.

There are other classes of pronouns, but they need not concern us here.

EXERCISES

1. Pick out the relative pronouns in the following sentences and name the antecedent of each.

(a) An account that is not regularly made up, presented, and settled is termed a current account.
(b) The receipt that you sent me was for an amount exceeding £2.
(c) The girl who answered the phone is my secretary.
(d) He is a man whom I have often wished to meet.
(e) The clerk whose car was stolen this morning works in the accounts department.
(f) The pen that you found in the corridor is mine.
(g) The book which I recommended is worth reading.
(h) The agent whom we appointed last year has now terminated his agreement.
(i) The results of the examination for which we sat during the summer are not yet published.
(j) The terms of the settlement that were arranged through your Mr. Parker provided for a quarterly account.

2. Copy the following letters, making them read sensibly and smoothly by replacing nouns in parentheses by appropriate pronouns:

(*a*) Dear Mr. Williams,
(Mr. Parker and I) have received your letter of 5 July and will call on you next Monday. (Mr. Parker and I) shall then be prepared to discuss the claim of the manufacturers against (Mr. Parker and me) and make (the manufacturers) an offer of compensation.

Mr. Parker and I very much regret that (the manufacturers) should have had any cause for complaint concerning the consignment referred to by Mr. Williams. There have been no complaints about the earlier (consignments) and it is most unfortunate that there should now be dissatisfaction with the present (consignment).

Yours sincerely
F. Johnson

(*b*) Dear Mr. Bowden
(Mr. Parsons and I) were glad to receive an enquiry from (Mr. Bowden) concerning Dupont & Co. (Mr. Parsons and I) have known this firm for many years. (Dupont & Co.) are in fact very old customers of (Mr. Parsons and me), and you may rely upon (Dupont & Co.) as being a very respectable firm. (Dupont & Co.) pay their accounts well within the time (Mr. Parsons and I) allow for payment of (the accounts), and (Mr. Parsons and I) do not hesitate to allow (Dupont & Co.) credit to an amount considerably beyond the sum mentioned by (J. Bowden).

Yours sincerely
R. Spencer

The adjective

An adjective is a word that amplifies the meaning of a noun or pronoun, at the same time narrowing its application. It is employed to qualify a noun or pronoun that would otherwise have too wide an application. By adding to the meaning of the noun or pronoun the adjective necessarily restricts the number of things to which it can apply, and identifies the object of thought more precisely.

Thus, the noun *piano*, unaccompanied by an adjective, can be applied to any one of countless pianos. But if the adjective *grand* is added the noun so amplified can be applied only to pianos of a certain type. If the meaning of the noun is further amplified by the addition of the word *baby* the application of the noun is still further restricted. The application of the noun *piano* becomes progressively restricted each time its meaning is amplified by the addition of further adjectives. Thus, the phrase:

My baby grand piano

identifies the piano precisely.

The adjective may also qualify a pronoun, as in the sentence:

I will have *this* one; you can have the *other* one.

It may be mentioned that certain adjectives (e.g. *this, that, each, either, some, other, any*) may also be used as pronouns.

I will have *this*; you can have the *other*.

Compound nouns

A noun and an adjective together make a kind of compound noun and in fact many compound nouns, such as *bookstall, halfpence, handwriting,* are today written as single words.

The retention of the hyphen in words such as *time-table, trademark, work-box,* marks an intermediate stage in the development of language from complete separation of adjective and noun in the first place to ultimate complete union. There is indeed a strong modern tendency to dispense with the hyphen in many common words such as *today, tomorrow, tonight, handbook, textbook, stocktaking,* and in future many words now written with the hyphen will no doubt come to be written without it.

Compound adjectives

A compound adjective consists of two or more words related to express a single quality. Together the words form a single adjective and are connected by hyphens to signify their unity.

A *dark-brown* suit; a *world-wide* organization; an *air-tight* container; a *razor-like* edge; the *above-mentioned* facts; an *up-to-date* version; a *never-to-be-forgotten* experience.

There is a strong, and desirable, tendency to dispense with the hyphen in compound adjectives of frequent occurrence, where no awkwardness results from the omission:

A *bloodthirsty* villain; a *lifelong* friend; a *lukewarm* reception; a *fireproof* curtain.

Definite and indefinite article

The definite article *the* (a modification of *that*) and the indefinite articles *a,* and *an* before a vowel, (abbreviated forms of *one*) are, of course, adjectives, since their function in a sentence is to amplify the meaning and narrow the application of the nouns they qualify.

The letter was posted at five o'clock (i.e. the particular letter previously alluded to, or understood).
A letter was found behind the door (i.e. *one* of a number of letters).
An entry was made in the book.

Kinds of adjectives
Adjectives are used in two different ways:

(*a*) to qualify their nouns directly—
   a *difficult* situation; an *angry* parent;

(*b*) to qualify their nouns indirectly—
   The situation is *difficult*. The parent became *angry*.

The first kind of adjective stands with, usually before, its noun, and is known as an attributive adjective because it expresses an attribute. The second kind is used in association with the verb to form the predicate, and is known as a predicative adjective.

Some attributive adjectives denote possession; they are then known as possessive adjectives. Care must be taken not to confuse the possessive adjective with the possessive pronoun.

Possessive adjectives	*Possessive pronouns*
my, our	mine, ours
your	yours
his, her, its	his, hers, its
their	theirs
whose	whose

The adjective phrase
A phrase that performs the function of an adjective is an adjective phrase.

Mine is the desk *near the window.*

The phrase in italics identifies the desk; it is an adjective phrase.

The adjective clause
A clause that performs the function of an adjective is an adjective clause.

We regret that the samples *we sent you last Friday* did not arrive in time.

The clause in italics explains *which samples.* It is an adjective clause.

EXERCISES

1. Supply adjectives corresponding to the following nouns.

access	economy	presumption
account	error	pretence
advantage	example	probation
benefit	felicity	problem
column	habit	regret
commerce	island	remedy
comparison	labour	reputation
conscience	opportunity	secretary
contribution	discipline	spectacle
crisis	practice	terminus

2. Copy the following sentences, inserting any necessary hyphens. *(Caution: not all sentences require them.)*

(a) Arrange for the timber to be cut into three foot lengths.
(b) Even the most prejudiced anti trade unionist cannot object.
(c) I wish to make a long distance call.
(d) A first class ticket to Manchester will cost £10.50.
(e) As a player he is in the first class.
(f) A well written article on the subject appeared in *The Times* last week.
(g) The suggested advertisement will occupy a full page.
(h) A full page advertisement will cost £350.
(i) Various government financed projects have been suggested.
(j) Additional staff have been appointed, both whole time and part time.

3. Explain the different meanings intended by the following sentences and, where necessary, insert articles to make the intended meanings clear.

(a) The Chairman and Managing Director *has* resigned.
   The Chairman and Managing Director *have* resigned.
(b) The whisky and soda *was* on the side-board.
   The whisky and soda *were* on the side-board.
(c) The red and blue flag *floats* high on the tower.
   The red and blue flags *float* high on the tower.
(d) The Youth Fellowship have agreed to provide the *bread and butter*.
   The Youth Fellowship have agreed to provide the *bread and the butter*.
(e) The fourth and last paragraph *is proving* to be the most difficult.
   The fourth and last paragraph *are proving* to be the most difficult.

4. Place in four groups the noun phrases, noun clauses, adjective phrases and adjective clauses printed in italics in the following sentences.

(a) *The delay in delivery* has caused great inconvenience.
(b) The contract *for the purchase of rayon* was a disastrous one.
(c) The typewriter *on the table near the window* is on ten days' approval.
(d) The executive *for whom I work* is a most reasonable person.
(e) *This is hardly the time* to ask why we have run into such difficulties.

(f) We regret *to have to complain* about the quality of the cotton recently delivered.

(g) We find *that the missing dress material was shipped after all.*

(h) We have transferred the premium to a *new policy for the sum of* £5,000.

(i) *Our liability for the damage to the goods* is covered by insurance.

(j) The form *accompanying your letter* was completed and returned yesterday.

The verb

The verb is a word that makes a statement about something else. It is the key word in every sentence, around which the other words revolve. It is not possible to frame a sentence or express a thought without a verb. A verb may indeed form all that part of the sentence which is expressed, the remainder being implied or understood. Thus, we can say *Stop!* to imply that *you* must stop, and the word by itself makes sense. Similarly, with *Laugh! Come! Go!* meaning *you* laugh, *you* come, *you* go.

The verb may make a statement, ask a question, or give an order.

The consignment *arrived* late last night. (A statement.)
Have you *received* the invoice? (A question.)
Invite Mr. Jackson to dinner. (An order.)

Finite and non-finite verbs

Verbs may be finite or non-finite. A finite verb is so called because its use is limited or restricted to a subject in the same person (first, second, or third) and number (singular or plural).

I *come* (first person singular)
You *come* (second person singular)
He (she, it) *comes* (third person singular)
We ⎫
You ⎬ *come* (plural, all three persons)
They ⎭

You will notice that the verb forms in these examples are restricted to their respective subjects through person and number. *Comes,* for example, is restricted to the third person singular and cannot be used for any but a singular subject in the third person. These forms of verb are, therefore, *finite* or *limited* to particular subjects and cannot be used generally for all subjects.

The non-finite forms of a verb are those which, by themselves, cannot say anything about a subject, e.g. *to come, coming.* They may, however, be converted into finite verb forms by use in association with other verbs, called auxiliary verbs.

I shall (to) come (omitting the preposition)
I was coming
We should be coming

Auxiliary verbs

In the last example *coming* is associated with two other verbs to make the finite verb form *should be coming*. *Coming* is the main verb; the verbs *should be* merely "help" the main verb to say something, and are therefore called auxiliary or helping verbs.

Active and passive verbs

Verbs may also be classified as *active* or *passive*. Active verbs are those whose subject *does something* to something or someone else.

> The secretary *typed* the letter.

Passive verbs are those whose subject is said to *suffer something* from something or someone else.

> The letter *was typed* by the secretary.

Verbs used passively tend to make a statement more impersonal; they are sometimes used in this way to convey unpopular news with which the communicator does not wish to be personally associated.

> Your claim for compensation *is not accepted.*

Mood in the verb

The mood of a verb shows the mode or manner in which the action of the verb is performed, i.e. whether it expresses a statement, a command, a wish, or the like. There are three finite moods.

(a) The indicative makes a statement, positive or negative, or asks a question.

> We came home yesterday (positive).
> He will not arrive till tomorrow (negative).
> When did you come home? (interrogative).

(b) The imperative expresses a positive or negative command, or advises.

> Bring me a drink (positive).
> Don't do that (negative).
> Be good and you are sure to be happy (advice).

(c) The subjunctive is used to express doubt, supposition, wishing, indeed anything rather than a fact.

> If he *comes,* I shall leave.
> Though it *kill* me, I will do it.

The subjunctive mood is old-fashioned and the verb *to be* is the only verb now used in the subjunctive to any extent. It survives mainly in the use of *were* for the first and third persons of the past tense, as often as not in *"If"* constructions.

> I wish I *were* (for *was*) coming with you (first person).
> If he *were* (for *was*) to fall he would hurt himself (third person).

The adverb

What an adjective does for a noun or pronoun an adverb does for any other part of speech—it amplifies the meaning of the word and thereby narrows its application. The part of speech limited or modified in this way may be a verb, an adjective, another adverb, or even a preposition or a conjunction.*

> Some people find it difficult to spell *correctly* (modifying the verb *spell*).
> He is an *intensely* keen musician (modifying the adjective *keen*).
> She plays the piano *remarkably* well (modifying the adverb *well*).
> The organ was built *just* under the gallery (modifying the preposition *under*).
> We are offering it to you, *only* because you are one of our best customers (modifying the conjunction *because*).

The adverb may similarly modify a whole sentence.

> *Unfortunately,* I was not in when you called.

In accordance with the general rule of proximity (*see* pp. 259—60) adverbs are placed as near as possible to the words they modify:

(a) immediately after verbs, but   as in the
(b) immediately before other parts of speech   above examples

In compound tenses the adverb may be placed immediately after the auxiliary.

> He had *suddenly* noticed the letter.

Positioning of the adverb is important; it sometimes affects meaning.

---

*An adverb cannot modify an interjection, since an interjection is not, properly speaking, a part of speech (*see* p. 235).

He is *also* taking his case to court (i.e. he is doing other things besides).

He *also* is taking his case to court (i.e. there are others doing the same thing).

The adverbial phrase

A phrase that performs the function of an adverb is an adverbial phrase.

We should like to hear from you *as soon as possible.*

The phrase in italics answers the question *hear when?* It is an adverbial phrase.

The adverbial clause

A clause that performs the function of an adverb is an adverbial clause.

When he had finished speaking the manager rang for me.

The clause in italics modifies the verb *rang;* it is an adverbial clause.

EXERCISES

1. Construct sentences using each of the following commercial terms as *(i)* a noun, *(ii)* a verb.

(a) combine, transfer, report, credit, guarantee.

(b) order, return, market, supply, stamp.

(c) refund, commission, sample, tender, export.

(d) stock, invoice, estimate, advance, account.

(e) contract, discount, indent, mortgage, share.

2. Copy the following sentences, selecting from the alternatives given in brackets the correct form of the finite verb.

(a) The entire system of road and rail communications (appear, appears) to be closely co-ordinated.

(b) It is one of the finest tributes that (has, have) been paid to any man.

(c) Tales from Shakespeare (was, were) written by Charles and Mary Lamb.

(d) We have received two reports from our surveyor neither of which (seem, seems) encouraging.

(e) Everyone, as all are aware, (know, knows) the answer.

(f) A large crowd of men, women and children (is, are) gathered in the square.

(g) The chairman, with the directors, (deny denies) the reports circulated.

(h) Your car, and mine too, (need, needs) overhauling.

(i) Economics (is, are) nowadays included as a subject in most professional examinations.

(j) A large number of applications (has, have) been received.

3. Place in three groups the adverbs, adverb phrases, and adverb clauses printed in italics in the following sentences.

(a) I will meet you at *two o'clock tomorrow afternoon.*
(b) *As soon as the new session begins* we shall join typewriting classes.
(c) The tribunal dealt with the case *fairly.*
(d) You will find the papers *in the right-hand tray on my desk.*
(e) *Now and then* I am required to help in the wages office.
(f) We shall attend to your order *as soon as supplies are received from the manufacturers.*
(g) *The urgent letters having been dealt with,* we were able to relax.
(h) She writes shorthand *nearly as fast as I do.*
(i) *When* will you be taking up your new post?
(j) The consignment was delayed *because of the dock strike.*

The preposition
The preposition is a word that shows the relation in which one thing stands to another. It always comes immediately before a noun (or the equivalent of a noun). It is for this reason that the word is called a *pre-position.* The noun or noun-equivalent is known as the object. The function of the preposition is to show in what relation this object stands to some preceding word in the sentence.

The letter *in* the tray.
The letter *under* the tray.
The letter *behind* the tray.

In, under, and *behind* all link together the words *letter* and *tray,* and express the relationship between them.
Similarly in:

We correspond *with* an agent in Australia (correspond—agent).
Shakespeare was born *at* Stratford-upon-Avon *in* Warwickshire (born—Stratford; Stratford—Warwickshire).

Certain words are always followed by special prepositions. No definite rules can be given, the use of the special prepositions being a matter of what is called *idiom,* that is, the accepted mode of expression. Apart from custom, there often seems no particular reason why one preposition should be used rather than another; yet the use of the right preposition is one of the principal tests of ability to speak and write good English.
The following is a list of the more common prepositional phrases:

absolve *from* (blame)   adequate *to* (or *for*)
accede *to* (a request)   agree *to* (a proposal)

accompanied *by* (not *with*,
   e.g., a friend)
acquiesce *in* (a suggestion)
acquit *of* (a charge)
adapt *to* (a thing)
adapt *for* (a purpose)
adapt *from* (something previously done)
approve *of* (a thing)
associate *with* (a person)
averse *from* (or *to*)
centre *in* (or *on*, never *round*,
   e.g. the mind)
compare *to* (when comparing
   one thing to another)
compare *with* (when comparing
   resemblances and differences
   between two things)
compatible *with* (a condition)
compensate *for* (a loss)
comply *with* (a request)
concerned *at* (some occurrence)
concerned *for* (someone's welfare)
concur *in* (not *with*, e.g. a
   suggestion)
conducive *to* (an effect)
confer *on* (a subject)
confer *with* (a person)
confide *in* (i.e. place confidence in)
confide *to* (i.e. entrust to)
conform *to* (a pattern)
connive *at* (an act)
conscious *of* (a circumstance)
consequent *upon* (an event)
consist *of* (i.e. composed of)
consist *in* (defines the subject
   referred to)
contemporary *with* (a person or
   thing)
contrary *to* (a belief)
conversant *with* (a thing)
correspond *to* (a thing)
correspond *with* (a person)
defer *to* (an opinion)
derive *from* (a thing)
desist *from* (an action)
differ *from* (a person in some
   quality)

agree *with* (a person)
agree *upon* (a plan)
amenable *to* (an idea)
analogous *to* (a thing)
angry *at* (a thing)
angry *with* (a person)
anxious *for* (someone's
   recovery)
anxious *about* (an event)
differ *with* (a person in
   opinion)
different *from* (no longer *to*)
divide *between* (two)
divide *among* (more than two)
encroach *on* (or *upon*)
enter *upon* (a duty)
enter *into* (an agreement)
impatient *with* (a person)
impatient *at* (an event or circumstance)
impatient *of* (criticism)
interfere *in* (a matter)
interfere *with* (a person)
invest *in* (an enterprise)
invest *with* (authority)
jump *at* (a bargain)
jump *to* (a conclusion)
oblivious *of* (not *to*, e.g. his
   surroundings)
opposite *to* (a thing)
part *from* (a friend)
part *with* (money)
personal *to* (an individual)
presume *on* (a kindness)
prevail *upon* (not *on*, e.g. a person)
profit *by* (experience)
profuse *in* (apologies)
reconcile *with* (a friend)
reconcile *to* (a condition)
replace *by* (not *with*, e.g. something
   else)
similar *to* (a thing)
substitute *for* (not *by*, e.g.
   something else)
synonymous *with* (a thing)
tendency *to* (an action)
tendency *towards* (a state)
typical *of* (a person or thing)

There is a half-hearted rule that the preposition, being a link word, should not come at the end of a sentence. For formal written work this may be good advice, but strict observance of the rule frequently produces a forced artificiality that it is better to avoid.

What are you doing that <u>for</u>? has a smoother flow and a more natural ring than *<u>for</u> what are you doing that?* and *It is something I will not put up <u>with</u>* is certainly better than *It is something up <u>with</u> which I will not put.*

The conjunction

The conjunction is a word used to join together sentences expressing related ideas.

> The pitch was water-logged, *and* the match could not be played.
> The manager is unpopular *because* he is ill-tempered.

The conjunction must not be used where there is no relation between the ideas separately expressed. One cannot say:

> The manager is unpopular *and* there will be a full moon tonight.

The conjunction is also used to join words and phrases, as well as sentences.

> Secretary *and* accountant are both at the meeting.
> It was left to the Chairman to decide the date of the next meeting, *as well as* the place.

The conjunction is simply a connecting word and, unlike the preposition, does not denote a relationship between the words and phrases joined, e.g.

> We adjourned to the lounge *after* dinner was finished (conjunction).
> One should rest awhile *after* dinner (preposition).

Both prepositions and conjunctions are linking words, but the preposition may readily be distinguished from the conjunction, since it is always followed by an object consisting of a noun, or noun-equivalent. The conjunction, on the other hand, is not followed by an object, but has the simple function of joining words, phrases, and sentences.

Conjunctions are divided into three classes—co-ordinative, subordinative, and correlative. Do not allow these technical terms to worry you. They are quite simply explained.

Conjunctions that co-ordinate

A co-ordinating conjunction is one that joins together words and sentences of equal grammatical value; hence the name *co-ordinate,* which means of *equal status.* Neither of the words or sentences joined by a co-ordinating conjunction is in any way dependent upon the other, or in any way enters into the construction of the other.

> Norway *and* Sweden together form Scandinavia.
> I must go tonight, *otherwise* I shall be too late.
> I have made a mistake, *but* I could not help it.

In the larger sentences of which they become part, the separate sentences joined by conjunctions are known as clauses.

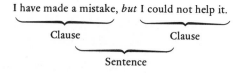

Conjunctions that subordinate

One clause is said to be subordinate to another when it depends upon that other, thus forming part of its construction. The clause on which the subordinate or dependent clause depends is called the principal or main clause.

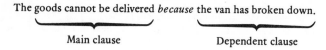

A subordinate or dependent clause may perform the function of a noun, adjective or adverb.

Main clause	Con-junction	Dependent clause	Function performed
We hope	*that*	the goods will reach you in good time.	Noun
This is the office	*where*	I started work.	Adjective
I cannot leave	*until*	I have finished these letters.	Adverb

A dependent clause may also be introduced by a relative pronoun.

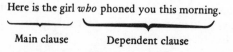

The following are among the conjunctions commonly used:

Co-ordinating	Subordinating
and	after
but	although
however	because
nevertheless	before
or	if
otherwise	since
then	that
therefore	unless
yet	until
	where
	while

Conjunctions used in pairs
When conjunctions are used in pairs they are said to be correlative.

both . . . and
either . . . or
if . . . then
neither . . . nor
not only }
not merely} . . . {but also
           {but even
rather . . . than
whether . . . or

Each word in a correlative conjunction must be accompanied by its own partner. Thus, *either* must always be followed by *or,* and *neither* by *nor.*

> *Not only* is she a good pianist, *but* she *also* plays the violin well.
> I am undecided *whether* to go tomorrow, *or* to wait until next week.
> I would *rather* go to work *than* go to school.

Conjunctions and Prepositions
Some words may be used both as conjunctions and as prepositions.

> A wide expanse of beautiful country lay *before* me (preposition).
> I want to be at the station in good time *before* the train leaves (conjunction).
> I cannot decide *until* tomorrow (preposition).
> I cannot decide *until* I see you tomorrow (conjunction).

The interjection
The interjection is a word *interjected* or *thrown into* a sentence to express some feeling or emotion, but it forms no part of the grammatical structure of the sentence.

> Alas!   Oh!   Hurrah!

Groups of words such as *What a pity!* (i.e. What a pity it is), *How disappointing!* (i.e. How disappointing it is) are not interjections, but elliptical sentences, i.e. sentences not fully expressed. Nor are words such as *Go! Hurry! Listen!* interjections; they are complete sentences, the subjects of which are not expressed.

Go! means YOU *go;* Hurry!— YOU *hurry;* Listen— YOU *listen.*

The two most important parts of speech are the noun and the verb; both are, in fact, indispensable. Without either of them intelligible communication between persons is impossible. Other parts of speech serve the purpose of extending the use of the noun or verb to enable different shades of meaning to be conveyed.

WORD GROUPS

As we have seen, the functions performed by certain parts of speech may also be performed by groups of words.

To reply to an enquiry is no more than common courtesy.

The words in italics form a phrase equivalent to a noun, because they name the object of thought that forms the subject of the verb.

The book *that was lost* was found yesterday.

This means that *the lost book* was found yesterday. The words in italics form a clause equivalent to an adjective, because they describe or further define the book.

The manager rang for him *as soon as he had finished speaking.*

This means that the manager rang for him immediately. The words in italics form a clause equivalent to an adverb, because they modify the verb *rang*.

EXERCISES

1. Supply the correct prepositions to fill the gaps in the following sentences.

A

(a) John deferred _____ Mr. Harvey's greater experience and did not press his preference _____ a bolder policy.

(*b*) Yours is a very different story_____ the one I heard yesterday.

(*c*) The employer was averse_____giving details concerning the profits of the firm.

(*d*) Genius consists_____ an infinite capacity for taking pains.

(*e*) We may correspond_____them on the subject, but politely point out that their accusations do not correspond_____the facts.

(*f*) I agree_____ you _____the proposals for an extension to the premises.

(*g*) My friend was impatient_____me, and also_____the suggestion I made.

(*h*) This sketch has been adapted_____the play by us, and is quite suitable _____ children.

(*i*) The whole question centres_____the results of the examination.

(*j*) He is likely to be acquitted_____ stealing.

B

(*a*) I will confer the powers_____you.

(*b*) I will make an early opportunity to confer_____the family_____the matter raised.

(*c*) It is typical_____him that he should wish to be reconciled_____his friend.

(*d*) I hope to prevail_____ her not to replace the model_____a more recent one.

(*e*) Every typist should be conversant_____the basic rules of grammar.

(*f*) The smaller amount was divided_____the two sisters, and the larger _____ the four brothers.

(*g*) Engrossed in her novel she was oblivious_____the storm outside.

(*h*) I take the precisely opposite view_____the one you yourself hold.

(*i*) The children entered_____the task of memorizing the poem.

(*j*) It would be unwise to interfere_____ the couple_____the plans they are making for their holiday.

2. We *accuse* a person *of* some wrongful act. What prepositions are used after the following?

adequate; amenable; acquiesce; associate; confide; compatible; conduce; derive; desist; contrary.   (*R.S.A. Inter.*)

3. Use each of the following conjunctions in a sentence of your own construction.

although	that
because	then
both . . . and	therefore
neither . . . nor	unless
otherwise	yet

4. Write a sentence which contains all the following, and indicate where each of them occurs in it.

    (a) a relative pronoun;
    (b) an infinitive verb;
    (c) a conjunction;
    (d) an adverbial clause;
    (e) a passive construction.

CHAPTER SIXTEEN

Sentence Building

The turn of a sentence has decided the fate of many a friendship, and, for aught we know, the fate of many a kingdom.

Jeremy Bentham

A sentence is a combination of words expressing a complete thought and making complete sense. The sentence may be one of four kinds. It may:

(*a*) make a statement

A bird in the hand is worth two in the bush.

(*b*) ask a question

How long have you been learning Spanish?

(c) issue a command

Take this letter to the post.

(*d*) be an exclamation

What a lovely day it is!

SUBJECT AND PREDICATE

But whatever its form, and however long or short, the sentence always consists of two parts, the *naming* part or subject and the *doing* part or predicate. The subject is the word or words that denote what we are talking or writing about. The predicate consists of the word or words used to say something about the subject, and must contain a verb, for otherwise no expression of thought is possible. The subject, on the other hand, as in example *(c)*, may be omitted as being understood.

Subject	*Predicate*
(a) A bird in the hand	is worth two in the bush.
(b) You	have been learning Spanish how long?
(c) (You)	take this letter to the post.
(d) It	is what a lovely day!

In speech we frequently use groups of words, or even single words, that are not sentences, but which perform the work of sentences when used in a context that supplies the missing element needed to make sense. *Tomorrow morning* standing by itself is meaningless, but in the context of the question *When can you deliver the goods?* it becomes intelligible as a part of a sentence which, when expressed in full, would read *We can deliver the goods tomorrow.*

There are also situations where even a single word serves as a complete communication unit; in reply to a question.

Did you attend the meeting last night? *Yes.*
Which do prefer, opera or ballet? *Ballet.*

These single words are not sentences, but as units of communication they serve the same purpose.

When issuing commands and instructions to a person or group we do not as a rule include a grammatical subject. We say, *Stop; Mind the step; Report to me next Friday; Give me a week to think about it.* In each case we address the person or group directly and so there is no need to include *You* as the subject element of the sentences.

PHRASES AND CLAUSES

All the examples on the previous page consist of simple sentences, because each contains only one verb and expresses only one thought. But if language were restricted to the use of simple sentences monotony would result. To afford variety and interest of speech and writing this simple structure of the sentence is often extended and elaborated by the inclusion of word patterns in the form of phrases and clauses. The difference between the phrase and clause is that the clause contains a finite verb, but the phrase does not. Consider the following.

I well remember the house.
I well remember the house *on the hill.*
I well remember the house *that stood on the hill.*

On the hill is a phrase; *that stood on the hill* is a clause, because it contains a finite verb, *stood.* By helping to identify the house both phrase and clause perform the function of an adjective and are, therefore, the equivalent of adjectives (see above, p. 225).

KINDS OF CLAUSES

Phrases and clauses may also perform the functions of nouns and adverbs (see above pp. 220, 230).

The adjective clause
The function of the adjective clause is to define or qualify some noun or pronoun in another clause. In so doing a clause simply performs the work of an adjective proper.

All adjective clauses are introduced by relative pronouns or their equivalents, either expressed or understood. As a rule, the relative pronoun is placed next to the noun to which it is related.

Main clause	Adjective clause
It is an ill wind	*that* blows no-one any good (pronoun).
The plate marks the spot	*where* (meaning "on which") King Charles stood his trial (pronoun equivalent).
The explanation is satisfactory	*(which)* you gave me (pronoun understood).

Care must be taken not to confuse the adjective clause, the function of which is to define or qualify some word in another clause, with that type of main clause which is similarly introduced by a relative pronoun or pronoun equivalent, but which makes a separate and independent statement.

Main clause	Adjective clause
We called at the office	where I started my career (explaining which office).
This is the house	which was built by my father (explaining which house).
Here comes the girl	who is eighteen today (explaining which girl).

Each of the above sentences makes only one statement, but in the following sentences the second clause does not qualify any word in the first; it makes a separate statement that is independent of the statement made by the first clause. Each sentence makes two statements.

Main clause	Main clause
We called at John's office,	where (meaning "and there") I started my career.
This is St. Paul's Cathedral,	which (meaning "and it") was built by Wren.
Here comes Miss Jones,	who (meaning "and she") is eighteen today.

The last three sentences could have been written as follows to give precisely the same meaning.

We called at John's office.	I started by career there.
This is St. Paul's Cathedral.	It was built by Wren.
Here comes Miss Jones.	She is eighteen today.

The adjective clause can always be distinguished because it answers the question *which?* e.g. which office? which house? which girl?

If, on the other hand, the introductory pronoun or equivalent can be replaced by a connective phrase such as *and there, and it, and she,* as in the examples of two linked main clauses above, then the clause introduced is a main clause, whose function is not to define any word in the preceding clause but to make a separate and independent statement of its own.

In the matter of punctuation it should be noted that a comma should never be used to separate the adjective clause from the word in the main clause that it is intended to define.

The adverbial clause

An adverbial clause is one that does the work of an adverb of any kind.

Main clause	Adverbial clause
The man stood	where I could see him (place).
We were late for the theatre	because the car broke down (reason).
The men fought	as if they were demons (manner).
The sea is deep	as the mountains are high (comparison).

The adverbial clause may, and often does, precede the main clause.

Adverbial clause	Main clause
If it is fine	I shall go hiking tomorrow (condition).
When the dentist came in	my tooth stopped aching (time).
So that you may be convinced	I will provide proof (purpose).
Although he was poor	he was honest (concession).

The noun clause

A noun clause is one that does the work of a noun.

A noun may perform a variety of functions, and a noun clause can be similarly used:

(*a*) sometimes as subject of a verb;

(*b*) sometimes as object of verb or preposition;

(*c*) sometimes as verb complement (i.e. words without which the verb is meaningless);

(*d*) sometimes in apposition to a noun (i.e. referring to the same thing).

In the following sentences the noun clauses are printed in italics.

What you have achieved will make you famous (subject of verb *will make*).
She really believed *there were ghosts in the house* (object of verb *believed*).
The horse will sell for *what it is worth* (object of preposition *for*).
This seems to be *what he bargained for* (complement of verb *seems to be*).
The rumour *that war had been declared* was unfounded (in apposition to the noun *rumour*).

Constructions in which a noun clause forms the subject of a verb often sound cumbersome and affected.

That his name appeared in the Honours List is true.

Noun clause

That we should have to pay one hundred and fifty pence a gallon for petrol

is ridiculous.   Noun clause

The modern tendency is to avoid using a noun clause at the beginning of a sentence and instead to use *It* as a provisional subject. The noun-clause subject is then placed at the end and is said to be *in apposition* to the provisional subject *It*.

It is true *that his name appeared in the Honours List.*
It is ridiculous *that we should have to pay one hundred and fifty pence a gallon for petrol.*

HOW TO RECOGNIZE CLAUSES

A clause can always be recognized because it contains a verb and has a subject and predicate of its own. What type of clause it is will depend, not upon its form, but upon its function. For example, the clause *when we were married* may serve as either adjective, adverb, or noun equivalent.

> The day *when we were married* was a memorable one (adjective clause qualifying *day*).
>
> *When we were married* we bought a bungalow (adverb clause of time to the verb *bought*).
>
> I shall never forget the day *when we were married* (noun clause, object of verb *shall forget*).

EXERCISES

1. From each of the following phrases form a complete sentence by adding a suitable predicate.

(a) Your letter of 15 July . . .
(b) With regard to the question of insurance, we . . .
(c) Four cases, each containing 500 metres of cloth . . .
(d) The reason for the increase in price . . .
(e) Confirmation of your order . . .
(f) The spare parts for the machine . . .
(g) The consignment that left here on the 14th . . .
(h) The cheque contained in your letter of yesterday . . .
(i) The terms of our offer . . .
(j) The explanation you gave . . .

2. Avoiding the use of pronouns, form sentences by adding suitable subjects to the following predicates.

(a)   . . . awaits your reply with interest.
(b)   . . . makes it necessary to keep our prices as low as possible.
(c)   . . . should reach you in good time.
(d)   . . . is reduced to a minimum.
(e)   . . . awaits further instructions.
(f)   . . . are not easy to overcome.
(g)   . . . caused considerable damage.
(h)   . . . will receive our careful attention.
(i)   . . . is as required for Customs purposes.
(j)   . . . causes endless expense.

3. Write out the main clauses in the following passages.

(a) Letter of Introduction

I have much pleasure in introducing Mr. James Hawkins, who has been a member of the clerical staff of this firm for the past five years. Owing to his wife's illness it is necessary for him to move to the south coast, where he hopes to obtain work as a book-keeper.

If you have a vacancy in your accounts department I should like you to consider Mr. Hawkins for it. He has had good accounting experience with us and we have always found him to be very conscientious and trustworthy.

(b) Letter of Recommendation

In reply to your enquiry of 3 April, I am glad to be able to report favourably on Messrs. Dupont & Co. They are a small but highly respectable firm and very old customers of ours, and have been established for nearly thirty years.

They do not as a rule qualify for cash discounts, but on the other hand they pay their accounts promptly. We ourselves have no hesitation in giving them credit to an amount considerably beyond the sum you mention.

(c) Circular

We regret to inform you that our premises at 17 Broad Street were partly destroyed by fire earlier this week. Fortunately, we have been able to obtain temporary factory accommodation at 25—27 Morley Road and hope by the end of this week to be able to fulfil the orders we now have on hand, including your own.

Although the damage to our premises is serious, production will not be unduly hampered, and we look forward to a continuance of your own custom, which we have always valued.

(d) Letter Regarding Agency

Thank you for your letter of 20 June. We are glad you think that a good market can be found for our goods, but confess that credit on the scale you mention opens up a far from attractive prospect.

We are, however, quite willing to appoint you *del credere* agent on a basis of 20% commission if, as we presume, you are willing to lodge adequate security with our bankers here.

Provided security is deposited we shall of course be willing to safeguard your own position by entering into a formal agreement giving you the sole agency for a period of five years.

Will you please let us know whether you are willing to accept the agency on the terms mentioned.

4. State which of the following clauses, printed in italics, are *adjective clauses* and which *main clauses.*

(a) I read through the policy, *which gave me all the information I wanted.*

(b) The director *whom you met this morning* is in charge of our sales department.

(c) Mr. Jackson, *whose salary is £15,000 a year,* is our managing director.

(d) The letter *which we received from our sales representative this morning* is enclosed for you to see.

(e) We visited the warehouse *where the fire had started.*

(f) We are sending you a consignment of sisal, *which please dispose of on the best terms possible.*

(g) You promised to send us a cheque, *which we have not yet received.*

(h) You will find details in the report *which is enclosed.*

(i) The delay *of which you complained* was caused by a strike in our export department.

(j) The directors adjourned to the board room, *where the proposal was discussed in detail.*

5. Using a table similar to the following analyse the sentences given below into main and subordinate clauses. In the last column name the type of subordinate clause (adjective, adverb, or noun) and state the function it performs in the sentence.

Examples

(a) We understand from the owners that the vessel will not arrive until Monday.

(b) The invoice which you mentioned in your letter was not enclosed.

Sentence	Main clause	Subordinate clause	Type and function
(a)	We understand from the owners	that the vessel will not arrive until Monday	Noun, object of *understand*
(b)	The invoice was not enclosed	which you mentioned in your letter.	Adjective, qualifying *invoice.*

(c) You may rest assured that your interests will be attended to carefully.
(d) As the factory is very busy we cannot guarantee delivery before Saturday.
(e) The fact that a fire occurred in our warehouse will not affect delivery.
(f) We shall be glad to know whether there is a prospect of early delivery.
(g) Thank you for the catalogue which you left for me to see.
(h) If money transactions are on a large scale cheques are more convenient than cash.
(i) Commerce is wider than trade, because it includes commercial operations other than trade.
(j) The customer who had been examining the patterns placed a large order.
(k) As soon as you have finished typing the letters I will sign them.
(l) The company we formed in 1950 had branches in all parts of the country.

6. Expand each of the main clauses given below by adding a suitable subordinate clause, and state the type of clause you add. (The added clause need not necessarily be at the end.)

(a) We have received the letter . . .
(b) We are prepared to allow you a special discount . . .
(c) The closing sentence in your letter promises to overcome the difficulty . . .
(d) The directors visited the warehouse . . .
(e) With this letter we are enclosing an invoice . . .
(f) The salesman made a good impression . . .
(g) We have passed the claim to our insurance department . . .
(h) The office manager was absent today . . .
(i) The goods are required for shipment abroad . . .
(j) We trust the explanation will be satisfactory . . .

7. Use the following clauses in sentences of your own making and state whether the clause, as used, is an adjective, adverbial, or noun clause.

(a) whom   we met recently
(b) how the damage occurred
(c) which we built at a cost of £7,000
(d) where the conference was held
(e) to whom we wrote last week
(f) where the fire broke out
(g) as soon as we can
(h) which was granted immediately
(i) before we were expected
(j) that you are mistaken

8. Construct sentences to include each of the following clauses (i) as an adjective clause, (ii) as an adverbial clause, (iii) as a noun clause.

(a) when the work is completed
(b) where the secretary lives
(c) when I receive your cheque
(d) where the meeting is to be held

SENTENCE STRUCTURE

To analyse a sentence means to break it into its component grammatical parts for the purpose of determining the relationship of these parts to one another. The structure of the sentence may be:

(a) simple;
(b) compound;
(c) complex;
(d) compound-complex.

The simple sentence
This is the sentence in its simplest form. It contains only one finite verb and can therefore make one, and only one, complete and independent statement.

Wealthy people are not always the happiest.

The compound sentence
A compound sentence is one consisting of two or more co-ordinate main clauses, that is clauses of equal grammatical value, none of which is in any way dependent upon any other, or in any way enters into the construction of the other.

It is formed by linking together two or more simple sentences by the use of co-ordinating conjunctions (see above p. 234).

> She arrived in England last February.
> She sang in my opera.   } Three simple sentences
> She was not a success.

Linking these sentences we have:

> She arrived in England last February, *and* (she) sang in my opera, *but* (she) was not a success.

This forms a compound sentence, better expressed by the omission of the pronouns in brackets.

The complex sentence
The complex sentence consists of two parts:

(a) one main clause; and

(b) one or more subordinate clauses, which may be adjective, adverbial or noun clauses, linked to the main clause.

> The man *who lives next door* is an architect (adjective clause).
> She will succeed *because she is persevering* (adverbial clause).
> I know *that my Redeemer liveth* (noun clause).

The following complex sentence includes two subordinate clauses.

(a) When he learned (adverbial clause modifying *left* in clause *(c)*)
(b) that you could not see him (noun clause, object of *learned* in clause *(a)*)
(c) he left immediately (main clause).

The following complex sentence includes three subordinate clauses.

(a) The representative (subject of main clause)
(b) who called this morning (adjective clause qualifying *representative*)
(c) when you were out (adverbial clause modifying *called*, in clause *(b)*)
(d) promised (verb forming predicate of main clause)
(e) (that) *he would call again* (noun clause forming object of *promised*).

The compound-complex sentence
We often meet with sentences that are neither wholly compound (two or more main clauses) nor wholly complex (one main clause and one or more subordinate clauses), but a mixture of both. Such sentences are called *compound-complex.* They consist of:

(a) two or more main clauses (like a compound sentence);
plus
(b) one or more subordinate clauses (like the complex sentence).

(a) As soon as the enemy had left it (adverbial clause modifying *entered* in clause *(b)*)

(b) he entered the town (main clause)

and

(c) (he) occupied the largest building (main clause)

(d) (that) *he could find* (adjective clause qualifying *building* in clause *(c)*).

EXERCISES

1. Say whether each of the following sentences is simple, compound, or complex.

(a) The ship, carrying a load of timber from the Baltic, put into Kiel for repairs.

(b) The ship, which was carrying a load of timber, put into Kiel.

(c) The ship was carrying a load of timber and put into Kiel for repairs.

(d) There have been disturbances in Algeria, which may have the effect of bringing about an improvement in prices.

(e) The disturbances in Algeria may have the effect of raising prices.

(f) There have been disturbances in Algeria and a rise in prices is likely to be the result.

(g) The paper we have been using is unsatisfactory because it will not keep its colour on the walls.

(h) Because of its tendency to fade the paper we have been using is unsatisfactory.

(i) The paper does not keep its colour on the walls and is therefore unsatisfactory.

(j) The paper, being liable to discoloration, is unsatisfactory.

2. Turn each of the following sentences into a compound or complex sentence, stating whether your sentence is compound or complex.

(a) Having dealt with the firm for so many years I have no hesitation in recommending them.

(b) I had the pleasure of meeting your director yesterday for the first time.

(c) The premises in Victoria Park are for sale.

(d) The ship sailed from the Port of London at dawn.

(e) We are enclosing samples showing the various colours we stock.

(f) Prices, including delivery to your works, can be arranged.

(g) Acting on the instructions of the chairman, the secretary signed the contract.

(h) To help you to decide we are sending you samples separately.

(i) Having heard of your recent move into the district we are sending you a copy of our catalogue.

(j) We thank you for your letter enclosing a copy of your latest price-list.

CHARACTERISTICS OF THE GOOD SENTENCE

Since we express our thoughts in sentences, the sentence should be regarded as the unit of composition. If we wish to write a good piece of composition we must first learn how to write a good sentence. To consider how this is done let us examine three aspects of the sentence:

   (a) its form;
   (b) its length;
   (c) the qualities it should possess—clarity, unity, coherence, and variety of structure.

The form of the sentence

There are two forms of sentence—the loose and the periodic.

The loose sentence

The distinguishing characteristic of the loose sentence is that it makes the principal statement at the beginning. It is in fact a grammatically complete statement followed by one or more explanatory or qualifying phrases or clauses. It continues running on after grammatical completeness has been reached and when it may be thought that the sentence has come to an end.

> *We are not surprised to learn that the cheque has been dishonoured,* / as there have been rumours that the financial position of the drawers is unsatisfactory / on account of their inability to raise capital / necessary to finance their new extensions.

The main idea in this sentence is contained in the first clause. The sentence is grammatically complete at the word *dishonoured* and could have finished there. It could also have finished at either of the other two line divisions.

The periodic sentence

The distinguishing characteristic of the periodic sentence is that it reserves the principal statement for the end. It is not grammatically complete until the end of the sentence is reached, and in consequence the mind of the reader is kept in suspense until the sentence is finished.

> As there have been rumours that the financial position of the drawers is unsatisfactory on account of their inability to raise capital necessary to finance their new extensions, *we are not surprised to learn that the cheque has been dishonoured.*

Loose and periodic sentences compared

Loose	Periodic
I have written to the man's employer, / as suggested.	As suggested, *I have written to the man's employer.*
We do not feel justified in declaring a dividend / until these claims have been settled.	Until these claims have been settled, *we do not feel justified in declaring a dividend.*
It is a matter of serious concern to us / that your account has remained unpaid for so long.	That your account has remained unpaid for so long *is a matter of serious concern to us.*
Your daughter will be given a copy of her new time-table / when she reports next Monday / and has paid the tuition fees / due for the term.	When your daughter reports next Monday and has paid the tuition fees due for the term, *she will be given a copy of her new time-table.*
The steps taken at the time were justified, / since there were no circumstances that would have caused anyone to suspect / there was anything wrong.	Since there were no circumstances that would have caused anyone to suspect there was anything wrong, *the steps taken at the time were justified.*

In the examples given of loose sentences the statements preceding the obliques are grammatically complete in themselves and the sentences could have finished there, whereas there are no intermediate points in the periodic sentences at which the statements could end. In the periodic sentences the full meaning is suspended until the end of the sentence is reached.

The periodic style is more dignified and forceful than the loose style. It tends to induce brevity and precision, and above all to maintain the unity of the sentence, and leaves one with a sense of completeness. On the other hand, it demands greater concentration, and if the sentence is long the thread of the various subordinate statements made may have been lost by the time the main statement at the end of the sentence is reached.

The loose sentence has the advantage of being easy, flowing and natural, and is thus admirably suited to a plain straightforward style of narrative. It is more in keeping with the style of the spoken language and calls for less effort on the part of the reader. It is therefore particularly suitable for business letter-writing. Its danger is that it may degenerate into slipshod construction and become involved and obscure.

Whether the loose or the periodic style is preferable depends upon the connection in which it is used. Each form of sentence has its own special advantages and drawbacks, and neither can be regarded as superior to the other. The practice of the best writers is to make use of both forms, though for letter-writing it is better that the loose form should tend to predominate.

EXERCISES

1. Analyse the following complex sentence into its constituent clauses, writing each one out in full. State what kind of clause each is, and show its connection with the rest of the sentence.

Here is the sentence.

When I asked the boys if they would be responsible for any damage that might occur while they were using the premises, they said they hadn't thought about that.   *(R.S.A. Elem.)*

2. Recast the following loose sentences in periodic form.

(a) He gave me an order the first time I called, and with little or no trouble on my part.

(b) Cost of production is a vital factor for the manufacturer, in fact just as vital a factor as the selling price.

(c) The chairman's report provided almost unlimited opportunities for questions and criticism, and this was not surprising in view of the difficult time through which the company had just passed.

(d) We should be very glad to go into this matter in greater detail on receiving further particulars from you, including the submission of drawings and estimates.

(e) At today's sale the price of tea made a sudden jump owing to rumours that a severe drought had adversely affected the crop.

(f) We shall be glad if you will cable the name of the container-ship and the date of sailing to enable us to make arrangements for the collection of the containers as soon as it arrives.

(g) Having regard to the high rate of duty payable we could wish that the quality of the cloth was better, as it does not pay us to import any but the highest grades.

(h) We shall be glad if you will present the shipping documents not later than next Thursday morning, as we understand from the owners that the vessel will begin discharging in the afternoon.

(i) It is obvious that the difficulties in the way of prompt dispatch are not easy to overcome, seeing that more than two-thirds of our business passes through the hands of small parcel carriers, who require all parcels to be handed in by two o'clock.

(j) The responsibility for managing such a large organization was more than he could carry, as he had never had any previous experience of the sort that would help him.

3. Recast the following periodic sentences in loose form.

(*a*) As soon as I arrived, and almost before I had sat down, the office manager began asking me about my previous job.

(*b*) In spite of all the indications to the contrary present trends in market prices are likely to be reversed.

(*c*) Although the conduct of the accountant in the matter of the loans was open to criticism, no one doubted his honesty.

(*d*) Although, looking back, it seems only like yesterday, it is now five years since we placed our first order with you.

(*e*) Before the haulage company will accept any parcels for dispatch they require a consignment note to be signed.

(*f*) Because in our view the proposal has not been carefully thought out, and consequently has little chance of success, we have decided to oppose it.

(*g*) Although the firm about which you enquire is not an old-established one and its products are not yet very well known, it enjoys a good reputation in this part of the country.

(*h*) As Mr. Baxter is a thoroughly good business man, I should have no hesitation in granting him a credit to the amount you mention.

(*i*) Should you be unable to deliver the goods by the time stated please get in touch with us immediately.

(*j*) If you will confirm these terms we will arrange for a formal agreement to be drawn up.

The length of the sentence

The length of a sentence is a matter of no less importance than its form, but no hard-and-fast rule can be laid down as to what the length of a sentence should be.

The short sentence has the merit of simplicity and directness, and is particularly suitable for effective introductions and conclusions, for driving home leading points in argument, and for summing up. A succession of short sentences, however, tends to produce an unpleasant jerky effect.

> We shall be leaving at 10.30. We hope the car will be ready. My sister will be coming with us. You know her. You met her at the dance last week. She will be twenty-three tomorrow.

The long sentence is more suitable for the development of reasoned argument and complex thought. But it calls for skill and practice, as well as the power to think clearly and coherently. In unskilful hands it tends to become obscure. Moreover, a succession of long sentences is cumbersome and is apt to produce a heaviness and formality that would be out of place in business correspondence.

Broadly speaking, a preponderance of long sentences sets a dignified and lofty style and a preponderance of short sentences a style that is light and conversational. The short sentence is therefore more suitable for letter-writing though, to avoid monotony, there must be a judicious blending of the short with the long.

The foregoing short sentences sound much better when rewritten as follows in sentences of varying length.

> We hope the car will be ready at 10.30, when we shall be leaving *(Medium)*.
> My sister, whom you know, since you met her at the dance last week, will be coming with us *(Long)*. She will be twenty-three tomorrow *(Short)*.

Short separate sentences are easily understood, but they either leave the reader to discover for himself the connection between them, or require the use of such extra words as *consequently, further, moreover, therefore, hence, on the other hand, as a result, at the same time* to make clear the logical connection between the parts that are linked. Linking words and phrases help to produce a smooth and flowing style of writing, but if used to excess they lead to long and involved sentences of a kind that may be confusing. What is required is a prudent blend of sentences of various kinds, suited to the type of subject-matter and the intelligence and educational level of the reader. This is an important part of the art of communication.

And and *also* are both commonly used as link words. As a link word *and* is the conjunction most often used. There is a tendency to use it much too freely. This is something we must try to avoid, for two reasons:

> *(a)* its too frequent use makes for monotonous reading;
> *(b)* unlike such link words as *consequently* and *because* it adds nothing to meaning.

Compare:

> *He was worried because he was late.*

with

> *He was worried and he was late.*

The former gives the reason for·his worry; it shows the connection between the two sentences. The latter does not; it merely links the two separate statements.

Also is an adverb and by itself should not be used as a conjunction. It may, however, be used as a conjunction with *and* or *but,* which are themselves conjunctions (see p. 293).

EXERCISES

1. The following paragraph is made up of many short, jerky sentences. Re-write it in an easy-flowing style by combining them to form a smaller number of larger sentences. You may alter or omit words here and there, and re-arrange the order of the sentences, but do not change the meaning.

Tom Thumb had heard everything they had said. He heard their voices. Then he got out of bed. He had come softly to the fireplace. He had got under his father's seat. He had not been seen. He knew what his father and mother were going to do. The little boy went back to bed. He had no more sleep that night. He was turning over in his mind how to keep himself and his brothers safe from a cruel death. Early morning came. He went down to the river. He filled his pockets with small white stones. Then he came back to the house. A short time passed. All the boys then went out together with their father and mother.   *(R.S.A. Elem.)*

2. Combine each of the following groups of short sentences into not more than two sentences each, making only minor changes.

(a) The train ran through the station. It was a fast train. It did not stop. There were crowds of passengers. The passengers were waiting on the platform. Most of the passengers were in a great hurry.

(b) The old man settled in his chair. It was his favourite armchair. He was tired. He had done a hard day's work. He had reached home. His wife was busy. She was preparing his tea.   *(R.S.A. Elem.)*

3. Combine the sentences in each of the following groups into one good sentence.

(a) I locked him in his room. I pocketed the key. I then returned to the kitchen. I made a blazing fire. I lay down and fell asleep.

(b) By this time my ears had grown accustomed to the quiet. I could hear the ticking of the clock inside. It slowly counted out the seconds. The fellow kept deadly still. He must have held his breath.   *(R.S.A. Elem.)*

4. Rewrite each of the following groups of sentences as one long sentence. Do not use *and, but, so* or *then.* No information must be omitted, but the order of the sentences may be changed.

(a) The garden was beautiful. It contained flowers of many different colours. I was very impressed by it.

(b) The letter was long. It was very badly written. I did not read it.

(c) The man worked hard. He deserved to succeed. He never gave up trying. He had failed many times.   *(R.S.A. Elem.)*

5. Show your skill at sentence structure by combining the following in the way that seems most suitable.

The sugar cane is a perennial. It belongs to the same botanical order as wheat and oats. It attains a height of 15 to 20 feet. It is propagated from cuttings. These are taken from the stem. It takes about 270 days to mature. This is near the equator. In sub-tropical countries it grows more slowly. The ripe canes are cut. They are sent to the factory. The buried root-stock lives on. It produces new crops. These are called ratoons. This continues for several years. Juice is extracted from the sugar cane. The stem is crushed. A series of mills is needed. Water is sprayed on the canes. This is done during the crushing process. The crushing is done slowly. It is very thorough. About 96 per cent of the sucrose is extracted.   (*R.S.A. Inter.*)

6. Show your skill at sentence structure by combining the following sentences in the most interesting and suitable ways.

The word "electric" comes from the Greek word "elektron". This word means "amber". Amber is the name given to a fossil. This fossil is made of resin. This substance must be briskly rubbed. Then it attracts other substances. These must be small and light. William Gilbert first studied frictional electricity. He lived at Colchester. This is a town in England. He has been called "the father of electricity". He wrote a book. It was published in the year 1600. It concerned the magnet, magnetic bodies, and our earth as a magnet. All over Europe, men became interested in electricity. Sometimes progress was made. Chance played a certain part. There is an example. Two Germans tried to electrify water. They took a hand machine. This machine could produce electricity. They suspended an iron chain from it. The other end of the chain was dipped into water. This was in a jar. The result was interesting. It was the starting point. From this point were developed condensers. These condensers play a part today. They are important. They are used in wireless apparatus and in telephones.   (*R.S.A. Inter.*)

The qualities of a good sentence
A good sentence must have clarity, unity and coherence; it must pay regard to emphasis, and be varied in structure.

Clarity
The great merit of writing, and especially of business writing where money is often at stake is to be clear — clear about what you want to say and clear about the way you say it. You must express yourself so clearly that your reader cannot fail to grasp your meaning without trouble, and certainly that he cannot interpret what you say in a manner different from that which you intended. Careless writing sometimes produces sentences that can be interpreted in different ways — ambiguous sentences we call them: the writer understands the sentence in one way, the reader in another. Both may be sincere in their interpretations, but there is always the danger that the reader may deliberately interpret an ambiguous statement to his own advantage. What, for example are we to make of the following?

The chairman told the managing director that he had been awarded an increase in salary.

To whom had the increase been awarded — the chairman or the managing director?

The manager gave his secretary·a cheque, and her husband a watch.

Who gave the watch, and to whom? Was it the manager to the husband, or the husband to his wife? It is not clear.

To ensure that their mutual relationship is clear, those parts of a sentence which are closely connected in thought should be placed as near as possible to one another in the sentence. Consider the following.

No child shall be employed on any weekday when the school is closed for more than four hours.

The meaning probably intended is that no child may be employed for more than four hours, in which case *for more than four hours* should be placed immediately after *employed.*

Unity
The sentence is built up on a regular plan, with each part grammatically related to some other part. But this grammatical unity is not by itself enough; there must in addition be a unity of thought; that is to say the sentence must contain one, and no more than one, main idea, each of the several parts being closely related to the main thought the sentence is intended to convey.

It would be quite logical to write:

A cheque for £15 was sent by post yesterday, and I hope you received it safely.

because the second statement is related to the first. But we cannot write:

A cheque for £15 was sent by post yesterday, and you will be interested to know that I shall be going to Manchester tomorrow.

since the sentence contains two main ideas—the cheque and the visit to Manchester—that are not related. Each of these main ideas should appear in a sentence of its own.

Again:

We were very interested in the opera, which was performed entirely by amateurs, who are all members of the local youth club, which is connected with the parish church, and is a considerable asset to the town.

This sentence contains three main ideas relating in turn to:

(a) the opera;
(b) the performers; and
(c) the youth club.

These separate ideas are more clearly represented in three separate sentences, as follows.

We were very interested in the opera *(Short)*. The performers, all of whom are members of the local youth club, are amateurs *(Medium)*. The club, which is connected with the parish church, is a considerable asset to the town *(Medium)*.

The suppression of subordinate clauses in favour of separate sentences, as in the above examples, is desirable only when the ideas to be expressed are not associated. Complex sentences rather than separate simple sentences should be used when the ideas to be expressed may be definitely associated.

Some time ago there was a king. He had a palace surrounded by most beautiful gardens. They contained the rarest trees and shrubs.

The ideas contained in these three sentences are closely associated and are better expressed in one complex sentence.

Some time ago there was a king, who had a palace surrounded by most beautiful gardens, which contained the rarest trees and shrubs.

The following are less obvious examples of false unity.

The Bank of England, which now employs some 2,000 men and 3,000 women, always consults the British Government about proposed changes in its minimum lending rate.

The separate facts stated here are inappropriately linked, since there is no logical connection between the number of persons employed, on the one hand, and consultation with the Government, on the other. The two ideas should therefore be expressed in separate sentences.

The Bank of England now employs some 2,000 men and 3,000 women. It always consults the British Government about proposed changes in its minimum lending rate.

Similarly with:

Your letter, which I did not receive until my return from Scotland, confirms our fears that the proposed structural alterations will not be satisfactory.

This sentence should be rewritten:

> I did not receive your letter until my return from Scotland. It confirms . . . .

Coherence

A sentence is not a good sentence if it is not coherent, that is to say unless its component parts are arranged in good logical order. Incoherence may result either from lack of balance or from failure to observe the rule of proximity.

(a) Balance. A balanced sentence is a stylistic device by which those parts of a sentence similar *in thought* are made similar *in form.*

> Reading maketh a *full man;* conference a *ready man;* writing an *exact man.* (Bacon).
> Every lesson is a *lesson in English,* and every teacher a *teacher of English.* What is needed today is not *broad, unenforceable promises,* but *precise, enforceable agreements.*

A well-balanced sentence has an attraction that is lacking in one that is not. It makes for simplicity and sounds well. It is useful in making comparisons and contrasts, but it must not be carried to excess, because it tends to become monotonous with over-use. It should, therefore, be used with moderation.

(b) Proximity. Those parts of a sentence that are closely connected in thought-sequence should be placed as near together as possible. This is known as the Rule of Proximity.

> We shall be pleased to show you samples, if you will call tomorrow, of the goods advertised.

This sentence is awkwardly arranged. The phrase *if you will call tomorrow* should be placed at the beginning of the sentence.
Failure to observe proximity sometimes results in absurdity.

> Erected to the memory of Rowena Smith, accidentally killed as a mark of affection by her brother.

The adverbial phrase *as a mark of affection by her brother* should follow the verb *erected,* which it modifies.

> A piano is offered for sale by a lady with carved oak legs.

The adjective phrase *with carved oak legs* should follow *piano,* which it qualifies.

Lack of proximity may also produce ambiguity.

He took a note from his wallet, and with an angry gesture, threw it on the
counter.

Threw what; the note or the wallet? If it refers to the note the sentence should be rearranged so that *threw it on the counter* follows
note.

From his wallet he took a note and, with an angry gesture, threw it on the
counter.

The adverb *only* needs careful watching (see pp. 293—4).

Emphasis

The purpose of emphasis is to heighten effect by giving prominence
to a particular word, phrase, or clause. It is obtained in a variety of
ways.

(a) By inversion of word order. The normal order of words in a
sentence is

subject + predicate + object

qualifiying words and phrases being placed as near as possible to
the words they qualify.

Any variation of the normal order is a most effective way of
securing emphasis. It occasions surprise and therefore attracts attention to the word or words abnormally placed, especially if placed at
the beginning of the sentence or the end.

Normal: The amount owing on your account is £500.
Emphatic: On your account the amount owing is £500 (emphasizes *your
account*).
Normal: I had a meeting yesterday with the works superintendent.
Emphatic: Yesterday, I had a meeing with the works superintendent (empha-
sizes date of meeting).

A qualifying phrase or supporting clause normally *follows* the
word or words it qualifies. The phrase or clause is emphasized if it
is placed *before*.

Normal: He resigned on grounds of health.
Emphatic: On the grounds of health he resigned (emphasizes cause of resig-
nation).
Normal: He did not realize what had happened until I told him.
Emphatic: Until I told him he did not realize what had happened (empha-
sizes time of realization).

(b) By contrast. Effect is also heightened when a word or phrase is contrasted with another.

> *Down* came the rain; *up* went the umbrella.
> Men *build houses:* but women *make homes.*
> A prodigal robs *his heir;* a miser robs *himself.*

(c) By means of correlative conjunctions (see p. 235).

> *Normal:* She is young and beautiful.
> *Emphatic:* She is *not only* young *but also* beautiful.
> *Normal:* If you can allow credit we will place an order.
> *Emphatic: If* you can allow credit *then* we will place an order.

(d) By a prefatory "It is", "It was".

> *Normal:* We regret to have to complain.
> *Emphatic: It is with regret* that we have to complain.
> *Normal:* Fortunately, your letter arrived before I left.
> *Emphatic: It was fortunate* that your letter arrived before I left.

Variety of structure

The normal word order of subject + predicate + object is the most suitable order for making statements of fact or intention, which form the subject-matter of most business letters. At the same time sentences must not be built to a uniform pattern, otherwise the writing will soon become monotonous. Some ways in which variety of construction may be achieved have already been mentioned.

(a) By a mixture of loose and periodic sentences (pp. 250–2).

(b) By using sentences of varying length (pp. 253–4).

(c) By the judicious introduction here and there of balanced sentences (p. 259).

(d) By changing normal word order (p. 260).

(e) By varied openings. Monotony may also be avoided by beginning sentences with different words and by avoiding repetition of the same parts of speech, especially when the parts of speech are similar in form.

> The board did not favour the original plan. *They* do not think it has been sufficiently considered, and *they* do not believe it can succeed; consequently *they* have decided to reject it.

This may be improved.

The board did not favour the original plan because, in their view, it had not been sufficiently considered, and consequently has little chance of success. They have therefore decided to reject it.

Again:

Invariably he calls on his way home, *usually* about six o'clock, but *occasionally* a little later.

The repeated use of adverbs of similar form can be avoided as follows.

He always calls on his way home, usually about six o'clock, but sometimes a little later.

(*f*) By varying the plan of the sentence. Most ideas can be expressed in several ways, and a practised writer is able to obtain variety by planning his sentences differently.

We will certainly send the coats if we can.
Certainly we will send the coats if possible.
If we are able to send the coats we shall certainly do so.
If it is at all possible we shall certainly send the coats.
You may rely on our sending the coats if we possibly can.
Unless prevented from doing so we shall certainly send the coats.

EXERCISES

1. Point out the ambiguity or absurdity in each of the following sentences and, by changing the order of the words or phrases and making any other necessary changes, rewrite or type the sentences to give the meaning probably intended.

(*a*) Every now and again the trader goes for a talk with his manager to find out how he stands.

(*b*) The accounts should be passed to me for payment not later than 30 September.

(*c*) The manager told his clerk he was a careless man, and could not keep his accounts properly.

(*d*) Bills are requested to be paid in advance.

(*e*) I shall return the copy of the book which you sent me for inspection during the course of next week.

(*f*) I should be glad if you would let me know the number of children attending the classes before the end of the month.

(*g*) We learnt that the parcel reached you with much satisfaction.

(*h*) The speakers for next week will be found pinned on the notice board.

(*i*) I can recommend him for the post he applies for with complete confidence.

(j) He gave an account of his travels soon after his return to one of the leading newspapers.

2. Recast the following sentences so as to improve them in any way that you think necessary.

(a) A retailer would keep his reserve capital in a deposit rather than a current account to gain interest and to work for him instead of lying idle.

(b) The goods in a department store can soon be found by boards indicating where to look for them.

(c) Goods taken by road is a much better form of transport than goods taken by rail.

(d) The shopkeeper must have somewhere he can keep and fetch his goods from.

(e) The importance of transport in connection with commerce is so great that it could not function properly without it.

(f) The bank provides a safe place to deposit money instead of keeping it in the house.

(g) Without transport goods, if they were perishable, would be no use at all.

(h) A current account does not earn interest, the reason being because it is not kept by the bank for a long period.

(i) Goods that are easily broken are not advised to be transported by rail.

(j) A department store often has a restaurant which is very convenient and also very reasonable prices.

3. Explain two ways in which each of the following sentences can be interpreted. Rewrite each sentence so that it has only one possible meaning.

(a) The manager was as anxious to please his customers as his staff.

(b) The appeal for the founding of a scholarship fund by the staff representative is worthy of consideration.   *(I. of B.)*

CHAPTER SEVENTEEN

The Paragraph

But true Expression, like th' unchanging Sun,
Clears and improves whate'er it shines upon.

A. Pope: *Essay on Criticism*

FUNCTION

The purpose of paragraphing, like that of punctuation, is to help the writer to convey his message more clearly and thus to make things easier for the reader.

A paragraph may consist of a single sentence, but it will more usually consist of a collection of sentences closely related to one another because they deal with the same subject-matter—the same topic or theme, or at least a new aspect of the topic under consideration.

Each paragraph should deal with only one idea, and every sentence in the paragraph should have a distinct bearing upon the sentences that precede and follow it. As soon as the idea dealt with is exhausted another paragraph should be begun. It follows that there is a greater break of thought between paragraphs than between sentences.

To try to deal with more than one topic in the same paragraph confuses the reader. The opposite fault of dealing with one topic in two or more paragraphs is no less confusing, though it is common practice nowadays for articles in newspapers, advertising copy and popular magazines to be presented in very short paragraphs to make for easy reading for a mass audience, many of whom do not find reading easy. No rules can be given for what is a suitable length for a paragraph. What is suitable depends upon the length and scope of the total subject-matter and the writer's assessment of the reader's intelligence and level of understanding. It may be said, however, that in business writing we tend to divide our material into small topics and to use much shorter paragraphs than is customary for literary work.

If a paragraph deals with a new aspect of the topic dealt with in the preceding paragraph it will often be introduced by a connective or link word or phrase, such as *Again, Besides, However, Nevertheless, In short, On the other hand,* etc. While such connectives are

264

often useful, and sometimes necessary, it is better to avoid using them to excess, and wherever possible to frame sentences in such a way that extraneous aids of this sort are unnecessary.

The function of the paragraph is best understood if we think of a chain as consisting of a number of separate links. Each link is a complete unit in itself; it serves in addition to connect the links immediately before and immediately after it. In the same way each paragraph is a unit, since it deals with only one topic; at the same time it serves to carry the reader forward to the next stage in the development of the writer's theme.

ESSENTIAL QUALITIES

The essential qualities of a good paragraph are unity and coherence.

Unity

Unity means that the paragraph deals with only one main idea or topic. Every sentence in the paragraph should bear upon this topic; any sentence that does not should be excluded and transferred to a new paragraph. This concentration of the paragraph upon a single topic helps the reader to follow the writer's train of thought one step at a time, and thus makes for clarity and assists comprehension.

A Business Letter

The Borough Treasurer
The Town Hall
LYNTHAM ST. ANNES
FY8 1AA

5 February 19..

Dear Sir

No. 1 Margate Road

I have recently brought the property at the above address from Mr. A. Pigott. The purchase was completed on 7 December, and in the completion statement received from Messrs Leslie, Harris & Fisher, Solicitors, is included the sum of £62.33 for General Rates already paid by Mr. Pigott up to 31 March next.

I am not able to occupy 1 Margate Road immediately, and shall not be able to do so until I can sell my present property in London. In the meantime the house in Margate Road will remain unfurnished.

I take it that rates will not be payable during the period the house remains unfurnished, and that the sum of £62.33 paid by me for the period 7 December to 31 March, or such a portion of it as is applicable, will be accepted as a set-off against the rates due for me when eventually I do move in. I should, however, be glad if you would kindly confirm that this is so.

Yours faithfully

M.A. Smith

M.A. Smith

This letter is well paragraphed. Each of the three paragraphs deals in turn with a separate topic, and no irrelevant matter is introduced. The three topics dealt with are:

(a) purchase of the property;
(b) inability to occupy it;
(c) payment of rates.

Coherence

It is not by itself enough that all the sentences forming a paragraph should relate to the same point; they must develop the point naturally and logically. In other words, the paragraph should be so constructed that one sentence leads naturally to the next, otherwise it may fail to make its point clear and leave the reader with an uncertain notion of what it is all about.

The following paragraph fails to develop its point naturally.

(a) Punctuation in business is usually left to the typist. (b) Not infrequently a sentence will be dictated that depends for its meaning upon the punctuation marks used. (c) Such sentences may not be good sentences, (d) but it is the typist's duty to see that the punctuation used conveys the meaning intended. (e) The typist is taught punctuation as part of her professional training.

Following the natural sequence the paragraph would be improved if recast in the order (e), (a), (b), (c), (d).

Punctuation is taught to the typist as part of her professional training, and in business is usually left to her. Not infrequently a sentence will be dictated that depends for its meaning upon the punctuation marks used. Such sentences may not be good sentences, but it is the typist's duty to see that the punctuation used conveys the meaning intended.

THE TOPIC SENTENCE

As we have seen, a good paragraph will deal with only one topic or point. This topic will usually be announced in one of the sentences, the function of the other sentences being to elaborate the point made in the topic sentence, as it is called, by the addition of explanatory or supplementary information relating to it.

The topic sentence serves as a signpost to the meaning of the whole paragraph, and accordingly calls for emphasis. Attention must therefore be given to its position in the paragraph. As with the sentence, the emphatic positions in a paragraph are at the beginning and the end, and as a rule the topic sentence should appear in one of these two places. If it comes at the beginning of the paragraph the construction is said to be *loose,* and if it comes at the end, *periodic.*

The loose paragraph

The preferred position for the topic sentence, especially in business letters, is at the beginning of the paragraph, for then it has the double advantage of being both prominent and also capable of natural and logical development through the remainder of the paragraph. We must be on the lookout, then, for the sentences that introduce new topics representing changes in the thoughts of the writer as he develops his general theme. These sentences tell the reader what the paragraph is about and help him to follow the writer's train of thought. In the following example the topic sentences are in italics.

Dear Mr. Loeber,

We are contemplating publication of a new edition of our 800-page, blue-bound, English and Shorthand Dictionary. Our first problem is to find someone able and willing to prepare a list of new words that have come into general use since the Dictionary was last edited, and to delete those that have fallen into disuse to such an extent that their inclusion in a dictionary of this kind could not reasonably be expected.

The purpose of this letter is to invite you to undertake the required revision for us at a fee to be agreed upon. Until a start has been made on the work it is impossible to estimate the length of time it is likely to take, and consequently I am unable to suggest a fee. It occurs to me, however, that the most satisfactory arrangement would be to base payment upon an agreed rate of so much a day, and leave it to you to decide what constitutes a day's work.

The dictionary position in this country at the present time is not very good. Few dictionaries are sufficiently up to date to be of very much help. Even the Oxford Dictionary is out of date, and its most recent Supplement, not yet available in bound form, does not take the revision beyond 1976. Some of the smaller dictionaries have been revised more recently, and of these the most useful appear to be *Concise Oxford, Chambers,* and *Collins.*

I hope you will be able to accept my invitation. May I suggest that you join me for lunch one day next week when, after a discussion of some of the problems involved in the revision, you could perhaps give me your decision.

I shall look forward to hearing from you.

Yours sincerely

In this letter each paragraph deals with only one topic. As each new topic is introduced a new paragraph is begun, the writer's thoughts moving naturally from one point to the next—from publication in the first paragraph, to invitation in the second, to the dictionary position in the third, and on to the final appeal. Each paragraph is introduced by a sentence that refers so suitably to the subject-matter that the reader is left in no doubt as to what the paragraph is about.

The periodic paragraph

Less usually the topic sentence will be placed at the end of the paragraph. This is done when the paragraph begins by clearing up some preliminary matter, or when the aim is to gather evidence leading to a conclusion or to build up an effective climax. Again, in the following example the topic sentences are in italics.

Dear Sir,

We understand that you have been established in the South African market for many years, and that you have built up a wide connection among buyers there. We also understand that you specialize in the marketing of electrical appliances and machinery. We have recently extended our factories at Luton and Bedford and are now anxious to widen the market for our increased output. *We are therefore writing to invite you to accept appointment as our sole agents for the Republic on terms to be arranged, and hope you will accept.*

Yours faithfully,

DISPLAY

If it is to serve its purpose of helping the reader the paragraph must be displayed so as to "catch the eye". With sentences this is done by leaving a space (two or three strokes of the space bar in typewriting) after the full-stop. In paragraphing it is done by commencing the first sentence on a new line and by displaying the paragraph in a variety of ways. Three different devices are used.

The indented paragraph

This was previously by far the commonest type of display normally found in business letters. The first word of the paragraph is set back (in typewriting, five spaces from the left-hand margin for pica type and six for élite type, though more extended spacings are sometimes preferred).

          I have recently bought a bungalow in Bexhill
and would like to have central heating installed. Your
name and address have been given to me by the manager
of Barclays Bank, and I should be glad to know whether
you could undertake this work for me very soon, as my
move from London has now become a matter of urgency.

The blocked paragraph

This type of display is now firmly established for main paragraphs
in the business letter (see p. 162) and also for inset paragraphs and
for quotations that appear within the body of the letter. Each line
in the paragraph, including the first, begins at the same vertical
point of the paper.

    If you can undertake the work I should like to have an
    estimate of the cost. I enclose a rough plan of the property,
    and give below a list of my proposed needs:

        Existing boiler to be replaced by a Crane Cavendish,
        No.4 size, automatic solid fuel boiler, provided this
        size of boiler is adequate for heating both domestic
        water supply and seven radiators, and also a towel
        rail in the bathroom.

        The work to be carried out from under the floor, in
        order to avoid cutting or lifting flooring.

The hanging paragraph

This type of paragraph is used only as a special device. Its effect is
to throw the first few words into prominence. The first word of the
paragraph begins at the left-hand margin, the remaining lines being
indented—usually two to five spaces in typewriting. It is thus a
reversal of the device used for the indented paragraph.

Our reward for self-discipline and the acceptance of social
    responsibility is not necessarily money or power, but self-
    respect and the respect of others.
If a man is not the sort to seize upon discipline as something
    contributing mightily to his life's happiness - a constructive
    force, a protective force - then he just must bear with it,
    for he cannot escape it.
It is better to make discipline something that will help us to
    get what we want out of life than to be driven into accepting
    it as a pitiless force.

(Royal Bank of Canada: Monthly Letter)

Headed paragraphs

If a letter is lengthy, containing a number of paragraphs each dealing with a separate point, it may be convenient either to number the paragraphs or to give them headings, or even both. This makes subsequent reference easier, and is an advantage where subsequent correspondence is likely to deal with the various points separately.

```
Referring to your quotation of 29 November and our conversation
last Thursday afternoon, I shall be glad if you will now arrange
to put the following work in hand:

Box Room. Brick walls to be plastered; exposed floor boards
under dormer window to be boarded in with suitable material; space
for radiator to be left under window, struts to be fully covered
with Swedish hardboard or other suitable material; ceiling beams
behind radiator to be boarded in; spaces on both sides of the
radiator to be fitted with sliding panel doors on suitable runners
to give access to storage space behind and to roof.

Electric Points. Points to be supplied in lounge, in front and
back bedrooms downstairs; one independent bed light to be fitted
in ceiling in each room above points indicated by chalk marks
on floor, the lights to be operated by a pull switch; one point
to be fitted in bathroom to take 1 kw electric heater.

Garage. Door to be made in existing brickwork, to give entrance
to back of garage from garden.
```

If numbers are used for the paragraphs they may or may not be placed within brackets. An unbracketed number is followed by a full-stop, but numbers within brackets are sufficiently distinctive to make the use of full-stops unnecessary. Thus:

> 1.   2.   3.   or   (1)   (2)   (3)

Paragraph headings may be typed in either upper-case or lower-case characters, followed by a full-stop or colon, or even by a dash. If lower-case characters are used they should be underlined to make clear the distinction between heading and text.

Subsidiary paragraphs

For inset or subsidiary paragraphs any one of the three forms of paragraph display may be used. To emphasize the distinction it may, however, be advisable to adopt different forms of display for main and subsidiary paragraphs, the blocked form of subsidiary paragraph being the one most commonly used with indented main paragraphs.

LENGTH OF PARAGRAPH

There is no hard-and-fast rule about the length of the paragraph. Some paragraphs will be long; others short. Length will vary with circumstances and will be dictated by the *unity* of the subject-matter.

In the business letter short paragraphs are preferable to long. Short paragraphs not only give the letter an attractive appearance but also enable the reader to grasp the writer's points more quickly. A solid unbroken text has an uninteresting appearance and often proves tiresome to the reader; to divide the same text into paragraphs gives it a touch of lightness and stimulates interest. On the other hand, a series of very short paragraphs may produce a jerky effect, and far from helping the reader may prove a hindrance to him. The need for care in paragraphing is therefore obvious.

Where a letter deals with a number of separate matters its arrangement into paragraphs will not be difficult. In lengthy reports of a technical character, for example, the natural breaks in the text will usually be clear. But when a letter deals in detail with only one topic, the division of the text into paragraphs calls for prudence and discernment. Care must be taken to discover the logical changes in the writer's thoughts, and with each change of thought to begin a new paragraph.

EXERCISES

1. Type, or write, a short paragraph, say five or six sentences, on each of the following topics.

A	C
Using the telephone	Dictation machines
Choosing your job	The power of the Press
Petty cash	Good manners
Holidays abroad	"Eleveneses" in the office
A tidy desk	International trade

B	D
Nuclear warfare	The value of good speech
The value of punctuality	Filing in the office
The typewriter in business	The private secretary
Equal pay	Making up the post
Television	Personal appearance

2. As secretary of a commercial college draft five short paragraphs for a circular, each dealing respectively with:

(*a*) advantages of a full-time secretarial and commercial training;
(*b*) outline of courses provided;

(c) qualifications for admission;
(d) enrolment arrangements and fees;
(e) examinations prepared for.

3. Type, or write, five short paragraphs on the career you would like to follow, dealing in turn with each of the following topics:

(a) the kind of career;
(b) reasons for choosing it;
(c) the qualifications needed;

(d) how you propose to prepare yourself;
(e) the prospects it holds out.

4. Type, or write, a short paragraph on each of the topics included under the headings given below.

A. Commerce
Meaning of commerce
Branches of commerce
Benefits derived from commerce

E. Retail Trading
Meaning of "retail" trade
Types of retail organization
Self-service selling

B. Money
Meaning of money
Types of money
Services performed by money

F. Insurance
Spreading risks
Forms of insurance
The insurance contract

C. Banking
Importance of modern banking
Kinds of banks
Services rendered by banks

G. Transport
Importance
Various types
Transport in the future

D. Cheques
What a cheque is
Comparison with other forms of money
Reasons for popularity

5. Read carefully through the following letters and decide the points at which new paragraphs should begin. Then type, or rewrite, them, using blocked paragraphs:

A

Letter to a New Student

Dear Miss Williams,

I am writing with reference to your application for admission to a full-time day secretarial course to inform you that the new session begins on Monday 10 September, and shall be glad if you will attend college on that date at 9.0 a.m., in Room 25 on the ground floor, where arrangements will be made for your enrolment. There will be an opportunity after enrolment for you to meet other students and also the various members of staff concerned with the course you will be taking. Matters concerning textbooks, stationery, arrangements for meals, etc., will then be explained to you. Lessons will begin on the following day. Morning classes will be held from 9.15 a.m. to 12.30 p.m., with a short break at 10.45, and afternoon classes from 1.30 to 4.30 p.m., with a short break at 3.0. In view of the intensive nature of the course, homework will form a part of it and will be set in two subjects for each evening, while a little additional work will be set for the weekends. The course aims at high standards and will call for serious application from the beginning. It is broadly based to continue general education, and in particular the importance of English for successful secretarial work is stressed. The need for good standards in handwriting and neatness is also emphasized. I hope you will take full advantage of the excellent facilities provided by the College, and that your session with us will be a successful and happy one.

Yours sincerely.

B
Application for a Post

Dear Sir,

I am writing to apply for the post of private secretary advertised in today's *Daily Telegraph*. I am 24 years of age, received my general education at the Walthamstow County High School, and my secretarial training at the Bloomsbury Secretarial College. My secretarial training included shorthand, typewriting, English, office practice, accounts, and general principles of English law, and in the examinations held at the end of the course I was awarded the college secretarial diploma, with speeds of 120 and 50 words a minute in shorthand and typewriting respectively. Upon completion of my training I obtained a post as shorthand-typist with Messrs. Baxter, Lloyd & Smithson, Solicitors, 125—129 High Road, Woodford, and for the past three years have been private secretary to Mr. Baxter, the senior partner. He seems to have been well satisfied with my work and would, I feel sure, give me a good recommendation. I enclose copies of two testimonials—one from my former Headmistress, and one from the Principal of my secretarial college, and hope that my qualifications and experience will commend themselves to you. I should be pleased to attend for an interview at your convenience, when I could give you further details concerning myself.

Yours faithfully.

C
A Testimonial

Dear Sir,

In reply to your enquiry of 21 September, I have much pleasure in support-ing the application of Miss R. Golding for the post of private secretary to your director. She joined my staff five years ago, and for the past three years has been my personal secretary. I have been greatly impressed by her conscientious attitude to her work, by her patience, her tact, and unfailing good humour. Her shorthand is very good, and her standards in typewriting I have not seen equalled for a long time. She holds the Teacher's Certificates of the Royal Society of Arts in both these subjects. Miss Golding is a very competent person in all she undertakes, and is thoroughly reliable in every way. Although I should be very sorry to lose her services I can recommend her to you with every confidence for the post she now seeks with you.

Yours faithfully,

D
A letter of Complaint

Dear Sirs,

We are sorry to inform you that, on opening up the ten cases of glass delivered here yesterday by Messrs. Brash & Jones, we found about 10% of the glass to have been broken, nearly half shows bubbles, and most is badly scratched. I should be glad if you would arrange for your London agents to inspect the consignment and report to you upon it, because I am afraid we shall have to claim on you for a 30% reduction in the amount of your invoice—the balance representing our estimate of the value of the glass as it stands. As we are under contract to deliver assorted sizes of this kind of glass immediately, and are awaiting your decision before cutting up, I should be glad if you would kindly attend to the matter immediately, and let me know when your representative may be expected to call.

Yours faithfully,

CHAPTER EIGHTEEN

Pitfalls and Traps

From the errors of others, a wise man corrects his own.

Syrus

Though language changes with the generations and what was incorrect yesterday may become correct by usage tomorrow, there are certain rules of good English that never change, and you cannot afford to ignore them. The wrong use of words and phrases not only offends the sense of those who know and respect the right use of language but also robs language of its effectiveness and interferes with its purpose—the clear and unambiguous communication of thought.

The following list is by no means comprehensive, but it includes some of the mistakes most commonly made and, if you master it thoroughly, it will help you to avoid many of the faults that now appear in correspondnece.

THE WRONG USE OF VERBS

Two singular nouns
When two singular nouns joined by *and* refer to the same person or thing, or are closely related in meaning, they take a verb in the singular.

New plant and machinery *was* (not *were*) ordered early this year (meaning *new equipment* was ordered).
Our chairman and managing director *spends* (not *spend*) a good deal of time abroad (meaning *the man* who is our chairman and managing director spends a good deal of time abroad).
The rise and fall in prices *results* (not *result*) from movements in supply and demand (meaning *the change* in prices results from movements in supply and demand).
Reading and the patient use of the dictionary *is* (not *are*) the best means we have of increasing our knowledge of words (meaning *careful reading* increases our knowledge of words).

Nouns not joined by "and"

When two nouns, the former of which is in the singular, are joined by any word other than *and*, or by a phrase, they take the verb in the singular.

> *Compare:* The plane *and* its crew *were* lost.
> *But:* The plane, *with* its crew, *was* lost.
> Good appearance, *with* good manners, *is* (not *are*) part of the equipment of the perfect secretary.
> Minimum lending rate, *as well as* other interest rates, *moves* (not *move*) in response to official policy.

Error of attraction

When a plural noun forms part of an expression introduced by a singular noun the verb is in the singular. The tendency to make the verb agree with the plural noun immediately before it is known as the "error of attraction".

> *A block* of flats *remains* (not *remain*) for sale.
> *His intimate knowledge* of materials, sources of supply, and prices *was* (not *were*) invaluable.

The true subjects of these sentences are *a block* and *his intimate knowledge;* the plurals *flats, materials,* etc. serve merely to enlarge their respective subjects.

On the same principle, when a singular noun forms part of an expression introduced by a plural noun the verb is in the plural.

> *The immediate results* of this procedure *were* (not *was*) apparent.
> *The best efforts* of management *fail* (not *fails*) unless supported by those of the staff.

Each; every; any; either; neither

These pronouns take their verbs in the singular, since they refer to each individual in a group and not the group as a whole.

> *Each* of the clerks *has* (not *have*) a desk of his own.
> *Everyone has his* (not *have their*) price.
> *Neither* of the solutions proposed *is* (not *are*) satisfactory.

None

None = no one, no person or persons. It was formerly held that it should be followed by a singular verb, but according to the *Oxford Dictionary* the plural construction is now more common.

None were pleased at having *their* bonus reduced.

reads more easily than

None was pleased at having *his* bonus reduced.

Or; nor
Two singular nouns separated by *or* or *nor* take a verb in the singular.

Either the personnel manager *or* his assistant *interviews* (not *interview*) all applicants.
Neither the secretary *nor* the accountant *was* (not *were*) willing to make the decision.

Complications occur when the separate subjects are in different numbers or persons. Though not unanimously approved by grammarians, the following rules are usually applied.

Different numbers
Where the subjects differ in number the verb is in the plural.

Neither the workmen *nor* the foreman *are* aware of the arrangement.

Different persons
Where the subjects differ in person the verb agrees with the nearer subject.

Neither the sales manager *nor* I *know* the result.

It is, however, better to accept the advice of Fowler* and to avoid such doubtful constructions by recasting the sentences.

The workmen are not aware of the arrangement, nor is the foreman.
The sales manager does not know the result, nor do I.

Collective nouns
A noun is collective when it denotes a single group of similar individuals.
There is no strict rule for the use of the singular or the plural with such nouns. Thus, we may say:

The Commission has (or *have*) recently published *its* (or *their*) report.
The Borough Council regret (or *regrets) their* (or *its*) need to increase the rate.

Modern English Usage (2nd ed.), p. 387, H.M.S.O.

depending on whether we wish to stress the idea of the group or of the individuals composing it.

The important thing, however, is not the choice of verb, but the consistent use of the singular or the plural throughout the same document. Failure to observe this rule is a common source of error. We can hardly say, for example:

> *The audience is* requested to keep *their* seats.

But while there is no hard-and-fast rule, general practice favours a distinction between:

(*a*) the true collective, used to denote the group as a whole; and

(*b*) the noun of multitude, used to denote the members forming the group.

The former takes a verb in the singular; the latter a verb in the plural.

Collective noun
Stressing the group.

> *The Committee consists* of ten elected and two co-opted members.
> *The firm has* just celebrated its centenary.
> *The crew is* the best the ship has ever had.

Noun of multitude
Stressing the members forming the group.

> *The Committee are* not all able to attend.
> *The firm were* unanimous in rejecting the proposal.
> *The crew wish* to consult their union.

Collective with "of"
A difficulty arises when the collective is followed by "of" plus a noun in the plural. Are we, for example, to say:

> *A number of typists leaves* at 4.30.

or

> *A number of typists leave* at 4.30?

The phrase *a number of* is a generalization that stands for an unspecified number (four, five, etc.), thus giving a sort of plural force to the group. It is better, therefore, to treat this collective as plural. This is in keeping with the treatment of the collectives *A lot of* and *A few*, which are always treated as plurals. Thus it is better to say:

A number of typists leave at 4.30.
A number of machines need repairing.
A number of callers are expected before 11.0.

just as we should always say:

A lot of people are late this morning.
Only *a few customers were* interested.

In the examples given the true subject is not *A number*, but *A number of typists*, etc.; hence the need for the plural verb.

But in sentences such as the following, in which the true subject is *The number*, the collective is treated as singular.

The number of typists now employed *is* double that (i.e. the number employed) of a year ago.
The number of machines available *was* inadequate.

When *a number of* can be replaced by *some, several*, or *many*, these forms are to be preferred if only because they use one word instead of three.

Singular nouns plural in form

The names of sciences and branches of study ending in *ics*, though plural in form, are treated sometimes as singulars and sometimes as plurals, the singular being preferred in definitions, and the plural when the names are used in a more general sense.

Athletics is the practice of physical exercise (singular).
Athletics form part of every school curriculum (plural).
Mathematics is both a science and an art (singular).
My *mathematics are* very rusty (plural).

When a compound noun is plural in form, but may be considered as a single object, the verb may be either in the singular or in the plural.

Twelve metres of silk at one hundred and seventy-five pence *is (are)* sufficient.
Three-quarters of the earth's surface *consists (consist)* of water.

Relative pronouns

A relative pronoun agrees with its antecedent, that is with the preceding noun to which it refers.

He is one of those men who *are* never content with anything less than perfection (not *is*, since *who* refers to *men*).

Winchester is one of the few schools that *have* a golf course (not *has*, since *that* refers to *schools*).

Shall; will

Shall and *will* are often confused. Their main use is as ancillary verbs to express the future.

Person	Singular	Plural
1st	I *shall post* this letter on my way home.	We *shall send* the goods as soon as they are ready.
2nd	You *will find* the price reasonable.	You *will enjoy* the performance.
3rd	He *will consider* the suggestion.	They *will postpone* delivery till next week.

When the use of *shall* and *will* is reversed, however, the words cease to express the future and have other uses. Thus, *will* is used in the first person to express willingness or determination.

I *will phone* him at once (expresses willingness).
We *will arrive* not later than ten o'clock (expresses determination).

Shall is used in the second and third persons to express either compulsion or some form of obligation.

They *shall return* all they have borrowed (expresses compulsion).
Your application *shall be considered* carefully (makes a promise).

It is important not to confuse these different uses of *shall* and *will* and to remember that *shall* in the first person and *will* in the second and third express the simple future, and that when their use is reversed they no longer help to express the future but have a special significance.

Since *will* used with the first person relates to an act of the will, the forms *will I* and *will we* cannot be used to begin sentences that form questions. To ask a question about one's own intentions would be absurd. Questions therefore should be in the form *shall I, shall we.*

Generally speaking, *should* and *would* follow the use of *shall* and *will.*

Wrong tense sequence

When a sentence contains an *If* clause both verbs must refer to the action in the same mood or manner.

I *shall* be pleased if you *will* or *can* (not *would* or *could*).
I *should* be pleased if you *would* or *could* (not *will* or *can*).
If you *will* phone me as soon as you arrive I *shall* (not *should*) be grateful.
If you *would* phone me as soon as you arrive I *should* (not *shall*) be grateful.

Shall, will, and *can* are in the indicative mood, and *should, would,* and *could* in the subjunctive, and in conditional sentences of the kind illustrated these two moods must not be mixed.

Error due to ellipsis

Ellipsis consists in the omission from a sentence of words that can be inferred; its purpose is to avoid repetition. A common error is to omit from the sentence words that form part of its grammatical structure.

You can say:

She *was not* and *could not have been* present.

but not:

They never *have* and never *will know* the truth.

Since *have* and *will know* require different forms of the verb *know,* you must say:

They never have *known* and never will *know* the truth.

Similarly, you cannot say:

They *did not* and *could not have won* the match.

since *did not* must be construed with *win* and not with *won.* Hence you must say:

They did not *win* and could not have *won* the match.

Lay; lie

You will avoid the frequent confusion between *lay* and *lie* if you remember that they are quite different verbs. Their principal parts are as follows.

Lay		Lie	
Present	*Past*	*Present*	*Past*
I lay		I lie	lay
You lay		You lie	(i.e. reclined)
He lays	laid	He lies	*or*
We lay		We lie	lied
You lay		You lie	(i.e. told an
They lay		They lie	untruth)

Since *lay* is a transitive verb it always takes an object (expressed or understood) while *lie* is intransitive and does not take an object.

> He *lays bricks* for a living.
> She *laid the directory* on the table.
> She *lies* (not *lays*) down after dinner.
> She *lay* (not *laid*) down for a short time.

Loan; lend
The use of *loan* as a verb is now confined chiefly to the United States, the preferred verb in this country being *lend*.

> The Banks *lend* (not *loan*) to their employees for house purchase on very favourable terms.
> It was announced by the chairman that the company had *lent* (not *loaned*) £50,000 during the past year.

The split infinitive
By a split infinitive is meant an intrusion of any word between *to* and the remainder of the verb. Though the splitting of the verb in this way is not in itself desirable, it is preferable to split the infinitive than to make a very obvious attempt to avoid it.

Thus, it is quite natural to say *to understand clearly, to consider carefully, to phone immediately,* and *merely to enlarge,* and for this reason these forms are to be preferred to *to clearly understand, to carefully consider, to immediately phone,* and *to merely enlarge.*

But the principle of non-splitting must not be pushed too far.

> The directors decided *to refuse flatly* any wage increase.
> The men are said *to favour strongly* a strike.

These are both awkward constructions with a pronounced artificial ring, and it is better here to split the infinitives and to say *to flatly refuse* and *to strongly favour.*

The splitting of the infinitive must not be confused with expressions such as:

> *to be* carefully examined;
> *to have* just arrived; and
> *to be* greatly increased.

Here, the infinitives consist of the first two words, and the phrases are expressed in faultless English.

EXERCISES

A

1. A few only of the following sentences are correct. Identify them, and then copy the remaining sentences, making such corrections as may be necessary.

(*a*) Each of the parts have been made separately.

(*b*) The United Nations Charter is one of the most important documents that has ever been prepared.

(*c*) We wish you to thoroughly and completely investigate the matter.

(*d*) The great variety of styles we are able to offer to customers ensure our ability to please.

(*e*) A complete set of patterns were sent to you by post yesterday.

(*f*) All being well we will be able to complete the work on Saturday.

(*g*) If neither of them are to be trusted there is little point in referring to them.

(*h*) I wish categorically to deny the accusation.

(*i*) Mr. Smith, as well as Mr. Jones, are coming here today.

(*j*) Mr. Martin has four clerks and every one of them is capable.

B

(*a*) We hope you will be able to finally settle your account by Saturday.

(*b*) He lay in bed until ten o'clock yesterday morning.

(*c*) Customers are requested to always examine their change before leaving.

(*d*) The main warehouse with its entire contents were damaged.

(*e*) Every member of the club have their own views on the matter.

(*f*) We have arranged to seriously consider your suggestion.

(*g*) Neither Mr. Brown nor Mr. White were at the meeting.

(*h*) He is one of the keenest buyers that has ever been here.

(*i*) The building, with all the firm's records of its customers, were completely destroyed in the fire.

(*j*) The number of employees have increased by more than half.

C

(*a*) A new set of files have been prepared.

(*b*) He is one of those who is never happy unless he is in the limelight.

(*c*) His bread and butter are at stake should he lose his job.

(*d*) To carefully overhaul the machine is a matter of urgency.

(*e*) Tact and discretion is an essential part of a secretary's make-up.

(*f*) Which of the two men are likely to be appointed.

(*g*) We hope to speedily finish the job.

(*h*) The financial results were as good and even better than ever.

(*i*) He laid there for an hour, as if in a dream.

(*j*) A suite of furnished rooms were available, but at a prohibitive rent.

D

(*a*) The committee adds these comments to their report.

(*b*) He never has and never will blame anyone but himself.

(*c*) The problem of making entirely new preparations were considerable.

(*d*) The box of carpenter's tools were left at the station.

(*e*) The office manager as well as the sales manager are abroad at the moment.

(f) He enquired whether either of the applicants were suitable.

(g) I am not one of those who never makes a mistake.

(h) You would be wise to carefully reconsider your proposal.

(i) The party were thoroughly disheartened by their election results.

(j) Gloucester has one of the finest cathedrals that is to be found in Britain.

2. Insert the appropriate verb, *is* or *are*, in each of the following sentences:

(a) Economics ——— the science of wealth.

(b) The statistics submitted to the meeting———misleading.

(c) Geriatrics ———the medical care of the aged.

(d) Tactics ———the science and art of disposing forces for battle.

(e) The acoustics of this large room———very good.

(f) Pediatrics ———the treatment of children's diseases.

(g) The aerobatics of the pilot———interesting to watch.

(h) Athletics ——— an essential part of school life.

(i) The politics of this speaker———those of a communist.

(j) Tactics ———subordinate to strategy.

THE WRONG USE OF PRONOUNS

The subject forms and the object forms of the personal pronouns are frequently confused, *me* being used for *I*, *him* for *he*, *them* for *they*, and vice versa.

Following the verb to be

The various forms of the verb *to be* take the nominative, that is the subject, form of the pronoun. It is incorrect to use the object form.

> Our suppliers are convinced that it *is we* (not *us*) who are at fault.
> It *is* I (not *me*) who must make the final decision.

Though it is grammatically incorrect to say *It is me*, the expression has established itself as good idiomatic English and, when standing alone, may now be defended on the ground of widespread usage.

Following than, as

When used for the purpose of comparing two pronouns or things *than* and *as* are conjunctions and are followed by the subject form of the pronouns. The pronoun and the other subject with which it is compared are then in the same, i.e. the nominative, case.

> Our competitors have been more successful *than we* (not *us*).
> We are not as well equipped to serve the market *as they* (not *them*).

These sentences are in fact elliptical, and any grammatical difficulty disappears when we express them in full and say *than we have been, as they are.*

You should note the difference in meaning between sentences such as the two following. Both are grammatically correct.

> The manager blamed the cashier more than *me* (that is, more than he blamed *me*).
> The manager blamed the cashier more than *I* (that is, more than *I* blamed her).

Who, whom

Whether the subject form *who* or the object form *whom* is correct depends upon whether the pronoun is the subject or the object of the clause to which it belongs.

> I met our new representative, *who* (not *whom*), I should imagine, will do well (subject of *will do*, e.g. I should imagine *he* will do well).
> We cannot even guess *whom* (not *who*) he will appoint (object of *will appoint*, i.e. He will appoint *him* or *her*).

Each other; one another

Each other and *one another* are reciprocal pronouns, that is they signify an exchange of action. The former is generally used in reference to two things, and the latter in reference to three or more.

> The chairman and his deputy toasted *each other* (not *one another*) before the meeting.
> The three discussed the matter with *one another* (not *each other*) for over an hour.

According to *Modern English Usage* (H.W. Fowler), failure to observe the distinction between *each other* and *one another* is no longer regarded as an error. Even so, it is better to retain the distinction.

Which

When used as a relative pronoun *which* must relate to some noun (or pronoun), known as its antecedent, previously mentioned. A common error is to use *which* without an antecedent. Thus, it is not strictly grammatical to say:

> He completed his report in good time, *which* pleased the directors.

It is evident that the pronoun *which* in this sentence relates neither to *he* nor to *report,* but to the fact of *completion,* but as this word is not included in the sentence the pronoun is without an antecedent. The sentence should be rewritten in some such form as the following.

His completion of the report in good time pleased the directors.

It is nevertheless common and convenient usage to employ *which* with an antecedent consisting not of a single word but of a phrase or clause.

He paid his debts in full, *which* is clear proof of his honesty.

But such usage requires careful handling if ambiguity is to be avoided.

No-one objected to his suggestion, *which* was disappointing.

What was disappointing?—The suggestion, or the fact that no-one objected?

And who; and which: etc.
A not uncommon error is the use of a superfluous *and* with the relative pronouns *who, whom, which. And* is correctly used only when the pronoun introduces a second relative clause.

The new operator is an excellent worker, *who* (not *and who*) knows his job.

but:

The new operator is an excellent worker, *who* knows his job, *and who* enjoys it.

Similarly:

We have just built a new factory, *which* is well sited, *and which* should double our output.
The personnel manager is a person *whose* experience is considerable, *and whom* we all respect.

Myself
The pronouns (*myself, himself,* etc.) cannot stand by themselves in the subject of a sentence.

James and *I* (not *myself*) will investigate the matter.

We can, however, say *I myself, John himself, the staff themselves,* etc., when wishing to emphasize the personal pronoun.

I *myself* will see to it.

Indefinite pronouns

Indefinite pronouns are those which refer to persons or things in a vague or general way, such as *each, everyone, any, anyone, either, neither,* etc. They refer to each individual of a class, and must therefore be treated as singular.

Everyone knows that *he* (not *they*) will receive a bonus.
Neither of the typists *is* (not *are*) able to claim that *she is* ready for promotion.

Another common error occurs from mixing the indefinite pronoun *one* with a personal pronoun. If we begin with *one* we must continue with *one* and not lapse into *he,* or some other personal pronoun; the use of pronouns within a sentence must be consistent.

If *one* wishes (*you* wish) to drive a car, *one* (*you*) must first get a licence.

Whose; of which

Grammatical purists object to the use of *whose,* except as a relative pronoun referring to living objects. But the objection often leads to cumbersome and artificially sounding constructions, and the use of *whose* for *of which* is sanctioned, on grounds of convenience, by no less an authority than Fowler.

Exhibitions are an important educational medium *whose* popularity has greatly increased in recent years. (Instead of "an educational medium the popularity *of which* . . . .")
The Stock Exchange is an institution *whose* members consist of jobbers and brokers. (Instead of "an institution the members *of which* . . . .")

Its; it's

These are commonly confused. *Its* without an apostrophe is a possessive pronoun; with the apostrophe it is an abbreviation meaning *it is* or *it has* (see p. 353).

It's (It is) the best machine of *its* kind.
It's (It has) proved *its* worth and served *its* purpose.

EXERCISES

1. A few only of the following sentences are correct. Identify them, and then copy the remaining sentences, making such corrections as may be necessary.

A

(a) He is the person whom we thought was to blame.

(b) One must safeguard his own interests.

(c) We have examined three catalogues, but found nothing suitable in either.

(d) Mr. Baxter and his assistant arranged to meet one another at Victoria Station.

(e) I decline to do business with dealers who I know are dishonest.

(f) They blame me for the mistake, which is most unjust.

(g) Everyone must either pay their subscription or resign.

(h) Every man, woman, and child have a right to be considered.

(i) Someone, we don't know whom, addressed the parcel incorrectly.

(j) I can type faster than she.

B

(a) One can usually see another's faults, but rarely his own.

(b) We have three typists neither of whom is competent.

(c) Who do you think called yesterday?

(d) His car broke down, which caused him to be late.

(e) If I were him I should be disappointed.

(f) The trader had little or no capital, which I suspected.

(g) He examined Mr. Brown's letter, who expressed himself in strong terms.

(h) One must be tactful as well as capable if they wish to succeed.

(i) He was first messenger, then clerk, then porter, but didn't do well in either capacity.

(j) I hope I can do the job as well as he.

C

(a) I am certain it was not him who phoned.

(b) He is hard-working and in consequence has been more successful than me.

(c) I suggest you and me try to settle the matter amicably.

(d) The fire spread rapidly, which caused considerable alarm.

(e) Each retired to their rooms to reflect on the matter separately.

(f) This is an excellent site, and which we should like to acquire.

(g) The girl whom you met just now is my secretary.

(h) Both our agents and ourselves regret the difficulties that have arisen.

(i) She is not nearly as good a typist as me.

(j) Mr. X is retiring, which will be a big blow to his firm.

2. Rewrite the following sentences and, where a word is missing, choose one from the given list. Note that not all the words in the list will be needed. If necessary, a word may be used more than once.

One, his, our, their, there, we, he, they, was, where, were, lying, laying, laid, lain, lay, who, whom, which, what, sang, sung.

(a) Each must do——share.

(b)——should always try to do one's best.

(*c*) —— you are.
(*d*) Everyone did what —— could to help.
(*e*) If any person saw this happen ——should come forward.
(*f*) We —— out when it happened.
(*g*) His mother is ill and is ——down.
(*h*) She felt ill and—— down.
(*i*) The boy——you wish to see has gone home.
(*j*) She —— that song last night.   (*R.S.A. Elem.*)

THE WRONG USE OF ADJECTIVES

Demonstrative adjectives
The demonstrative adjectives are *this, that, these, those.* Their use in the singular or the plural must agree with the nouns they qualify.

> I have listened to *this sort* (or *these sorts*) of excuse before.
> We rejected *those kinds* (or *that kind*) of desk as being quite unsuitable.

Comparatives and Superlatives
Great, greater, greatest; clever, cleverer, and *cleverest,* and similar groups provide three degrees of comparison know respectively as:

(*a*) *the positive,* which is the ordinary form of the adjective denoting the simple quality of the thing referred to;
(*b*) *the comparative,* which is used to compare the qualities of two things;
(*c*) *the superlative,* which is used to express the highest degree of quality when three or more things are referred to.

Thus, we say, the *better* of two machines, but the *best* of three.

> Which is the *quicker*—road or rail?
> Which of these three patterns is the *best?*

A common fault is the use of the superlative instead of the comparative when two things only are compared.

Any; either
Either means any one of two; *any* means any one of three or more.

> *Either* (not *any*) of the two patterns is quite suitable.
> *Any* (not *either*) day next week will be convenient.

Any signifies only one; hence, in comparatives and superlatives it cannot stand alone.

Woman's Life has a larger circulation than *any other* (not *any*) journal.
The *Echo* has the largest circulation of *all newspapers* (not *any newspaper*, since *largest* implies at least three things; *any* signifies only one).

Same

Same is an adjective, and it must never be used as a pronoun.

We received your letter this morning, and thank you for *same* (wrong).

say:

We thank you for your letter, which we received this morning.
The parcel was received early last week, and we forwarded *same* to Malta immediately (wrong).

say:

. . . and we forwarded *it* to Malta immediately.

The two first; two last

It is impossible to have more than one first or last of anything, and the expressions *the two first, the three last,* etc., are therefore quite wrong.

Your *first two* (not *two first*) orders were completed last week.
None of the *last three* (not *three last*) quotations were acceptable.

EXERCISES

1. Some of the following sentences are correct; others are not. Identify the correct sentences, and then copy the remaining ones, making such corrections as may be necessary.

A

(*a*) Of the two proposals we think the first is the most attractive.
(*b*) Smith knows more about the job than any person on the staff.
(*c*) I have chosen the willow pattern, and wish you to deliver same next week.
(*d*) Of the three clerks Thompson is by far the more reliable.
(*e*) I dislike those sorts of complaints more than I can say.
(*f*) The oldest of the two partners is the one with the grey beard.
(*g*) I sent him half a dozen samples, but he was unable to choose from either.
(*h*) I regret that the last three pages are missing.
(*i*) Having received your cheque this morning, we are writing to thank you for same.
(*j*) These kind of ribbons are more expensive, but they last longer.

B

(*a*) We have a wider selection than any firm in the town.
(*b*) This is the rarest specimen of any I have.

. PITFALLS AND TRAPS

(c) It is precisely those sort of mistakes that result in loss of custom.

(d) Young people have little interest in these kinds of film.

(e) Of French and Spanish, which is the easiest to learn?

(f) Either of the three applicants will be quite suitable.

(g) The first two to leave were faced with long journeys.

(h) Red, blue, or green—either of these colours will do.

(i) Which is it best to do—buy now, or to wait a while?

(j) Any of them will do; they are both the same size.

CHAPTER NINETEEN

More Pitfalls and Traps

Error is a hardy plant; it flourisheth in every soil.

Martin F. Tupper: *Proverbial Philosophy*

THE WRONG USE OF ADVERBS

Less and fewer

Less means a smaller amount. It is used in reference to quantity; *fewer* is used in reference to number. It is a common fault to use *less* where *fewer* would be correct.

> He now owes *less* (not *fewer*) than five hundred pounds.
> *Fewer* (not *less*) than a dozen applications have been received.

Scarcely; hardly

Scarcely and *hardly* are both followed by *when,* and not, as so frequently happens, by *than. Than* is used only in comparisons.

> *Scarcely* had the phone rung *when* (not *than*) I was called away.
> We had *hardly* left the bank *when* (not *than*) we were attacked.

A correct alternative to *scarcely* and *hardly* would be *No sooner,* which takes *than.*

> *No sooner* had the phone rung *than* I was called away.

Quite

Quite means completely, entirely, absolutely, and is an adverb. The practice of using it to qualify nouns as if it were an adjective is one to be avoided.

> The firm continues to do *quite* well (modifying the adverb *well*).
> We are *quite* prepared to meet your claim for compensation (modifying the adjective *prepared*).

But you cannot say:

> The chairman was given *quite* an ovation (say instead, a *great ovation*).
> *Quite* a number of people agreed with the policy adopted (say instead, a *large number . . ., a great many . . .*).

Also

Also is an adverb, but it is often wrongly used as a conjunction to introduce afterthoughts where the correct form would be *and, and also, but also,* or *as well as.* This wrong use of the unsupported *also* may be acceptable in conversation, but in writing it must be supported by the conjunctive forms *and* or *but,* or better still, avoided altogether by structuring sentences to express the complete thought in a single statement.

It is wrong to say:

> We sent the goods last week, *also* the invoice.

Say instead:

> . . . the goods *and (and also, as well as)* the invoice.

> Britain's chief imports consist of food, *also* raw materials.

Say instead:

> . . . consist of food *and (and also, as well as)* raw materials;

or

> . . . consist not only of food *but also* of raw materials.

Nor should *also* be used instead of *furthermore, moreover, besides, in addition* and similar terms to introduce new sentences or their equivalents, e.g. after a semicolon.

> When washed the dress shrank; *also* (say *moreover,* etc.) the colour ran.

Misplacement of only

It is a general rule that an adverb should be placed as near as possible to the word it qualifies.

Special care is needed with *only.* Its correct grammatical position is next to, preferably before, the word it qualifies.

> *Only* he borrowed £15. (i.e. he, and no else, borrowed).

He *only* borrowed £15 (i.e. he did not seek the money as a gift, but merely borrowed it).

He borrowed *only* £15 (i.e. he borrowed £15, and no more).

But if there is no ambiguity *only* may be allowed to take what is felt to be its natural place in the sentence. Thus you may say:

She *only* sang one song.

which sounds more natural than the strictly correct

She sang *only* one song.

All right

The spelling of this adverb as a single word *alright* is incorrect, and is no doubt due to confusion with words like *almost, already,* and *altogether.* It should always be written as two separate words—*all* and *right.*

EXERCISES

1. Recast the following sentences to include any necessary corrections:

A

(*a*) One member of staff only arrived late this morning.
(*b*) We received less than half a dozen letters by this morning's post.
(*c*) It will be quite a problem to get the work finished in time.
(*d*) Scarcely had I replaced the receiver than the phone rang again.
(*e*) We only deliver in your district on Tuesdays.
(*f*) In winter we find ourselves with less than ten hours of full daylight.
(*g*) Quite a lot of responsibility falls on the deputy.
(*h*) He had hardly begun dictating than he was called away.
(*i*) The newly appointed assistant is quite a good typist.
(*j*) There were less of us at the meeting than usual.

B

(*a*) Mathematical tables can only be learned by rote memorization.
(*b*) There is quite a lot of truth in what you say.
(*c*) Hardly had I arrived than I was invited to play.
(*d*) The school only taught commercial subjects at the elementary level.
(*e*) The present economic position calls for more rather than for less restrictions.
(*f*) The word capital is used as a noun, meaning accumulated wealth; also as an adjective, meaning most important.
(*g*) That is quite a different story.
(*h*) I had scarcely reached home than it began to rain.

(i) The value of the experiment can only be measured by results.

(j) Although we work less hours and less hard than formerly, we enjoy a higher living standard.

(k) His late arrival created quite a problem.

THE WRONG USE OF PREPOSITIONS

Between

Between signifies two, so that you cannot say:

Leave a space between each paragraph.

since *each* signifies only one. You must say:

Leave a space *between* the paragraphs.

or

Leave a space *after each* paragraph.

Between is a preposition, and its following nouns and pronouns must be in the objective case.

Between you and *me* (not I).

Among

Among signifies three or more, and some grammarians claim that we cannot "divide something *between* three", but must say *among three*. According to the *Oxford Dictionary,* however, *between* is the only word we have to express the relationship of one thing to a number of surrounding things. It is, therefore, correct to say:

The space lying *between* the three buildings.
There is nothing to choose *between* the four of them.

When you wish to express a relationship to things collectively or in a general way, however, *among* is correct.

The profits will be shared *among* the workers.
What is £50 *among* so many?

Among; amongst

Although either form of this preposition is correct, *among* is the more usual, except immediately before a vowel, when *amongst* is preferred because it sounds better.

The letter was found *among* the papers in the drawer.

but

The letter was found *amongst* a set of price lists.

Till; until

Till is now the usual form of this preposition, except at the beginning of a sentence.

A decision will not be known *till* Saturday.

but

Until tomorrow, a decision cannot be given.

Different to

Although *different to* has the sanction of writers of all times and cannot be regarded as wrong, accepted usage requires that *different* should take *from* and not *to* as its following preposition.

The bulk is *different from* the sample we submitted.

Due to; owing to

Due to and *owing to* are frequently misused. The former means *caused by* and should be associated with a noun or noun equivalent; the latter means *because of* and should always be associated with a verb.

The late *arrival* of the goods was *due to* a strike at the docks (*due to* is associated with the noun *arrival*).
The goods *arrived* late *owing to* a strike at the docks.
The high *quotation* was *due to* an error in calculation.
We *quoted* incorrectly *owing to an error in calculation.*

It should be noted that the verbs *to be, to seem, to appear,* always take *due to.*

It *was* largely *due to* her inexperience.
That some prices *have been* increased *is due to* the higher cost of materials.

Try to; try and; come to; come and

Try and and *Come and* are often used when *Try to* and *Come to* would be more correct.

Try *to* (not *and*) succeed.

Here, *trying* refers to *succeeding* and the sentence implies a single activity—trying for the purpose of succeeding.

"Try *and* succeed", on the other hand, implies two separate activities—*trying* and *succeeding*.

Try (e.g. work harder) and succeed.

Similarly with:

I hope you will come *to* hear me play (a single activity—coming for the purpose of hearing me play).

I hope you will come *and* hear me play (two separate activities—*coming* and *hearing*).

Like; as
It is a vulgarism to use *like* as if it were a conjunction, and to substitute it for *as.*

Prices rose considerably, *as* (not *like*) I expected.
He is a good salesman, *as* (not *like*) his father was.

The use of *like* as a conjunction in such sentences as these is the result of careless writing and loose thinking and is unpardonable, but in the sentence:

He is a good salesman, *like* his father.

like is correctly used as a preposition governing *his father.*

Except; without
Except and *without* must not be used as conjunctions; they must be replaced by *unless.*

We cannot quote *unless* (not *except* or *without*) you can provide a sample.
Unless (not *except* or *without*) the transport position improves delivery will be delayed.

Prepositional endings
The end of a sentence is a position of emphasis. It is therefore better to avoid ending a sentence with a preposition, unless the result sounds stilted and artificial.

By what date do you want the work finished? (not *What date . . . finished by?*)
He is the person to whom I gave the money (not *gave the money to*).
They are a firm with whom we frequently do business (not *do business with*).

But the rule must not be applied too rigidly, otherwise artificiality and even absurdity may result, as when Mr. Churchill humorously referred to: "The sort of English up with which I will not put", thus:

That person isn't worth listening to.

sounds much more natural than:

That person isn't one to whom it is worth listening.

and:

That by Mr. X is the only suitable book I know of.

sounds better than:

That by Mr. X is the only suitable book of which I know.

The distinction between short forms and contractions is one we ought to get rid of.

is preferable to:

. . . is one of which we ought to get rid.

The ear is a good guide in such cases.

EXERCISES

1. Recast the following sentences to include any necessary corrections.

A

(a) The goods you sent us were of a quality very different to that we had counted on.

(b) The manufacturers informed us they could not deliver by the weekend like they had hoped.

(c) Without his parent signs it the agreement is of no legal value.

(d) His way of doing things is very different to his manager's.

(e) She hadn't the least idea it was me she was talking to.

(f) There must be no secrets between you and I.

(g) This youth does not work like his father did.

(h) X, Y, and Z shared the profits equally between them.

(i) The delay in replying is owing to the secretary's illness.

(j) Due to the strike we may not be able to deliver as promised.

B

(a) We are able to reduce prices due to a lowering of costs.

(b) We cannot increase wages except we can increase output.

(c) Prepare a credit note just like you did the one yesterday.

(d) Who were you typing that letter for just now?

(e) Do like I do, and decline to take part.

(f) The outcome is very different to that we had been led to expect.

(g) He was energetic and capable, just like his father was.

(h) It is unfortunate there is no-one to discuss the problem with.

(i) Due to a blackout the works were plunged into darkness.

(j) The breakdown in negotiations is owing to the unreasonable attitude of the management.

THE WRONG USE OF CONJUNCTIONS

Correlative conjunctions

Correlative conjunctions are those used in pairs as *both . . . and, either . . . or, neither . . . nor, not only . . . but also* (see p. 235).

Each of the words forming the pair must be followed by the same part of speech.

Thus, you cannot say:

The parcels are suitable for transit *both* by road *and* rail.

because the first correlative *(both)* is followed by a preposition *(by)* and the second correlative *(and)* by a noun *(rail)*.

The mistake is rectified if you include *by* before *rail.* Both correlatives are then followed by prepositions.

Nor can you say:

The secretary may *either* be in his office *or* in the warehouse.

because the first correlative *(either)* is followed by a verb *(be)* and the second correlative *(or)* by a preposition *(in)*.

You must reverse the position of *either* and *be.* The sentence then correctly reads:

The secretary may be *either in* his office *or in* the warehouse.

Similarly, you cannot say:

We were *not only* impressed by his speech *but also* by his manner.

since the first correlative *(not only)* is followed by a verb *(impressed)*, and the second correlative *(but also)* by a preposition *(by)*.

You must say:

We were impressed *not only by* his speech, *but also by* his manner.

Both correlatives are then followed by prepositions.

Though; although
Either of these forms of the conjunction may be used, though the former is more usual, except at the beginning of a sentence.

No decision was reached *though* the meeting lasted an hour.

but:

Although the meeting lasted an hour no decision was reached.

While; whilst
While is the more usual form of this conjunction, though the use of *whilst* as an alternative is permissible.

Look after the office *while* I am away.

EXERCISES

Recast the following sentences to include any necessary corrections.

A
(a) They not only decline to pay their account, but also to proffer any explanation.

(b) The book you are seeking is neither in the desk nor the bookcase.

(c) Neither he or I approve of the steps taken.

(d) The accused neither admitted the charge, nor did he deny it.

(e) His success is neither due to hard work nor to unusual abilities.

(f) The premises were not only fitted with electricity but also with gas.

(g) The script contained an error both at the beginning and the end.

(h) He is neither inclined to listen to advice nor to act for himself.

(i) I have a higher shorthand speed than her.

(j) A study of trends both within the national economy and the undertaking itself has become necessary.

B
(a) You can either pay me now, or later.

(b) The proposed changes not only apply to shorthand but to typewriting.

(c) The two schools differ considerably both in outlook and achievement.

(d) A lecture may either be read, or delivered without notes.

(e) We found it necessary not only to provide him with clothes but also with money.

(*f*) To ensure the fullest benefit from homework, regulation both of its quality and its quantity is necessary.

(*g*) The agent's principal must either be named or clearly identified in some other way.

(*h*) The organization is not only concerned with attaining its objectives in the present, but in the future.

(*i*) Though he may be poor he is honest.

(*j*) She had more mistakes in her homework than me.

THE WRONG USE OF PARTICIPLES

A participle is a verbal adjective, that is, a word which is part verb and part adjective; it is verbal in form but adjectival in function.

A participle may be either past, like *waited,* or present, like *waiting.*

I was *irritated* by the experience.
It was an *irritating* experience.

The unattached participle

Because a participle is a kind of adjective, it must always be related to a noun. One of the commonest faults committed by English writers, and one that occurs frequently in business letters, is that of starting a sentence with a participle and then failing to provide it with its noun (or pronoun), thus leaving it unrelated or unattached. The participle then tends to become associated with the subject of the following main clause, sometimes with absurd results.

While *reading* your letter the *telephone* rang.
While *engaged* with a representative, the *telephone* rang.

Both these sentences are wrong. *Reading* and *engaged* clearly relate to some person, but as the person is not specified, the participles tend to associate themselves with *the telephone,* the subject of the following main clauses. The association is manifestly absurd, and the sentences should read as follows.

While *I was reading* your letter, *the telephone* rang.
While *I was (he was,* etc.*) engaged* with a representative, *the telephone* rang.

The following is another example of this faulty construction.

The contractors are waiting for the licence, and as soon as *received building* can begin.

Received in this sentence is grammatically related to *building,* though it is intended to relate to *the licence.*

To put the sentence right the addition of *it is* immediately before *received* is necessary.

The participle in correspondence
One of the commonest faults in business letters is that of the unattached participle in the opening and concluding sentences of the letter.

Introductory phrases
Failure to associate opening phrases such as *Referring to your letter, Replying to your enquiry* with their appropriate nouns or pronouns is a common cause of error.

> *Referring* to your letter, *our agents* inform us that the consignment has now been shipped (*incorrect*).

In this sentence *referring* is wrongly associated with *our agents,* though it is clearly the intention to associate it with the writer of the letter. You must therefore write:

> *Referring* to your letter *we* have been informed by our agents (*correct*).

Again:

> *Referring* to your complaint of yesterday, there is little we can do in the matter (*incorrect*).

In this sentence there is nothing to which *referring* can be attached, and the sentence must be rewritten to include the pronoun that is clearly intended.

> *Referring* to your complaint, *we* (or I) regret there is little we can do in the matter (*correct*).

Closure
A practice now much less common than formerly is to bring business letters to a close by phrases beginning with a participle. Phrases of this kind must be followed by expressions such as *I am, We are, I remain, We remain,* otherwise the participle is unattached.

> *Regretting* the delay that occurred,
> *I am,*
> Yours faithfully

> *Thanking* you for your help,
> *We are,*
> Yours truly

The expression *Yours truly* is now somewhat old-fashioned and little used in business. Being rather less formal than *Yours faithfully* it is sometimes used between persons well known to each other, or where a personal relationship exists, as with solicitors, bankers and doctors.

Participles used as prepositions

Words like *provided, providing, seeing, regarding, concerning, considering, supposing, having regard to, owing to,* are sometimes used, not as participles, but as prepositions. When they are used in this way no question of attaching them arises, and sentences such as the following are grammatically quite correct.

> *Provided* no one objects, the suggestion will be adopted.
> *Considering* the amount of time spent on the enquiry, the results are disappointing.
> *Supposing* the facts to be as reported, the position would be serious.
> *Notwithstanding* the strike, the year's profit is satisfactory.

Not all participles have established a right to be used as prepositions, and the danger of the unattached participle needs to be constantly watched. The important thing is to make sure that a sentence says just what it means.

The gerund, or verbal noun

Consider the following examples.

> The secretary dislikes Joan typing.

In this sentence the grammatical subject is *the secretary,* and what the sentence says is that he dislikes Joan. It is much more probable that what he dislikes is not Joan but *her typing,* that is the *typing of Joan,* in other words *Joan's typing,* in which case the sentence should read:

> The secretary dislikes *Joan's typing.*

Similarly:

> She hates her fiancé smoking.

What is it that she hates? Not her fiancé, surely, but the smoking; that is she does not like her fiancé to smoke, in other words *her fiancé's smoking,* so that the sentence should read:

She hates her *fiancé's smoking*.

again:

The train travelling at one hundred and twenty miles an hour frightened everyone.

What was it that frightened everyone? Certainly not the train, and certainly not the travelling, but *the travelling at one hundred and twenty miles an hour,* in other words, *the train's travelling* at a high speed, and the sentence must be recast with *train* as a possessive.

The *train's travelling* at one hundred and twenty miles an hour, etc.

In the three examples given, *typing, smoking,* and *travelling* are not participles, but verbs used as nouns, i.e. verbal nouns, or gerunds as some grammarians call them. With their preceding nouns *Joan, fiancé*, and *train* they represent a single idea that can be expressed only by taking the verbal noun and using it to form a possessive construction.

To understand the proper use of this possessive construction is important, because there is sometimes a significant difference between it and the non-possessive construction, as in the following sentences.

Come and see *me* typing.
Come and see *my* typing.

The two sentences mean different things and the difference is obvious. In the first, the object of *see* is *me,* and *typing* is a true participle, meaning *when I am typing.* In the second, typing is a verbal noun serving as the object of *see*, used with the possessive adjective *my* to give the possessive construction needed.

Care is necessary with sentences of this kind, since it is nearly always the possessive construction that is intended, though the non-possessive (i.e. the participle) construction is often mistakenly used for it.

EXERCISES

1. Recast the following sentences to include any necessary corrections.

A

(a) Replying to your enquiry, the goods were sent by rail yesterday.

(b) Referring to the account you sent us last week, you have omitted to allow the usual trade discount.

(c) Having established a good business connection, an effort is now being made to extend operations.

(d) Referring to our letter of the 18th, it must be stressed that we cannot accept any further delay.

(e) Being the only product of its kind on the market, we are naturally optimistic concerning sales.

(f) Thanking you for your interest in the matter, Yours truly.

(g) The chairman decided that, being Christmas, the offices would close until next Wednesday.

(h) Whilst not agreeing with all you say, you certainly have some ground for complaint.

(i) Hoping to hear from you very soon, Believe me, Yours faithfully.

(j) Having been advised of the ship's arrival, a busy time may now be expected.

B

(a) Having labelled the parcels, they were taken to post.

(b) Referring to your enquiry, the invoices were posted yesterday.

(c) Being an old friend of mine, I did my best to help him.

(d) Entering the room, it was found to be empty.

(e) Being both tired and hungry, the hotel was a welcome sight.

(f) Entering the kitchen, the door closed with a bang.

(g) After enjoying the dance, all thoughts turned to supper.

(h) Scanning the policy quickly, several mistakes were noted.

(i) Being Saturday, the trains were packed.

(j) Arriving late, our attendance at the meeting wasn't recorded.

2. Write out the following sentences, making whatever corrections you consider to be necessary to indicate the meaning probably intended.

A

(a) Have you any objection to me waiting till he comes?

(b) What do you think about him being appointed secretary?

(c) You may rely upon me doing all I can for you.

(d) The news of a woman being appointed bank manager was most interesting.

(e) The secretary travelling all night wasn't a good preparation for the following day's conference.

(f) Everyone was surprised at him being promoted.

(g) It was not until after the first World War that women working in offices became at all common.

(h) He phoned to ask whether there was any objection to him applying for the job.

(i) Well, gentlemen, our past year's record profit is offset by the treasurer having absconded with every penny of it.

(j) There was no objection to the examination being taken at different times.

B

(a) He had no knowledge of the money having been stolen.

(b) When teaching typewriting the machines should be carefully arranged.

(c) The bus strike will prevent us arriving at the office on time.

(*d*) There is no objection to the examination starting an hour earlier.

(*e*) When buying goods on hire purchase, payments are spread over an extended period.

(*f*) Air transport carries goods with little risk of them being stolen.

(*g*) The insurance covers loss resulting from the ship running into trouble.

(*h*) A probation officer's job can be very arduous, often working twelve hours a day.

(*i*) Perishable goods are placed in a refrigerator to prevent them going bad.

(*j*) The chair should be carefully adjusted when typing.

3. The following letters contain a number of grammatical errors. Recast the letters, making whatever corrections you consider to be necessary.

A. *Application for a Post*

Dear Sir,

Having seen your advertisement in the "Daily Telegraph", my qualifications and experience may interest you.

I am 25 years of age, have had eight years' office experience and am quite an experienced shorthand-typist. The promise of better prospects, together with easier travelling, are my main reasons for wishing to change my present job. I have recently applied for two other posts nearer my home, but neither were to my liking.

My present employer is one of those men who is always willing to help those who work for him to improve themselves. I am therefore sure that he will be willing to give me a reference should you approach him for one. He and myself have now worked together for the past five years, which has been very enjoyable. Everyone, however, should broaden their experience, and that is another reason for my present application.

Should you wish to interview me I could call to see you on either of the three first days of next week.

Yours faithfully,

B. *Letter reporting Damage*

Dear Sirs,

Referring to your advice note of 18 July, the lantern slides arrived yesterday in a badly damaged condition; quite a number were broken. We do not know who to blame for the damage, but we shall make a full investigation, which should enable us to place the responsibility. Each of the carriers concerned are aware that they will be liable for any damage due to their negligence. The two first to handle the package have already informed us that they have had no less than three other complaints of a similar nature during the past month, but that in each case the goods complained about were alright when they passed them on.

We not only feel concerned about the amount of damage that has occurred, but also about the number of occasions on which we have had similar cause to complain.

Hoping however that we will soon have information that will enable us to lodge a claim in the right quarter.

Yours faithfully,

C. *Letter of Complaint*

Dear Sirs,

Replying to your letter of 20 January, our customers now inform us that the shirting supplied last November was too light in shade, which is unfortunate, since they are customers who we do considerable business with. They also report finding quite a deterioration in the quality of some of the rolls, owing, they suggest, to breaks in the thread during spinning.

This complaint, together with others we have recently received from several other customers, are a matter of serious concern to us, and we will be grateful for your assurance that you will take all possible steps only to supply shirting of first-class quality against future orders. We look forward to you doing everything you can to ensure this.

Hoping there will be no further difficulties of this kind.

Yours faithfully,

D. *Letter concerning Building Site*

Dear Mr. Baxter,

Referring to your report of 30 March, the work indicated by you on the charts you sent us appears to continue to satisfactorily progress, and we congratulate you not only on the progress made to date but also because of the happy relations you have established between all who are working on the site. New plant and machinery were provided at the beginning of the year, and each of the men responsible for its maintenance have been given full instructions concerning it.

We should be glad if you will continue to keep us informed of progress. During the past year the number of workmen engaged on the site have been increased by 25%, so that we shall have to carefully watch the question of labour costs and ensure that they do not rise unnecessarily. Very soon now we hope to appoint the new Clerk of Works, but whom it is likely to be we have no idea. Until the appointment is made we trust you will continue to supervise operations for us.

Thanking you for all your help and co-operation.

Yours sincerely,

4. Rewrite the following sentences, correcting any definite errors (but otherwise altering the sentences as little as possible).

(*a*) He said that those sort of sweets aren't his favourites.

(*b*) Walking home yesterday, a car going very quick came past me, nearly knocking me down and which didn't stop.

(*c*) Mary and I am rather tired and don't feel like eating no supper; we'll go and lay down for a while instead.

5. Rewrite the following correctly, and give reasons for your corrections.

(*a*) Due to your not writing last month, everybody in the bank thought you were seriously ill.

(*b*) In every branch, customers exist at whom we all sneer yet secretly admire.

(*c*) Referring to your letter of the 13th instant, details of the proposed mortgage were despatched to you last month.   (*I. of B.*)

6. Correct the following sentences and give reasons for any alterations you may make.

(*a*) Having only received your order today, it is impossible to despatch the new machine before next week.

(*b*) To effectively dispose of this problem, the result of the shareholders' meeting should have given more authority to him and I.

(*c*) The reason why the new sales programme failed was because it had not been planned as it should have been.   (*I. of B.*)

CHAPTER TWENTY

Reported Speech

For nothing goes with sense or light,
That will not with old rules jump right.
Butler: *Hudibras*

Since a précis is a reported version of what someone else has written it is necessary to write in the past tense and to use the form of expression known as reported speech. This involves changing what is known as direct or first-person speech into indirect or third-person speech. There should be no difficulty in this. The change from direct to indirect speech is a constant though quite unconscious daily process with all of us; we are constantly reporting by word of mouth something we have seen, or read, or what someone else has said. If your chief says, "Will you type this letter for me straight away?" you would report this by saying, *He asked me* to type *that letter for him* straight away. And if your friend says, "I don't understand the use of documentary credits", you would report, without thought or hesitation, *He said he didn't* understand the use of documentary credits.

You will notice that the inverted commas used in direct speech are omitted from indirect speech. This is because the words reported are not those of the original speaker, but those of the person reporting.

The process of converting direct to indirect speech is a perfectly natural one, performed in everyday life without reference to any rules for guidance. There are, however, a few simple rules which must be known and carefully followed in précis writing. They are summarized as follows.

(*a*) provide an introductory clause;
(*b*) use the past tense throughout;
(*c*) put pronouns in the third person;
(*d*) change proximate into remote expressions;
(*e*) omit words of address.

These rules will now be considered more fully.

The introductory clause

Because we are providing a reported version of what someone else has already said or written it is natural to begin with an introductory reference in the past tense, and if the source of the original is known it must be acknowledged.

> Writing recently in *The Guardian, the music critic* said that . . . .
> In a leading article on race relations *it was alleged that* . . . .

If the source of the original is not known, then an introductory clause in general terms is used—*The writer said that* . . ., *The speaker was of the opinion that* . . ., *he thought* . . ., *he noticed* . . ., *he wished to know* . . ., or whatever other may be the appropriate verb.

Use of the past tense

The same tense must be employed throughout, and since the verb in the introductory clause is in the past tense all other verbs must be in the past tense, verbs in the present tense being turned into the past—*am* and *is* into *was*, *are* into *were*, and so on.

> "At what time *do you expect* to arrive in Paris?" I asked him *(direct)*.
> I asked him at what time *he expected* to arrive in Paris *(indirect)*.

Similarly, *shall* and *will* become *should* and *would*, and *may* and *can* become *might* and *could*.

> He said, "They *will* send the goods by passenger train *tomorrow* if they *can (direct)*.
> He said they *would* send the goods by passenger train *the next day* if they *could (indirect)*.

If, however, the statement makes reference to something that is *permanently* true, the appropriate verb is kept in the present tense.

> "Banking", he told us, "*assists* trade, since it *provides* a safe and easy means of making payments" *(direct)*.
> He told us that banking *assists* trade, since it *provides* a safe and easy means of making payments *(indirect)*.

Notice also that the past simple (i.e. the preterite) tense in direct speech becomes the past-perfect tense in reported speech.

> He said, "I *wanted* to be present at the ceremony" *(direct)*.
> He said that he *had wanted* to be present at the ceremony *(indirect)*.

Use of third-person pronouns
Pronouns in the first and second person must be changed into third, so that *I* becomes *he* or *she; we* becomes *they; you* becomes *he, she, they* (subject) and *him, her, them* (object), etc.

"*I* have no doubt *you* will agree with *me*", said the chairman *(direct)*.
The chairman said *he* had no doubt *they* would agree with *him (indirect)*.

But if the person referred to in the quotation is the one reporting, second-person pronouns are changed into first.

He told me, "*You* cannot have an overdraft unless *you* can provide security" *(direct)*.
He told me *I* could not have an overdraft unless *I* could provide security *(indirect)*.

Should there be any danger of misunderstanding, the noun referred to in the quotation must be repeated (within brackets) after the pronoun in the reported statement.

Speaking to his assistant, the manager said, "*I* have to attend a meeting at four o'clock" *(direct)*.
The manager told his assistant that *he (the manager)* had to attend a meeting at four o'clock *(indirect)*.

Replacement of proximate expressions
Words expressing nearness of time or place must be replaced by words expressing remoteness.

this	becomes	that
these	becomes	those
now	becomes	then, at that time
here	becomes	there
come	becomes	gone
today	becomes	that day
yesterday	becomes	the day before, the previous day
tomorrow	becomes	the next (following) day
last (week, etc.)	becomes	the week (etc.) before
next (week, etc.)	becomes	the week (etc.) after, the following week (etc.).

The speaker said, "*I have come here this* afternoon . . ." *(direct)*.
The speaker said *he had gone there that* afternoon . . . *(indirect)*.
"*I saw him yesterday*", said the foreman *(direct)*.
The foreman said *he had seen him on the previous day (indirect)*.

"We shall meet *here* again at the same time *tomorrow"*, announced the chairman *(direct)*.

The chairman announced that *they would* meet *there* again at the same time *on the following day (indirect)*.

Omission of words of address

Words of address, such as *Ladies and Gentlemen, Sir, Dear Sir, Mr. Chairman,* must be either turned into an equivalent phrase or, if unimportant, omitted altogether.

"Dear Sir—I did not receive *your* letter until *this* morning" *(direct)*.

He (She) replied saying that *he (she)* did not receive *his (her, their)* (i.e. the writer's) letter until *that* morning *(indirect)*.

The chairman said, *"Ladies and Gentlemen—*It *is my* pleasure to report that . . ." *(direct)*.

Addressing those present (or *the meeting*) the chairman said it *was his* pleasure to report that . . . *(indirect)*.

A worked example

The foregoing rules make the exercise of putting a passage into reported speech appear a very formal and rather complicated matter. But, as we have seen, reported speech is something we are practising unconsciously and quite naturally every day of our lives. In the process of conversion we must be careful not to alter the form in which the sentences in the original passage are cast, since we are not asked to make a paraphrase or to attempt in any way to improve the language of the original. As far as possible, therefore, the words and punctuation marks used in the original must be preserved, except for the necessary logical variations outlined in the foregoing rules. The following example should be carefully studied.

Direct speech

"Then I will drink," said Mr. Micawber, "if my friend Copperfield will permit me to take that social liberty, to the days when my friend Copperfield and myself were younger, and fought our way in the world side by side. I may say of myself and Copperfield, in words we have sung together before now:"

Reported speech

Mr. Micawber said *he would* drink, if *his* friend Copperfield *would* permit *him* to take that social liberty, to the days when *his* friend Copperfield and *himself had been* younger, and *had fought their* way in the world side by side. *He might* say of *himself* and Copperfield, in words *they had* sung together before *then:*

Notice that all the inverted commas of the original have disappeared and that the original is left more or less untouched, except for the words and phrases in italics.

Some special cases

Because a report of what has been said or written always comes later it is natural, as mentioned at the beginning of this chapter, to begin with an introductory reference using a verb in the past tense, but where what is reported continues into the present it is not uncommon to use introductory verbs in the present tense. The tenses of verbs in the passage quoted then remain unchanged.

The secretary said, "I put the document in the safe this morning".

Introduced by a verb in the customary past tense the report would read:

The secretary said he *had put* the document in the safe *that* morning.

But introduced by a verb in the present tense the verb *put* in the original statement would remain unchanged.

The secretary *says* he *put* the document in the safe that morning.

It is not always possible to change what is said into reported speech in the way suggested by the rules. This is so especially with instructions and commands. If the secretary says:

"Don't allow the documents to be taken away by anyone."

the version in reported speech would be in some such form as:

The secretary gave instructions that no-one must be allowed to take the documents away.

EXERCISES

1. Turn the following into reported speech.

(a) The captain said, "I shall require William to take my place today".

(b) I said, "I was quite unable to pay the account before the end of the month".

(c) He then replied, "I have never before been asked to do such a thing".

(d) "We have done all we can", said the colonel, "until our supplies reach us tonight".

(e) The pilot declared, "I have not had the slightest trouble with my engine".

(f) They said, "It was our first visit to that theatre".

(g) The girl replied, "I will finish the coat as soon as I can".

(h) The chairman announced, "No seats will be given to candidates who canvass votes".

(i) The speaker said, "I have no doubt you will agree with me when I say the question is not one for discussion".

(j) "In my opinion", said the head, "this boy has a lot of good in him".

2. Turn the following passage into direct speech.

The chairman said that he spoke on behalf of his fellow-directors when he said that they had no interest in the matter except where it affected the financial security of the company. They thought that Mr. Summers' proposal was one that should not be adopted then, even if it were later on. The essential thing to do at that time was to make the company stable by raising the reserve fund. If they made the purchase suggested, the whole future life of the company would depend on the success of that venture alone. *(U.L.C.I.)*

3. Turn the following passage into direct speech.

The manager of the department called a meeting of his assistants and said that as they all knew the firm had that week changed hands. The new board of directors had, however, decided to make no changes in the staff providing that the employees proved suitable and loyal. He wanted them to understand that he personally was satisfied with their co-operation. He was sure that, if they determined to continue with the same diligence and punctuality as they had shown in the past, the new directors could not but be satisfied with the work of that department. They had their difficulties but these had been overcome. Once more he urged them to support him by their efforts and he felt confident that he could assure them that they need have no worries as to the security of their positions. *(U.L.C.I.)*

4. Convert the following passage into "indirect" (i.e. reported) speech.

"Well I never!" shrieked the somewhat hysterical landlady. "Here I am, an honest widow, such as never has done, nor ever will do a wicked thing, and this is what I get for my pains. My poor dear husband, rest his soul, would shiver even where he is now, if he knew how I am being treated. Yes! Mrs. Harris, you are right. You know well enough how I hate going to court (although circumstances have compelled me several times during the last year) but I shall have to do it. Either that lodger promises faithfully never to pass nasty remarks about dear Tibby, or I get him a rejection order immediately." *(U.L.C.I.)*

5. Rewrite the following passage in reported speech. Begin thus: The speaker said that . . . .

"Westland Engineers Ltd. has had a successful year. The range of Welrise 'up-and-over' Garage and Industrial doors manufactured by this company is

becoming increasingly popular. A new type of vertical lifting door, the Welpak, has been developed, is now in production, and has been ordered by a number of important firms at home and abroad. We have good expectations of the continued expansion of this subsidiary. I know that the shareholders will support me in thanking all those whose work has made this year's success possible."
                                                                                                (R.S.A., Inter.)

6. Rewrite the following passage in reported speech, beginning "The speaker said . . ." Keep the meaning of the original words, without using any of the figurative expressions printed in italics.

I propose that we let the hut at a *peppercorn rent* to the Boy Scouts. They have *left no stone unturned* in their search for a place to meet, and since we use the hut *once in a blue moon* we shall be acting *like a dog in the manger* if we *give the cold shoulder* to their request.

7. Rewrite the following in reported speech.

Counsel: Do you admit, Mr. Smith, that you could have gone to the rescue of the bank messenger when he was first attacked by the accused?

Witness: I can only repeat that my surprise on seeing a masked intruder made any action on my part momentarily impossible.

Counsel: But, surely, you must have been spurred to action when the intruder proceeded to attack your old friend the cashier?

Judge intervening: I think my learned friend must accept the testimony of the witness. Apparently, surprise, or some other agency, prevented the witness from taking any action to help his friends and colleagues.   (I. of B.)

8. Rewrite the following in indirect speech.

Clerk: Good morning, madam. What can I do for you?

Customer: I am Miss Jane White. I have recently come from London and my account has been transferred to this branch. I have the necessary credentials with me.

Clerk: I am pleased to meet you. Are you not the Doctor White who has recently taken up an appointment at the University? We shall be very pleased to help you in any way we can.   (I. of B.)

9. Rewrite the following in indirect or reported speech.

Policeman: Do you realize, sir, that parking is not permitted in this street?

Motorist: I'm sorry, constable. My engine has been running very irregularly for the last fifty miles. I think there's some fault in the ignition, but I haven't been able to trace it. I've stopped at several garages but, as it's a Sunday, none of them had a mechanic available. Now the wretched thing has failed completely.

Policeman: We shall have to move the vehicle into the next side-street, sir. Otherwise, you will be causing an obstruction.   (I. of B.)

10. Turn the following into indirect speech.

"How many here?" asked Budd.

"A hundred and forty, sir," answered the page boy.

"All the waiting rooms full?"

"Yes, sir."

"Courtyard full?"

"Yes, sir."

"Coach-house full?"

"There's still room in the coach-house, sir."

"Ah, I'm sorry we haven't got a crowded day for you, Doyle. Of course we can't command these things. Now then, make a gangway, can't you?" he bawled to his patients. "Come here and see the waiting-room. Pooh! What an atmosphere! Why on earth can't you open the windows for yourselves? I never saw such folk! There are thirty people in this room, Doyle, and not one with sense enough to open a window to save himself from suffocation."   (R.S.A. Inter.)

CHAPTER TWENTY-ONE

Précis Writing

Since brevity is the soul of wit,
And tediousness the limbs and outward flourishes,
I will be brief.
                              Shakespeare: *Hamlet*

THE TECHNIQUE OF SUMMARIZING

The widespread use of telephones, typewriters, tape recorders, intercom systems and other forms of mechanical and electronic equipment has greatly widened the sources and increased the amount of communicated material the business executive has to contend with. To operate as an effective competitor in a business world that is constantly changing he must keep himself informed and up to date, but the flow of information is now so considerable that he cannot absorb it or even know of it unless it is fed to him in a summarized form that reduces it to a nucleus of essentials, a process that involves the use of a number of special skills. These include:

(a) ability to absorb and understand a general body of subject-matter;

(b) ability to identify what is relevant to a particular purpose;

(c) ability to distinguish what is important for the purpose in hand and what is not;

(d) ability to express a summarized version in language that reflects the tone and character of the original.

Making a summary is nothing new; it is a process familiar to every one of us, for we are summarizing one way or another every day of our lives. We are often asked to give an outline of a book we have read, or a film we have seen, or what happened at the office yesterday. We do this in a few sentences, relating only the essential facts and leaving out much of what is less important. And that, quite briefly, is the art of summarizing or, what is often referred to as précis writing if the summary is written. But though précis writing is a form of summarizing it has a different purpose. The précis seeks to shorten the length of an original passage and to reproduce it as a faithful miniature. A summary on the other hand is selective in that it aims to serve a specific purpose; it selects and deals only with those points that are relevant to that purpose. Successful précis writing and summarizing both call for close concentration, a critical eye and a thoughtful and analytical mind. An orderly and methodical approach to both is essential. The beginner is advised to proceed by easy stages and to master the use of certain simple techniques; before attempting to précis full-length passages it is just as well to practise summarizing the component parts—first the phrase or clause, then the sentence and finally the paragraph.

SUMMARIZING THE PHRASE OR CLAUSE

Not infrequently, the idea expressed in a phrase or clause can be reduced to a single word.

(a) The scheme was *one that could not be put into practice* (impracticable).

(b) Every man is *liable to be called upon to account* for his own actions (accountable).

(c) The secretary's proposal was adopted *with the full agreement of all the members* (unanimously).

(d) The committee *suspended proceedings and dispersed* until the following Thursday (adjourned).

The most important parts of a sentence are the subject-word, the finite verb and the object-word; if the verb has an object, this must be retained in any summary of the sentence. Qualifying words and phrases may usually be omitted, except where they form an essential part of the meaning. The important parts of the following sentences are printed in italics.

(a) A further complication arises from the fact that *most things are made*, not to the order of the consumer, but *in anticipation of demand*.

(b) In the light of factors of this nature, and because of the competition of large retailing units, *the small retailer might well be thought to be on the way out*.

(c) *The chairman*, a very prominent member of the Manufacturers' Association, *began business with very little capital and extensive debts*, owing to the upkeep of his estate.

The important part of a complex sentence is, of course, the main clause and this, or some portion of it, must form part of the summary. Of the dependent clauses those that limit some word in the main clause will usually be more important than those that limit some word in another dependent clause. Some examples are given below, the most important sections of the main clauses being printed in capitals and the more important of the dependent clauses in italics.

(a) *If I am free,* I WILL CALL ON YOU TOMORROW, *when we can talk about the meeting* which you mention in your letter.

(b) *Because of* the nature of *the banks' obligation* to their depositors *to repay balances at short notice,* LOANS MADE ARE SHORT TERM IN CHARACTER, that is, the type repayable within a period of six months.

(c) THE EPISTLE TO THE ROMANS, one of the four principal epistles of St. Paul, WOULD SEEM TO HAVE BEEN WRITTEN FROM CORINTH towards the end of the apostle's third missionary journey, *so that the way might be prepared for a visit to the Roman Christians,* which he was hoping soon to make.

SUMMARIZING THE PARAGRAPH

The fact that a well-constructed paragraph deals with only one main idea or topic is of considerable help when we come to summarize its contents. The essence of the paragraph is to be found in the theme or topic sentence (see pp. 266—7). After that, the important things are the inferences or conclusions that may be drawn. Merely illustrative or explanatory matter can usually be omitted and, not infrequently, the contents of the paragraph can be expressed in a single sentence.

When making a summary of a lengthy passage not already paragraphed it is a good plan to mark it off into sections and to underline the topic sentences. When these are arranged in their right order, they provide a useful basis for the summary.

In the following paragraph the main ideas are given in italics and the sentences numbered for reference.

1. *Tidiness is one of the hallmarks of an efficient secretary.* 2. Her dress, her appearance, her room, her desk and her work must all be tidy. 3. *Her shorthand notebook will be a model of tidiness.* 4. Each day's work will be dated; there will be a margin down the left-hand side for notes and each letter will be numbered and each will be separated by a blank line from the letter before it. 5. *Far too many typists use their notebook as if it were a rough book.* 6. They take no pride in its appearance, no pride in orderly setting out, *so that they cannot easily turn up a particular letter.* 7. *The efficient secretary* on the other hand *realizes that her notebook may be useful for reference* in an emergency and will keep it methodically and tidily.

(135 words)

The theme or topic of this passage taken as a whole is the secretary's shorthand notebook and the topic sentence is No. 3. Sentence 4 merely serves to illustrate the form taken by the tidiness referred to in the topic sentence, while sentence 7 mentions the purpose tidiness serves. The effect of sentences 5 and 6 is to stress the value of a well-kept notebook by referring to the consequences of its alternative. Sentences 1 and 2 do no more than serve as an introduction to the main topic.

If we accept these points, a summary of the paragraph would appear somewhat as follows.

A methodically and tidily kept shorthand notebook is one of the marks of an efficient secretary, and has the advantage of being available as a source of reference, whereas a badly kept notebook cannot be conveniently used for this purpose.   *(40 words)*

EXERCISES

1. *(a)* Find a single word for each of the following.

(i) a fertile spot in the desert;
(ii) the study of animals;
(iii) one who looks on the worst side of things;
(iv) a period of ten years;
(v) the room where an artist works.

   (b) Explain, in phrases similar to the above, the meanings of these words.

   (i) horizon;   *(ii)* mutiny;   *(iii)* coroner;   *(iv)* antidote;   *(v)* panic.
                                                                    (R.S.A. Elem.)

2. Give a one-word equivalent for each of the following short definitions:

(a) able to speak two languages equally well;
(b) introduce something new;
(c) a brief summary of the decisions reached at a meeting;
(d) not having made a will;
(e) the giving of false evidence in court;
(f) a person's life story, written by himself;
(g) curved outward;
(h) government by the people;
(i) incapable of being read;
(j) instrument measuring atmospheric pressure used for forecasting weather.
                                                                    (N.W.R.A.C.)

3. Write one word for each of the following:

(a) an instrument for measuring minute distances;
(b) an instrument for increasing the volume of a voice;
(c) the art of cultivating and managing gardens;

(d) the study of ancient buildings and remains;

(e) the study of coins;

(f) the study of mankind;

(g) a disease affecting many persons at the same time and place;

(h) a picture facing the title-page of a book;

(i) a book of names and addresses;

(j) not keeping to the subject.   (R.S.A., Inter.)

4. Supply a single word for each of the following phrases:

(a) living at the same period of time;

(b) a period of ten years;

(c) a person with an exaggerated respect for wealth and social position;

(d) the area which an M.P. represents in Parliament;

(e) the supply of water for cultivated land by artificial means;

(f) a room for sleeping in, containing many beds;

(g) the same in every respect;

(h) the crime of giving false evidence on oath;

(i) not biased in favour of either side in a contest or argument;

(j) pension payable on retirement.   (U.E.I.)

5. Give single words that express the sense of the words printed in italics in the following sentences.

A

(a) One does not like to see men whose behaviour and manners are *more like those of a woman than of a man.*

(b) The problem set for homework seemed to be *one that was never likely to be solved.*

(c) Some writers are fond of using words *that are no longer in use.*

(d) It is to be feared that doctors will never find a *remedy for all diseases.*

(e) He is famous as a *man who is generous to his fellow men.*

(f) Some of his remarks were *capable of bearing more than one meaning.*

(g) The two authors decided to *work in association with each other* in the production of a book on Queen Mary.

(h) The two men were *university teachers of the highest grade.*

(i) His remark seemed *to lack any bearing on the subject under discussion.*

(j) The policy advocated would cause *an increase in available currency that would raise general prices.*

B

(a) *The interchange of merchandise between nations and people* involves the services of transport, the banks and the insurance houses.

(b) *A commodity consisting of coins and notes* is what we use when we buy goods from a shop.

(c) They are *counting all the goods* in the warehouse to find out what further supplies need to be ordered.

(d) *Goods brought into the country from abroad* are paid for by *goods sent out of the country for sale.*

(e) Trade *between this and other countries* greatly increases the variety of goods we are able to enjoy.

(f) Most business transactions today are settled by means of *documents addressed to bankers instructing them to pay money to the persons named.*

(g) It is evident that we could not do without *the means of carrying merchandise from one place to another.*

(h) Many wholesalers supply to their retailers *a book containing particulars of goods and prices.*

(i) Wholesalers usually supply goods to retailers on *an arrangement under which payment is to be made at a later date.*

(j) When he receives the goods ordered a buyer should check the *statement giving particulars of quantities and prices.*

6. Write out each of the following sentences, replacing each of the phrases in italics by a single word which has the same meaning.

(a) The judges were *all in agreement* that John's essay was the best.

(b) One of the clerks in our office is *able to use either hand with equal skill.*

(c) My uncle went into the hall to look at his *instrument for measuring atmospheric pressure.*

(d) I had a bad cold which I *made worse* by going to the football match.

(e) Many of the merchants were *persons of mixed Asian and European parentage.*

(f) The mayor's hobby was *collecting postage stamps.*

(g) The *distance from the centre of the circle to the circumference* was six inches.

(h) There was a lecture at the museum by the *man in charge of the collections.*

(i) The report said that his conduct was *a good example to others.*

7. Copy out each of the following sentences and underline the most important parts.

(a) Since the end of the Second World War a good deal has been done to improve efficiency in the office.

(b) Standardized production makes it difficult to meet the needs of different customers for variations in the design, quality and price of a product.

(c) The purpose of capital as one of the agents of production is to assist labour by increasing the output from a given amount of effort.

(d) A cheque that appears to have been paid by the banker on whom it is drawn is evidence of the receipt by the payee of the sum payable by the cheque.

(e) Since the commercial banks close at 3.30 p.m. and many shops remain open and receive cash several hours after that time, traders who do not wish to keep cash on their premises may have a night-safe account.

(f) Our present currency issue is what is called a fiduciary issue, which means that its value depends on faith and confidence in the banking and government systems behind it.

(g) With the co-operation of the banking and business worlds, a government can halt inflationary tendencies and bring about deflationary tendencies by using various measures which it is authorized to apply.

(*b*) There is a place in business for both the audio-typist and the shorthand-typist and neither can claim to be generally better than the other, for there will always be circumstances to which one is more suited than the other.

(*i*) When shares are issued in two or more classes, the ordinary shares are the shares most likely to benefit from the success of the company as regards both dividend payments and capital appreciation.

(*j*) Since the computer works mainly by electric pulses operating at incredibly high speeds, measured in nano-seconds,* it can complete in an hour or two work that would take clerical staff days or even weeks to perform.

8. Using your own words, express briefly the meaning of each of the following sentences.

(*a*) Whatever may be the controversy between the humanities and the scientific disciplines, the fact that barely more than half the number of candidates who sit for the O-level examination in English each year manage to pass is evidence of a lamentable failure, which both must equally deplore.

(*b*) "Although man's qualities belong more to the head, and woman's more to the heart—yet it is not less necessary that man's heart should be cultivated as well as his head, and woman's head cultivated as well as her heart." (S. Smiles: *Character.*)

(*c*) Signs of the approach of winter are different in the town and in the village. To a certain northern city, whose spires fret my skyline of a morning, this proximity is made known by the departure of the last tourist and the arrival of the first student, by the reassembling of schools, and by advertisements in newspapers relating to the opening of the university.

(*d*) The former legal maximum of twenty for partnerships bore hardly on large stockbroking firms that offered a comprehensive service to their clients, involving the provision of a great deal of statistical and similar information, domestic and overseas, as well as the multitudinous services and routine tasks that a long list of clients inevitably demands.

(*e*) Young people are too frequently discouraged from scientific careers by being given the impression, at school, that science consists of obscure rituals and pedantic definitions which must be remembered by heart; that scientists are people with prodigious memories and a capacity for splitting hairs; and that society's need of science is narrowly bound up with the balance of payments and military research.

9. Summarize each of the following paragraphs, using not more than half the number of words in the original. In each case supply a heading.

A

Children of a former generation were expected, as a matter of course, to study Shakespeare and to get passages of verse, sometimes even of prose, by heart. Was their appreciation of the great masters of English stunted by too early and too forced an acquaintance with them? Most would claim that it was not. Schools must, of course, teach English in some definable

*One billionth of a second.

manner and help children to pass some definable tests. But proper appreciation of language, and fluency in its use, depend on the convergence of many factors and so tend to become indefinable.   *(95 words)*

B

Punched-card systems have numerous applications. In business they can handle the bulk of the repetitive and uninteresting work involved in accounting procedures, and this they do with extraordinary rapidity and unfailing accuracy. Sales analysis, stock control, costing and the preparation of invoices, pay rolls, bank statements, gas and electricity accounts and trial balances are only some of their many applications to business problems. Punched cards are also used as one of the media for feeding data into electronic computers and for recording the results achieved by these high-speed robots.   *(91 words)*

C

The chief benefits of the computer have so far been to eliminate much routine clerical work and to increase the amount of detailed information and the speed with which it can be obtained. Further developments are bound to have important effects on the kinds of work undertaken by office staff and on the type and form of records kept. It is unlikely that the computer will create vast unemployment; in fact, it helps to create other jobs, and much of the clerical work eliminated will be replaced by work on programme preparation, operation and maintenance of machines and on the uses to which the increased information made available is put.   *(110 words)*

D

The increased mechanization associated with methods of mass-production has been taken a stage further by recent technical developments known as *automation,* a term first used in the 1930s to describe the automatic handling of products between progressive stages in the manufacturing process. More broadly, the term is applied to any machine process that is automatically controlled, and also to electronic computation, by which intricate calculations are carried out and the resulting data made available with incredible speed. In chemical manufacturing, oil refining, food processing and newspaper production complete operations have become almost entirely automatic.   *(96 words)*

E

Work study is a combination of time, motion and method study. It is used to measure the time taken to perform specific tasks, and by eliminating unnecessary movements and improving methods of operation to increase output and achieve greater efficiency in production. At one time suspect by the worker, work study is now widely accepted in industry as a detached method for determining what is a fair output for an average worker. Its techniques were used in industry for a generation before it was realized that they had an application to office procedures also.   *(94 words)*

F

Key-operated machines for producing characters resembling print were invented as early as the eighteenth century, but the first commercially successful writing machine embodying all the essential mechanism of the typewriter as we know it was invented in 1873 and manufactured in quantities by Remington in America. The arrangement of the keyboard, originally designed to prevent the characters most frequently used from jamming at the printing point, has remained practically unchanged from the beginning. The advantages of a keyboard arranged according to letter frequency have often been urged, but the difficulties associated with the proposed change have so far proved too compelling.   *(94 words)*

G

The effectiveness of transport is determined by considerations of cost, speed, safety and convenience. The cost of moving a commodity from the point of production to the point of sale forms part of the price the buyer must be prepared to pay, and since transportation costs increase with distance they are an important factor in determining the limits of the area within which any given commodity can be marketed. Anything that increases the cost of moving his product weakens the competitive power of the producer and reduces the distance over which he can profitably market his goods, while anything that lowers the cost strengthens his hand and extends the range of his market.   *(115 words)*

H

There is a popular tendency to associate the term "production" with the physical operation of producing goods for use by the general population and to regard the provision of services as unproductive and therefore outside the meaning of the term, merely because they do not provide anything in tangible form. It needs very little thought to see that the distinction thus drawn is indefensible. The object of producing goods is to satisfy certain of man's needs and in so doing to contribute to his standard of living. The production of goods is merely a means to an end. Those workers who provide services contribute to precisely the same end and it is therefore much more reasonable to regard as productive any kind of work that helps to satisfy mankind's needs and to maintain or raise the standard of living, be it factory work, office work, or work in one of the professions.   *(152 words)*

NOTE-MAKING AND PRÉCIS WRITING DISTINGUISHED

Ability to condense a passage into brief, clear and intelligible notes is of great value. It is useful when information is being collected for an essay, or a lecture, and for purposes of revision. The making of notes is also an important part of the work in preparing an abstract or summary of a passage.

But précis writing is something very different from note-making, with which it is sometimes confused. A précis is a summary in the form of a continuous narrative, with connected thoughts linked together and expressed in sentence form. It should be a well-constructed piece of carefully worded composition, free, like any other piece of written composition, from all faults of style and grammar. Note-making, on the other hand, produces a series of disconnected jottings, which, more often than not, are not in sentence form.

SUGGESTIONS FOR PRÉCIS WRITING

Having learned earlier in this chapter how to condense the sentence and the paragraph, and realizing the importance of comprehension as a first step in précis writing, you should now be ready to summarize fairly lengthy passages of prose. What you have already learned applies equally to the longer passages, but in dealing with these you will find the following additional suggestions helpful.

Supply a title
Give the passage a first, fairly quick reading to catch its main theme and supply an appropriate title consisting of a short phrase that expresses the essence of the passage as a whole and covers the entire subject-matter. Consistent with these aims the title should be eye-catching and as short as possible.

> How to choose words   (for passage A on p. 330)
> The road to happiness   (for passage E on p. 331)
> The decline of profit sharing (for passage on pp. 334–5)

The title should convey some idea of the theme of the passage, and single-word titles cannot do this. They should not be used. An examiner may not always ask for a title, but one should invariably be given.

Establish comprehension
Having decided on a title, read over the passage again, this time carefully—once, twice, or as many times as may be necessary to gain a thorough grasp of its subject-matter *as a whole*. Full comprehension of the passage to be summarized is the essential basis for a satisfactory précis.

Make notes of main points
Then read through the passage once more and, paying special attention to main clauses and topic sentences, underline the essential

points. If the passage is a short one, consisting of no more than 200 to 300 words, memorize these points, put the passage aside and jot down the main ideas as you remember them. If the passage is too long to be treated in this way, make notes of the points underlined. These notes provide the framework for the précis.

Provide an introductory clause
Remember to provide an introductory clause in the past tense and to retain this tense throughout, except where the statement makes reference to something that is permanently true (see pp. 310 and 313).

> Writing in the *Observer* Mr. Spencer *said* that in recent years few other forms of investment *had proved* as popular as unit trusts, and that in one way that *was* natural enough since they *appeal* strongly to the small investor.

Prepare a rough draft
Without referring to the original, use your notes to prepare a rough draft, *using your own words and avoiding as far as possible the language of the original.* Avoid at all costs two possible temptations:

(*a*) the temptation to make a sort of paraphrase of the passage; and

(*b*) the temptation to select sentences here and there and to combine them to form a piece of composition.

Précis prepared in these ways gain very few marks in an examination.

If, as often happens, you find you finish up with more than the permitted number of words, you can reduce their number in several ways:

(*a*) by further pruning of the unessential;

(*b*) by using more economical language;

> The firm had insufficient liquid capital and was being pressed by its creditors. Say: *The firm was in financial difficulties.*

(*c*) by combining sentences.

> No man has the time to produce everything he wants. Nor has any man the skill or the means. He therefore concentrates on producing some particular thing.
>
> Say: *Man specializes because he has neither the time, the skill nor the means to produce everything for himself.*

Check your draft
Check your draft carefully against the original, making sure that

you have neither omitted anything from nor added anything to the sense of the original.

Observe proportion
Make sure that your précis is well proportioned. Deal with each part according to its relative importance and not according to the space it occupies in the passage for summarizing.

Write the précis in good prose
Using indirect speech in the third person and working from your draft, write your précis. It should consist of one paragraph only and should emerge as a piece of well-written and "finished" composition. Reduction in the size of the passage is likely to result in a number of short sentences and some loss of smoothness. To some extent this can be overcome by the use of linking words to get rid of very short sentences. It is usually advisable, but not essential, to present facts in the order in which they appear in the original; there is no objection to rearranging the order if it improves the logical sequence.

State the number of words used
If the instructions stipulate the word limit be sure to observe them carefully. *In not more than 150 words* means what it says and on no account must your précis exceed this limit. *In approximately 150 words* may reasonably be taken as permitting a margin of about 5 per cent on either side. If no word limit is mentioned it is usually assumed that a précis about one-third the length of the original is expected. Even if the number of words used is not asked for, these should be stated at the end as an act of grace that assists the person marking the précis.

A WORKED EXAMPLE

Suppose you are required to make a précis of the following passage.

> *The story of the Rochdale Co-operative Society, in 1844,* which became the working model for thousands of others, *is a most romantic one,* and in some of its aspects the history of its progress reads like a fairy tale. *A hundred and forty years ago wages were very low,* and *it was a terrible struggle for working people to secure a bare subsistence. They were compelled to buy* the necessities of life from small retail shopkeepers, who usually supplied wretched provisions at extremely high prices; the price of bread alone created a serious problem.
>
> In the midst of this poverty, *twenty-eight poor* but intelligent *weavers of* Rochdale determined to try to improve their lot. As this could not be done

by increasing their earnings, they *decided upon a plan whereby they could lessen their expenditure,* purchase better provisions with their money, and at the same time *keep in their own pockets the profits previously secured by the shopkeepers* from whom they bought their provisions. *They soon discovered that by buying in large quantities, and by paying cash, they could buy at a cheaper rate* and thus obtain greater benefits; but this required ready money, which they did not possess. *They determined,* however, though it cost each one a severe struggle, *to give twopence a week to raise some capital. Afterwards,* by great self-sacrifice, their weekly contribution was *increased to threepence, until their combined savings amounted to twenty-eight pounds. A room was taken in Toad Lane as a store,* and from this small beginning *a society gradually developed,* which now numbers its members by thousands, and its annual business by hundreds of thousands of pounds, while in place of the humble room is a huge central warehouse *with numbers of branch stores.*   *(297 words)*

Choice of title

Informative and suitable titles that suggest themselves are "The Rochdale Co-operative Society", "The Rochdale Pioneers" and "The Birth of the Co-operative Movement".

Notes of main points

The following notes are based on the key words given in italics.

> Rochdale Co-operative Society (1844). Forerunner of thousands. Wages poor at the time and prices of necessities high. Hence, working-class poverty. Twenty-eight weavers sought to improve conditions. Higher earnings not possible, but bulk buying for cash economical. Capital needed. Obtained from weavers' small weekly contributions. Premises taken in Toad Lane. Society flourished. A model for others.

Précis of passage

The notes in the preceding section provide the basis for the following précis.

> The writer said that in 1844, when the Rochdale Co-operative Society was founded, the working class were living in a state of poverty, owing to conditions of low wages and the extortionate prices charged for the necessities of life. Since earnings could not be increased, improved conditions were possible only through a lowering of prices. Realizing that prices could be cut by buying in bulk on a cash basis, twenty-eight weavers raised, but only with difficulty, the necessary capital by each contributing small weekly sums. They acquired premises in Toad Lane and gradually developed a prosperous society that became the prototype of many others.   *(107 words)*

EXERCISES

1. Write a précis, about one-third the length of the original, of each of the following passages. Supply a heading to each.

A

The dictionary contains many thousands of words and is always available to tell you what a word means. But it doesn't tell you which word to choose, and prolonged study of a dictionary may simply leave you feeling that there are far too many words in the English language. There are at least three safe rules in choosing words. First, pick out the shortest word that will say what you mean. Those who use long words when a short one would do just as well show, not their education, but their lack of it. Long words may be useful in a spelling-bee, but they are out of place in a business letter except to convey some technical meaning. The second rule is to be accurate. A good craftsman uses his tools with precision, and those who seek to write good English must do the same, choosing always the word that expresses just the meaning they wish to convey. The third rule is to choose the appropriate word. English is a rich language which has taken over words from many other languages. In writing poetry the appropriate word may well be one that would sound far-fetched in more mundane surroundings. In a business letter the appropriate word is nearly always the shortest and simplest that will express your meaning. *(221 words)*

B

To write a good letter one does not need to be an expert in language, but it calls for practice and an appreciation of the simple mechanics of language. Aristotle said that what we have to learn we learn by doing, and if one would become skilled in letter-writing one must practise letter-writing. Only when we come to reproduce our thoughts in writing do we cultivate the discipline of clear thinking and exact expression. There are people with worthwhile thoughts who cannot express them because they have never learned how. Most unfortunate are those who express themselves so badly as to be misunderstood. In business this is dangerous; the art of clear expression is an essential part of every business-man's equipment.

Writing a business letter is not just a matter of routine, a mere chore. It is an opportunity. It is an opportunity to achieve a purpose. It may be seeking information, giving information, cultivating a friendship, placing an order or inviting one. Whatever the purpose, the writer must keep it in mind, because it will dictate the style and tone of his letter.

A well-written business letter pays dividends. Not only does it create a good impression and produce better results, but it also leaves the writer with a feeling of satisfaction. *(217 words)*

C

Three important words in our language, or for that matter in any language, are courtesy, kindness and consideration. Stop for a moment and actually let your thoughts picture for you the conduct of somebody who has thoroughly understood and lived up to the ideas expressed by these three words. Try to imagine such a person and what he or she would do during the course of a day; I mean just the ordinary things one would do daily.

Such a person works quickly but in a quiet manner; he gets through his breakfast and out of the house with as little excitement as possible. Walking down the street, or in the station, or getting on the train, he does not try to force others out of his way. Upon entering the office he shows his regard for others by speaking in a pleasant manner, whether it be to a clerk or to a superior. Thus he goes through the day, and can see that he has secured approximately every result desired, and is in a better state of mind than those who do not appreciate the value of these words. Best of all, those with whom he works will regard him with respect, and he will enjoy the friendship of everyone.

If you have not been thinking in terms of how you can help other people, it would be well for you to begin now.   *(235 words)*

D

If you are still at school you will one day be applying for a post. If so, then first and most important of all you must have the qualifications needed. The best letter in the world will not make up for lack of experience or ability. But if you really believe that you can competently handle the job, then go ahead and apply.

You may make your application in either of two ways. You may write a letter and with it enclose a summary of your experience and background, or you may write a comprehensive letter containing all the information you need to give. The former arrangement has two merits to commend it. First, the letter you write gives you a chance to reveal something of your attitude to work; secondly, the summary provides a ready means of referring to factual details. Your prospective employer will appreciate both.

You must not neglect the opportunity it affords to show your ability to write a good business letter, and to stress those aspects of your qualifications most likely to be of special interest. You must express yourself concisely, yet attractively. Your letter must be correctly addressed, sensibly punctuated and properly spelt. It must be business-like in appearance, that is to say well arranged, and not written or typed on paper more suitable for social than for business purposes. The slightest failure in any one of these matters may be enough to seal your fate at once; carefully prepared, however, your letter may put you in the lead right away.   *(258 words)*

E

Happiness should not be looked upon as a reward for a good life, but as the natural effect of it. You will be happy if you are exercising your powers along the lines of excellence in a life that affords full scope for their development. Nor is happiness a negative or passive thing. It is the outcome of things you do, the product of positive thinking and active living. It may be made up of little, everyday incidents; of having something to do, something to love and something to hope for. A man who was Roman emperor for twenty stirring years wrote after his retirement: "Could you but see the five cabbages in my garden, which I have planted and raised with my own hands, you would not ask me to relinquish such happiness for the pursuit of power".

Happiness is not the means to something else, but is the end in itself. Every person chooses the stepping-stones towards it that suit his stride, his temperament and his ideals. You do not need the word of the philosophers for this: search your memory, and you will find that your happy hours were those following an achievement in some area of life where you had made yourself proficient.

The seeker after the happy life will never be satisfied with things as they are. Having reached a plateau, he will not be content to stay there. He will not be content to treat an accomplishment like a jewel, to be enshrined in a casket for achieving contemplation. He will be conscious of his natural gifts and bent upon developing them.   *(269 words)*

F

How can we define good manners? To be well-mannered is to do the thing you should do although you are not obliged to do it. This means being considerate of others, avoiding personalities that hurt people, taking no unfair advantage, and never being intentionally impolite. Manners can be more important than laws. The law touches us only here and there and now and then; manners vex or please us, exalt or debase us, constantly. Moses is known as the "great law-giver", particularly because he inscribed the Ten Commandments, but he entered the field of manners, too. He went beyond the "musts" of well-organized society, and prescribed the conduct of a gentleman: to be gentle with those who are afflicted, to refrain from gossip, to respect the aged, and to be kind even to strangers. No matter to what station in life you belong, or how highly educated you may be, you owe courtesy to your fellow men. Here is an illustration from the life of Sir Winston Churchill. On a day in May 1941 when he had already been on his feet in the House of Commons with some hard news about the fighting in Crete, he rose for a second time with some welcome news, but he apologized all the same for interrupting the House. Good manners include tact, which means taking pains, and some trouble to see that others are not neglected, and doing the kind thing in a pleasant way. Great leaders are always tactful in dealing with people at all levels.   *(259 words)*

2. Your managing director drew up this report but now finds it is too long. You are asked to reduce to approximately 100 words.

Your directors are happy to report that the company as a whole has had another satisfactory year's trading to which every department of the business has made a most useful and substantial contribution.

The consolidated profit is approximately £100,000 more than in the previous year. This profit is, of course, the balance after all the ordinary outgoings of the business have been paid, and to accomplish this result, as you will readily realize, the company has had an increased turnover and this has occurred in all its various departments.

The debtors have increased considerably and this is of course some measure of the increased activities of your company. All branches of your business, whether large or small, continue to operate and develop normally.

We are all aware that taxation takes a very heavy toll of the profits of any business undertaking and in our case this taxation amounts to £96,000.

Shareholders will be pleased to note that the Directors again recommend a final dividend of 33 per cent, less tax.

Additions to the Plant and Machinery have been made during the year and you will gather that they and other assets are well maintained and that the Directors are doing all in their power to keep your assets in an efficient condition for carrying on the many and varied undertakings of your business.

The financial position of your company is sound and the total reserves now amount to £177,000. *(274 words)* *(R.S.A., Inter.)*

3. Using your own words, as far as possible, make a précis of the following passage in not more than 105 words. Count the number of words you use, and write it at the end of your précis.

If a shipowner decides to set aside tradition he may let a newly-built vessel slide down the ways unblessed and without the customary baptism in champagne. But in no country can he escape from the obligation of declaring to the Registrar of Shipping the time and place of birth of the latest addition to his fleet. Having done so, and provided that earlier formalities have been complied with, the shipowner will receive a certificate of registration.

The register is the most vital of the ship's "papers" and must at all times be kept aboard in the custody of the master. Although all ships must display their names in clear lettering on the bows and again (together with the port of registry) on the stern, only the certificate of registration is legally valid as evidence of identity.

Because a ship at sea is officially a territorial extension of the country under whose flag she sails, production of the register to qualified people ashore or afloat entitles a ship and those on her to protection and assistance from her own country's forces and those of its allies. In time of war (provided that international law is respected and the ship is not trying to run a blockade) the exhibition of the certificate of registration ought to ensure immunity from capture or seizure.

A ship not officially registered would be "stateless" and, lacking any flag to protect her, might even be regarded as a pirate vessel. That is why registration of merchant tonnage is compulsory throughout the world, save for small coastal ships which never venture outside territorial waters, some fishing vessels and small pleasure craft in private ownership.

Moreover, official registration of merchant ships contributes to safety at sea in that it is conditional on the observance of certain principles of construction and on the vessel not being allowed to load deeper than a stipulated maximum draft. *(316 words)* *(L.C.C.I., Inter.)*

4. Carefully read the following passage, which contains about 400 words. Then, *using your own words as far as possible,* write a summary of it in not more than 120 words. Finally, supply an appropriate title for your summary.

The character and appearance of a well equipped modern office are as far removed from those of the Victorian office, as is an up-to-date motor vehicle from the primitive horse and cart. In place of a grimy and dimly lit interior, furnished with tall sloping desks and high stools, muddy inkpots, dog-eared ledgers, copy-presses, dusty shelves and pigeon-holes which were formerly characteristic of the typical "city" office, one now expects to find light and often spacious rooms, pedestal writing and typing tables, comfortable chairs, possibly desk-top computers, accounting machines, electric type-writers and many other modern features, all conceived with a view to reducing labour, saving time and enhancing efficiency.

The modern office, or as it may more accurately be called, the administration department, is the nerve-centre of the business, from which emanate the direction and control of every branch of its activities, and in which the details and effects of the operations are recorded and collated. The functions of the office are numerous and varied.

In a business of any size the normal organisation would provide for buying, production, research, selling and accounting and probably the heads of the first four of the above mentioned departments would each require a small personal secretarial or clerical staff. The accountant's department would comprise sections for the bought ledgers, sales ledgers, cashiers and cost office. The administrative head, who might be the chief accountant (sometimes called the treasurer) or the company secretary would be responsible for the general office services, e.g. correspondence, the reproduction and filing of documents, the engagement and supervision of staff and the general maintenance of the establishment. The heads of the departments referred to above would each be responsible to the managing director, who, in turn, is responsible to the board of directors.

In a small business many of the functions referred to above will be carried out by the same individual, and the office will be confined to, perhaps, one or two rooms, with one or more private rooms for the principals and managers.   (L.C.C.I., Inter.)

5. Write a summary of the following passage reducing it to about one-third of its length.

Profit-sharing is a name given historically to a method of applying some of the revenues of a company to the benefit of its employees. It relates to the distribution, in cash or in credit, of a proportion of the net profits in advance by an undertaking on the part of the owners or managers.

It is sometimes used as a general term to include the acquisition of shares in the company by its employees, but its use in this sense is strictly appropriate only in the small number of cases in which the method of distributing all or part of the proportion of the net profits takes the form of a free issue of company shares. There is, however, an element of "profit-sharing" in the numerous cases of employee shareholding in which the purchase of shares by employees is assisted by the company, either by enabling them to buy at a reduced price or by adding a bonus of additional shares to those bought, or by some system of guaranteeing a dividend rate on them in excess of the dividend rate on shares held by the public.

Both terms "profit-sharing" and "employee shareholding" are frequently comprised in the phrase "co-partnership". Co-partnership is normally a much wider conception, covering the development of good relationship between owners, managers and employees in the business, based upon common objectives and interests.

No special significance attaches to profit-sharing (in the limited sense) or to employee shareholding except as manifestations of this co-partner relationship. It is not the experience of companies today that they perform, to any measurable extent, the functions which have been historically attributed to them.

At various periods in the past, companies in this country, Europe and the U.S.A. have found that they had value as substitutes for pay increases, as stabilizers on the movement of labour, deterrents to strikes, or as incentives. Today, with well-established trade unions and a high level of wage rates, and with national insurance and other State welfare services, there is little evidence that they serve such particular purposes. For a company which already has good industrial relations, either or both can have value in setting the seal on those relations.

To introduce a scheme of profit-sharing or employee shareholding in expectation of a particular benefit, or in expectation that it will have the effect of improving a not very satisfactory condition of industrial relations is to risk severe disappointment. Half the schemes introduced in this country in the last 100 years have ceased to exist after shorter or longer runs. Many of them have faded away in bad times; many of the employee shareholding systems have collapsed when share values have collapsed in periods of slump. In a number of other cases they have been abandoned by companies for failing to produce expected results.   *(478 words) (L.C.C.I., Priv. Sec. Dip.)*

6. Write a précis of the following passage in not more than 150 words. Your version should avoid as far as possible the words and phrases of the original. State the exact number of words you have used.

Few other forms of investment have proved as popular as unit trusts. In one way this is natural enough. They are tailor-made for new investors and particularly for people who are building up their capital out of savings. If it were not for the unit trusts, a £1,000 stake spread over a hundred equities would be virtually impossible to achieve.

Unit trusts are basically the same animal as investment trusts. In both cases experts are engaged in investing money with the object of benefiting members as much as possible. But there are important differences in their legal status and structure. Unlike investment trusts, unit trusts really are trusts, set up under a trust deed which has to be approved by the Department of Trade. Under this arrangement there have to be two independent organisations involved in the formation of a unit trust. One is the trustee, which looks after the cash and securities. This has to be a concern of substance, with a paid-up capital of over £500,000, and in practice it is usually a bank or an insurance company. The other, independent of the trustees, is a management company, which is responsible for the investment policy of the trust. The management company usually also makes the market in the trust's units.

It is important to get clear in your mind what part the trustees play in a unit trust. Many people wondering whether to buy a trust's units draw encouragement from the prestige and authority of its trustees, as though that

provided some guarantee of the performance of their investment. This is not so. True, the trustees carefully check the standing of any management company associated with them They also take other, general steps to safeguard the position of unit holders. For example, they ensure that an adequate reserve fund is set up so that the trust could be kept going if anything happened to the management. Again, at the formation of the trust they like to approve the general outline of the managers' investment policy. Other functions include checking the calculations of unit prices occasionally and keeping an eye on transactions to see that the trust's income is not boosted unnaturally by buying shares just before a dividend and selling them again just afterwards. But apart from that, it is wrong to imagine that trustees guarantee units in any way at all. Their day-to-day duties involve looking after the trust's cash and securities. They take no responsibility for the choice of individual investments. That is the duty of the management company. (ROWLATT and DAVENPORT: *Saving and Investment.*)   *(434 words)*
                                                                        (I. of B.)

CHAPTER TWENTY-TWO

Punctuation

> The pipe, with solemn interposing puff,
> Makes half a sentence at a time enough;
> The dozing sages drop the drowsy strain,
> Then pause, and puff—and speak, and pause again.
>
> William Cowper: *Conversation*

IMPORTANCE

Punctuation is the device used in writing to do for the reader what pauses and inflexions do for the listener—it helps to convey the meaning of what is written. It does no more, and no less. Approached in this way, punctuation is not nearly so formidable a matter as it may seem to be.

It consists of a series of stops or signs inserted to mark off words from one another either to show their grammatical relationship or to give emphasis to them. Some signs, such as the full-stop and the comma, merely denote the length of a pause; others like the question mark and exclamation mark, denote inflexion of the voice; while signs for quotations and parentheses serve to bring external matter into the basic text.

In business letter-writing the signs used to denote pauses are by far the most important, since without pauses a writer cannot convey his message in words that are meaningful and readily understood.

THE BASIC RULES

The basic rules for punctuation are simple enough:

(*a*) a paragraph marks off a group of sentences which together form a connected train of thought;

(*b*) a full-stop marks the end of a sentence;

(*c*) a semi-colon marks a pause only less strong than a full-stop;

(*d*) a comma marks only the mildest pause—no more than a slight check in the reading.

These are the most common of the punctuation marks, and if you remember that punctuation should be kept to the minimum necessary to help the reader to understand, they can serve as a basis for much excellent writing. Punctuation marks are signposts for the reader, and since the multiplication of signposts can be more embarrassing than helpful, we must learn to be intelligent in our placing of them. If a letter is well written it will not require much punctuation.

It is, then, the main purpose of punctuation to help the writer to present his ideas clearly and effectively, and to save the reader the trouble and annoyance of having to read a passage twice to grasp its meaning. Punctuation is thus not only a matter of necessity but also a matter of courtesy.

INDIVIDUAL TASTE

"But", it is often said, "no two people punctuate alike". This is broadly true, because punctuation does not follow detailed rules so inflexible that they leave no room for the exercise of personal taste. Punctuation is, indeed, very much a matter of combined taste and common sense, though there are certain underlying principles every writer must observe if he is to be clearly understood without difficulty.

The safest guide to correct punctuation is a proper appreciation of sentence structure and a recognition of the elements of which the sentence is composed — subject, predicate and the different kinds of clause. Generally speaking, the better the construction of a sentence, the fewer the signs needed to make its meaning clear, and if copious punctuation is necessary to make the meaning of a sentence clear it is fairly safe to assume that the sentence is a bad one. The best constructed sentence is in fact that from which all punctuation marks could be removed without in any way impairing the clearness of what is said or the ease with which it is understood.

The meaning of the following rather long sentence, for example, is perfectly clear and readily understood without the help of punctuation.

> Contracts for the sale of goods are governed not only by the Sale of Goods Act 1893 but also by the rules of common law except where these rules are inconsistent with the provisions of the Act.

Nevertheless, the insertion of punctuation marks to indicate pauses after *1893* and *common law* would no doubt make the reader's task somewhat easier.

NEED FOR CLARITY

Without punctuation some passages would be almost unintelligible, while others might convey meanings very different from those intended. Consider the following.

> I learned from the reputation and remembrance of my father modesty and a manly character from my mother piety and beneficence and abstinence and further simplicity in my way of living.

A first reading of this passage conveys little or nothing of its meaning, because there is nothing to show how the words should be grouped. With the insertion of the appropriate punctuation signs, however, the meaning becomes quite clear:

> I learned from the reputation and remembrance of my father, modesty and a manly character; from my mother, piety and beneficence and abstinence; and further, simplicity in my way of living.
> (Marcus Aurelius: Meditations)

AVOIDING AMBUGUITY

Now consider the effect of omitting all punctuation marks from the following sentences:

> The chairman, said the managing director, is quite incapable of understanding the problem (i.e. the chairman is incapable).

> The chairman said the managing director is quite incapable of understanding the problem (it is now the managing director who is incapable).

> I was given a rise of seventy-five pence—more than I expected (i.e. the rise was seventy-five pence exactly).

> I was given a rise of seventy-five pence more than I expected (i.e. the rise was more than seventy-five pence).

From these examples it is evident that punctuation has an important part to play not only in making reading easier but also in helping the writer to make his meaning clear.

SUMMARY OF ADVICE

(*a*) Try to write sentences that are clear without the help of stops.
(*b*) *Don't* punctuate to excess; you will hinder rather than help

your correspondent if you do. Use as few stops as will do the work.

(c) If in doubt about the comma, leave it out.

(d) Don't use stops to remedy a badly constructed sentence—rewrite it.

(e) Be consistent throughout; decide on the form of punctuation you wish to adopt, and stick to it.

(f) Concerning the use of the full-stop it is difficult to give practical guidance. It is, of course, used to mark the end of each sentence, but where one writer would close a sentence, another would delay the closure by adding some further thought. Perhaps the most one can say is that the modern style of writing prefers the shorter sentence to the long, rambling kind of sentence popular with many writers of the past.

THE SPECIAL CASE OF THE COMMA

A special word is necessary about the comma. It is at once the most frequently used and the most troublesome of all the stops. As we have seen, its inclusion or omission may completely alter the sense of a passage. Two special misuses of the comma should be carefully noted and avoided.

Subject and predicate

Since the grammatical relationship between the subject of a sentence and its verb is an intimate one, it is a general rule that they must not be separated by punctuation marks. The insertion of the comma in the following cases is quite wrong.

> The inability of the managing director to attend the meeting last Friday, was due to the sudden illness of his wife (*wrong*).
> The question whether the goods are to be sent by road or by rail, has not yet been decided (*wrong*).

If, however, the subject is a lengthy one, or consists of an enumeration with separating commas, the conclusion of the subject in speech would be marked by a slight pause; it is therefore permissible to insert a comma to mark this pause.

> The choice of a good business site, the employment of suitable assistants, attractive display of the goods for sale, and careful treatment of customers, are all important factors making for success in business (the comma after *customers* is legitimate).

Relative clauses

Care is necessary with relative clauses i.e. clauses introduced by relative pronouns (*who, which, that,* etc.). Such clauses are of two kinds and have already been referred to on p. 241. For purposes of punctuation the distinction between the two types of clause is important, and is now dealt with more fully.

The adjective (or defining) clause

When the clause serves to define some noun or pronoun in some other clause it performs the function of an adjective, and *must not be separated by a comma* from the word it qualifies and to which it is therefore closely related.

> The postman *who delivers our letters* has a distinguished war record (the clause in italics explains *which* postman).
> We did not receive the cheque *which you sent us last week* until yesterday (the clause in italics explains *which* cheque).

The main (or non-defining) clause

Clauses introduced by relative pronouns often serve to make statements of their own and not to define or qualify some word in some other clause. Clauses of this kind are grammatically independent, and *must be separated from the preceding clause by a comma.*

> I met our postman, *who told me he had been ill* (the clause in italics does not explain *which* postman, but makes a separate statement about him).
> Your cheque for £25, *which we received yesterday,* was paid into the bank this morning (the clause in italics plays no part in explaining *which* cheque, but makes the separate statement that it was received yesterday).

Rule in doubtful cases

There are many who find this distinction between the defining clause (not requiring commas) and the non-defining clause (requiring commas) confusing. There should be no difficulty if it is remembered that the defining clause is adjectival, and therefore answers the question *which?*

> The man who rang for you just now is the sales manager (i.e. *which* man?).

If, on the other hand, the relative pronoun *who, which, that,* etc., can be replaced by *and it, and he,* and similar phrases the clause is not defining anything but is making an independent statement of its own.

> Our sales manager, who (i.e. *and he*) has been with the company twenty-five years, will retire at the end of next month.

That; Which

There are many who feel that something more than a mere comma is needed to mark the distinction between the two types of relative clause. They prefer to use *that* for the defining clause and restrict *which* to the non-defining clause. The arrangement provides a distinction that is unmistakably clear and its use is recommended.

> The invoice *that you sent me* is wrongly totalled (*defining clause*).
> Your invoice No. 425, *which I received this morning*, is wrongly totalled (*non-defining clause*).

The pronoun in the defining clause is often suppressed, especially in speech:

> The work (that) I had to do was not difficult.
> He attributes his success to the training (that) he received at school.

Business correspondence

The main purpose of punctuation is to make meaning clear. But many of the commas, and some of the full-stops, used in business letters are purely conventional. They serve no useful purpose and there is a strong modern tendency to omit them. The conventional style of punctuation, sometimes referred to as "closed" punctuation, is rapidly giving way to what is termed "open" punctuation, a style that omits all but essential stops outside the body of the letter, i.e. from the date, the inside name and address, the salutation and the complimentary close. The "semi-open" style is a compromise between the two styles mentioned. The closed and semi-open styles compare as follows.

Closed punctuation	*Semi-open punctuation*
10 August, 19..	10 August 19..
R.B. Jackson Esq., O.B.E., M.A.,	R.B. Jackson Esq. O.B.E. M.A.
Managing Director,	Managing Director
Fylde Motor Co. Ltd.,	Fylde Motor Co. Ltd.
Folkestone Road,	Folkestone Road
PRESTON, Lancs.	PRESTON Lancs.
PR1 OLD	PR1 OLD
Dear Sir,	Dear Sir
Yours faithfully,	Yours faithfully

You will notice the following points.

(a) Semi-open punctuation omits all commas.

(b) Both styles of punctuation retain full-stops to mark abbreviations, e.g. initials. The full-stop after *Lancs.* follows the general rule and would be used after any other abbreviated county name as detailed in the *Post Office Guide,* but is omitted after county names typed in full, e.g. *Yorkshire,* since the inside name and address does not make a sentence.

The form of punctuation recommended for use in civil service departments is the fully "open" style*. It omits from all but the body of the letter not only all commas but also the full-stops marking abbreviations, e.g. for a person's initials, decorations, degrees, etc. and county names. Spaces are left between the initials preceding the surname but not between the letters in abbreviations of decorations and qualifications after the name. Following recommended civil service practice the above examples would be typed as follows.

Fully open punctuation

10 August 19..

R B Jackson Esq OBE MA
Managing Director
Fylde Motor Co Ltd
Folkestone Road
PRESTON Lancs
PR1 OLD

Dear Sir

Yours faithfully

Civil service practice influences the attitude of business firms considerably, but it is unlikely that all firms will follow the style recommended by the Civil Service Department.

Whichever style of punctuation is adopted for the non-functional markings outside the body of the letter, i.e. from the inside name and address, etc., standard punctuation is always used for the text in the body of the letter itself.

A comma is used after the introductory reference:

In reply to your enquiry of 3 July, we are pleased to enclose a copy of our catalogue. Confirming our telegram of this morning, we can supply the copper piping you require.

*Civil Service Department: *Manual for Civil Service Typists,* H.M.S.O., 1974

Numbers

To assist the eye commas are inserted in large numbers to mark off the figures for thousands and millions.

£28,627   23,547,346

EXERCISES

1. Remembering the close grammatical relationship between the subject of a sentence and its verb, copy the following sentences, removing commas where you think they are wrongly inserted and inserting them where you think they are wrongly omitted.

A

(a) The practice of allowing trade discounts to customers other than those who are genuine retail shopkeepers, is not one we can recommend.

(b) It is just possible that the advice posted at the close of business on 6 July, missed the last collection.

(c) The late arrival of the goods, the inferior quality of some of them, and the damage sustained by a large number of them as a result of faulty packing, are all matters we are bound to take into account when we place future orders.

(d) The question of compensation for the damage caused by prolonged exposure to the weather, has not yet been decided.

(e) Particulars of his age, his education and professional qualifications, and his business experience, have been noted.

B

(a) A formal agreement for payment of a salary of £7,000 a year subject to termination by three months' notice by either side, will now be prepared for you to sign.

(b) A reduction since last October of four in the number of full-time staff employed at our warehouse in Mincing Lane, has been necessary owing to a falling off in trade.

(c) The invoice, bill of lading, and insurance policy, together with a draft bill of exchange for acceptance by the consignee, are enclosed.

(d) Because of our wish to expand our business with this customer, credit considerably beyond the amount originally agreed upon, has been extended to him.

(e) Our contacts with all the leading merchants in this part of the world and our experience in dealing with goods of the kind you wish to market, will enable us to be of considerable service to you.

2. The following include both defining and non-defining clauses. Copy the sentences, inserting commas where you think they are necessary to give the meaning intended.

(a) All orders which are entrusted to us receive careful attention.

(b) The order for two dozen pairs of blankets which was received yesterday has already been dealt with.

(c) The business carried on by us in Gracechurch Street has now been taken over by Messrs. Paulden & Co. who will transfer it to their own well-known premises opposite.

(d) The representative who called this morning represents H. Roberts & Co.

(e) Our new managing director whom I first met in Zimbabwe takes over at the beginning of next month.

(f) The man whom you met just now is the master of s.s. *Victoria.*

(g) We regret we shall be unable to meet our acceptance for £185 which matures at the end of this month.

(h) Please pay any warehouse charges that may have accrued and debit our account.

(i) The matter will be considered at the end of March when the year's accounts are prepared.

(j) He is longing for the day when he can retire.

3. Type the following examples of "semi-open" punctuation, using blocked style.

(a) S. Gedge Esq. F.S.C.T.
    The Lyceum
        OLDHAM Lancs. OL1 8DN

(b) Dr. L. Blair M.B. Ch.B.
        115 High Road
        WALTHAMSTOW E17 3DT

(c) Messrs. Clayton Baxter Brown & Co.
        Chartered Accountants
            The Crescent
                ROMFORD Essex RM1 4EF

(d) The Secretary
        W.G. & F. Musgrave & Co. Ltd.
        126−130 Gartinall Road
            SOUTHGATE Middx. N14 3NZ

4. Using "semi-open" punctuation, type the following letters.

(a) The Secretary,
    Macdonald & Evans Ltd.,
    Publishers,
    Estover Road,
    PLYMOUTH PL6 7PZ

Dear Sir,

In reply to your enquiry of 10 October I am pleased to be able to inform you that 500 copies of *A History of Red Tape* by Craig have been sent to your Southend warehouse today.

I remain,
Yours faithfully,

(b) Messrs. Anderson Johnson & Co.,
   25 Woodstock Street,
   DURHAM DH4 7JR

Dear Sirs,

Confirming my telephone message this morning I give below the estimated cost of the work to be carried out at your factory in Carpenter Road:

      External painting £2,460
      Extension to existing warehouse £25,500
      Installation of central heating in the office block £2,600

Upon receiving your instructions we will proceed with the work immediately.

Yours truly,
for Reginald Harris & Co. Ltd.
R. WATKINS
Secretary

(c) The Works Manager,
   Crescent Engineering Co. Ltd.,
   Longsight Works,
   MANCHESTER M2 3AT

Dear Sir,

In answer to your advertisement in yesterday's *Daily Telegraph* I should like to be considered for the post of Works Accountant.

I remain,
Yours faithfully,

5. Copy the following sentences, inserting commas where necessary.

(a) We have just placed an order for 2 dozen leather purses ½ dozen handbags 1 dozen pairs of gloves and 1 dozen shirts.

(b) The applicant explained that he had just arrived in England that he was looking for a suitable post and that he had every hope of finding one.

(c) An invoice normally includes the catalogue numbers the quantities the descriptions the prices and the total cost of goods supplied on credit.

(d) In business houses public offices Government departments and in fact wherever correspondence is considerable an efficient filing system is necessary.

(e) Tact courtesy understanding great patience good temper a knowledge of accounts and competence in both shorthand nad typewriting are among the qualifications that make an efficient private secretary.

Sign	Function	When used	Examples
The period or full-stop (.).	Denotes the longest pause.	(a) The full-stop is used to mark the end of a sentence that takes the form of a statement. It is always followed by a space (two or three spaces on a typewriter), the following sentence beginning with a capital.	(a) Thank you for your letter of 29 July. I am glad to learn that you still undertake repairs to television and radio equipment. The information will be of interest to a number of our customers.
		(b) The full-stop is used: (i) after abbreviations; and (ii) single letters representing a full word.	(b) (i) Esq. (Esquire), Hants. (Hampshire). (ii) J.B. Cameron, w.p.m. (words per minute), C.O.D. (cash on delivery). *Exception:* 75p
		(c) The full-stop may be omitted from abbreviations in very common use, though it is often retained.	(c) memo, per cent, per pro
		(d) (i) Full-stops are omitted from abbreviations consisting of initial letters that make pronounceable words called *acronyms*.	(d) (i) NALGO, NATO, UNO, UNESCO
		(ii) There is a growing practice to omit the full-stop from unpronounceable letter combinations.	(ii) BBC, HMSO, OED
		(e) The full-stop may be omitted when the abbreviation retains the first and last letters of the complete word (though it is the more usual practice in typewriting to retain it).	(e) Mr, Mrs, Messrs, Ltd, Dr (Debtor or Doctor), ft, fcp.
		(f) The full-stop is not used after forms that may appear to be, but which are not, abbreviations.	(f) 1st, 2nd, 3rd, 4to (quarto), 8vo (octavo), £, Cu (copper) and all other symbols for chemical elements.

Sign	Function	When used	Examples
		(g) The full-stop is not used after metric symbols.	(g) m (metre), kg (kilogram), l (litre). Note also p (new pence).
		(h) Full-stops in a series are used to indicate the omission of words, especially from passages quoted—three if the omission is from the middle of a sentence and four if it is the end (i.e. including one to mark the end of the sentence).	(h) "It is a sound principle that as few stops should be used as will do the work. . . everyone should make up his mind not to depend on his stops." (Extract from Fowler's *The King's English*.)
Comma (,)	Denotes the shortest pause of all, and is the most frequently used and the most troublesome of all stops.	(a) Commas are used to mark off items in a list or series. *Note:* Omission of the comma before *and* is optional, except that:	(a) The invoice, bill of lading, insurance policy, and draft bill of exchange, have been sent to your bankers in Cape Town today. The price quoted includes cost, insurance, and freight.
		(i) it is retained in some cases to avoid ambiguity;	(i) The college provides classes in short-hand, typewriting, secretarial practice, music, and drama (signifying that music and drama are provided in separate classes.)
		(ii) it is omitted when the enumeration consists of only two items.	(ii) The project is one that calls for enterprise and initiative.
		(b) Commas are used to mark off separate clauses in a sentence, unless the clauses are very short, when the comma may be omitted.	(b) As I have not heard from you in reply to my letter of 4 January, the goods will now be offered to another customer. We feel sure you will find the appliance satisfactory and look forward to further business with you.

(c) Commas are often used instead of brackets or dashes to mark off a parenthesis, i.e. an explanatory expression that does not form part of the normal construction of the sentence. (But if the parenthesis is lengthy it is more helpful to the reader if brackets or dashes are used instead of commas.)

(d) The comma is used to mark off adverbs and adverb phrases at the beginning of a sentence.

(e) Commas are used to mark off adverbs and adverb phrases occurring in the middle of a sentence. (But there is a modern tendency to omit the commas unless emphasis is sought.)

(f) The comma is used to mark the omission of some word or group of words that is understood.

(g) Commas are used to mark off non-defining clauses introduced by a relative pronoun (see p. 341). It will be noticed that such clauses are in the nature of parentheses.

(c) John Strauss, *our managing director*, has been with the company since its formation.
Compensation is also due, *in my opinion*, for loss of time in attending meetings.

(d) *Nevertheless*, we hope to deliver the goods tomorrow. *Notwithstanding the difficulties*, I shall travel to Liverpool next week.

(e) We are, *however*, disappointed with the results of last year's trading.
I shall, *of course*, do my best to be present. There is no need, *in the circumstances*, to make a decision immediately.

(f) The first column shows the date; the second, the name of the payee; the third the nature of the payment.
The fabric is low in price; the quality, excellent; the dye, fast, and the appearance, attractive.

(g) Miss Barrett, *who holds a shorthand certificate for 120 w.p.m.*, is the chairman's private secretary.
The enclosed account, *which has been carefully checked*, is due for payment at the end of this month.

Sign	Function	When used	Examples
Comma (,) (*continued*)		(b) The comma is used to introduce a *short* direct quotation, i.e. where the exact words of a person or passage are given. (For lengthy quotations the colon is preferred.)	(b) The chairman replied, "I have nothing more to add to the statement already made."
Semicolon (;)	Denotes a pause mid-way between the comma and the full-stop.	(a) A comma is normally sufficient to mark off the items forming an enumeration; but the semicolon is used to indicate a longer pause and thus to emphasize the separate items.	(a) If you like the house; if the price is reasonable, and if you can obtain a mortgage; then buy it.
		(b) The semicolon is used to mark off two or more separate statements, not connected by conjunctions, but which are related in thought. It warns the reader that more on the same topic is to come. (c) The semicolon instead of the comma may be used before conjunctions when it is desired to emphasize some contrast, explanation, etc.	(b) We do not condemn the civil servant who looks for a safe job; the teacher who looks for a pension; the barrister who looks for a high income; nor must we condemn the businessman who looks for good profits. (c) On this occasion a discount will be allowed; but in future the full price will be payable. If you cannot accept the goods at the price invoiced you may return them; otherwise, please send your cheque for the amount due.
		(d) The semicolon is used to mark off separate statements which themselves contain commas.	(d) We are sending you the following goods by passenger train today: silk handkerchiefs, 5 dozen; nylon stockings, 50 pairs; woollen jackets, 2 dozen.

Colon (:)		
The former use of the colon, denoting a pause longer than the semi-colon has been discontinued. It is now used almost exclusively to denote that there is something to follow.	(a) (i) The colon is used to introduce a list or enumeration, especially after expressions such as *namely*, *thus*, *as follows*. (ii) At the end of a paragraph the colon is sometimes followed by a dash, thus (:–), but as the modern tendency is towards plainness, it is better to omit the dash. (b) The colon is used to introduce a quotation, *especially if the quotation is a lengthy one*. (But if the quotation is short a comma will usually be sufficient to introduce it.) (c) The colon is used between two sentences too closely connected in thought to justify separation by a full-stop. (d) The colon is used to introduce a remark that expands or explains an idea just referred to.	(a) (i) Those present were: His Worship the Mayor, the Mayoress, and the two local Members of Parliament. (ii) The course includes the following subjects: shorthand, typewriting, English, secretarial duties, and French. (b) Addressing the annual meeting the chairman said: (c) Mr Redgrave will be calling at eleven o'clock: be sure to let the secretary know when he arrives. (d) He is a thorough rogue: he would swindle his own mother.
Parentheses ( )		
To enclose a parenthesis or "aside".	(a) Brackets, like the dash, are used to denote a strongly marked parenthesis. (b) Brackets are used to repeat sums of money.	(a) Our prices (which have not been increased for over twelve months) compare favourably with those of our competitors. We invite your attention (see price-list enclosed) to some remarkable bargains in cotton goods. (b) We can offer you an attractive three-bedroom bungalow for £35,750 (Thirty-five thousand seven hundred and fifty pounds).

Sign	Function	When used	Examples
Dash (—)	Is used freely for a variety of purposes.	(a) The dash is used as an alternative to parentheses to denote a strongly marked "aside" or break in the sense of a passage. (For denoting a short or less strongly marked parenthesis the comma is usually sufficient.)	(a) The prices quoted are very low—lower than they have been for years—and we hope you will find them acceptable. We can supply any quantity you need—500 or more—at the price stated.
		(b) The dash is used to mark an abrupt change of thought.	(b) If only I could attend the meeting on Thursday—but then, that is out of the question.
		(c) The dash is used to bring together several subjects belonging to the same verb.	(c) Furniture, carpets and linos, kitchen utensils, and electric appliances—all were included in the sale.
		(d) The dash is used where a word or phrase is repeated.	(d) Our competitor's policy must have repercussions on our overseas trade—repercussions that are likely to prove serious for us.
Hyphen (or short dash) (-)	To form compounds.	(a) (i) A hyphen is used to form compound nouns.	(a) (i) Mother-in-law, subject-matter, St. Annes-on-Sea, dining-room.
		(ii) There is a strong modern tendency to omit the hyphen from compounds consisting of two short words and to write the words as one.	(ii) Today, tomorrow, textbook, footbridge.
		(b) (i) The hyphen is used to form compound adjectives.	(b) (i) A *head-on* collision, *first-aid* equipment, an *up-to-date* catalogue.
		(ii) But a hyphen is not used between	(ii) A *very good* performance, a *highly*

Mark	Purpose	Rules	Examples
		an adverb and its adjective. (*Exception:* When the adjective is a participle, past or present, a hyphen is frequently attached if the adjective is attributive, but not if it is predicative.) (*c*) The hyphen is used after certain prefixes, especially when it is necessary: (*i*) to indicate the pronunciation of two separate vowels; (*ii*) to distinguish words similarly spelt. (*d*) The hyphen is used to join the numbers from 21 to 99, and also parts of fractions. (*e*) The hyphen is used to mark division of words at line-endings.	skilled worker, a *most unusual* result. But note: a *well-earned* holiday, a *well-known* person, an *oft-repeated* phrase, an *ever-increasing* difficulty (Attributive); a person *well known*, a phrase *oft repeated*. (Predicative). (*c*) Ex-officio, ante-natal, anti-aircraft, post-war. (*i*) Co-education, pre-eminent, pre-estimate, re-enter, re-examine. (*ii*) Re-cover, re-creation, re-form, re-sign. (*d*) Twenty-one, twenty-first, five-and-twenty years, three-quarters, five-eighths. (*e*) *See* pp. 384–6 for examples and rules.
Apostrophe (or raised comma) (')	To mark omissions and ownership.	(*a*) The apostrophe is used to mark the omission of some letter or letters from a word (unusual in business correspondence because of the colloquial and informal nature of words so treated). (*b*) (*i*) The apostrophe is used to denote ownership or possession, 's being added to the word. (*ii*) In compounds and in names consisting of more than one word only the last word is inflected; though for the	(*a*) *Don't* (do not), *there's* (there is), *it's* (it is). (*b*) (*i*) The *firm's* business, the *typist's* desk, Mr. *Jones's* office, *women's* and *children's* wear. (*ii*) Man-*servant's* quarters, Bank of *England's* premises.

Sign	Function	When used	Examples
Apostrophe (or raised comma) (') (*continued*)		sake of euphony it is better to avoid the possessive in compounds ending with s.	The examinations of the *Royal Society of Arts* (not Royal Society of Art's examinations).
		(*c*) The apostrophe without the *s* is used: (*i*) to avoid three consecutive *s* sounds; (*ii*) with plurals ending in *s*.	(*c*) (*i*) St. *Francis'* day, *Jesus'* disciples, for *goodness'* sake. (*ii*) Private *Secretaries'* Association, the *typists'* department, *members'* subscriptions.
		(*d*) As a general rule the preposition *of* and note the possessive form is used for inanimate things, though what seems to be usual or acceptable is often the determining factor.	(*d*) The success of the experiment (not the *experiment's* success), within the scope of the regulations (not the *regulations'* scope), but the *B.B.C.'s* programmes.
		(*e*) Possessive pronouns do not take the apostrophe.	(*e*) Hers, its, yours, ours, theirs.
		(*f*) (*i*) The apostrophe is used to give possessive form to words that are not in fact possessives (though there is a modern tendency to omit the apostrophe in such cases).	(*f*) (*i*) A *day's* journey, a three *days'* journey, one *month's* notice, three *month's* *notice, at death's* door.
		(*ii*) Conversely, some expressions having possessive force do not take the possessive form.	(*ii*) The *Railways* Act, *Entertainments* Tax, The *Companies* Act.

| Quotation marks (used doubly or singly) (" ") or (' ') | To mark the beginning and the end of a quotation. | (a) Quotation marks are used to enclose a quotation. (They may be used either singly or doubly, but Fowler* recommends the use of single quotation marks as normal practice, and double marks only for a quotation appearing within another.)

(b) Quotation marks are sometimes used as an alternative to italics (or, in typewriting, underscoring) for titles of books, plays, names of ships, etc., but for plainness the use of italics (or underscoring) is preferred.

(c) Normal punctuation marks are kept in the places to which they belong in the passage quoted (though many printers and publishers prefer to place *all* full-stops and commas *inside* inverted commas, because it simplifies the work). | (a) The chairman said: "I welcome you to this, our 27th annual general meeting".

(b) The "Duchess of Argyle" will sail to-morrow.
I will meet you at the "Corner House".

(c) (i) I cannot give any more time to this question just now
becomes
"I cannot", he said, "give any more time to this question just now."

(Since there is no comma in the original statement, the comma in the quotation belongs to *be said* and not to *cannot*, and is therefore placed outside the quotation marks.)

(ii) Why did you say, "I don't know"?
but
(iii) His letter included this question: "Will you please explain why the goods promised for January 27th have not yet been delivered?" |

*Modern English Usage (2nd ed.), p. 591.

Sign	Function	When used	Examples
Quotation marks (used doubly or singly)(" ") or (' ') (*continued*)			(In (*ii*) the question mark is placed *outside* the quotation marks because it does not appear in the original statement; in (*iii*) it is placed *inside* because it forms part of the passage quoted.)
		(*d*) When a quotation appears within another it should be placed within single quotation marks if the main quotation is in double, or within double marks if the main quotation is in single (the practice recommended by Fowler).	(*d*) He asked me: "Did the Chairman say, 'The meeting is adjourned', or not?" or He asked me: 'Did the Chairman say, "The meeting is adjourned", or not?' (The latter method has the advantage of giving the required prominence to the interior quotation.)
		(*e*) When the quotation consists of two or more paragraphs, quotation marks are placed at the beginning of each paragraph and at the end of the last.	(*e*) "An open telegram is one written in language whose meaning is apparent to all, including any foreign language written in letters of the English alphabet. "All necessary words forming part of the address after the name of the street or road count as a single word, e.g. St. John's Wood, London, NW8 7NG."
		(*f*) Inverted commas are also employed to indicate words used in a special sense.	(*f*) For example: some confirmed tea-drinkers prefer the "dust" of the tea-bag

Punctuation	Purpose	Rule	Examples
		(g) Inverted commas are also used in direct speech, but not in indirect speech. (*See* p. 309.)	(an uncomplimentary reference to the residue from blending, packing, etc.). There was another "incident" at the corner of West Street (a euphemism for something more serious than an incidental outcome). (g) He said, "I want you to telephone immediately." but He told me he wanted to telephone immediately.
Question mark (?)	To denote questions.	(a) The question mark is used to replace the full-stop when a direct question is indirect.	(a) What is the date of the next meeting? Are the goods now ready for delivery? but I asked what was the date of the next meeting. I enquired whether the goods were now ready for delivery.
		(b) The question mark is not used for polite requests made in question form.	(b) Will you please complete and return the enclosed form. Would you be good enough to deliver the goods tomorrow.
Exclamation mark (!)	To denote the expression of surprise or some other emotion. (It is not normally used in business correspondence.)	Following an exclamation, and exclamatory words and sentences.	Alas! the resolution had been passed before I arrived. Good gracious! I didn't expect to find you here. What a day we've had, to be sure!

EXERCISES

1. First read through the following letters and decide the points at which each sentence ends; then copy the letters, inserting full-stops and capitals as necessary.

A

Dear Sir

My daughter is a pupil at the Ilford County High School and will complete her five-year course there next July she was admitted to the school in September 19. . on the results of the Essex entrance examination and has a good record of achievement she has been entered for the school-leaving examination in seven subjects next June she has now decided to take up secretarial work and on the advice of her headmistress I am writing to ask you to send me full particulars of your secretarial courses at the same time perhaps you will suggest a day and time when I may call with my daughter to discuss her training.

Yours faithfully

B

Dear Sir

Thank you for your quotation of 26 March I notice that the Formafelt for which you quote is only half the yardage of the carpets I believe you mentioned that it was double width when we called to see you if this is so then I accept your quotation.

I think I told you that central heating was to be installed and until this work is finished it will not be possible for you to lay the carpets before then I shall be visiting St. Annes and will call to see you in the meantime I should be glad if you would put the work in hand so that there may be no delay once central heating is installed.

Yours faithfully

2. Type or write out in full the following abbreviations, frequently found in business letters.

(a) encl., Co., per pro., MS., E.C.2;
(b) H.P., etc., viz., c/d, e.g.;
(c) a.m., C.O.D., E. & O.E., f.o.b., P.S.;
(d) Ltd., c.i.f., pro tem., N.B.; P.T.O.;
(e) Esq., Messrs., inv., m.p.h., do.

3. Give the recognized form of abbreviation for the following, inserting full-stops where necessary:

(a) octavo, steamship, that is, manuscripts, kilowatts;
(b) inches, yards, kilograms, ounces, millimetres;
(c) Buckinghamshire,   Cambridgeshire,   Hertfordshire,   Gloucestershire, Leicestershire;

(d) Northamptonshire, Nottinghamshire, Oxfordshire, Staffordshire, Worcestershire;

(e) Lancashire, Bedfordshire, Lincolnshire, Wiltshire, Hampshire.

4. Copy the following sentences, inserting commas where necessary.

A

(a) As I have not heard from you in reply to my letter and as completion of the work has become a matter of urgency I now propose to approach another contractor.

(b) Having had long experience in work of this kind and controlling as we do large capital resources we are well able to undertake the building of your new factory.

(c) We are glad you think that a good market can be found for our goods but we confess that credit on the scale you mention opens up a far from attractive prospect and we hope something may be done at least to shorten the period for which credit is required.

(d) We have already written to you twice urging dispatch of the goods and because you have failed to deliver them by the date named we are now reluctantly compelled to cancel the order.

(e) We admit that we have made a mistake since we should have referred to the patterns supplied by you but on the other hand we think we have some claim to indulgence on account of the misleading specification supplied to us and if you could relieve us of the need to supply the last two items in your order we should be grateful.

B

(a) Your letter enclosing a specification of the work to be carried out prepared by you at the request of our managing director will be considered at the next meeting of the Board.

(b) For the first part of the work items 3 4 and 5 we quote you £620 and for the latter part items 6 7 and 8 we quote you £1,235.

(c) The instrument can be used and frequently is for a number of other purposes.

(d) Mr. James Legon our managing director acted as chairman.

(e) Mr. Harold Watson a prominent figure in local business circles opened the discussion.

C

(a) If it is at all possible the work you asked us to put in hand will be completed by the end of the month.

(b) We too are of the opinion that prices will fall before the end of the season.

(c) He arrived at the office looking very tired and immediately asked not to be disturbed for at least an hour.

(d) As soon as I know he has arrived I will deliver your message to the manager.

(e) The goods delivered yesterday for instance were damaged as a result of faulty packing.

5. Type or write out the following letters, inserting necessary full-stops and commas.

A

Dear Sirs

I was educated at King's College School where I obtained G.C.E. "O" levels in six subjects since leaving school last summer I have attended shorthand and typewriting classes and in these subjects have now attained speeds of 40 and 100 w.p.m. respectively I am very anxious to get into a merchant's office and should my application be successful I would do my best to give you satisfaction.

Yours faithfully

B

Dear Sirs

You will no doubt remember that you acted for me last December in the purchase of the property at No. 1 Margate Road St. Annes I recently received a demand note for payment of rates in respect of this property and upon enquiry am informed that the amount claimed namely £125 is for the period 5 April to 7 December last and that it should have been allowed to me upon completion of the purchase.

I am enclosing the demand note and also my correspondence with the local authority and since the borough treasurer is apparently looking to me for payment of the amount should be obliged if you would arrange for the necessary adjustment to be made in your completion statement.

Yours faithfully

C

Dear Mr Baxter

Since writing to you on 19 March about central heating for the bungalow at Frinton I have visited Cranes in London and seen their range of domestic boilers I did so because I think you mentioned that it was a Crane boiler which you proposed to install.

I am enclosing a leaflet giving particulars of the three sizes of "Cavendish" boiler supplied by Cranes for domestic purposes it seems to me that the No. 4 size is the one that would be needed for the number and size of radiators we have in mind I should be obliged if you would give me your opinion on this point and also inform me whether the tiled recess in the kitchen would be deep enough to take the No. 4 size.

Yours truly,

6. Copy the following sentences, inserting semicolons (and, where necessary, commas) at appropriate points.

(a) It happened at a time when the firm had very little working capital when exports were falling and when skilled labour was difficult to get.

(*b*) We are able to supply a ledger containing 400 pages ruled as follows:

250 pages with two accounts or sections 100 pages with three sections 50 pages with six sections.

(*c*) The Government as usual claims that the nation's affairs are running smoothly the Opposition on the other hand maintains that we are on the brink of disaster.

(*d*) We are prepared to pay you a fixed salary of £4,000 a year in addition we shall allow you a commission of 5% on all orders introduced by you.

(*e*) There are signs of prosperity everywhere farmers were never so well off manufacturers' books are bulging with orders the roads and railways are blocked with traffic and the public are spending as never before.

7. Punctuate the following paragraph replacing words by figures where customary and introducing an appropriate semicolon. Explain concisely the use of this semicolon.

A fifteen per cent dividend would cost with profits tax some thirty-one thousand pounds earnings after the tax for the year to september thirtieth last were over three times that figure net assets at september thirtieth were four hundred and forty-five thousand pounds.   (*R.S.A. Inter.*)

8. Copy the following sentences, inserting colons, semicolons, and commas at appropriate points.

(*a*) The section of the syllabus on finance includes the following the various means of payment the Bank of England including its main functions the British banking and currency systems including the cheque system a detailed study of the cheque itself and the remittance facilities of the Post Office.

(*b*) We have today dispatched the following by British Road Services 20 reams lined A3 paper 15 reams plain A4 paper ½ gross boxes large paper clips.

(*c*) We are able to offer you the property at a very reasonable figure namely £1,500 yearly for ten years and thereafter at £1,400 yearly.

(*d*) There are several things you should do before you attempt to type back your shorthand notes first read through them carefully and correct any obvious grammatical errors insert the punctuation signs you propose to use and finally check doubtful spellings.

(*e*) He was a chairman who inspired confidence to listen to him was to feel that here was a man of tremendous character.

9. Copy the following sentences, inserting dashes, parentheses, and commas as may be necessary.

(*a*) The quality of the coal now in stock is very good much better than we have had for some time and we hope you will like it.

(*b*) The representative left at two o'clock for I am afraid I have forgotton where.

(*c*) We are pleased to quote you for electrical fittings see pages 27—35 of catalogue enclosed any of which we can supply immediately on receipt of order.

(*d*) We have been informed and we have every reason to believe that supplies of the dictionary are likely to run out within six months.

(*e*) Our method or lack of method of spelling may be absurd but it is now fixed at least until the efforts of our spelling reformers meet with success.

10. Copy the following sentences, inserting hyphens and other necessary punctuation marks.

(*a*) Seven and twenty years have passed since he entered the company's service as an office boy.

(*b*) It was agreed that Mr. Herbert Spencer should be coopted to the Finance Sub-committee.

(*c*) The subject matter of the contract will not be made known until after the meeting.

(*d*) We have pleasure in sending you an up to date price list of our range of card index cabinets.

(*e*) The principal's secretary is a refined and well spoken girl and an excellent shorthand typist.

11. Write down, or type the possessive plural forms of the following nouns.

(*a*) jury, lawyer, cashier, lady, family;
(*b*) secretary, manager, man-servant, Lord-Mayor, shorthand-writer.

12. Copy the following sentences, inserting apostrophes and other necessary punctuation marks.

(*a*) The Boards decision regarding the purchase of Bartons bakery will be made known at the close of the meeting.

(*b*) The companys new offices overlook St. Jamess Park the typists department being on the front of the building.

(*c*) My pension becomes payable in two weeks time and my wifes in a months time.

(*d*) Members subscriptions to the Ratepayers Association are due in three months time.

(*e*) Teachers pensions are regulated by the Teachers (Superannuation) Act 1956 friendly societies activities by the Friendly Societies Act 1896 and shop assistants conditions of work by the Shops Act 1950.

13. Explain how the meaning of each of the following sentences would be changed if the commas were removed.

(*a*) The workers, who had completed their task in the alloted time, were granted a bonus.

(*b*) The statement, I believe, was made by the man in the dark suit,
(*c*) Why did you ask, John?   (*I. of B.*)

14. Each of the following sentences lacks *two* essential punctuation marks. Re-write them correctly, without changing the word order.

(a) However even pre war jewellery may have some antique value.
(b) "Do you wish to see Mr. Price the Manager"
(c) "Whos going to pay for this boys ticket?"
(d) "Theyre very simple minded and believe everything he says."
(e) "He's rich youre poor."
(f) "Im so sorry" he replied.
(g) Exhausted by the climb the girl fell into a deep dreamless sleep.

(E.M.E.U.)

15. Write out the following passage, supplying all the necessary punctuation.

Without effort we will achieve nothing even a genius must work hard indeed genius is said to be 99 per cent effort how often do people feel satisfaction after a job well done it may have cost them a lot in terms of discomfort and fatigue but the feeling of achievement makes it all worthwhile many who retire at 60 or 65 ask themselves this question what am I going to do with myself the obvious answer is to find some hobby or part-time job because it is this interest this searching for a sense of purpose and achievement that makes their lives meaningful.   (E.M.E.U.)

CHAPTER TWENTY-THREE

Capitals

A vile conceit in pompous words express'd,
Is like a clown in regal purple dressed.

A. Pope: *Essay on Criticism*

The effect of using capital letters is to emphasize a word by giving it importance or by adding dignity to it. Words with capitals stand out from the rest and attract attention.

To use initial capitals excessively is to be pompous, and should you have doubt as to whether a particular word requires a capital letter you should use a small letter.

The main rules for using initial capitals are summarized below.

For sentences
Give an initial capital letter to the first word of each new sentence, i.e. always following a full stop; but after a question mark or exclamation mark use an initial capital only when the mark occurs at the end of a completed sentence.

> Thank you for your letter of 20 March. We are glad to learn that the goods arrived safely.
> What a day you've had! You must be tired.
> Wait! Don't be so impatient.

but

> What! you didn't phone my apologies?
> Good heavens! it seems impossible.

For correspondence
Use initial capitals for the salutation and for the first words only in the complimentary close.

> Dear Sir (or Madam),

> We are, dear sir
> Yours faithfully

The use of initial capitals for such words as street, road, avenue, forming part of an address is optional.

For proper names
Use initial capitals for the names of persons, places, streets, buildings, etc., and for adjectives from them.

The letters were sent to Mr. Gilbert from Toronto.

Devonshire House
Normanshire Drive
CHINGFORD E4 5BN

The opera was in true Gilbertian style.

Some words which originated as proper names take small letters, since they are no longer closely associated with their origins:

brussels sprouts, french chalk, wellingtons, gum arabic, roman numerals, venetian blinds, alsatian dog.

For calendar names, etc.

Days, Months, etc.
Use initial capitals for days of the week and months of the year, and also for the names of special days and festivals.

Our representative will call on Monday afternoon 5 July.
Remembrance Sunday, Easter Day, Whitsuntide.

Seasons
The names of the seasons do not take initial capitals unless they are personified, as in verse.

Our new fashions will be ready in spring.

For titles
Use initial capitals:

For the important words in official titles of organizations and institutions

College of Preceptors
Institute of Marketing and Sales Management

But when such terms as *institute, university, college,* and *department* are used in a general sense and do not form part of a title or refer to a particular institution use small letters.

The College (referring to a particular college) offers courses in a wide range of subjects and fulfils the functions of a college of further education in every way.

Note: Some writers prefer to use small letters even to refer to particular institutions. There is no hard-and-fast rule, but the advice of Sir Ernest Gowers is, "Use a capital for the particular and a small letter for the general".

For Courtesy and Similar Titles

Send the letter to Professor L. James, care of Messrs. Holden & Co.

But, as above, when words such as *professor, headmaster, vicar,* and *chairman* do not form part of a title or refer to a particular individual, use small letters.

The Chairman (meaning a particular chairman) gave an encouraging report.

but

The chairman is the person responsible for the conduct of a meeting.

For the important words in headings, descriptive titles, titles of publications, plays, etc.

Use and Abuse of Leisure
Head of the Department of Management and Business Studies
Have you read *Gone with the Wind?*

For abbreviated titles

O.B.E., B.Sc.(Econ.), M.A., Ph.D., M.P.

For numercial sequences
Use initial capitals for nouns followed by numbers denoting a sequence:

No. 54,   Para. 23,   Ch. IV,   Section 21,   Invoice 3,624,   Grade III,
Stage II,   Page 125.

For enumerations
Use initial capitals:

For the chief names in a list of items (optional)

Please send the following items:

2 reams Duplicating Paper, A3, white;
500 Manilla Folders, A4, assorted colours;
2 gallons Ink, blue black;
1 dozen Typewriter Ribbons, ½″, black record.

To give emphasis to a particular word (optional)

The consignment of Sugar has not yet arrived.

For resolutions (optional)
Use initial capitals for the first word of a resolution.

It was Resolved, That future meetings be held on the first Monday in every month.

For quotations
Give an initial capital to the first word of a direct quotation

The secretary asked, "When was the telegram received?"

If the quotation is indirect do not use initial capitals

The secretary asked when the telegram was received.

For the pronoun "I"

I am sorry, but I do not agree.

EXERCISES

1. Type or write out the following sentences, using capitals and punctuation where necessary.

(*a*) The college will not be able to move into its new buildings until the end of the summer.

(*b*) Our office manager always stressed make a point of answering or at least acknowledging every letter the day it is received.

(*c*) Address this letter to the rt. hon. sir edward wilson kcmg kbe president of the society for the protection of science and learning ltd 5 old burlington street sw1n 5dh.

(*d*) Our representative will arrange to call on you on the thursday in easter week or if this is not convenient on any day in whitsun week.

(*e*) You will find the salary scales for grade I shorthand typists set out on page 5 of appendix IV in the current edition of conditions of service.

(*f*) Sir james portman has agreed to give a lecture on tuesday 7th march on the educational and practical value of a commercial course.

(*g*) Following a long discussion it was resolved that consideration of the claim for increased pay be deferred to the next meeting of the society.

(b) The houses of parliament and the offices of the main ministries of the government are all to be found in westminster.

(i) The advertisement for an assistant to the personnel manager should appear in all wednesday and friday editions during July.

(j) Prepare an order for the following items and send it to messrs. r j holden & co ltd 10–14 gracechurch street bolton bo4 7gh.

    3 dozen sweeping brushes, size 4
    ½ dozen peruvian carpet brooms
    1 dozen no 5 sponge bags
    2 dozen knife boards

2. Type or write out the following passages, capitalizing and punctuating as necessary.

A

from the daily telegraph

private secretary required by the central electricity generating board for a principal assistant clerk in the planning department salary £7,000/£8,000 per annum modern offices near london bridge and waterloo stations staff restaurant permanent pensionable appointment candidates should be competent shorthand typists of good education applications stating age qualifications experience present position and salary to the appointments officer 24–30 holborn london ecln 2hn not later than 4 April

B

messrs fennell & Co 26 burlington avenue maidstone kent me4 2bn
gentlemen

in answer to your advertisement in todays times for a foreign correspondence clerk i would like to apply for the post.

i was born of english parents in paris and have passed several years of my life in mannheim and cologne and can speak and write both french and german with fluency i also have a fairly good knowledge of spanish

i am 32 years old and for the past four years have been correspondence clerk to messrs saurel et cie of 31 mincing lane ec3t 7dp who have extensive foreign connections especially with france and germany during the whole time i was employed by them i was in charge of continental correspondence

i look forward to hearing from you

i am
yours faithfully
james mahon

C

messrs m power & sons 16–20 abbots crescent sunderland sn8 8at
dear sirs

i am writing to inform you that owing to the death of my friend and partner mr william morris i have taken into partnership mr robert constance late of messrs rowbotham & co 19 renfield street glasgow gw4 2rd and with his co-operation will carry on this business under the style of

smithson & constance

all accounts of the late firm of smithson & morris will be settled by mr constance and me

thanking you for the support you have hitherto given us and trusting to maintain our friendly business relations

i am
yours faithfully
r.l. smithson

3. Write out the following passage, with capital letters and punctuation marks where necessary:

well if they wont answer ill see if i can go in he said he lifted the latch the door was not locked it opened before him hullo you inside harry called i am a friend is anyone here hey hey is anyone here at all

4. Write out the following passage with correct spacing, punctuation and capital letters.

did you ever read jane austens emma mary joan asked no replied mary but ive often meant to have you got a copy yes but my brother jack wants it to take on holiday to spain next wednesday ill lend it to you when hes back thank you joan.

5. Re-write the following passage inserting all necessary punctuation marks and capital letters.

i hope my dear said mr bennet to his wife that you have ordered a good dinner today because i have reason to expect an addition to our family party whom do you mean my dear i know of nobody that is coming the person of whom i speak is a gentleman and a stranger
(Adapted from *Pride and Prejudice:* Jane Austen)   *(N.W.R.A.C.)*

CHAPTER TWENTY-FOUR

The Technique of Spelling

It is a pity that Chawcer, who had geneyus, was so unedicated; he's the wuss speller I know of.
Aretmus Ward

SPELLING AND BUSINESS

A firm's correspondence is often enough the principal means, and sometimes the only means, by which business relations with the outside world are established. It is therefore of the utmost import- ance that letters sent out should create a good impression. If they are to do this they must be attractively displayed, and unblemished by errors in grammar, punctuation, and spelling. High standards in correspondence suggest high standards of service generally, and a well-typed letter on attractive notepaper may well pave the way to an important business connection.

Current spelling standards are not good. One of the main reasons advanced is careless and superficial reading, due partly to pressure of other interests. Careless pronunciation (*Feb-uary* for *Feb-ruary*, *tempor-y* for *tempor-ary*, etc.) also accounts for mis-spellings of many common words. The involved rules of English spelling may be too much for many of us, yet it remains something of a mystery why so many continue to spell *necessary* with two *c's*, *occurred* with one *r*, *privilege* with a *d*, *receive* with *ie*, *develop* with a final *e* and *business* with *buis* as the first syllable. These and other notorious mis-spellings must have been corrected for us many times, yet they persist.

With attention to a few simple rules many of the errors commonly committed could be avoided. This is not to suggest that English spelling is controlled by any tidy set of rules; it is, on the contrary, notoriously illogical and leaves numerous loopholes for error. This is so mainly because it is a language derived from many sources. There is the further difficulty that we use a restricted alphabet of twenty-six letters to represent over forty different sounds, and in consequence English spelling cannot be phonetic. Moreover, many of the letters we use are not sounded at all, as in *comb, Wednesday, psychology, answer,* and numerous others.

A good deal of bad spelling is due to carelessness. We all know the difference between *to* and *too,* and between *there* and *their,* and yet how often do these and other simple mistakes creep into our writing!

If you would spell well you will need to think about words clearly, and to pronounce them carefully—to think of them, not as a jumble of letters but as a group of syllables. Divided into syllables the longest words become as easy to spell as the short ones; *me-te-o-ro-lo-gy* will give you no more trouble than *commerce.*

The first rule of good spelling, then, is—pronounce carefully. It will help you to avoid many of the commonest errors.

> *affi*-davit not affa-
> *assimi*-late not assimu-
> auxil-*iary* not -ary
> compar-*ative* not -itive
> defi-*nite* not -nate
> dete*rior*-ation not -ri
> Feb-*ruary* not -uary
> gov-*ernment* not -erment
> gov-*ernor* not -enor
> honor-*ary* not -y
> *minia*-ture not mina-
> *quar*-ter not qua-
> tempor-*ary* not -y
> ultima-*tum* not -tim

Some of the more general rules of spelling are given below, but they are by no means rigid, and are open to many exceptions that need to be learned. These rules may be conveniently grouped under the headings:

> (*a*) primary words;
> (*b*) prefixes;
> (*c*) suffixes;
> (*d*) plurals.

PRIMARY WORDS

"ie" and "ei"
When the sound is that of long *ee* (as in *me*) the *I precedes the E,* except after *C;* when the sound is other than *ee,* the *E precedes the I.*

be*lie*ve, ch*ie*f, f*ie*ld, rel*ie*f

but

rece*i*pt, ce*i*ling, dece*i*ve (after *c*),

and

either, foreign, Leicester, their, (where the sound is not *ee*)

Exceptions: seize, counterfeit, ancient, and some proper names such as Sheila, Keith, O'Neill.

Words with "ll"
Some words ending in *-ll* drop one of the *ls* in derivative words.

> *all* but *al*most, *al*ways, *al*ready
> *full* but *ful*fil, care*ful,* truth*ful*
> *till,* but un*til*
> *well* but *wel*come, *wel*fare

> *note carefully: all right* (two words—never *alright*).

PREFIXES

When the prefixes *il, im, in* (also *en* and *un*) and *ir* are added to words beginning respectively with *l, m. n,* and *r* the double consonant is retained.

> *il*legible, *im*mortal, *in*numerable, *en*noble, *un*necessary, *ir*relevant

SUFFIXES
Short, stressed syllables
When the last syllable of a word contains a short, accented vowel, but not otherwise, the final consonant is doubled before a vowel suffix in order to preserve the short sound of the vowel.

> begin, begin*n*ing   occur, occur*r*ed
> transfer, transfer*r*ed   deter, deter*r*ent

but

> benefited ⎫
> credited ⎬   where the accent does not fall on the last syllable of the
> different ⎭   primary word

Endings in "l"
When the last syllable of a word ends in "*l*" preceded by a short vowel, the *l* is doubled before a vowel suffix, irrespective of the position of the accent.

> travel, travel*l*ing   label, label*l*ed
> equal, equal*l*ed   council, council*l*or

> *(Exception: paralleled)*

Mute "e"

Words ending in mute *e* drop the *e* before a vowel suffix, but retain it before a consonant suffix:

endorse,	endorsing,	but	endorsement
value,	valuable,	but	valueless
care,	caring,	but	carefree

and similarly with:

debatable	excitable	likable
movable	ratable	salable

though, except for *excitable,* the *Oxford English Dictionary* gives alternative spellings *with* mute *"e"* for the words in the last two lines (e.g. *debateable, likeable*), but usage tends to follow the rule for the omission of the *"e"*, and is supported by Fowler.*

Exception 1
The final *e* is retained after *c* and *g,* when it serves to preserve the soft sound.

noticeable	manageable	advantageous

Exception 2
Words ending in *ee, oe,* and *ye* retain the *e* before *ing.*

agreeing	hoeing	dyeing

Exception 3
The final *e* is dropped before a number of consonant suffixes.

acknowledgment	truly	argument

Note: In words such as *acknowledgment, abridgment, judgment,* and *lodgment* the *Oxford English Dictionary* prefers to retain the *"e"* of the primary word and to use the spellings *acknowledgement, judgement,* etc. The retention of the *"e"* is also recommended by Fowler.† Choice between the alternative spellings must therefore be left to the individual taste. (*See* "Alternative Spellings", pp. 376–7.)

---

*Modern English Usage (2nd ed.), p. 376.
†*Modern English Usage* (2nd ed.), p. 319.

Endings in "y"

Y preceded by a consonant is changed to *"i"*, except when the suffix itself begins with *i* (otherwise there would be the awkward combination of two consecutive *is*).

apply,	applied,	but	applying
rely,	reliable,	but	relying
copy,	copier,	but	copyist

Endings with related forms

It is sometimes difficult to know which of two endings is correct. The correct form may often be deduced from the spelling of the primary word.

-able, -ible

irritate	and so	irritable
terminate	and so	terminable
exhaustive	and so	exhaustible
permissive	and so	permissible

Of these two endings *-able* is the preferred form, though *-ible* must not be tampered with where it is already established as the accepted form, as in aud*ible*, discern*ible*, resist*ible*, access*ible*, etc.

-cial, -tial

commerce	and so	commercial
office	and so	official
resident	and so	residential
potent	and so	potential

Although the last two words have the corresponding forms *residence* and *potency*, *-tial* is the preferred spelling.

-city, -sity

public	and so	publicity
scarce	and so	scarcity
universe	and so	university
verbose	and so	verbosity

-sion, -tion

revise	and so	revision
possess	and so	possession
enumerate	and so	enumeration
appreciate	and so	appreciation

It may be noted that verbs ending in *d* take *-sion:*

| exclu*de* | and so | exclus*ion* |
| provi*de* | and so | provis*ion* |

-ance, -ence, -ant, -ent

These endings are particularly difficult, and in cases of doubt the choice must be settled by reference to the dictionary.

persever*ance*	but	occurr*ence*
further*ance*	but	infer*ence*
depend*ant* (noun)	and	depend*ent* (adj.)
toler*ant*	but	solv*ent*

-cle, -cal

If it is remembered that princi*ple* is a noun and princi*pal* an adjective there should be no difficulty in choosing between *-cle* and *-cal* in similar words.

Nouns	*Adjectives*
arti*cle*	typi*cal*
recepta*cle*	mechani*cal*
obsta*cle*	criti*cal*

Note: Principal is sometimes used as a noun to mean the principal or chief master of a school or college, the principal or capital sum of money, etc. In such cases the adjective serves as a noun by virtue of the ellipsis.

-ce, -se

Because of their different pronounciations it is easy to remember that *advi*CE is a noun, and *advi*SE a verb. Other related nouns and verbs follow the same pattern.

Nouns	*Verbs*
devi*ce*	devi*se*
licen*ce*	licen*se*
practi*ce*	practi*se*
prophe*cy*	prophe*sy*

Note: American practice is different, *-se* being used for nouns such as *defense, license, offense, pretense,* and *-ce* for the verb *practice.*

-ceed, -cede

There is no rule for distinguishing between these two suffixes, which often cause trouble. They must be memorized.

pro*ceed*	but	pre*cede*
ex*ceed*	but	ac*cede*
suc*ceed*	but	con*cede*

Only the above three words take *-ceed;* the rest take *-cede.*

Note: proce*dure,* supers*ede.*

-ise, -ize

Whether words like *deputize* and *specialize* should be spelt with "*s*" or "*z*" is a matter on which authorities differ. The standard practice of many printers is to use *ise,* but on the other hand, the modern trend favours *ize. Ize* is the spelling recommended in the *Oxford Dictionary,* since this suffix is always either Latin or Greek in origin and in both languages is spelt with z. The *ize* spelling is also used by the Cambridge University Press, by *The Times,* and by the *Encyclopaedia Britannica.*

The choice between *ise* and *ize* does not apply to words such as

advertise	enterprise	supervise
analyse	comprise	merchandise
advise	exercise	revise

where *ise* is not a suffix, but part of the primary word. With other words it is better to follow the modern practice set by the best authorities and to use *ize* in all those cases where alternative spellings are given in the dictionary.

Words with alternative spellings

Some words may be spelt in two ways. The following are among those commonly used in business, the preferred spellings, according to Fowler,* being the ones in the first columns.

by-law	bye-law	instil	instill
carcass	carcase	loth	loath
connexion	connection [†]	manilla	manila
disk	disc	medieval	mediaeval
dispatch	despatch [†]	moneyed	monied

*Modern English Usage (2nd ed.).
[†] Usage favours the latter spelling.

employee	employé	moneys	monies
enquire	inquire (see p. 56)	net	nett
enrol	enroll	ratable	rateable
gram	gramme	reflection	reflexion
grey	gray	show	shew
guild	gild	waggon	wagon
install	instal	whisky	whiskey
		(Scotch)	(Irish)

(See also "Mute 'E'." p. 373.)

Whether to use one spelling or the other is of much less importance than the consistent use of the one adopted.

Some foreign words, too, have alternative spellings, among them:

Tsar	Czar	Mahomet	Mohammed
Tsarina	Czarina	Moslem	Muslim

PLURALS

General rule
Add *s* to the singular:

meeting, meetings;   office, offices;   telephone, telephones

Note: Nouns ending in *s, ss, ch, sh, x* and *z* take *-es:*

buses,   processes,   matches,   brushes,   boxes,   waltzes

Endings in "y"
Nouns ending in *y* preceded by a consonant take the plural *ies:*

company, companies;   deputy, deputies;   duty, duties

but

convoy, convoys
holiday, holidays   } where *y* is preceded by a vowel
journey, journeys

Endings in "o"
Most nouns ending in *o* preceded by a consonant take the plural *oes:*

cargo, cargoes;   hero, heroes;   potato, potatoes

(Exceptions: pianos, dynamos, provisos.)

but

folio, folio*s*   } where *o* is preceded by a vowel.
ratio, ratio*s*

Endings in "f" or "fe"
Most nouns ending in *f* or *fe* take the plural *ves*:

   leaf, lea*ves*;   knife, kni*ves*;   thief, thie*ves*;   wharf, whar*ves*; *(or wharfs)*;

but there are numerous exceptions:

         chiefs. reliefs, roofs.

Special plurals
The English language contains many unusual plurals, among them
the following.

Change of Inside Vowel

         man, men; foot, feet; mouse, mice; tooth, teeth.

"En" Endings

         children, brethren (but usually "brothers"), oxen

Retention of Singular Form

         sheep, deer, grouse, salmon, trout

Plurals with no Singulars

Some words have no singular forms.

         means, news, scissors, trousers, whereabouts

Although plural in form some of these are treated as singulars.

This news *is* welcome.
This was the only means possible.

Compound words
In compound words the plural is given to the noun element.

aides-de-camp, consuls general, coups de grâce, deeds poll, Lord Mayors,
men-servants (both elements)

But many familiar compounds are treated as single words and take the plural at the end.

charabancs,   gin and tonics,   knock-outs,   spoonfuls

Foreign words
Some adopted foreign words take the plurals of their original language.*

addendum	addenda (L.)	basis	bases (Gr.)
agendum	agenda (L.)	château	châteaux (Fr.)
alumnus	alumni (L.)	corrigendum	corrigenda (L.)
crisis	crises (Gr.)	parenthesis	parentheses (Gr.)
criterion	criteria (Gr.)	phenomenon	phenomena (Gr.)
datum	data (L.)	stratum	strata (L.)
erratum	errata (L.)	tableau	tableaux (Fr.)
genus	genera (L.)	trousseau	trousseaux (Fr.)
hypothesis	hypotheses (Gr.)		

For some foreign words, however, there is a tendency to use the anglicized s form of plural, as in *portmanteaus* (Fr. *portmanteaux*), especially for the popular or colloquial use of words also used in a formal or scientific context. The following are some examples.

Word	Plural in formal use	Plural in popular use
appendix	appendices	appendixes
bureau	bureaux	bureaus
formula	formulae	formulas
index	indices	indexes
plateau	plateaux	plateaus

HOW TO IMPROVE SPELLING
Good spelling is largely a matter of visual memory, and whether your spelling is good or bad depends very largely upon the way you read. If you read with keen, critical interest you form mental pictures of the printed words, whereas a perfunctory skimming of the page will leave you with no more than a blurred impression. There is a degree of truth in the saying, "Lazy readers make bad spellers".

*Fr. = French; Gr. = Greek; L. = Latin.

(a) The first step, then, towards good spelling is—careful reading.

(b) The second step, already mentioned on p. 371 is—careful pronunciation.

(c) The third step is to keep a notebook and in it to write down the correct version of any words whose spelling causes you trouble. The value of the notebook will be proportionate to the extent to which you use it for systematic revision. If you learn only two new words a day in this way you will have mastered over 600 in a year.

(d) The final step is to use the words you have noted; this will consolidate what you have learned.

The following are some of the words most commonly mis-spelt. You might do worse than make those in Section 1 the starting-point for your own personal list:

WORDS TO WATCH

Words to make sure of

In the following lists, (A) in brackets indicates words that, according to *Thorndike's Junior Dictionary,* occur at least fifty times in every million words in general use. Within the specialized vocabulary of business many of the other words not marked in this way occur just as frequently.

accommodate	embarrass	principal (adj.) (A)
address (A)	exceedingly	principle (noun) (A)
argument	February (A)	privilege
beginning	fulfil	procedure
benefited (A)	governor (A)	quarter (A)
business (A)	gramophone	receive (A)
committee (A)	harass	recommend
comparative	interrupt	referred
convenient	licence (noun)	separate (A)
correspondence	license (verb)	stationary (adj.)
definite	necessary (A)	stationery (noun)
dependant (noun)	occurred (A)	success (A)
dependent (adj.)	omitted	transferred
develop (A)	practice (noun) (A)	until (A)
disappear (A)	practise (verb)	Wednesday

Other words used in business and commonly mis-spelt

abbreviate	accelerate	accessory
abridge	accentuate	accompany (A)
accede	accessible	accomplish (A)
accrue	auditor	concurrence

achieve
achievement
acoustics
acquaint
acquiesce
acquire
across (A)
adhesive
adjourn
adjudicator
adjusting
admissible
adolescent
advantageous
advisable
adviser
advisory
aerial
affidavit
agreeable
aggrieved
allege
allocate
allotment
allotted
altar (a table)
ambassador
ambitious
amicable
anaemic
analysis
announce (A)
annul
anonymous
anxious
appalling
appetite
appreciate
apprentice
article (A)
ascertain
assess
assessor
assimilate
atrocious
attitude (A)
attorney
audible

audience
auditor
auxiliary

barrister
battalion
believe (A)
beneficial
biased (or biassed)
bicycle
biscuit
bouquet
budget
bulletin
buoyant
bureau

calendar
campaign (A)
cancellation
cancelling
canvass (to solicit)
carriage
casualty
catalogue
catarrh
ceiling
centre
centring
century (A)
chagrin
champagne
chaotic
charter
cheque (a document)
cipher
circuit
clientele
collateral
colleague
college (A)
collusion
colour (A)
commemorate
commission (A)
commissionaire
competent

concede
conceivable
concurrence
confident
connoisseur
conscientious
conscious
consensus
convalescent
convenience
corroborate
counsel (an adviser)
courteous
courtesy
creditor
credulous
criticism
curriculum
customary

dearth
debris
deceit
decipher
deferred
definable
demurrage
desultory
difference (A)
different (A)
disappoint
discern
discipline
discoloration
dissent (to disagree)
dissipate
dissolve
draught (air)
dubious
duplicator

eccentric
efficiency
eighteenth
elapse
eligible
eliminate
emigration

encyclopaedia -pedia
endeavour
enervate
ephemeral
erroneous
etiquette
evenness
eventually
evidence (A)
exaggerate
excellent (A)
exception
excessive
excise
excitable
exercise (A)
exhibit
expedite
expense (A)

facsimile
fallacy
fascinate
fatigue
feasible
flotation
foreign (A)
forfeit
freight
frontispiece
fullness or fulness

gauge
glossary
governor
gradient
grammar
grievous
guarantee
guest (A)
guilty

honorary
honourable
hygiene

illegible
illicit

illiterate
immersion
immigrate
imminent
incentive
inconvenience
incredible
indefensible
indelible
indemnify
independence
indispensable
infallible
inference
infinite
innovation
insolvent
installation
instalment
intellectual
irrelevant
irritation
issuing

labelled
lacquer
leisure
liaison
libellous
licensed
liquidator

maintenance
mannequin
manoeuvre
marriage
marvellous
mathematics
Mediterranean
metre (measurement)
miniature
miscellaneous
mischievous

necessitate
necessity
neighbourhood
nuisance

obsession
occasion (A)
occurrence
occurring (A)
omission
oscillate

paraffin
parallel
paralyse
parliament
pavilion
perceive
permissible
permitting (A)
persuade
pessimist
Piccadilly
platen
plausible
possession (A)
precede
precocious
preference
preferring (A)
preparation
procession
programme
proprietary
psychology
pursue

queue

receivable
receipt
reciprocate
reducible
referee
referring
regrettable
reimburse
remittance
repudiate
rescind
resistible
resources
resume

retrievable
retrogressive
review (to re-examine)
rhythm

schedule
secede
secondary
segregate
seize (A)
series (A)
skilful
stencilling
stevedore
storage
stupefy
suburb
successful (A)
summarized
superannuation

supersede
supervisor
susceptible
suing
synonymous
synopsis

tacitly
technique
television (A)
temporary
terrify
territory (A)
thermometer
thoroughly
tidily
tidiness
tobacco
tolerant
totally

transferable
transitory
traveller (A)
trial (A)
typical

ultimatum
unique
unmistakable
unnecessary
unveil
usable

vertical

wholly
wrench

yield (A)

Words commonly confused

advice (recommendation)
alternate (first one, then the other)
amend (to correct)
artist (a painter, etc.)
beside (close to)
biannual (twice yearly)
canvas (a cloth)
check (to restrain)
complement (a supplement)
council (an assembly)
current (now existing)
decease (death)
definite (clear)
device (a contrivance)
distinct (separate)
draft (a document)
dying (losing life)
economic (on business lines)
elicit (to draw out)
emigrate (to move out)
eminent (distinguished)

advise (to offer counsel)
alternative (either of two)
emend (to delete)
artiste (an entertainer)
besides (in addition to)
biennial (every two years)
canvass (to solicit)
cheque (money)
compliment (praise)
counsel (advice)
currant (dried fruit)
disease (illness)
definitive (final)
devise (to plan)
distinctive (characteristic)
draught (air)
dyeing (colouring)
economical (sparing)
illicit (illegal)
immigrate (to move in)
imminent (near)

ensure (to make certain)	insure (to protect)
envelop (to cover)	envelope (stationery)
faint (feeble)	feint (pretence)
impracticable (impossible)	impractical (not workable)
licence (a permit)	license (to authorize)
lightening (weight)	lightning (weather)
luxurious (in luxury)	luxuriant (profuse)
personal (private)	personnel (people)
practice (action)	practise (to exercise)
prescribe (to recommend)	proscribe (to outlaw)
principal (chief)	principle (a rule)
prophecy (a prediction)	prophesy (to foretell)
stationary (still)	stationery (paper, etc.)
stimulant (a drug)	stimulus (an incentive)
there (in that place)	their (belonging to them)

WORD-DIVISION

Words are divided at the end of lines in typewriting in order to avoid ragged right-hand margins. Some firms discourage the practice because, they claim, it wastes typing time. Word-division should be kept to a minimum, but there are occasions when available space makes it necessary. The following rules then apply.

General rule

Divisions should be based on etymology (e.g. *atmo-sphere, biographer, front-age, super-intend*); but where etymological structure is not obvious, divisions should correspond as nearly as possible to the way in which words are pronounced, the new syllable generally beginning with a consonant, except where this would affect the pronunciation of the preceding syllable:

busi-ness, divi-ded, privi-lege, propa-ganda

but

pref-erence, prem-ises, prop-erty, sched-ule.

Prefixes and suffixes

Where possible the division should be made after the prefix or before the suffix, except when the prefix or suffix consists of only two letters. (It is considered bad practice to have a division consisting of only two letters at the end or beginning of a line.)

mis-apprehension, *trans*-action, hop-*ing*, correspond-*ence,*

but

alto-gether (not al-together), recon-sider (not re-consider), smoo-ther (not smooth-er).

Where the final consonant of a word is doubled before a suffix the division is made between the consonants (see below):

occur-red, begin-ning, label-led

Double and treble consonants
The division is made between two consonants; and after the first of the consonants when there are three.

recom-mend, excel-lent, Feb-ruary, exag-gerate, frus-trate, accom-plish, disas-trous

But when two or more letters form a single sound they must never be divided.

ano-*ther*, *psy-ch*ology, roug*h*-ness, ma*tch*-less

Compound words
The division is made at the point where the elements join to form the compound.

half-penny, head-ache, over-awe, text-book

Words not divided
Words of one syllable

though, draught, blocked, straight

Words of two syllables, one or both of which contain only one or two letters

about, afloat, invoice, debit, reply, always

Proper names, unless they form compounds from separate words

Folkestone, Scarborough, Margaret, Alison

but

St. Annes-on-Sea, Ashton-under-Lyne, Newcastle upon Tyne

Nor out of courtesy should a person's initials be separated from his surname. Thus, you must not write or type *H.C.A.* at the end of one line and *Shawcross* on the next.

Words already hyphenated, except at the hyphen

   shorthand-typist, brother-in-law, post-mortem.

Dates

The day and the month, and if possible the year, must appear on the same line, thus:

10 February 1981

Sets of figures and sums of money

186,000   £25.31

Foreign words

Foreign words should not be divided, since it is not always possible to be sure of their pronunciation:

   garçon (French for *boy*)
   autobahn (German for an *arterial dual carriage-way*)
   incommunicado (Spanish for *in solitary confinement*)
   memorabilia (Latin for *things worth remembering*).

The last word on a page

To carry a portion of a word on to a continuation sheet hampers continuous reading.

EXERCISES

   1. Type or write out, the opposites of the following words, by adding a prefix to each.

(*a*) colour	resolute	legal	human	entangle
(*b*) mortal	limited	redeemable	measurable	relevant
(*c*) necessary	numerable	similar	mortal	rational
(*d*) service	resistible	material	logical	noticed

   2. Complete the following words by inserting *ie* or *ei* as may be required in the blank spaces, and check the results with your dictionary.

(*a*) gr . . vous	rec . . pt	dec . . ve	misch . . f	n . . ther
(*b*) w . . rd	s . . ze	fr . . nd	Mad . . ra	counterf . .t
(*c*) n . . ghbour	l . . sure	h . . ght	fr . . ght	K . . th

   3. Type, or write out, the following words, inserting the correct number of *l*s in the spaces shown by the dots.

(*a*) a . most	du . ness	doubtfu .	forete.	a . together
(*b*) reca .	unti .	a . though	ski . fu .	spoonfu .

> (c) we . being   we . fare   a . ways   we . come   a . right
> (d) chi . blain   enro . ment   insta . ment i . ness   disti .

4. Complete the following words by inserting the appropriate single or double letters; then use your dictionary to check them.

(a) begi(n)ing	envelo(p)ing	admi(s)ion	trave(l)er	refi(l)
(b) occu(r)ed	enro(l)	benefi(t)ed	we(l)fare	foresta(l)
(c) sti(l)ness	cance(l)ed	remi(t)ance	transfe(r)ed	unti(l)
(d) fu(l)fi(l)	omi(t)ing	a(l)ready	refe(r)ing	insta(l)ment
(e) debi(t)ed	acqui(t)ed	mode(l)ing	diffe(r)ed	doubtfu(l)

5. Some only of the following words are spelt incorrectly. Type or write out the incorrectly spelt words with the necessary corrections, then use your dictionary to check them.

(a) achievment	outragous	useable	endorsment	abridgment
(b) agreeing	blameable	valueing	chargable	pavement
(c) valuless	debateable	knowledge-able	commence-ment	likeable
(d) moveing	servicable	desireous	arguement	grieveous

6. Complete the following words by addition of i or y as may be necessary; then use your dictionary to check them.

(a) accompan . ment	stead . ness	suppl . ing	rel . able	happ . ness
(b) accompan . ing	injur . ous	magnif . er	env . able	cop . ist
(c) betra . al	suppl . er	anno . ance	satisf . ed	da . ly
(d) angr . ly	enjo . ment	ga . ty	ga . ly	bus . ness

7. Add the correct suffixes -able, or -ible to the following words, making any changes necessary to give correct spelling.

(a) advise	admit	compare	digest	endure
(b) permit	sense	access	rely	resist
(c) pity	exhaust	excite	defence	notice
(d) response	dispense	reverse	move	justify

8. Add the correct suffixes -ance, or -ence to the following words, making any changes necessary to give to correct spelling.

(a) continue	concur	excel	infer	depend
(b) remember	endure	abound	exist	hinder
(c) occur	correspond	further	ignore	persist
(d) insist	refer	prefer	persevere	recur

9. Complete the following words by adding the correct suffixes from those indicated.

(a) -ant, -ent
    compet . nt   independ . nt   intoler . nt   promin . nt   relev . nt

(b) -cial, -tial
        commer . al   substan . ial   finan . ial   ini . ial   espe . ial
(c) -city, -sity
        inten . ity   publi. ity   capa . ity   genero . ity   univer . ty
(d) -sion, -tion
        quota. ion   exclu . ion   inten . ion   excep . ion   deci . ion
(e) -cle, -cal
        musi . . .   criti . . .   vehi . . .   period . . .   specta . . .

10. Complete the spellings of the following words; then use your dictionary to check them.

(a) compar . tive	acco . odate	misce . aneous	defin . te
(b) benefi . ed	Feb . ary	nec . ary	gov . nor
(c) permiss . ble	tempo . ry	proc . dure	assim . late
(d) sep . rate	gram . phone	We . esday	carr . ge
(e) super . ede	g . rantee	maint . nance	insta . ation

11. Type or rewrite the following, correcting all spelling mistakes.

In business it is necessary to render accounts accuratley. A small mistake may lead to considerable work for the firm's employees. Allways cheque and recheque your columns before makeing the final entry in ink. Remember that clear figures are allways helpfull. Don't allow one line of figures to get confused with another; separate each line. You shoud see that each entry in the ledger has a corrisponding reciept.

12. Write out the following passage, spelling all words correctly, and putting in any commas and full-stops you think necessary.

When the axident ocured to my bicicle I was releived to reckerlect that it was gaurented for to years as this period of time had not then past I had every exspectashun of haveing my bicicle compleatly overhorled without my inkuring any expens as you will redily beleive I siezed the opertunity imediatly and fortunatly was sucesful in my claim.   *(R.S.A., Elem.)*

13. Ten of the following words are spelt correctly, and ten incorrectly. Pick out the latter and write these down with the correct spelling.

gramaphone	proffessor	sincerly	business	prisioner
ridiculous	omission	successful	expierience	suprised
village	completly	pursuit	carriage	recommend
comparative	dectective	develop	bycicle	athelete

(R.S.A., Elem.)

Recommended Reading List

FICTION

Austen, Jane (1775–1817), *Pride and Prejudice*
Blackmore, R.D. (1825–1900), *Lorna Doone*
Brontë, Charlotte (1816–55), *Jane Eyre*
Buchan, John (1875–1940), *The Thirty-nine Steps, Mr. Standfast*
Bunyan, John (1628–88), *The Pilgrim's Progress*
Chesterton, G.K. (1874–1936), *Father Brown Stories*
Collins, W. Wilkie (1824–89), *The Moonstone*
Conrad, Joseph (1857–1924), *Lord Jim, Typhoon*
Cronin, A.J. (b. 1896), *Hatter's Castle, The Citadel*
Defoe, Daniel (1660–1731), *Robinson Crusoe*
Dickens, Charles (1812–70), *A Christmas Carol, David Copperfield, Oliver Twist, The Pickwick Papers*
Douglas, Lloyd C. (1877–1951), *The Robe, The Big Fisherman*
Doyle, Sir Arthur Conan (1859–1930), *Sherlock Holmes Stories, The Lost World*
Dumas, Alexandre (1802–70), *The Count of Monte Cristo*
Eliot, George (1819–80), *Adam Bede, Silas Marner*
Fielding, Henry (1707–54), *Tom Jones*
Forster, Edward M. (1879–1970), *A Passage to India*
Grahame, Kenneth (1859–1922), *The Wind in the Willows*
Haggard, Sir H. Rider (1856–1925), *King Solomon's Mines*
Hardy, Thomas (1840–1928), *The Mayor of Casterbridge*
Hemingway, Ernest (1898–1964), *For Whom the Bell Tolls*
Hilton, James (1900–54), *Good-bye, Mr. Chips*
Hughes, Thomas (1822–96), *Tom Brown's Schooldays*
Hugo, Victor (1802–85), *The Hunchback of Notre Dame*
Huxley, Aldous L. (1894–1963), *Brave New World*
Jerome, Jerome K. (1859–1927), *Three Men in a Boat*
Kingsley, Charles (1819–75), *Alton Locke*

Kipling, Rudyard (1865—1936), *Plain Tales from the Hills*
Lawrence, David H. (1885—1930), *Sons and Lovers*
Lytton, Lord (1803—73), *The Last Days of Pompeii*
Marryatt, Captain F, (1792—1848), *Peter Simple*
Maugham, W. Somerset (1874—1965), *The Moon and Sixpence*
Melville, Herman (1819—91), *Moby Dick*
Monsarrat, Nicholas J.T. (1910—1979), *The Cruel Sea*
More, Sir Thomas (1478—1535), *Utopia*
Priestley, John B. (b. 1894), *The Good Companions, Angel Pavement*
Reade, Charles (1814—84), *The Cloister and the Hearth*
Sayers, Dorothy L. (1893—1957), *The Nine Tailors*
Scott, Sir Walter (1771—1832), *Guy Mannering, Ivanhoe, The Fortunes of Nigel*
Shaw, G. Bernard (1856—1950), *Saint Joan*
Stevenson, Robert L. (1850—94), *Dr. Jekyll and Mr. Hyde, Treasure Island*
Swift, Jonathan (1667—1745), *Gulliver's Travels*
Thackeray, William M. (1811—63), *Vanity Fair*
Trollope, Anthony (1815—82), *Barchester Towers*
Wells, Herbert G. (1886—1946), *The War of the Worlds, Kipps*

NON-FICTION

Bacon, Sir Francis (1561—1626), *Essays*
Belloc, Joseph H.P. (1870—1953), *The Path to Rome*
Clark, Kenneth (b. 1903), *Civilisation*
Heyerdahl, T. (b. 1914), *The Kon-Tiki Expedition*
Lamb, Charles (1775—1824), *Essays of Elia*
Lawrence, Thomas E. (1888—1935), *The Seven Pillars of Wisdom*
Morton, H.V. (1892—1979), *In Search of England*
Pepys, Samuel (1633—1703), *Diary*
Ruskin, John (1819—1900), *Sesame and Lilies*
Smiles, Samuel (1812—1904), *Self Help*
Van Loon, Hendrik W. (1882—1944), *The Story of Mankind*
Walton, Izaac (1593—1683), *The Compleat Angler*

The Business Education Council
(Assignment-based Courses)

The role of BEC is to establish and administer a unified national system of non-degree courses for people whose occupations or prospective employment fall within the broad area of business and public administration. Omitting higher national awards the courses available at approved centres replace those for the former Ordinary National Certifice and Diploma in Business Studies, and are as follows.

BEC General Certificate } BEC General Diploma }	Intended for young students with few, if any, academic qualifications.
BEC National Certificate } BEC National Diploma }	For students who have already obtained a reasonably good school-leaving standard qualification or equivalent qualification.

A general award may be considered either as a foundation course, complete in itself, or as a springboard to a national award, which is career oriented.

BEC courses operate through a system of practice assignments derived from business contexts. Assignments are grouped in modules, each representing a unit of work with specified objectives. The number of modules prescribed for an approved course of study varies with the level of the course, from a minimum of four for a general certificate course to a maximum of twelve for a national diploma. Module 1, entitled *People and Communication,* consists essentially of a series of assignments which, taken as a whole, provide a range of such learning activities as speaking, listening, note-making, summarizing, reading and writing, and is compulsory as a unit of study forming part of all BEC courses. It is the module with which *English for Business Studies* is directly concerned. It is comprised of assignments arising out of business situations, actual or hypothetical, giving rise to tasks which those taking part are required to carry out. An example assignment of the kind suitable for inclusion in Module 1 is reproduced at the end of the Appendix by courtesy of the Blackpool and Fylde College of Further and Higher Education. It is a moderated assignment used by students followng BEC courses provided by the College at National Level.

Module 1 aims to contribute to the personal development of the students by fostering the ability to communicate and to encourage in them a sensitivity to the ideas and attitudes of others.

The Council is opposed to any suggestion that mechanical competence in English should be treated as a prerequisite for work on assignments, and strongly urges that such competence is best achieved through work on the assignments themselves and the motivation they can provide. But at the same time it emphasizes the importance of competence in the use of language as a central concern of the Module, and stresses the need for a rigorously maintained standard throughout the course. It emphasizes the need for lucid speech, correct spelling, competent punctuation, and a clear awareness of syntax and usage, all of which are vital to the students' self-esteem and their prospects in employment.

MODULE 1
PEOPLE AND COMMUNICATION

Example Assignment:
ROYSTON'S

Situation
Royston's Estate Agents, for whom you work as Assistant to Mr. Basil Royston, have recently advertised in the local press an administrative and clerical post which they wish to fill immediately. The duties include shorthand, typewriting and writing descriptions of properties for sale. High speeds and a good command of English are vital. Also there is reception work and accompanying of clients on property inspections. Irregular hours, including some weekend work, are inevitable.

Task 1 (Group)
The class will divide into four small groups, each of which will discuss *one* of the topics given below. No group will see the topics being discussed by the others.

1.1 Using the material given, say what it is like to be a member of the staff in this firm.

1.2 Define the kind of work that a clerical assistant in this firm would have to carry out.

1.3 Assess the kinds of qualifications, experience and personal qualities which would be appropriate to the post.

1.4 What career prospects would be offered to applicants for the post at Royston's?

A spokesman from each group will then report back to the whole class, summarizing the conclusions of his/her group and answering questions.

Task 2 (Individual)

2.1 Draft a full job description for the post of clerical assistant at Royston's.

2.2 Design an advertisement to be placed in the local press.

Task 3

The details attached are taken from letters of application received. Tabulate the information to enable your employer to compare the applicants more easily.

(*a*) Miss Belinda Potter, 28. Has worked for rival estate agents for last six years as secretary to senior partner who is retiring soon. Slightly disabled from polio from childhood, makes it clear that she occasionally needs time off for medical reasons. Unmarried. Shorthand speed 140 w.p.m., typing 50 w.p.m. Has often managed office of present employer in absence of partners and is studying for professional qualifications in evening school.

(*b*) Mrs. Rosemary King. Divorced, mother of three young children, aged 34. Educated to 'A' level and worked in offices for several years after leaving school. Has recently taken refresher course in shorthand and typing, now seeking employment. Speeds 120/40. Very stylish letter.

(*c*) Miss Naomi Nputo, 26. Graduate of Nigerian University. Has been in England for eight years and worked for last year as secretary/receptionist with a firm of accountants. Now seeking more variety of work and long-term responsibility. No ties, lives very close to office, car driver. Speeds 140/50 w.p.m. One month's notice required.

(*d*) Mrs. Nancy Thomson, 44. Married with teenage children. Has just completed 1 year full-time secretarial course, speeds 120/40 plus 'A' level English. Was leading student of her year. Address, small village four miles away. Would be happy to study for professional qualifications in own time.

(*e*) Miss Elaine Hamilton — age 21. Ex-student of top London secretarial college, speeds 150/50 w.p.m. Has worked for last year as secretary to an M.P. at Westminster, recently moved to area following engagement. Keen sportswoman, contributes articles to various magazines. Lists among hobbies "entering beauty contests".

(f) Miss Gladys Whittaker, 51. Already employed by Royston's (for last sixteen years). Speeds 100/20 w.p.m. Occasionally writes property descriptions already. Very reliable, at present paid much less than the salary for this post.

(g) Mr. Peter Leeming, 26. O.N.D. with distinction in Business Studies, speeds 110/40 w.p.m. acquired in early training for journalism. Variety of jobs, all involving selling including last 18 months in Life Insurance. Wife comes from this area and family reasons make a return to the district desirable. Car driver.

Task 4
Write brief notes on each application, saying why you would or would not select each individual to be one of the *three* called for interview.

Task 5
In groups of about six, simulate the interviews for this post, using the appropriate information given for each candidate. Half of the group should act the part of interviewers, the remaining three being interviewed in turn.

Criteria for Assessment

(a) Co-operation in group oral activity.

(b) In the job description, inclusion of appropriate and clear details relevant to the job; with headings.

(c) Appropriate layout and content of advertisement.

(d) Tabular presentation under appropriate headings. Data clearly organised for easy comparison.

(e) Convincing arguments in Task 4 for choice or rejection of candidates.

(f) Successful participation in role playing.

(g) Correct language, spelling and punctuation in all written work.

Learning Objectives
Lists setting out the learning objectives for this and other Modules are given in *BEC National Awards Course Specification*. The following are those included for Module 1.

A2. To use the skills involved in obtaining and interpreting information.

A5. To prepare abstracts and summaries of information.

B1—4. To obtain and give information as listeners, speakers, readers and writers.

C1. To select and use appropriate standard formats of certain documents.

C2. To spell and punctuate and use conventional layouts for letters, etc.

G1. To help others to communicate effectively.

J1. To make appropriate selections from the different forms of communication available, e.g. oral, written, Telex, etc.

Index

noun, 220
Pitch, in speech, 147
Plain words, 27—8, 33, 139
Plurals
    compound words, 378—9
    foreign words, 379
    spellings, 377—8
Poetry, in speech training, 148
Possessive adjective, 225
Possessive pronoun, 221, 225
Précis
    business correspondence, 188—
        97
    comprehension, importance of,
        100
    note-making distinguished, 325—6
    reported speech, 309
    skills involved, 317
    steps in arranging, 326—8
    summarizing paragraphs, 319—20
    summarizing phrases and clauses,
        318—9
    techniques employed in, 317—8
    topic sentence in, 319—20
    worked example, 189—92, 319—
        20, 328—9
Predicate, function of, 239—40
Prefixes, *il-, im-, in-*, etc., in spelling,
    372
Preposition
    conjunction disinguished, 233,
        235
    defined, 231
    function of, 231
    list of, in idiom, 231—2
    participles used as, 303
    wrong uses of, 295—7
Prepositional endings, 297—8
Prepositional phrases
    list of, 2
    examples of unnecessary, 22—3
Principal clause — *see* Main clause
Pronoun
    conjunctive (i.e. connective), 222
    defined, 220
    indefinite, 287
    personal, 221

possessive, 221, 225
relative, 222, 241, 279—80
wrong uses of, 284—7
Pronunciation
    aid to spelling, 371
    use of dictionary for, 47—9
Proper names
    not to be divided, 385
    use of capitals for, 365
Proximity, rule of, 229—30, 259—60
proximo, use of, 163
Punctuation
    ambiguity in, 339
    basic rules, 337
    closed and open, 161
    in business letters, 342—3
    need for, 338, 339
    personal taste in, 338
    summary of rules, 339—40

Question mark, use of, 357
Quiller-Couch, Sir Arthur, 43
quite, misuse of, 292—3
Quotation marks, 355—7
Quotations
    Dictionaries of, 139
    price, 177
    use of capitals in, 367

Reading
    aloud, 149
    efficiency in, 134—6
    for information, 132
    for study, 132
    literature and, 133—4
    recommended list, Appendix I
    technique, 136
    to improve speech, 149
    value of, 131
    vocabulary and, 132—3
Recorded dictation, 153
Recorded speech, 148
Reference books, 137—9
Reflective writing, 88—9
Relative clauses, use of comma,
    241—2, 340—1